IMAGINATION AND HEALING

Imagery and Human Development Series

Editor: Anees A. Sheikh

Baywood Publishing Company, Inc.
FARMINGDALE, NEW YORK

Library of Congress Catalog Card Number: 83-27561
ISBN Number: 0-89503-037-3

© 1984 Baywood Publishing Company, Inc.

Library of Congress Cataloging in Publication Data
Main entry under title:

Imagination and healing.

(Imagery and human development series; 1)
Based on papers originally presented at a series of
conferences, entitled the Power of imagination, organized
by Marquette University in collaboration with the
Institute for the Advancement of Human Behavior.
Includes bibliographical references and index.
1. Imagery (Psychology) — Therapeutic use — Addresses,
essays, lectures. 2. Fantasy — Therapeutic use — Addresses,
essays, lectures. 3. Autogenic training — Addresses,
essays, lectures. I. Sheikh, Anees A. II. Series

RC489.F35I47 1984   615.8'51   83-27561
ISBN 0-89503-037-3

TABLE OF CONTENTS

Preface

For centuries, thinkers have paid tribute to the human gift of imagination.

"The soul never thinks without a picture"—*Aristotle*
"A strong imagination begets the event itself"—*A scholastic axiom*
"Imagination is the eye of the soul"—*Joseph Joubert*
"Imagination is the air of the soul"—*J. P. Bailey*
"Imagination is more important than knowledge"—*Albert Einstein*
"Imagination is not a talent of some men, but is the health of every man"
  —*Ralph Waldo Emerson*
"Keep the imagination sane; that is the truest condition of communion
  with heaven"—*Nathaniel Hawthorne*
"I dream the world, therefore the world exists as I dream it"—*Gaston
  Bachelard*
"The mind is its own place and in itself
Can make a heaven of hell and hell of heaven"—*John Milton*

Throughout the ages and in numerous cultures, imagination has been regarded as a powerful agent in the healing process. Unfortunately, this notion had fallen into disfavor during the last three hundred years among Western psychologists and physicians. In the seventeenth century, René Descartes had proposed the mind/body dualism, that the mind exists independently of the body and exerts no influence upon it. Descartes's ideas were suited to the times and he found a large and faithful following. Then, of course, the behaviorists did their part to ban imagination from the domain of legitimate concerns of psychologists.

But during the last decade, the climate has changed dramatically: psychologists and physicians again are proclaiming that imagination plays a vital role in both mental and physical health, and they have furnished numerous experimental and clinical investigations to support their contention. They have shown that mental images can bring about rapid and far-reaching emotional, psychological, and physiological changes. In fact, it now has become clear that imaginal events can have an impact which is as forceful as that of reality.

It is not surprising that the healing capacity of images is attracting the attention of an ever-widening circle of practitioners and researchers. *Imagination and Healing* represents a response to this blossoming interest. Contributors to this volume are widely recognized and the diversity of the applications of imagery which they provide, render the book unique. Undoubtedly, it will constitute an invaluable addition to the existing literature on the topic, and I feel that those readers who are not convinced of the power of the imagination upon opening this book, surely will be believers even before they reach its last chapters.

Chapter 1 provides a historical perspective of the importance accorded to imagination in the disease and healing processes. First Aristotelian theory of the arousal function of imagination is presented. Next, the belief in the role of images in pathogenesis as well as in therapeutic procedures is traced through the ages.

The remaining ten chapters, to varying degrees, furnish theoretical, empirical, and clinical evidence of the efficacy of imagery in healing. More specifically, imagery has been utilized successfully in the treatment of a wide variety of disorders; among them are allergies, skin disorders, warts, burns, abnormal bleeding, posttraumatic stress, cancer, depression, phobias, sexual problems, pain, and suicidal tendencies. Furthermore, this book contains not only procedures to combat disease, but also abounds with valuable suggestions for enhancing the quality of life, for fulfilling both one's biological and psychological potential.

In conclusion, I would like to express my appreciation to all who played a part in making this book happen. Foremost, I cordially thank all contributors for their vital role in bringing this volume into existence.

Most of the chapters of this book are revised versions of lectures presented at a series of conferences, entitled the Power of Imagination, organized by Marquette University in collaboration with the Institute for the Advancement of Human Behavior. I would like to pay tribute to Marquette University for its part in regaining for imagery its appropriate status.

Also I am indebted to Norm Cohen, president of Baywood Publishing Company, for his encouragement, guidance, and patience, and to Sundar Ramaswami for his generous assistance. Last but not least, I lovingly acknowledge the help and support provided by my wife, Katharina, throughout the preparation of this volume.

Anees A. Sheikh, Ph.D.

CHAPTER 1

Imagination in Disease and Healing Processes: A Historical Perspective

CAROL E. McMAHON
AND ANEES A. SHEIKH

Aristotle's understanding of human nature led him to regard imagination as causal in inducing physiological arousal. This theory was pervasive in premodern medical systems and contributed to a sophisticated conception of pathophysiology in the late European Renaissance.

In this chapter, first Aristotelian theory of the arousal function of imagination is presented. Secondly, the role of the image in pathogenesis from ancient through modern periods is reviewed. Next, the use of imagination in therapeutic procedures through the ages is examined.

The awareness that imagination was recognized as a contributor to health and disease already at the time of Aristotle inevitably leads to the question: Why is the concept so new to contemporaries? The explanation of this paradoxical state of affairs lies in the philosophical underpinnings of past and present theory. When Cartesian dualism became a determining philosophical basis of medical theory, the role of imagination lost its premodern status. The implications of dualism for modern formulations are of vital importance; thus, this philosophical issue is addressed throughout.

PREMODERN THEORY: IMAGERY AND PHYSIOLOGICAL AROUSAL

Ancient and Renaissance medical approaches were "holistic" in the true sense of the word. In place of the Cartesian mind, an immaterial "thinking thing," a spirit or soul was assumed. This biological soul formed the substrate of psychophysiologic events. Biological and psychological functions were governed and performed by the soul.

Imagination, along with sensation, digestion, and reason, were among the faculties of the soul. Sensation functioned by taking the object (minus its matter) from the external world into the heart where the soul was seated; and here the *sensus communis* (common or collective sense) worked upon sensations to form images, dreams and illusions, or hallucinatory images.

Emotional arousal, conceived in terms of humoral imbalances, was stimulated by images thus formed in the heart. "Emotion" is close in meaning to its root, the Latin *emovere*, which means "to move out" or "to stir up." Such movements of the biological soul varied according to whether the image provoked states of desire or aversion. According to Aristotle, the emotional system did not function in the absence of an image.

The theory explained both the activation and direction aspects of motivation. An object of desire or aversion, represented in imagination, directed the physiological arousal which led to specific actions of pursuit or avoidance [1].

According to Aristotle, images were "to the intellective soul as sense objects. But when it affirms or denies good or evil, it pursues or avoids." [2, p. 442] The image in the soul therefore was the prime motivating force in human action. It operated in two ways. The voluntary, where reason exerted control, was known as deliberative imagination. Irrational animals acted without deliberation and their behavior was controlled by sensitive appetite. An animal "is not capable of appetite without possessing imagination, and all imagination is either 1) calculative or 2) sensitive. In the latter all animals, and not only man, partake." [3, p. 559] In states of intoxication, fever, madness, and dreaming sleep, when persons functioned without the faculty of reason, imagination assumed absolute power.

Aristotle's interest was that of a natural philosopher rather than a physician, and he dealt only briefly with pathogenic effects. The theory, however, became central in medical and psychological concepts thereafter. Initially intended to explain human action, the theory soon became a powerful tool in understanding health and disease.

IMAGINATION AND PATHOGENESIS

It is not unusual to find post-Aristotelian thinkers defining images as "emotions," since images too were movements of the soul. Disturbing images enacted and indeed constituted the deviations from harmonious balance or proper proportioning of elements and humors which comprised health.

The Stoic Preoccupation with Prevention

The Stoic philosophers provide interesting examples of the effects of imagination because the psychophysiology of emotion was of great interest to them. To the Stoics, all emotion was a moral violation and a pathological state of body and spirit. They regarded the ideal condition of human nature to be a harmoniously balanced and tranquil state. Health was associated with "the unruffled flow of life." Anyone who attained such perfection was "absolutely free of any form of emotion." [4, pp. 34-35]

The Middle Ages brought a change in localization of function: The faculty of imagination was placed in the cerebral ventricles. It resided here in its psychophysiologic form as "vital spirits." These spirits travelled between brain and heart; the latter remained the seat of emotion.

Imagination led to pathology by arousing emotions and the deleterious effects related to the emotion's intensity. If an image provoked fear, for instance, "we see the whole spirit throughout the members join in the feeling; sweat and pallor occur over the whole body, speech is broken, words fade away, eyes are darkened, ears ring, limbs give way, until we often see men collapse from terror." [5, p. 84] In the many Stoic treatises on the emotions, the characteristic formula for health is: "Wipe out imagination: check desire: extinguish appetite." [6, p. 714]

Pathogenesis in Renaissance Medicine

Renaissance physicians ascribed to imagination a predominant role in pathology. Little change occurred in underlying theory. When imagination conceived an object pleasing or repellent, spirits carried activation from the brain to the heart, via nerves, and induced arousal. Nemesium in 1636 put it thus:

> The Instruments of *Imagination*, are the *former Panns* of the *braine*; the Vitall Spirits, which are in them; The *sinewes proceeding from the braine*; The *nerves moistened by the Vitall Spirits*, and the very frame of the places wherein the *Senses* are seated. [7, p. 180]

Humoral pathology entered at this point, because emotions tended to establish the internal milieu which favored their perpetuation. Spirits from the imagination created humoral imbalances, then the heart released spirits which ascended "into the imagination" and "moved diverse passions according to their nature." The ensuing circular pattern of disproportioning of humors instated illnesses or "distemperatures," such as melancholy which corresponded to a constitutional predominance of black bile. Such an imbalance corrupted the vital spirits which controlled all vital activities, including the higher mental processes. Madness, then, was as much a biological state as a psychological condition.

What we interpret today as the expressions of emotions, such as tears, sighs, respiratory changes, and redirection of blood flow, were understood during this period as functional processes. They operated as homeostatic mechanisms to restore balance or equilibrium.

In this context the heart was called the "domestic oracle." Its injunctions were to be followed, because they presaged action conducive to well-being. For instance: "If a man begins to imagine upon a minurie that hath been profered him, the blood of the arteries runs sodainly to the heart, and stirs up the wrathful part, and gives the same heat and forces for revenge." [8, p. 83]

In Shakespeare's *Macbeth*, imagining the future crime gives warning to Macbeth:

> Macbeth: Why do I yield to that suggestion
> Whose horid image doth unfix my hair,
> And makes my seated heart knock at my ribs,
> Against the use of nature? [9, Act 1, Scene 3].

Imagination prepared the organism for specific action: In Huarte's example of wrath, in response to an attack, blood and spirits perfused muscles used for striking. Julius Caesar Scaliger, a French physician of the late fifteenth century, examined individual differences in temperament to emotional responses. If an insult were imagined, brave men felt the force of activation in the muscles used for striking, and cowardly individuals felt the force of the insult in the muscles used for speaking.

Lovesickness provides a good example of the entire pathogenic sequence in operation. Imagination of a love object is first stimulated by the sexual organs. This promotes the production of "seed." Increased quantity of seed (manufactured from a portion of the blood by a digestive process) in turn reinforced the passion and the image of the beloved, resulting in production of still more seed. Emotion thus tended to its own increase. The principle "they tread in a ring" described the images, spirits, and humors sequence, and is analogous to the feedback concept used today in psychophysiology.

If the passion of love was not abated by obtaining the object in imagination, by consummation and release of seed, the following pathogenic process commenced. Constitutional imbalances affected the brain, causing cognitive and imaginative faculties to retain the object constantly in memory. This obsession accelerated the progressive deterioration of temperament and established a chronic disturbance called "erotomania."

Lovesickness in advanced stages was believed to be a deadly disease. The abundant quantity of blood around the lover's heart degenerated over time due to the heat of passion. It became transformed into melancholy, the most pernicious of humors. In early stages of erotomania, physicians used bloodletting to arrest the production of seed. If the disease went untreated, however, death ultimately ensued from a "withered heart all burned." An autopsy performed on a victim of love-melancholy disclosed "instead of a heart . . . nothing but a drie skinne like to the leaues in Autumne." [10, p. 141]

Imagination was the *"Medium deferens* of passions, by whose means they work and produce many times prodigious effects." [7, p. 180] The nature of the image determined the quality and quantity of the disturbance. An image leading to states of excitement, like joy or anger, propelled blood and spirits outward in all directions from the heart, reddening the face and perfusing the periphery. Depressing emotions, such as fear and dread, created the reverse effect: Blood and spirits, with their innate heat, retreated toward the heart.

Thomas Wright summarized the mechanism as follows:

> When we imagine any thing, presently the purer spirits, flocke from the brayne, by certaine secret channels to the heart, where they pitch at the dore, signifying what an object was presented, convenient or disconvenient for it. The heart immediately bendeth, either to prosecute it, or to eschew it: and the better to effect that affection, draweth other humors to help him, and so in pleasure concurre great store of pure spirits; in paine and sadness, much melancholy blood; in ire, blood and choller . . . [11, p. 45].

The effects of any emotion, including joy, could be pathogenic. In Shakespeare's *King Lear* [9] the death of Gloucester followed an emotional shock:

> . . . his flaw'd heart
> Alack, too weak the conflict to support!
> 'Twixt two extremes of passion, joy and grief,
> Burst smilingly (Act 5, Scene 3).

Similarly, in *King Henry IV, Part II* [9], the glad news of victory precipitated the monarch's death. Already weakened by prolonged emotional stress, the King did not survive the incident:

> King Henry: And wherefore should this good news make me sick?
> I should rejoice at this happy news;
> And how my sight fails, and my brain is giddy:
> O me! come near me, now I am much ill (Act 4, scene 4).

Because imagination sets the circular arousal sequence into operation, the image had greater powers of control than sensation or perception. Anticipation of a feared occurrence was presumed to be more damaging than the occurrence itself. The event given most consideration in this context was imaginary anticipation of death. Nymannus chose "horror of death" as the most pathogenic emotion, because its emotions inclined toward disease and morbidity. A strong imagination of a particular malady, such as fever, paralysis, or suffocation, was able to produce symptoms of that condition. Stigmata were explained by this theory:

> And thus did the contemplation of Christ nayled on the Crosse, imprint certaine strakes, stampes, and markes upon the hands and feet of Saint Francis [12, p. 150].

Images were the products of sensations, and thus imagery was a perceptual process. As such, an "imaginary pain" was a felt pain; "imaginary blindness" was an inability to see. Robert Burton, author of the oft cited *Anatomy of Melancholy* [13], believed disorders of imagination to be the only cause of melancholy. The sufferer's imagination was persistently engaged in conceiving states of ill-being:

> Imagination is eminent in al, so most especially it rageth in melancholy persons in keeping the species of objects so long, amplifying them by continuall and strong meditation, until at length it produceth reall effects, and causeth this and many other maladies [13, p. 122].

Depending upon the strength of their powers of imagination, parents could influence the characteristics of their offspring at the time of conception. According to Charron [14], imagination "marks and deforms, nay, sometimes kills *Embryos* in the womb, hastens Births, or causes Abortions." In 1657, Fienus attempted to explain how, despite parental efforts, imgination sometimes failed to "imprint its characteristics on the foetus." [7, p. 181]

Imagination and Premodern Psychopathology

During this era of holism, prior to the modern definition of mind, all illness was regarded to be psychosomatic. Given our present-day concerns, however, the psychological aspects of illness merit separate consideration. Let us consider the formation of delusions and hallucinations.

As we have seen, lovesickness tended to its own increase: Images disturbed the internal milieu and the internal milieu reinforced the disturbed imagination. An extensive disturbance of imagination had a proportional effect upon sensation and perception. External events were perceived in specific ways depending upon the type and magnitude of humoral imbalances. All that is seen "passeth by the gates of imagination, and, a clowdie imagination interposeth a mist" between one's understanding and objective reality.

Imagined blindness, paralysis, and loss of sensation were distortions of reality. External events met with the same transfiguration when processed by the deranged system. Delusions, such as imagined pursuit by enemies and the belief of being a king, fit into this framework. The victim of erotomania saw the face of the beloved in the countenances of others and heard the beloved's voice in others' voices. A melancholic interpreted events in keeping with his state of misery and debilitation. The choleric individual who suffered from anxiety, saw threats and assaults where the unexcitable phlegmatic individual saw nothing. Reports of spectres and like apparitions were imputed to the passion of terror "which above all other passions, begets the strongest imaginations." [7, p. 182]

Imagination and Pathogenesis after Descartes

The medical tradition of regarding the image as possibly pathogenic ended in the late seventeenth century. At this point Cartesian dualism of mind and body became a preeminent determining philosophical basis of medical and psychological theory. Before examining the impact of dualism on the traditional theory, it is necessary to understand the revolutionary nature of this philosophical redefinition of the biological soul.

In an effort to prove the immortality of the soul, René Descartes (1596-1650) defined the mind as an entity unto itself, an "immaterial substance" or "thinking thing," incapable of affecting matter in any way. According to Descartes, the mind's essence

> ... or nature consists entirely in thinking, and ... for its existence, has no need of place, and is not dependent on any material thing ... this soul is entirely distinct from the body, ... and would not itself cease to be all that it is, even should the body cease to exist [15, p. 119].

Descartes arrived at this definition in the following manner. His objective was absolute truth, knowledge beyond question. He sat in darkness doubting and systematically rejecting all which could be doubted. At length he arrived at the one notion which appeared indubitable: *Cogito ergo sum;* I think, therefore I am.

What then was this "I" he queried? It was not the biological soul, as he already had doubted and dismissed his body. Only one definition was possible—I am a thinking thing, a mind, a soul—and these three terms he used interchangeably.

It is important to note that the concept of mind (as mental functions of the soul) was traditionally assumed. What was revolutionary here was Descartes's use of the term "soul" as a synonym for "mind" or "thinking thing."

Two thousand years of meaning were thus expunged by a paragraph. The soul's faculties of imagination, passion, and reason were thenceforth regarded as "contents of the mind." Again, in a later work he wrote:

> I am a thinking thing. And although possibly I have a body with which I am very closely conjoined, ... in so far as I am only a thinking unextended thing, and ... in so far as it (my body) is only an extended unthinking thing, it is certain that I am truly distinct from my body and can exist without it [16, p. 237].

Several factors led to the acceptance of this unlikely view. Renaissance anatomists had tried with scant success to find the biological soul within the body. William Harvey's discovery of circulation of the blood conflicted with traditional concepts of the heart's functioning; "the pump" hardly seemed worthy to be the seat of the soul. Thus, Harvey's discovery strengthened mechanistic physiology.

When dualism converged with mechanistic physiology in the late 1600's, the weight of the proverbial last straw was added to the already weakened structure of soul theory. The dualistic metaphysic of Descartes gave philosophic justification to mechanistic interpretations of biologic functioning. In addition, the Church, which still exerted powerful influence, favored the Cartesian view. The topic of access to heaven by beasts had created considerable controversy within the Church. Descartes resolved this problem by defining animals as autonomously functioning mechanisms lacking an immaterial soul or mind.

A paradigmatic revolution brought a turmoil of protests. Thomas Hobbes wrote, "Had Descartes kept himself wholly to geometry . . . he had been the best geometer in the world, but his head did not lie for philosophy." [17, p. 643] Others were less generous: "I tell thee *DesChartes* is a whim and a wham without one *why* or *wherefore*." [18, p. 274] A notion thought to be pure nonsense by Descartes' contemporaries became axiomatic within half a century. The Cartesian view fit the Zeitgeist.

To explain the apparent existence of psychophysiologic events such as the influence of imagination, Descartes was at a loss. He suggested that we study mathematics and physics, as someday an explanation of "apparent unity" might be found therein.

The philosophic principle of parallelism emerged to replace the mysterious initial hypothesis of interaction, where divine intervention accounted for cause and effect across the dualistic barrier.

Descartes took the life out of the vital spirits, the mind and intelligence out of the body, and, as subsequent history teaches, the holism out of medicine. The body as subject matter was given to the physiologist and anatomist; the mind was assigned to the philosopher or psychologist, and their mutual influences to God. Consciousness, as an epiphenomenon of the body, was relegated to the domain of philosophy; and the body, as an automaton, was relegated to physiology or "animal mechanics." The ground plan for psychology and medicine now was designed as strictly prohibitive of the psychophysiological.

The meaning of the term "imagination" changed accordingly. In the pre-dualistic era, when the diagnosis put the malady "in the imagination," specific therapeutic action followed. In the post-Cartesian era, the expression, "It's all in your imagination," implied that the patient was untreatable at best, or it carried an accusation of malingering. Let us examine the historic steps in this process of redefinition where the image lost its biological basis.

According to the received view, whatever was caused by a psychological variable could itself be none other than psychological. An "imaginary ailment" was not a genuine ailment. This factor left many somatic complaints beyond the reach of orthodox medicine. In response, huge numbers of sufferers resorted to faith healing, mesmerism, and numerous forms of quackery. Cures purported to have derived from such practices were designated by orthodox physicians as cures of imaginary ailments.

Mesmerism, for instance, was directed at illnesses of a psychosomatic nature, including diarrhea, asthma, temporary blindness, depression, and transient attacks of paralysis. Mesmer (1734-1815) claimed success where standard procedures failed. A commission appointed by Louis XVI arrived at a negative decision regarding mesmerism. It was stated that in instances of apparent therapeutic success, "The imagination does everything, the magnetism nothing." [19, p. 207]

Braid and Esdaile were the foremost nineteenth century exponents of mesmerism. Braid's account of the phenomena was psychophysiologic. He proposed a role for imagination: "A strong direction of inward consciousness to any part of the body . . . is quite sufficient to *change the physical action of the part.*" [20, p. 6] Esdaile, however, was vehemently opposed to such a view. Like most thinkers of his period, Esdaile employed a mentalistic definition of imagination:

> I am convinced that Mesmerism is a physical power . . . and I should as soon adopt the diabolical theory as a satisfactory solution to the problem, as attempt to account for what I have seen and done by the action of imagination alone [21, p. 162].

Among other unconventional treatments, brass, iron, and zinc tractors were in common use in the late eighteenth century for treatment of disease by "galvanism." In 1800, John Haygarth argued that imagination, rather than galvanism, was the variable accounting for therapeutic success. Quite apart from being a vindication of the role of imagination, this statement meant that the symptoms and illnesses treated must have existed only in the patients' minds. Whatever was curable by imagination must have been imaginary.

By the middle of the eighteenth century, mechanism was instated where holism formerly had held sway. All bodily functions were accounted for by mechanical principles. To the influential Hermann Boerhaave (1668-1738), the greatest advance in the history of medicine was the demonstration of "the Human Body to be an Engine." [22, p. 41] Disease was caused by "morbific matter," and the physician's task was identification of that matter and expulsion or eradication of the substance.

The status of temperament theory declined, and medical authors discontinued use of psychophysiologic concepts. Radical reductionism transformed emotions into mechanical phenomena. "Anguish or Anxiety" for instance, was defined by Boerhaave as "the Blood being stopp'd in the very Heart; whence a cramp of the contracted Vessles, or an impossibility to the inflamed Matter of passing through them." [22, p. 144] Imagination was understood as an involuntary function like respiration, and the causes of "absurd imaginations" in madness were "sundry material things" like bile and phlegm.

The former psychosomatic approach to therapy was not to be found among orthodox practitioners. The new mechanical treatments frequently were satirized in literary works of the period. Shakespeare had praised former medical practice, but Molière denounced his medical contemporaries. In *Le Médecin malgré lui*, the patient's condition worsens after taking the remedy. "So much the better," Molière's doctor replies, "that's a sign it operates." [23, p. 284] John Cookley Lettsom, a prosperous physician of the early nineteenth century, was the butt of the following popular ridicule:

> When any sick to me apply
> I physics, bleeds, and sweats 'em;
> If after that they choose to die,
> Why verily! I Lettsom   [24, p. 420].

Descartes had initiated two independent intellectual movements, mentalism and materialism, and although one could adopt both without contradicting oneself, one could never hope for productive interchange between the two realms. Thus the data of psychophysiology became an embarrassing residue which was swept under the carpet until no room remained for more. The bulge became evident to the philosophers of the Age of Enlightenment, and those who brought it to the public attention suffered grievously for the indiscretion.

Imagination and Pathogenesis in the Eighteenth and Nineteenth Centuries

The eighteenth century thinkers criticized the implications of dualism for physiology and medicine. The Zeitgeist of Enlightenment was a revolutionary spirit: an *esprit critique*. Filled with revolutionary zeal, philosophers wielded weapons of satire, scientific demonstration, and empirical fact against the barren Cartesian conception of man as machine.

Ecclesiastic power declined, and science became an institution and a source of belief systems. The intellectual spirit of the age is captured in the words "reason and nature." Human beings became the subject of observation, experimentation, and rational inquiry.

A bold few dared to liberate science from religion where human nature was concerned. La Mettrie (1709-1751) approached the subject as a psychophysiologist. He hoped to disentangle the soul from spiritualism and to reinstate the ancient naturalistic understanding. La Mettrie found dualism to be the central problem in philosophy and medicine and claimed that pathophysiology led him to see the failure of dualism. All illness was equally represented in the machine and in the mind. Imagination was a mover along with instinct and was seated in the brain. As a manifestation of the functioning of the soul, imagination demanded the physician's attention.

La Mettrie's naturalistic approach to the soul was his undoing. He was ostracized for depriving the soul of its immortality, and he died in Prussia three years after being exiled from France, impoverished and friendless at the age of forty-two.

Enlightenment scholars had every intention of reinstating holism so that medicine "may be advanced and carried to the point where it was two thousand years ago." [25, p. 183] The predicted return to holism did not occur. Dualism was by then axiomatic, and parallelism presented a less controversial alternative and was popularized widely by the British Empiricists. The image was defined as a content of the mind and an end product of sensation. Aristotle's thinking on the subject was reproduced with one exception. Aristotle had linked imagination directly to arousal, but such causation was irreconcilable with dualism. As Hartley put it, an image may cause movement of the nerves "by no physical cause at all, but the immediate agency of God." [26, p. ix]

Pierre Jean George Cabanis (1757-1808) shared La Mettrie's interest in psychophysiology and in imagination in particular. Cabanis, however, accepted parallelism and his ideas had great longevity. Mental events, he proposed, caused physiological disturbances and the latter likewise caused distressful images. "Cheerful or sombre ideas, kindly or harmful sentiments are due . . . to the manner in which certain abdominal viscera perform their functions." [27, p. 278] He also gives an instance of causation in the reverse direction: A meal in a healthy person is followed by active digestion but "let this man receive bad news, or let sad and troublesome emotions arise in his soul; at once his stomach and his intestines cease to act upon the food which they contain." [27, p. 279]

In his early work, Cabanis regarded the soul as a faculty of the body. It was this premodern influence on his thinking which encouraged holistic concepts. However, he was out of step with his contemporaries. As use of the soul concept declined, no theoretical framework existed to accommodate psychophysiologic concepts. Organic illness was explained by Virchow's cell theory and Pasteur's germ theory. Neither interpretation took into account the sufferer's ideational or emotional experience.

Illnesses which displayed no organic derangement were classified as "nervous." Nervous disorders were not organic diseases but merely functional, involving "no independent disease." Among these were all conditions related to "emotions of the mind." Because emotions did not qualify as natural causes of disease, nervous disorders often were interpreted as instances of malingering.

It was agreed that a disturbance caused by a psychological variable could itself be nothing but psychological. The conversion reaction, known in the nineteenth century as "physical hysteria," was among the nervous disorders. Physical hysteria was "a malady of the imagination." A survey of the literature on somatic symptoms, referred to as "hysterical," appeared in 1864. The consensus was that such symptoms were "merely the fanciful productions of idle women of inferior constitution." [28, p. 34]

If the onset of such a disorder of imagination was associated with military training or active service, it was classified as "compensation hysteria." Not until

1913 were pensions granted for "nervous or hysterical disabilities;" and these were granted only when "the nervousness intended is a real and not a fictitious nervous condition." [29, p. 1038]

In 1859, Robert Macnish wrote, "When a physician pronounces a complaint to be *nervous*, it is a sure proof that he knows nothing about it." [30] Illnesses related to imagination and psychosomatic disorders generally were without theoretical explanations. Those who attempted to explain such phenomena were defeated by dualism. John Newport Langley (1852-1925), for instance, made such an attempt. Langley was the Cambridge anatomist who gave us the nomenclature in use today for the autonomic nervous system and its subbranches. Langley introduced the term "autonomic" with one misgiving:

> The word "autonomic" does suggest a much greater degree of independence of the central nervous system than in fact exists. It is untrue that the "involuntary" actions are out of all control by the will . . . the will exercises more or less control over unstriated muscles and glands by recalling emotions and sensations [31, pp. 6-7].

Langley ascribed a "mentalistic" role to imagination, and as such it found no place in the mechanistic physiology of the age.

However, to the early psychologists, mentalistic concepts were permissible. The "ideomotor-action" theory echoed the Aristotelian understanding of imagination and arousal. William James, the major exponent of this view, wrote as follows:

> Whether or not there be anything else in the mind at the moment when we consciously will a certain act, a mental conception made up of memory images of these sensations, defining which special act it is, must be there (1890, in [1, p. 477]).

The ideomotor theory was paralleled in psychopathology by the concept of the fixed idea or *idée fixe*. Alfred Fouillée was the principle exponent of this view. A fixed idea was a morbid conception or delusion which dominated the reasoning processes and at times instated symptoms of organic diseases [32].

Ideomotor theory was almost universally accepted by early psychologists. It seemed to furnish the necessary theoretical basis for understanding the role of imagination in pathogenesis. However, at the very height of the theory's popularity, it was terminated by the behavioristic revolution. Images had been linked to arousal, but now "drives" were substituted. If psychology aspired to scientific status, the contents of the Cartesian mind could not comprise its subject matter.

Twentieth Century Thought

If a link does exist between imagination and pathology, imagery must be theoretically based in physiology. Several thinkers at the turn of the century undertook to demonstrate that this was so. Alexander Bain's *The Senses and the Intellect* demonstrates such an approach [33].

Bain used the physiology of his time to challenge the view that "the brain is a sort of receptacle of the impressions of sense, where they lie stored up in a chamber quite apart from the recipient apparatus." [33, p. 337] Bain found the "cerebral-closet" notion incompatible with nervous functioning. He proposed instead "completed circles" where imagery occupies "the same parts and in the same manner as the original sensory activation." Bain further argued that no matter how "enfeebled these neural and muscular activities appear upon introspection, they do not take refuge in any chambers of the brain." [33, p. 377]

In 1931, Edmund Jacobson confirmed Bain's view: he applied electrical measurements in an attempt to determine what takes place in the neuromuscular system during various forms of mental activity [34]. Relaxed subjects were instructed to engage in particular mental activities when signaled to do so by clicks. When the polygraph registered minimal activity, subjects were signaled to imagine throwing a baseball, for instance. Significant activity was recorded in appropriate limbs and was observed to disappear when the signal to discontinue imaging was given. Jacobson's results led to numerous modern applications of imagery in the therapeutic context, most notably in the areas of biofeedback and self-regulation and desensitization [35].

Jacobson's research was conducted in an intellectual climate hostile to imagery. His work survived the attack on mentalism, because his results were not incompatible with behaviorism. The attack was directed at schools of thought, like Titchener's structuralism, which inspired an abundance of research on imagery that, however, in the long run, led to no consensus. The imageless-thought controversy was frequently cited as justification for banishing imagery as a subject of investigation along with the introspective method of study. According to John Watson [36, p. 3], "The behaviorist finds no evidence for 'mental existences' or 'mental processes' of any kind." What Jacobson measured, however, was considered "covert behavior" and thus was accepted as a suitable subject for research.

In subsequent decades, psychologists continued to prefer behavioristic variables to mentalistic constructs. The topic of imagery was neglected for nearly half a century, until verbal report, as an index of imagery, gained broad acceptance [37].

Today, an abundance of evidence links imagination and physiopathology. As noted in the concluding section, however, results suggesting this relationship are largely derived from correlational data and correlations fail to elucidate causal mechanisms [38].

IMAGINATION IN THE CONTEXT OF THERAPY

We return now to the predualistic era to investigate uses of the image in diagnosis and therapy.

Ancient and Renaissance Therapeutic
Uses of Imagination

The tradition of dream imagery interpretation dates to the ancient period. The distinguished second-century physician, Claudius Galen, used dream imagery to assist in diagnosis. Galen presumed that dream content reflected the nature and severity of humoral imbalances. For instance, images of loss, disgrace, or grief indicated excessive melancholy; images of terror, fighting, and wounds signified predominance of choler [7].

Premodern image arousal theory led to clinical use in diagnosis, therapy, and prevention. By the same psychophysiologic means that imagination induced pathological changes, it could remove them and restore health. The image arousal function

> can thus take away or bring some disease of the mind or body. For the passions of the soul are the chiefest cause of the temperament of its proper body. So the soul, being strongly elevated, and inflamed with a strong imagination, sends forth health or sickness (Cornelius Agrippa, 1510, in [7, p. 180]).

Removal of a pathogenic image was necessary to cure an existing disorder and prevent its recurrence. William Vaughan (1612) outlined one therapeutic procedure:

> The physitian . . . must inuent and deuise some spirituall pageant to fortifie and help the imaginatiue faculty, which is corrupted and depraued; yea, hee must endeauour to deceiue and imprint another conceit, whether it be wise or foolish, in the patient's braine, thereby to put out all former phantisies [7, p. 182].

However deranged the sufferer's imagination, it was still his/her reality. With sympathetic listening and attention to pulse, complexion, posture and gait, the physician analyzed the disturbed imagination. It was necessary that the patient "open his heart" to the physician or, in some cases, to the physician's ally.

The ultimate objective of therapy was to restore equilibrium by rectifying internal imbalances. To this end, the ancient principle of opposites was applied. An image leading to excitation could arouse the phlegmatic personality; an image provoking joy or laughter could be of benefit to the melancholic. During this period, melancholy received the most attention. The following medical advice was common during that period:

> *What is the principall naturall meanse to prolong life?*
>   Mirth.
> *What are the effects of mirth?*
>   Mirth enlargeth the heart, and disperseth much naturall heat with the blud, of which it sendeth a good portion to the face, especially

if the mirth be so great, that it stirreth a man to laughter. Mirth I say, maketh the forehead smooth and cleere, causeth the eyes to glisten, and the cheeks to become ruddy [39, p. 141].

Shakespeare, who evinced great respect for the medicine of his era, once remarked that the task of the physician was "To enforce the pained impotent to smile." [40, p. 279] In the Induction to *The Taming of the Shrew*, treatment for a case of melancholy was described:

For so your doctors hold it very meet:
Seeing too much sadness hath congeal'd you blood,
And melancholy is the nurse to frenzy:
Therefore, they thought it good you hear a play,
And frame your mind to mirth and merriment,
Which bars a thousand harms and lengthens life
(9, Act 1, scene 1).

Suppression or repression of emotion was judged to be especially perilous, because the pathogenic imagination, left to its own mechanism, could do no other than worsen the condition. A victim of suppressed love is described in Shakespeare's *Twelfth Night*:

She never told her love,
But let concealment, like a worm i' the bud,
Feed on her damask cheek: she pin'd in thought:
And with a green and yellow melancholy,
She sat, like patience on a monument,
Smiling at grief ([9], Act 2, scene 5).

As previously noted, the expressions of emotion were healthful releases; for instance, weeping expelled excess moisture through the eyes, and the increased respiratory rate of anger cooled the "boiling blood" of rage. In *King Richard II* [9], the king suffered from long repressed sorrow. In his looking glass he observed wrinkles:

Bolingbroke: The shadow of your sorrow hath destroyed the shadow
         of your face.
Richard: Say that again.
        The shadow of my sorrow? Ha!
        'T is very true, my grief lies all within;
        And these external manners of laments
        Are merely shadows to the unseen grief,
        That swells with silence in the tortur'd soul;
        There lies the substance (Act 4, scene 1).

If patients did not express their emotions, physicians would urge them to do so. They warned, however, not to go so far as to lose the controlling influence of reason. Balthasar Gracian discussed "the art of getting into a Rage:"

The first step in losing your temper is to realize that you are losing it, for you thus keep your emotions under control from the start, gauging the precise degree of rage that is necessary, and not going beyond it [41, p. 167].

Imagination and the Historic Use of Placebos

What we know today as the "placebo effect" refers to reliable alterations in conditions of control group subjects in experimental tests of the effects of drugs, for example. Premodern theory of imagination-induced physiological changes predicted and explained this phenomenon, and it became a standard form of therapy.

Renaissance physicians sought naturalistic explanations for the mysterious faith cures of the Middle Ages. Cures were reported to follow ingesting relics, performing magic rituals, wearing charms, and so on. The explanation of these phenomena was found in the traditional theory. On the basis of that theory, highly respected medical thinkers, like Robert Burton and Jerome Cardan, wrote defenses of the use of spells, charms, chants, and like remedies.

"All the world knowes there is no vertue in such charmes" argued Burton, save their power to dominate imagination "which forceth a motion of the humors, spirits, and blood, which takes away the cause of the malady from the parts affected. The like we say of all our magicall effects, superstitious cures, and such are done by Mountebanks and Wizards. An Empiricke many times, and a silly Chirurgeon, doth more strange cures than a rationall Physition" [13, p. 124].

To be effective, the placebo-type remedy had to be accepted with unqualified confidence and the corresponding imagination had to be firmly implanted and capable of persistence. This occurred only when the patient had absolute belief in the physician's competence. H. Cornelius Agrippa advised that both physician and patient

. . . affect vehemently, imagine, hope and believe strongly for that will be a great help. And it is verified amongst physicians, that a strong belief, and an undoubted hope and love towards the physician and medicine conduce much to health; yea, more, sometimes, than the medicine itself. For the same [reason] that the efficacy and virtue of the medicine works, the same doth the strong imagination of the physician work, being able to change the qualities in the body of the sick, especially when the patient placeth much confidence in the physician, by that means disposing himself for receiving the virtue of the physician and physic [42, p. 204].

Agrippa cited one extreme case of these principles in operation. He described a patient who

... at the sight of the medicine, was affected as much as he pleased; when, as neither the substance of the medicine, nor the odor, nor the taste, of it came to him, but only a kind of resemblance was apprehended by him [42, p. 198].

If its power was imagined to be pathogenic, a placebo substance could likewise induce a malady. Witchcraft was surrounded by an aura of fear during this period. Spells were cast and curses applied for the purpose of inflicting bodily harm. Burton described persons who are vulnerable to such suggestions [13]:

If they but see another man tremble, giddy, or sicke of some fearfull disease, their apprehension and feare is so strong in this kinde, that they will have the same disease. Or if by some South-sayer, Wiseman, Fortune-teller, or Physition, they be told they will have such a disease they will so seriously apprehend it, that they will instantly labour of it. A thing similar in *China*, saith *Riccius* the Jesuite, If it be told them they shall be sicke on such a day, when that day comes they will surely be sicke, and will be so terrible afflicted, that sometimes they will dye vpon it [7, pp. 182-183].

According to patients' beliefs, physicians who gave placebos accompanied by explicit prediction and their effects, administered charms, chants, spells, talismans, and magic rituals. However, after the Cartesian revolution, when images became "contents of the mind," physicians who advocated such therapy were stepping outside the bounds of standard practice. Therapy now was based upon a mechanical model incompatible with the influence of any psychological process on physiologic functions.

Imagination and the Placebo Effect
In Post-Cartesian Medicine

While physicians no longer addressed the issue, philosophers regularly included treatments of imagination in their works on human nature. Not long after Descartes, the topic of imagination in the context of physiology appeared in the influential works of David Hartley (1705-1757). Hartley was a parallelist who felt that two sets of lawful principles could be devised, one for mental events and one for somatic processes, and that these two sets of principles would lead to medical applications [26].

Dualism indeed did lead to two sets of laws but not to medical application, because causation could not logically enter the picture. Any causal influence across the dualistic barrier was logically impossible and causal principles, rather than correlations, were needed for medical application. As one early modern physician put it, with evident sarcasm: "How certain emotions of the mind should circulate through the arteries ... or should for a time obstruct the ordinary return of blood by the veins, is a subject into which we shall not presume to enter" (Carson, 1815, in [38, p. 113]).

Despite the implications of dualism, it was evident to Hartley that imagination exerted control on involuntary functions, that is, on the functions of the autonomic nervous system. Hartley felt that cardiovascular activity could be increased or diminished in the following way:

> We seem to have a semivoluntary Power to alter the motion of the Heart immediately, by introducing strong Ideas, our power of introducing these being semivoluntary: Nay it may be possible for Persons . . . to acquire still greater Degrees of Power over the Motion of the Heart [19, p. 207].

Physicians who addressed questions of mental influences were ostracized as quacks. William Falconer, Benjamin Rush, and Daniel Hack Tuke were among the few who dared to propose a role for imagination. Their credibility had been established through earlier works well received. All three addressed the image in the context of placebo mechanisms. Falconer argued that numerous cures

> . . . have been performed by medicines of little, or even of no medical efficacy whatever in themselves, which effect could proceed only from the opinion the patient entertained of their powers; as a proof of which we find that the certainty of the cure has almost always depended on the degree of the patient's confidence in the success of the remedy [43, p. 23].

Falconer recommended a general therapeutic procedure of "redirecting the mind" of the patient in order to eliminate memory images of disorders and their symptoms. He urged that this approach be utilized especially with hypochondriacs due to their highly pathogenic images. Falconer advised that a sufferer's imagination be prevented from "dwelling on itself." The imagination should be thoroughly occupied with other things "leaving no room for the apprehension and recollection of the disorder to operate." [19, p. 208]

D. H. Tuke (1827-1895) was the most prolific advocate of the role of imagination in the medical literature after Descartes. His confidence in the reality of the phenomenon derived not from familiarity with premodern literature but rather from a news report he had chanced upon. The article told of a bloody and dramatic railway accident from which one of the uninjured passengers emerged completely cured of a severe case of rheumatism. This aberration led Tuke to conduct a thorough search of the literature wherein he found the historic conception [44].

He attempted to restate traditional theory for a modern audience in a major work titled *Illustrations of the Influence of the Mind upon the Body in Health and Disease, Designed to Elucidate the Action of Imagination.* However, the numerous citations of imagination-related illnesses and cures were naught but medical curiosities to Tuke's contemporaries. Medical theory in no way could accommodate events that were by definition biologically and logically impossible.

Tuke strongly advocated the use of placebos, and he advised that physicians be present when such remedies were administered; for, at times the dosage might be too potent and perhaps dangerous. He cited a French contemporary's "remarkable success" with two sets of pills composed of bread crumbs and covered with silver leaf. One set, the "pilules argentées antinerveuses," was used to treat disorders of unexplained origin and termed "nervous." Nervous disorders were the nineteenth-century analog of what we now know as psychosomatic conditions [38]. The remaining containers were marked "purgatives" and the dosage prescribed was five capsules every 15 minutes for a period of several hours. Impressive results were claimed for this "most violent" purgative.

Benjamin Rush had an unorthodox liking for psychosomatic concepts and regarded imagination to be necessary in the workings of placebos. He frequently prescribed remedies of doubtful efficacy in the critical stages of acute diseases and claimed that "the success of this measure has much oftener answered than disappointed my expectations." [19, p. 208]

With the emergence of psychology as a separate discipline in the late nineteenth century, came many statements of imagery's role in arousal. Parallelism did not prevent William James from formulating a theory of "ideo-motor action." [45] In the psychology texts of the early twentieth century, we find James' theory accepted almost unanimously. It appeared that the time for a renaissance of Aristotelian theory had arrived. This was not to be the case however. The behaviorists were eminently successful in eliminating all mentalistic concepts from the arena of serious research. As Klinger notes, from 1920 to 1960, there was a moratorium in North American psychology on investigations of inner experience, including imagery; and not a single book on the topic of imagery appeared during this period [46]. However, this was not the case in Europe.

European Imagery Approaches in the 1900's

European clinical psychologists and psychiatrists continued to demonstrate a deep sensitivity to an involvement in the realm of imagination. This attitude was relatively unperturbed by the growing influence of behavioristic psychology in America. The reasons for the continuation of this largely subjective approach to imagery are many: 1) Many experimentalists fled Europe during the two World Wars. 2) The phenomenology of German and French origin permeated European clinical and scientific systems. 3) Jung's subjective approaches to the exploration of symbols in fantasies, dreams, and myths deeply influenced many European practitioners. 4) Europe had been affected by subjective Eastern psychology [47, p. 396, 48].

The notable contributors to the therapeutic use of imagination, of the early 1900's, include Carl Happich, Eugene Caslant, Oscar Vogt, Johannes Schultz, Ludwig Frank, Marc Guillerey, Pierce Clark, Sigmund Freud, Anna Freud, and

Carl Jung (See [47] for a review). More recently, Desoille and Frétigny and Virel in France, Leuner in Germany, and Assagioli in Italy have made significant contributions to the area and their influence has gradually infiltrated into North America [47, 49]. It is worth noting, however, that although European clinicians managed to elude the stranglehold of Watsonian ideas, they could not escape the powerful influence of Cartesian dualistic formulations. Consequently, with a few exceptions, imaginative skills were utilized in the treatment of the so-called psychological problems and not applied to the physical ones.

"Return of the Ostracized" in American Psychology

As Holt [50] and Watkins [51] point out, a renewed interest in imagery was initiated mainly by developments in areas peripheral to mainstream psychology, such as engineering psychology, sensory or perceptual deprivation research, biochemical and neuropsychological investigations, and studies of sleep and inactivity. However, gradually, psychologists realized that they could utilize the research techniques developed by the behaviorists, in investigations of topics that had been discarded but were critical to the understanding of human nature. And, ironically, behavior therapists themselves played a significant role in indirectly compelling clinicians to reexamine the relevance of imaginal variables. Experimental and clinical psychologists responded eagerly to Holt's invitation [50], "Come on in—the water is fine." The emergence of the "third force," the humanistic trend in psychology, lent the study and use of imagery further impetus and respectability. Recently, interest in widely varied image techniques has greatly expanded and intensified, and the therapeutic relevance of such techniques is being examined closely.

Bases for the Clinical Efficacy of Images

The imaginal mode has numerous characteristics that make it an eminently suitable vehicle for clinical work. A number of these are listed below:

1. It appears that imagery represents the functioning of vital components of the same psychological apparatus which is exercised in all activities . . . imagery represents the core of perceptual response and retrieval mechanisms [52]. Therefore, several researchers [52-55] propose that an experience in imagination can be regarded to be psychologically equivalent in many important respects, to the actual experience. Also, Perky [56], Leuba [57], Segal and Fesella [58], and Richardson [59], among others, have found that imagery and perception are experientially and neurophysiologically similar processes and share the same intrinsic qualities. Hebb and Pribram tend to support this view [60]. Furthermore, Penfield showed that the locus of image excitation corresponds to the locus of sensory functions in the brain [61].

2. Aristotle proposed that images are the source of action and guide behavior by presenting the goal object [1]. A number of modern psychologists [62-64], also believe that since images can represent situations and objects, they can act as motivators for future action. In fact, Shephard [65] and Tower and Singer [66], have found that people appear to act more according to imaginal consequences than to actual probabilities.

3. Apparently, meaning depends heavily on images; words elicit images which are accompanied by emotional responses, and these responses are the source of the words' meaning [67, 68]. Arieti adds that images render it possible to retain an emotional attitude toward an absent object [69].

4. Mental images furnish the opportunity to examine "the integration of perception, motivation, subjective meaning, and realistic abstract thought." [70, p. 99; 71]

5. Schachtel points out that as people are socialized, they generally rely increasingly on empty verbal clichés or abstractions and thus lose direct contact with experience [72]. But, as Singer and Pope state [73], this contact is implicit in the "concrete modality-specific imagery system," which therefore is a source of extensive details about past occurrences [74].

6. Imagery may provide the main access to memories encoded during a developmental stage when language was not yet present or not yet predominant [49].

7. Klinger maintains that the imaginal stream, present in image therapies, has a tendency to overrepresent the patient's problem area or "current concerns." "Unlike polite social discourse, imaginal techniques invite material that is likely to move selectively into the troubled areas of the client's life." [52, p. 12]

8. Also, Klinger observes that images are accompanied by emotional responses to internal and external cues contained in the situation [52]. Singer, too, states that the "imagery system increases the likelihood that we will experience more fully a range of emotions." [74, p. 36] Numerous other researchers have noted that focusing on images may uncover intense affective changes or elicit emotional reactions [47, p. 394]. "Images may have a greater capacity than the linguistic mode for the attraction and focusing of emotionally loaded association in concentrated forms: Verbal logic is linear; whereas the image is a simultaneous representation. The quality of simultaneity gives imagery greater isomorphism with the qualities of perception, and therefore greater capacity for descriptive accuracy." [49, p. 557]

9. Numerous researchers have shown that imagery is capable of producing very diverse physiological changes. For example, Barber et al. reported that the directive to imagine that tap water was sour led to increased salivation [75]. Simpson and Paivio observed alterations in pupillary size during imagery [76]. May and Johnson found that arousing images caused increased heart rate [77]. Yaremko and Butler noted that imagining a tone or shock and presentation of the actual stimuli led to comparable habituation [78]. Several investigators have observed changes in electromyograms caused by images [47, p. 294]. Furthermore, Barber reported that images could lead to blood glucose increases, inhibition of gastrointestinal activity, increased gastric-acid secretion, blister formation, and changes in skin temperature [79]. Several studies of meditation and biofeedback, which probably involved imagery, demonstrated reduction in blood pressure, heart rate, and oxygen consumption, and also alterations in gastrointestinal activity and body temperature [80]. Neal Miller has proposed that the utilization of imagery may be the only practical means of developing a measure of control over autonomic processes [81].

10. Therapists have observed that at times when individuals can no longer continue to express experiences verbally, spontaneous images may occur, filling in with perceptual, generally pictorial representations [49]. Also, when therapy seems to have come to a dead end, imagery often uncovers new areas of exploration [60]. Davé points out that if an impasse is reached on a certain problem, visualizing elements of the problem is more beneficial than utilizing a rational cognitive approach [82].

11. Researchers have shown that "free imagery," which is analogous to free association, is highly effective in circumventing even stubborn defenses and bringing to light repressed material [48, 52, 83]. The resort to imagery may catch the patient by surprise and outwit his defenses [60, p. 251].

12. Horowitz remarks that the image mode is best suited to unconscious organization [84]. It more readily allows for the spanning of the conscious-unconscious continuum than does overt or covert language; elements from the unconscious more easily enter imagoic cognition, and images more readily act as symbols [49]. . . . Images are less likely to be filtered through the conscious critical apparatus than is linguistic expression. In most cases, words and phrases must be consciously understood before they are spoken; for in order to assume a grammatical order they must first pass through a rational censorship. Imagery, perhaps, is not subject to this filtering process, and therefore may have the opportunity to be a more direct expression of the unconscious." [49, p. 556]

Imagery: Current American Approaches

From a position of near disgrace imagery recently has risen to be one of the hottest issues in both clinical and experimental cognitive psychology. Cognitive psychologists have extensively debated the question whether images represent a direct encoding of perceptual experiences, an artifact of propositional structuring of reality, or a constructive and reconstructive process [66]. But this issue has not been of any real concern to the majority of clinicians. "They assume that everyone experiences mental representations of objects and events, and these representations constitute their subject matter." [47, p. 395] A definition of imagery, such as the one provided by Richardson, is implicit in most of these approaches [59]:

Mental imagery refers to all those quasi-sensory or quasi-perceptual experiences of which we are self-consciously aware, and which exist for us in the absence of those stimulus conditions that are known to produce their genuine sensory or perceptual counterparts [59, p. 2].

Space limitations do not permit a detailed discussion of the various imagery approaches. Interested readers are referred to other sources [47].

But the multitude of existing imagery approaches can be classified perhaps into the following four broad categories.

1. The first group consists of a number of approaches that are based primarily on the Pavlovian and Skinnerian models. "They demonstrate the surface relationship between images and emotional reaction as well as the power of images to act as potent stimuli . . . . The methods consist of several variations of counterconditioning and emotional flooding." [47]
2. The second category includes the approaches of several clinicians who maintain that images very effectively provide individuals with a clear comprehension of their perceptual and affective distortions. Unlike the cognitive behavior therapists, they do not subscribe to the conditioning principles.
3. The third class basically deals with imagery rehearsal of physical and psychological health. The client may be asked to image a malfunctioning organ gradually becoming normal or to practice in imagination a healthy interpersonal relationship. No complicated interpretation or theories are offered except the assumption that "sane" imagination will gradually lead to sane reality.
4. The fourth category includes the "depth" imagery techniques that place the healing of the psyche back into the "magical" model which emphasizes a transformation through "irrational" procedures as opposed to rational or reflexive therapies.

Extensive claims concerning the potential of imagery for therapeutic benefits are being made. However, the claims, with a few exceptions, are based largely on the reports of clinicians and are not sufficiently backed by well-controlled investigations. Further systematic research on the therapeutic outcome of imagery approaches is sorely needed.

CONCLUDING REMARKS

In general, psychologists and physicians have explicitly or implicitly assumed dualism. Various attempts have been made to circumvent the problem, but never has dualism been rejected as inapplicable to, or irreconcilable with the phenomena of psychophysiology and psychosomatics. Recently, however, physicists have addressed the question of dualism's applicability to the life processes. Their consensus is that dualism must be replaced by a more reasonable conception.

Dualism is a form of reductionism, and because it simplified subject matter it led to great advances in the physical sciences. Only within the past few decades has its inadequacy been realized. Von Neumann [85] and Polanyi [86, 87] expressed doubts concerning the possibility of explaining the phenomena of life on mechanistic grounds. Several eminent physicists including Elsasser [88, 89], Wigner [90], and Schrödinger [91], founder of wave mechanics, have argued a need for a separate set of laws to account for organismic functioning. The consensus is that current knowledge in physics is neither adequate nor appropriate in application to living systems.

Elsasser's main thesis is that "the time-honored dualism of the mutually exclusive systems of thought, mechanistic biology on the one hand and vitalism on the other, express a pair of theoretical approaches which are both inadequate." [89, p. v] There are regularities in the organism, whose existence cannot be logicomathematically derived from the laws of physics. To Elsasser, life is a *"primary* phenomenon, not deducible from physics or anything else" [89, p. 52]. Life is a "process," and he introduced the term "biotonic" to apply to the phenomena of living systems.

Wigner gave rigorous mathematical proof that mechanistic reductionism is inapplicable in biology [90]. Schrödinger used the stability of hereditary transmission to show the inapplicability of physical laws [91]. Physics fails "not on the grounds that there is any 'new force' or what not, . . . but because the construction [of atoms within the living organism] is different from anything yet tested in the physical laboratory." [91, p. 81]

If the implications of dualism are prohibitive to physicists, how much more so are they to psychologists and health professionals generally. A solution may reside in the concept of a "biotonic phase" of existence. Many distinguished writers, including the physicists just cited, have argued for the acceptance of a biotonic phase. Within psychology, Weimer has accepted the concept and has presented an analysis of causation [92, 93]. If we accept the existence of three phases of existence, as distinguished from the Cartesian two, we are able to address causation without self-contradiction. These three dimensions of reality are 1) the psychic phase (where mnemic causality applies), 2) the material phase (as defined by classical and quantum physics), and 3) the biotonic phase, which is reducible neither to mental nor material phases.

The biotonic phase provides a substrate for psychophysiological functioning in the same manner that the biological soul of the pre-Cartesian era provided a substrate. It removes the burden of causation from mental events. It provides a rational basis for theory in psychophysiology and psychosomatics. With such a basis for theory we might easily restore the role of imagination to the position of prominence it once enjoyed.

REFERENCES

1. C. E. McMahon, Images as Motives and Motivators: A Historical Perspective, *American Journal of Psychology, 86*, pp. 465-490, 1973.
2. D. W. Stark (ed.), *The De Anima of Aristotle*, W. Browne, London, 1861.
3. R. McKean (ed.), *The Basic Works of Aristotle*, Random House, New York, 1941.
4. J. B. Gould, *The Philosophy of Chrysippus*, E. J. Brill, Leiden, 1970.
5. C. T. Lucretius, *On nature*, R. M. Geer (trans.), Bobs-Merrill Co., New York, 1965.
6. C. E. McMahon, Voluntary Control of Involuntary Functions: The Approach of the Stoics, *Psychophysiology, 11*, pp. 710-714, 1974.
7. C. E. McMahon, The Role of Imagination in the Disease Process: Pre-Cartesian History, *Psychological Medicine, 6*, pp. 179-184, 1976.
8. J. Huarte (1575), *The Examination of Men's Wits*, Scholars' Facsimilies and Reprints, Gainesville, 1959.
9. C. Knight (ed.), *The Stratford Shakespeare*, D. Appleton and Co., New York, 1876.
10. F. Coeffeteau, *A Table of Humane Passions with Their Causes and Effects*, E. Grimeston (trans.), London, 1621.
11. T. Wright (1604), *The Passions of the Minde in Generall*, University of Illinois Press, Urbana, 1971.
12. L. Lemnius, *The Touchstone of Complexions*, E. A. for Michael Sparke, London, 1633.
13. R. Burton, *The Anatomy of Melancholy*, John Lichfield and James Short, Oxford, 1621.
14. P. Charron, *Of Wisdom*, Bonwick, London, 1601.
15. R. Descartes, *Discours de la Methode* (1637), in *Descartes Philosophical Writings*, N. K. Smith (trans.), Random House, New York, 1958.
16. R. Descartes, *Meditations de Prima Philosophia* (1641), in *Descartes Philosophical Writings*, N. K. Smith (trans.), Random House, New York, 1958.
17. W. Durant and A. Durant, *The Age of Reason Begins*, Simon and Schuster, New York, 1961.

18. H. W. Jones, Mid-Seventeenth Century Science: Some Polemics, *Asiris*, *9*, pp. 254-274, 1950.
19. C. E. McMahon and J. L. Hastrup, The Role of Imagination in the Disease Process: Post-Cartesian History, *Journal of Behavioral Medicine*, *36*:2, pp. 205-217.
20. J. Braid, *The Power of the Mind over the Body*, J. A. Churchill, London, 1846.
21. F. Podmore, *Introduction of Mesmerism to India*, University Books, New York, 1963.
22. H. Boerhaave, *Aphorisms: Concerning the Knowledge and Cure of Diseases*, F. Delacoste (trans.), B. Cowse and W. Innys, London, 1715.
23. Molière, *The Plays of Molière* (Vol. 6), K. P. Wormeley (trans.), Little Brown and Company, Boston, 1909.
24. A. Wolf, *A History of Science, Technology and Philosophy in the Sixteenth and Seventeenth Centuries*, Allen and Unwin Ltd., London, 1935.
25. D. Diderot, *The Encyclopedia*, S. J. Gendzier (ed.), Harper and Row, New York, 1967.
26. D. Hartley, *Observations on Man* (1749), Scholars' Facsimiles and Reprints, Gainesville, 1966.
27. H. M. Gardiner, *Feeling and Emotion*, American Book Company, New York, 1937.
28. W. McDougall, *Outline of Abnormal Psychology*, Charles Scribner's Sons, New York, 1926.
29. J. H. Boyd, *Workmen's Compensation and Industrial Insurance* (Vol. II), Bobbs-Merrill, Indianapolis, 1913.
30. R. Macnish, *Book of Aphorisms*, W. R. McPhum, London, 1859.
31. J. N. Langley, *The Autonomic Nervous System* (Part I), W. Heffer and Sons, Cambridge, 1921.
32. A. Fouillée, La psychologie des idées fixes, *Philosophical Review*, *36*, pp. pp. 515-535, 1893.
33. Alexander Bain, *The Senses and the Intellect*, D. Appleton and Co., New York, 1872.
34. E. Jacobson, Electrophysiology of Mental Activities, *American Journal of Psychology*, *48*, pp. 677-694, 1931.
35. J. Wolpe, *The Practice of Behavior Therapy*, Pergamon Press, Elmsford, New York, 1974.
36. J. B. Watson, *Behaviorism*, W. W. Norton and Co., New York, 1930.
37. R. R. Holt, On the Nature and Generality of Mental Imagery, in *The Function and Nature of Imagery*, P. W. Sheehan (ed.), Academic Press, New York, 1972.
38. C. E. McMahon, Psychosomatic Disease and the Problem of Causation, *Medical Hypotheses*, *2*, pp. 112-115 (c), 1976.
39. W. Vaughan, *Approved Directions for Health*, T. S. for Roger Jackson, London, 1612.
40. C. E. McMahon, Psychosomatic Concepts in the Works of Shakespeare, *Journal of the History of the Behavioral Sciences*, *12*, pp. 275-282 (b), 1976.

41. B. Gracian, *The Oracle*, J. M. Dent and Sons, Ltd., London, 1953.
42. H. C. Agrippa, *Three Books of Occult Philosophy or Magic*, W. F. White-head (ed.), Hahn and Whitehead, Chicago, 1898.
43. W. Falconer, *A Dissertation on the Influence of the Passions upon Disorders of the Body*, C. Dilly, London, 1788.
44. D. H. Tuke, *Illustrations of the Influence of Mind upon Body in Health and Disease, Designed to Elucidate the Action of Imagination*, J. A. Churchill, London, 1872.
45. W. James (1890), *The Principles of Psychology* (2 Vols.), Dover, New York, 1950.
46. E. Klinger, *The Structure and Function of Fantasy*, Wiley, New York, 1971.
47. A. A. Sheikh and C. S. Jordan, Clinical Uses of Mental Imagery, in *Imagery: Current Theory, Research, and Application*, A. A. Sheikh (ed.), Wiley, New York, 1983.
48. C. S. Jordan, Mental Imagery and Psychotherapy: European Approaches. In *The Potential of Fantasy and Imagination*, A. A. Sheikh and J. T. Shaffer (eds.), Brandon House, New York, 1979.
49. A. A. Sheikh and N. C. Panagiotou, Use of Mental Imagery in Psychotherapy: A Critical Review, *Perceptual and Motor Skills, 41*, pp. 555-585, 1975.
50. R. R. Holt, Imagery: The Return of the Ostracized, *American Psychologist, 19*, pp. 254-264, 1964.
51. M. M. Watkins, *Waking Dreams*, Harper, New York, 1976.
52. E. Klinger, Therapy and the Flow of Thought, in *Imagery: Its Many Dimensions and Applications*, J. E. Shorr, G. E. Sobel, P. Robin, and J. A. Connella (eds.), Plenum, New York, 1980.
53. S. Kosslyn, *Image and Mind*, Harvard University Press, Cambridge, Massachusetts, 1980.
54. U. Neisser, *Cognition and Reality*, Freeman, San Francsico, 1976.
55. A. A. Sheikh (ed.), *Imagery: Current Theory, Research, and Application*, Wiley, New York, 1983.
56. C. W. Perky, An Experimental Study of Imagination, *American Journal of Psychology, 21*, pp. 422-452, 1910.
57. C. Leuba, Images as Conditioned Sensations, *Journal of Experimental Psychology, 26*, pp. 345-351, 1940.
58. S. J. Segal and Y. Fusella, Influence of Imaged Pictures and Sounds on Detection of Visual and Auditory Signals, *Journal of Experimental Psychology, 26*, pp. 458-464, 1910.
59. A. Richardson, *Mental Imagery*, Springer, New York, 1969.
60. J. L. Singer, *Imagery and Daydream Methods in Psychotherapy and Behavior Modification*, Academic Press, New York, 1974.
61. W. Penfield, The Brains Record of Auditory and Visual Experience—Final Summary, *Brain, 86*, pp. 595-696, 1963.
62. G. A. Miller, E. Galanter, and K. H. Pribram, *Plans and the Structure of Behavior*, Holt, New York, 1960.
63. O. H. Mowrer, Mental Imagery: An Indispensable Psychological Concept, *Journal of Mental Imagery, 1*, pp. 303-326, 1977.

64. T. R. Sarbin and W. C. Coe, *Hypnosis: A Social Psychological Analysis of Influence Communication*, Holt, New York, 1972.

65. R. N. Shepard, The Mental Image, *American Psychologist*, *33*, pp. 125-137, 1978.

66. R. B. Tower and J. L. Singer, The Measurement of Imagery: How Can It Be Clinically Useful?, in P. C. Kendall and S. Holland (eds.), *Cognitive-Behavioral Interventions: Assessment Methods*, Academic Press, New York, 1981.

67. B. R. Bugelski, Words and Things and Images, *American Psychologist*, *25*, pp. 1002-1012, 1970.

68. B. L. Forisha, The Outside and the Inside: Compartmentalization or Integration, in *The Potential of Fantasy and Imagination*. A. A. Sheikh and J. T. Shaffer (eds.), Brandon House, New York, 1979.

69. S. Arieti, *Creativity: The Magic Synthesis*, Basic Books, New York, 1976.

70. J. E. Shorr, Discoveries about the Mind's Ability to Organize and Find Meaning in Imagery, in, *Imagery: Its Many Dimensions and Applications*, E. Shorr, G. E. Sobel, P. Robin, and J. A. Connella, et al. (eds.), Plenum, New York, 1980.

71. S. K. Escalona, Book Review of Mental Imagery in Children by Jean Piaget and Barbel Inhelder (New York: Basic Books, 1979), *Journal of Nervous and Mental Diseases*, *156*, pp. 70-77, 1973.

72. E. G. Schachtel, *Metamorphosis: On the Development of Affect, Perception, Attention, and Memory*, Basic Books, New York, 1959.

73. J. L. Singer and K. S. Pope, The Use of Imagery and Fantasy Techniques in Psychotherapy, in *The Power of Human Imagination*. J. L. Singer and K. S. Pope (eds.), Plenum, New York, 1978.

74. J. L. Singer, Imagery and Affect Psychotherapy: Elaborating Private Scripts and Generating Contexts, in *The Potential of Fantasy and Imagination*, A. A. Sheikh and J. T. Shaffer (eds.), Brandon House, New York, 1979.

75. T. X. Barber, H. M. Chauncey, and R. A. Winer, The Effect of Hypnotic and Nonhypnotic Suggestions on Parotid Gland Response to Gustatory Stimuli, *Psychosomatic Medicine*, *26*, pp. 374-380, 1964.

76. H. M. Simpson and A. Paivio, Changes in Pupil Size During an Imagery Task without Motor Involvement, *Psychonomic Science*, *5*, pp. 405-406, 1966.

77. J. May and H. Johnson, Physiological Activity to Internally Elicited Arousal and Inhibitory Thoughts, *Journal of Abnormal Psychology*, *82*, pp. 239-245, 1973.

78. R. M. Yaremko and M. C. Butler, Imaginal Experience and Attenuation of the Galvanic Skin Response to Shock, *Bulletin of the Psychonomic Society*, *5*, pp. 317-318, 1975.

79. T. X. Barber, Hypnosis, Suggestions and Psychosomatic Phenomena, A New Look from the Standpoint of Recent Experimental Studies, *The American Journal of Clinical Hypnosis*, *21*, pp. 13-27, 1978.

80. A. A. Sheikh, P. Richardson, and L. M. Moleski, Psychosomatics and Mental Imagery: A Brief Review, in *The Potential of Fantasy and Imagination*, A. A. Sheikh and J. T. Shaffer (eds.), Brandon House, New York, 1979.

81. N. E. Miller, Interactions between Learned and Physical Factors in Mental Illness, in *Biofeedback and Self-Control*, D. Shapiro et al. (eds.), Aldine, Chicago, 1972.
82. R. P. Davé, The Effect of Hypnotically Induced Dreams on Creative Problem Solving, unpublished master's thesis, Mighican State University, 1976.
83. J. Reyher, Free Imagery, an Uncovering Procedure, *Journal of Clinical Psychology, 19*, pp. 454-459, 1963.
84. M. J. Horowitz, *Image Formation and Cognition*, Appleton, New York, 1970.
85. J. Von Neumann, *Theory of Self-Reproducing Automats*, A. Burks (ed.), University of Illinois Press, Urbana, 1966.
86. M. Polanyi, *Personal Knowledge*, Harper, New York, 1958.
87. M. Polanyi, *The Tacit Dimension*, Doubleday, Garden City, 1966.
88. W. M. Elsasser, *The Physical Foundations of Biology*, Pergamon Press, New York, 1958.
89. W. M. Elsasser, *Atom and Organism: A New Approach to Theoretical Biology*, Princeton University Press, Princeton, 1966.
90. E. P. Wigner, *Symmetries and Reflections*, Indiana University Press, Bloomington, Indiana, 1967.
91. E. Schrödinger, *What Is Life?*, Cambridge University Press, Cambridge, 1944.
92. W. B. Weimer, Manifestations of Mind: Some Conceptual and Empirical Issues, in *Consciousness and the Brain*, G. Globus (ed.), Plenum Publishing Co., New York, 1976 (a).
93. W. B. Weimer, *Structural Analysis and the Future of Psychology*, Erlbaum Associates, New York, 1976 (b).

CHAPTER 2

Psychophysiology of Imagery and Healing: A Systems Perspective

GARY E. SCHWARTZ

INTRODUCTION AND OVERVIEW

The purpose of this chapter is to present a general, biopsychosocial theory of the relationship between imagery and healing. The chapter is based on an invited lecture and is written to maintain as much of the flavor of the lecture as is appropriate in written form. The chapter should be viewed more as a sketch than as a complete picture—a sketch which the reader can elaborate.

It has long been claimed that imagery can have unique, if not profound, effects on physiological activity and health. With few exceptions [1], most of these observations have been ignored by mainstream medicine and psychology. I believe a major reason for this lack of interest, if not downright hostility, is the lack of a comprehensive theory that can integrate the biological, psychological, and social mechanisms implied by these observations. I believe that systems theory [2,3], as recently applied to behavioral medicine [4-7], has the potential to provide a metatheoretical framework for integrating the biological, psychological, and social consequences of imagery on health and illness.

The general theory sketched in this chapter follows directly from a general theory recently described for integrating biological, psychological, and social processes involved with biofeedback [8]. As will become clear, since the general theory is actually a metatheory, it can be applied equally well to cognitive and affective processes and to overt behavioral processes (with biofeedback being a particularly good example). Table 1 (adopted from [8]), illustrates the nine

*This chapter was stimulated in part by the insightful and creative work of Jeanne L. Schwartz in the Yale Behavioral Medicine Clinic. The theory emerged during the period of my father's illness. This chapter is dedicated to the memory of Howard Schwartz, with love.

Table 1. Nine Major Levels of Processes Linking Imagery and Physiology

The levels are synthesized using a systems perspective. The processes are organized from micro to macro levels. Note that each higher-numbered process incorporates processes described by the lower-numbered processes.

9. Social interactions
8. Motivation and belief
7. Education and insight
6. Cognitive-emotional-behavioral-environmental self-control
5. Discrimination training
4. Motor-skills learning
3. Operant conditioning
2. Classical conditioning
1. Homeostatic-cybernetic self-regulation

Note: (See text for details, adopted from [8]).

major levels of processes involved with biofeedback and, as proposed here, with imagery.

Note that these levels of processes are organized hierarchically, from the more micro to the more macro, from the physical and biological, through the psychological, to the social. We can therefore posit the existence of biological imagery, psychological imagery, and social imagery. Then we can consider the levels of psychoneurophysiological processes involved with each of these levels of imagery. The theory suggests that as imagery becomes more macro, so too should the combination of neurological and physiological processes associated with the imagery.

The chapter begins with two clinical examples that highlight multilevel, multiprocess effects involved in complex self-generated imagery. Then, some principles of systems theory are presented which are fundamental to understanding the application of the general theory to the imagery/healing question. This is followed by a brief discussion of each of the nine levels of imagery processes, showing how each process emerges and interacts as one moves from the simple to the more complex, from the micro to the more macro. As this general picture is sketched, the reader will see how the theory not only integrates these observations, but also suggests new experiments and potentially new clinical applications that can be tested empirically.

TWO CLINICAL EXAMPLES

"Hot Thoughts" for Cold Feet and "Hands—You're Hot!"

The first clinical example occurred almost fifteen years ago when I was just beginning to apply biofeedback to cardiovascular problems. This early experience taught me the importance of studying the effects of imagery on healing.

The second example is current. The imagery effects in the second clinical example are even more dramatic than in the first and stimulated the writing of this chapter.

The first example occurred in the late 1960's, while David Shapiro, Bernard Tursky, and I were doing research at Harvard University on biofeedback for the treatment of hypertension (reviewed in [9]). At that time a man in his early sixties came to our laboratory suffering from cold, painful feet. His disorder was medically diagnosed as Reynaud's disease. What was unusual about this particular patient was that he was a practicing psychoanalyst who had come for behavioral treatment of his problem. If the reader recalls that this was the late 1960s, it should be apparent that in many ways this was a last-ditch effort for this man!

Although at that time, very little was known about the psychophysiology of Reynaud's disease, we decided to try to help him. We recorded blood flow from the big toe of each foot and began giving him binary feedback and rewards for relative increases in blood flow in his left foot. The patient was instructed to try to make the binary feedback (tones and lights) come on as often as possible. He was told that as an incentive for making the tones and lights come on, every now and then a reward in the form of a slide would appear on the screen. Although he was psychodynamically oriented, he was enthusiastic about trying the biofeedback procedure.

Over the course of about ten sessions, the patient showed dramatic increases in blood flow, primarily in his left foot. This specificity of biofeedback was interesting and was consistent with our theory of specificity of learning [9]. At this point, unbeknownst to him, we switched to giving the feedback and reward for relative increases in blood flow in his right foot. Over the next few sessions, the blood flow in his right foot caught up to that in his left foot.

Importantly, a fortuitous accident occurred for the patient. This accident, in fact, dramatically changed the course of my academic and clinical career. Being a psychoanalyst, the patient was prone to free associate. It turned out that he interpreted the slide reinforcers as being diverse material to which he should free associate! For example, if a picture came on of Boston, he free associated to scenes of the city. If a picture came on of a piece of artwork, he imagined art-related scenes. If a picture came on showing a nude female, he imagined sexual activities. Needless to say, he probably had the most active and complex imagery of any subject we had studied to date.

The fortuitous accident occurred in one of the middle sessions. The slide projector inadvertently jammed, and, rather than showing a slide, it displayed a bright, white light on the screen. Given his proclivity toward imagery and free association, the patient began imagining the sun, beaches, warmth, and so forth. These bright-light rewards led him to develop a class of what he called "hot thoughts." Once he developed this class of hot thoughts, he was ecstatic because he could carry these images with him anywhere. So he requested that we continue to use only the bright-light rewards. He informed us that his hot thoughts were very practical, since he could use them even on the job. If his feet started getting cold during therapy, all he had to do was tune his patient out, turn his hot thoughts on, attend to his feet, and then come back to his patient, all this unbeknownst to the patient (since the patient was free associating at the time!).

I recall being amazed by the elegant simplicity and potential power of this patient's biofeedback-aided imagery discovery. His discovery sounded curiously similar to claims made for hypnosis and autogenic training concerning imagery of warmth and blood flow. In the late 1960's, few researchers in psychophysiology took such claims seriously. I wondered, "How could hot thoughts lead to such changes in blood flow in the feet?" At that time, except for classical-conditioning theory (to be described as Level 2 below), there were few theories that encouraged one to take these claims seriously.

The hot-thoughts discovery of this patient was applied to the second clinical example provided by a patient currently being treated in the Yale Behavioral Medicine Clinic. This patient represents the other end of the spectrum. Rather than being an elderly, creative, and warm (pun intended) professional, this patient is a very young, creative, and now warm, lay child. The patient began treatment at age three. He suffered from serious migraine headaches which had no apparent biological or psychiatric basis. Jeanne Schwartz, who is very skilled in working with young children and families, decided to take on the task of seeing whether she could teach this young child to self-regulate his physiology in ways that might reduce his headaches.

Needless to say, trying to do biofeedback with a three-year-old child is quite a task. Jeanne began the treatment by developing a therapeutic relationship with the child. She played with the child and encouraged him to view the biofeedback equipment as being playful and friendly. For example, she and the child would put electrodes on "Jeremy the Frog" (a stuffed animal in Jeanne's office), as well as on the child's mother, and on Jeanne herself. The child was told that learning to control his body would be a healthy, enjoyable game. Jeanne concluded that a potent reinforcer for the child would not be slides of New Haven (or children's art, etc.) but something more immediate—a snack called cheese doodles. The child initially was given electromyographic biofeedback for reducing tension in his forehead, with substantial food and social reinforcement for reducing his muscle tension levels. He learned this rapidly in a few sessions. Then Jeanne taught him to warm his hands using temperature biofeedback. The child was very adept at learning to warm his hands, and in the process, his daytime headaches decreased by over 80 percent (though his nighttime headaches were not helped).

In the process of teaching the child to warm his hands, Jeanne encouraged the child to use hot thoughts to help him make the temperature feedback increase. The child loved the imagery and began playing with the imagery at various times during the day. What was striking to me, however, was not the fact that the child could effectively use imagery to help warm his hands, but rather that he rapidly graduated from the imagery to direct overt, verbal commands! This graduation to verbal commands was not suggested by Jeanne but was discovered by the child himself. He simply would say out loud, "Hands—you're hot!" and his hands would. In 1 or 2 minutes his hands would warm by 10 to 15°F. When he stopped trying to warm his hands, his hands would cool off again. Then he would again quietly but emphatically say, "Hands—you're hot!" and they would. He had clearly mastered the hand-warming game.

How is it possible for a three-year-old child to be able to learn to warm his hands, not only by visual and kinesthetic imagery, but also by verbal commands? If this is a real phenomenon (and I think the data speak for themselves), the question arises, how this profound control can take place.

I will propose that the command, "Hands—you're hot!" is deceptively simple and may for this child involve an integration of nine major levels of social psychoneurophysiological processes. I will propose that instead of thinking about this phenomenon as being a biological phenomenon versus a psychological phenomenon versus a social phenomenon (recall all the social factors, such as social praise and suggestion, involved in the training of both the elderly psychoanalyst and the young child), we should think of it as being a biopsychosocial phenomenon. In fact, for the child, the image he developed may well be an integrated biopsychosocial image. Systems theory helps us tease apart and integrate the potential combination of processes involved in this kind of imagery/physiology control.

INTRODUCTION TO SYSTEMS THEORY: METAPRINCIPLES OF METATHEORY

The fundamental metaprinciples of systems theory were derived by a number of people [2, 3] from the biological, psychological, and social sciences [7, 8]. These individuals proposed that fundamental metaprinciples exist in nature and can be applied to all levels of nature, from subatomic particles to ecology and beyond (e.g., astronomy). Furthermore, specific new principles may arise at each level as systems become more complex, such as the evolution of living systems as described by Miller [3]. However, these new principles are hypothesized to reflect basic expressions of the fundamental metaprinciples. The metaprinciple of emergent property described below is a case in point.

Briefly, a system is an entity (a whole) that is composed of a set of parts (which are subsystems). These parts interact. Out of the parts interaction emerge unique properties that characterize the new entity or system as a whole. These emergent properties represent more than the simple, independent sum of the properties of the parts studied in isolation. It is hypothesized that the emergent properties appear only when the parts are allowed to interact.

A classic example of emergent property is water—a chemical (molecule) that is composed of hydrogen and oxygen, two basic atoms. These atoms, at room temperature, themselves have a set of system/whole properties—they are both gases, they both have no smell, cannot be tasted, and so forth. However, when these two atoms (and only these two atoms) are connected under the right circumstances, a new, molecular system is formed, called water. Water has unique emergent properties that are very different from the individual properties of hydrogen and oxygen—at room temperature, water is a liquid, has no obvious smell, can be tasted, and so forth. It is impossible to predict from the individual properties of hydrogen and oxygen all the unique emergent properties of water.

What systems theorists propose is that emergent phenomena are universal in nature and occur at all levels of complexity. Atoms combine to form new molecules, molecules combine to form new more complex molecules, some of these complex molecules combine to form new living cells, living cells combine to form new organ systems and organisms, organisms combine to form new social groups, and so forth. The different disciplines of knowledge reflect the study of emergent phenomena that occur at each of these levels. Organized hierarchically, the disciplines emerge from philosophy and mathematics, to physics and physical chemistry, to chemistry and biochemistry, to cellular biology and organ physiology, to psychophysiology and psychology, to social psychology and sociology, to political science and economics, to government and ecology, and so forth.

It follows from this general principle of parts interacting to form unique, emergent wholes, that when two or more parts interact, they regulate each other. It is out of their mutual control/regulation that emergent properties occur and systems become whole, ordered structures. Note that it is very critical for the parts of a system to be connected properly. Connection is necessary for parts to interact to form a system. If connections occur, then regulation can occur, and a system can occur. Mutual connection leading to mutual regulation is called self-regulation. All systems regulate themselves, and out of their self-regulation, new properties emerge. If the system is an open system, it also is regulated by its environment—which is a suprasystem, of which the system is a part. Depending upon the level you look at, one person's part (subsystem) is another person's whole (system).

Cannon described one aspect of mutual regulation in his lovely book, *The Wisdom of the Body* [10]. In this book he described homeostasis, the process whereby the brain and body interact in mutual regulation to maintain the internal milieu. Homeostasis refers to the process whereby the body maintains certain critical levels of functioning despite stresses imposed upon it. For example, human body temperature is regulated to be about 98.6°F despite wide changes in external temperature. This stability requires multiple levels of self-regulation between brain and body, including the evolution of new brain-body-behavioral strategies, such as clothing and climate control subsystems in new environmental systems (e.g., heating and air-conditioning subsystems in houses). Regulation that leads to stabilization is termed negative feedback, for the feedback is used to counteract stresses by subtracting information around a set point.

Homeostasis is a prerequisite for all living systems. Negative feedback is a prerequisite for all systems. Weiner described this fundamental principle in his development of cybernetic/control theory, which is a subset of systems theory [11]. Positive feedback, by contrast, leads systems to accentuate processes as a function of external stresses. What most people do not recognize is that 1) positive feedback also is essential, at least for living systems (e.g., the hunger/eating relationship initially begins as a positive-feedback process), and 2) positive feedback is also a self-regulatory process (e.g., if the parts are not connected and cannot interact, positive-feedback effects cannot occur).

In summary, positive- and negative-feedback effects are properties of self-regulating systems and can occur at all levels. Cannon noted at the end of his book that homeostasis applied not only to the biological level but also to the social level [10]. Social homeostasis, he proposed, explained how people maintained families and friendships.

It follows from the above that if connection is a prerequisite for self-regulation, then disconnection should lead to impaired self-regulation. If a system becomes disconnected at some level, the system should become less ordered, less structured, less regulated. In the process, it should lose some of its emergent properties. I have developed the concept of disregulation to refer to the logical opposite of self-regulation [4, 5, 12]. In essence, self-regulation is to order in a system as disconnection is to disorder in a system. If connection leads to self-regulation which in turn leads to order, then disconnection should lead to disregulation which in turn should lead to disorder.

Note that disregulation also is a general concept, a metaprinciple of systems theory. Disregulation conceivably can occur in any system at any level. Disregulation at a subatomic level can lead to atomic explosions. Disregulation at a cellular level can lead to cancer. Disregulation at a psycholgoical level can lead to thought or behavior processes that are clearly out of control (e.g., schizophrenia). This is a general principle for conceptualizing how systems can become disordered and go out of control. I propose that imagery can be used not only to foster negative and positive feedback loop self-regulation, but also to foster disregulation. In fact, following the logic of systems theory, the potential for imagery to promote self-regulation or disregulation may be more profound than we currently recognize.

There are two other points implied by the above that must be understood before systems theory can be applied to the imagery/healing question. The first point is quite controversial and borders on the mystical. That is, when two parts interact and self-regulate, the system self-regulates "automatically." That is, if the parts are connected in a particular way, the system will "know" what to do and do so automatically. Consider, for example, self-regulation in a heating system. When the thermostat is appropriately connected to the furnace in a negative-feedback fashion, the question arises as to what makes the system self-regulate? Does the thermostat control the furnace, or does the furnace control the thermostat, or do they both control each other? Systems theory proposes that the behavior of the heating system emerges out of the parts' mutual regulation. This system, when connected properly, operates automatically. It does not have to be instructed to work in this fashion. It simply does, and does so quite effortlessly. The system will act with "ease" if it is in the appropriate environment and all the pieces are connected properly and functioning appropriately. This automatic "ease" in system self-regulation is presumed to be a general principle, one that applies to self-regulation at all levels. How consciousness and learning fit into this theory is particularly interesting and will be discussed below.

The second point (which also is controversial and borders on the mystical) is that systems behave with a sense of purpose. Once a system is connected, it will work to meet specific, emergent goals. In the heating system example, once the parts are connected, the system will work to maintain temperature around the set point. Connection, therefore, leads to purpose. Early systems theorists recognized the profound philosophical implications of this conclusion [2]. In essence, once connections are made, a system, so to speak, takes on a life of its own. If we change these connections, we change the way the system functions, and therefore change the system's purpose. I propose that a major effect of imagery is the making and breaking of connections, all kinds of connections at biological, psychological, and social levels, and this alters the system's purpose.

What, therefore, is essential to make a system work? First of all, the parts must be connected. How the parts are connected will determine how the system behaves. Second, how the information is interpreted by each of the connected parts will determine how the parts regulate each other and therefore how the system behaves. If the information is interpreted in a "negative" way, the information/feedback usually will lead to moderation. If the information is interpreted in a "positive" way, the information/feedback usually will lead to extremism. How each connection is interpreted will determine whether each connection contributes to moderation/stabilization or to extremism in the system. Third, the feedback may be intensified or amplified. The stronger the feedback, the stronger will be the connection, and the more the system will self-regulate. I emphasize amplification because imagery not only 1) makes or breaks connections and 2) determines how the connections will be interpreted, but also 3) determines whether existing connections will be amplified or minimized.

This, in brief, is an elementary sketch of key concepts of systems theory. How these concepts can be applied to the imagery/healing question should logically follow from the above, and some novel (emergent) suggestions for future research and applications should be apparent. The analysis will follow from Table 1, which lists nine basic levels considered here. We will use the seemingly simple command of "Hands—you're hot!" to illustrate how imagery can operate at various levels.

BASIC LEVELS

Level 1: Homeostatic/Cybernetic
Automatic Control

It follows from the above that when a person attends to some part of his/her body, s/he is making (or amplifying) specific connections between brain and body and breaking (or minimizing) other specific connections between brain and body. All things being equal, if the self-attention leads to self-connection, self-regulation should occur automatically, without the subject trying to control the physiological response consciously. The phenomenon of attention leading to automatic self-regulation has been described in the biofeedback literature and is reviewed in detail elsewhere [4, 8].

When a person says, "Hands—you're hot," the word and image of "hands" per se directs his/her attention to the hands. Theoretically, this should by itself promote self-regulation of the hands. A recent experiment by Schwartz and Rennert illustrates this attention self-regulation phenomenon [8]. We instructed subjects simply to attend to their breathing (sense their breathing go in and out) or to attend to their heart rate (sense of the heart's rhythm). As a control for self-directed attention, we had subjects attend to an external sound that was generated about once a second (similar to a heartbeat). On half of the trials, the subjects were instructed to attend without additional feedback amplification. On the other half of the trials, the subjects were instructed to amplify the feedback by natural kinesthetic biofeedback. That is, the subjects were told 1) to place their fingers in front of their nose to feel their breath going in and out, and 2) to place their fingers on their pulse to feel the effects of their heart beating. As a control for kinesthetic sensations, subjects were instructed to place their fingers directly on the speaker so that they could literally feel the vibrations of the speaker cone that generated the sound.

Our prediction was that self-attention, especially when amplified by the natural kinesthetic biofeedback, would lead to automatic and selective self-regulation. Even though subjects were not instructed to control their physiology, we predicted that, to the extent that they interpreted the feedback in a relaxed, safe fashion, the increased attention automatically would promote the natural homeostatic stabilization processes selectively involved in the control of respiration and of heart rate. The data confirmed this prediction. These data support the general hypothesis that the first and most fundamental effect of imagery is the making of connections by the direction of attention which will have automatic self-regulatory effects predicted by cybernetic/control theory. Needless to say, there is a need to conduct systematic research to test the generality of this fundamental hypothesis.

Once this connection is made, how is the information interpreted and possibly amplified? Implicit in the command "Hands—you're hot" are the processes

1) "Interpret the information as hot," and 2) "Amplify the sensations of hot." According to cybernetic/control theory, these two processes should each facilitate the warming of the hands. Moreover, it is critical that the sensation of warmth not trigger aversive thoughts and images, especially learned images. Though we will discuss learning below, it is valuable here to illustrate how interpretation of the feedback can potentially alter the effects of attentional self-regulation.

There are no data currently available that directly test the hypothesis predicated by the present theory that the interpretation of physiological sensations will effect the regulation of these processes. However, a clinical example of Engel provides important suggestive evidence. Engel and colleagues were conducting pioneering biofeedback research in the late 1960's, teaching patients to reduce their PVC's (preventricular contractions) by control using their heart rate. Engel discovered that, for some patients heart rate increases were associated with reduced PVC's, for other patients heart rate decreases were associated with reduced PVC's, and for some patients heart rate was unrelated to PVC's. As a result, Engle taught patients to both increase and decrease their heart rates in order to maximize the likelihood of finding clinically meaningful results (and also to increase the patients' skill in heart rate control).

The particular clinical example involved a woman who ended up being one of Engel's most successful biofeedback patients. She first was taught to increase her heart rate, which she learned quite rapidly. During this period, her PVC's increased dramatically. Then, when she was taught to decrease her heart rate, her PVC's decreased dramatically. However, despite her cardiologic improvements, she became quite upset and wanted to quit the program. When Engel interviewed the patient, the reason became clear. She was afraid that she was dying, and that her heart beat was stopping. She had concluded that she was okay if she could feel her heart beats—which actually were PVC's. When she was taught to lower her heart rate, she came to the conclusion that her heart was stopping, and she became very upset.

Engel explained to the woman that she should change her interpretation of her cardiologic perceptions. She should relabel the experience of cardiac sensations as unhealthy, not healthy, and relabel the absence of cardiac sensations as healthy, not unhealthy. When she did this, she felt happy about decreasing her heart rate, and she became quite successful in voluntarily controlling her potentially dangerous PVC's. Did her initial interpretations have a positive feedback effect on her PVC's, and did her reinterpretation facilitate the development of more healthy, homeostatic control over her PVC's? Future research is clearly needed to test this fundamental hypothesis.

Finally, brief mention should be made of amplification of physiological sensations by attention. Theoretically, people who can focus on their bodily sensations well and can amplify these sensations should show more automatic self-regulation of these processes. Also, certain kinds of instructions and social variables (high-level processes, see below), potentially should facilitate attention and thereby amplify the self-regulation. Though research findings on attentional absorption [14] and hypnosis are consistent with this hypothesis, there is currently no systematic research that has examined ways of amplifying internal feedback signals and their effects on automatic self-regulation. This is clearly a challenge for future research.

Level 2: Classical Conditioning

Once Level 1 processes are understood, it should follow how learning, including social learning, can be superimposed on these fundamental feedback processes. Cybernetic theory was based on the assumption that a system does not learn, that is, change the nature of its connections as a function of experience. However, living systems in general, and now computers as well, do change their connections as a function of experience. Levels 2-9 refer to different levels of learning processes that can occur, from the micro to the macro. Each higher-order learning process builds upon the lower-order learning processes in a hierarchical fashion. Note that this same logic, at least theoretically, might be applied to the basic thermostat-furnace example. A micro computer using modern artificial-intelligence programs could be added to the heating system. Therefore it could learn through experience to anticipate certain heating changes and make preparatory adjustments accordingly.

Classical conditioning, in essence, is the making of associations to environmental stimuli. Association learning, in systems terms, can be thought of as connection learning. Association learning involves the making and amplifying of connections. Extinction is therefore the breaking of connections. Association learning increases the probability of making certain connections and decreasing the probability of making others. As reviewed by Schwartz, modern theories of classical conditioning include biological preparedness as facilitating the making of certain connections [8]. It follows that through classical conditioning, we learn that the word "hot" is associated with feelings of warmth in our hands, elicited, for example, by placing our hands in warm water or by being out in the sun. The images, therefore, become classically conditioned to these natureal biological associations and combine with the Level 1 cybernetic processes when we attend to our hands and generate a warm image.

Note that classical conditioning with imagery implicitly involves Level 1 cybernetic processes. Moreover, it follows that the cybernetic/classical-conditioning connection may be strengthened by techniques that foster their association and integration. This is clearly a researchable question for the future.

Level 3: Operant Conditioning

It follows that operant conditioning includes cybernetic (Level 1) and classical-conditioning (Level 2) components. In operant conditioning, reinforcement is provided for making certain cybernetic and classical-conditioning associations. When the child was reinforced with cheese doodles for warming his hands, the warm image/warm physiology connection was strengthened by the food reinforcer. Hence, we can posit that reinforcement potentially aids the connecting of Level 1 and Level 2 imagery processes.

Level 4: Motor Skills Learning

Motor skills learning is a more complex form of operant learning. In motor skills learning, such as in the playing of musical instruments, the coordination of multiple processes is usually involved. Motor skills learning can be thought of as connecting layers of cybernetic-classical-operant patterns to achieve a complex goal. From a systems point of view, it becomes clear that images are remarkable in their ability to compactly organize complex patterns of multilevel processes. Consider the complex set of integrated processes involved with the instruction "Imagine that you are a three-year-old child . . . and you are on the beach . . . and you feel the sun . . . and you smell the salty air . . . etc." The image connects multiple processes in a temporal sequence. Following Lang [15], I propose that each time we add a component by imagery, we make a more complex psychoneurophysiological connection. The more complex the connections, the more complex the pattern of psychobiological processes should be. The image "Hands—you're hot" may have become for the child a shorthand means of integrating multiple Level 1 to 3 processes in an orchestrated Level 4 manner.

Levels 5 to 8

The reader should be able to fill in how higher-order processes can be layered, one on top of the other. Level 5 involves discrimination training. It relates to how successful people are in connecting physiological sensations to specific thoughts and environmental events. As people develop better Level 4 skills, their ability to make Level 5 discriminations should improve. This should foster advanced imagery/physiology connections.

Moving to Level 6, we can see that just as the psychoanalyst discovered that "hot thoughts" led to specific temperature changes in his feet, so too can people learn by experience to integrate various combinations of cognitive, emotional, somatic, and environmental processes to alter their physiology. At this stage, imagery control over physiology is quite voluntary and conscious. Whereas in Levels 1 to 3, self-regulation can occur without conscious awareness of physiological control, in Levels 4 to 6 consciousness is added as a higher-order, voluntary control process.

At Level 7, we begin to approach the concept of scripts and their relationship to even higher-order, organized control of behavior [16]. The command "Hands —you're hot" is a relatively simple script. Scripts become more and more complex as children mature and become adults. Since learning continues throughout the lifespan, so too does the development of images that can integrate complex, organized scripts. Scripts can be regarded as higher-level skills. In this context, skill learning would be a prerequisite for the development of scripts. (On the other hand, one can use the term "script" more in a systems sense and conclude that even classical conditioning is a script, albeit a very simple one.) The important point to recognize is that the organization of images involves the layering of psychological processes, and therefore, theoretically, the layering of underlying biological processes.

At Level 7, processes of education and insight arise. People may discover that particular conflicts in their lives are associated with certain physiological changes, and that resolving these conflicts can lead to the reduction of the physiological symptoms. It appears that the young child who learned to warm his hands had developed an elementary insight into some of his problems and also an insight into his ability to control his hand temperature. We can hypothesize that this would facilitate actual conscious control.

Level 8 is most intriguing, because it is the level of motivation and belief. Belief can be thought of as a metascript, a script that truly organizes our perceptions and actions. Clinical and experimental literature attest to the fact that motivation and belief influence the effectiveness of imagery in altering physiological processes. The art of good therapy, in part, is to help the patient believe in what he/she is doing, and to make new connections (and break other connections) in order to solve his/her problem. How does belief relate to the question of "Hands—you're hot"? Belief facilitates two major underlying processes.

One is that positive belief increases the likelihood that people will do what they are supposed to do. If one believes that something will happen, one is likely to practice things. Hence, all the Level 1 to 7 processes should be facilitated by positive belief. This, in turn, should increase the likelihood that new, emergent connections will be made, and that these connections will have consequences for health.

The second major process is that positive belief encourages people to realize that they are succeeding, and this may make them feel good about themselves. In psychobiological terms, this should facilitate the generation of positive affective states, and these physiological states may interact with the specific images to promote healing. Thinking happy thoughts in general may facilitate healing because of the psychoneurophysiological patterns associated with positive emotions [17]. This may include all the biochemical processes associated with positive states, including changes in immune function. Hence, a positive belief not only should foster practice and the making of multiple connections, but also should generate a particular psychobiological state (happiness) which may facilitate healing in general.

Level 9: Social Interaction

Up to now we have discussed mostly the biological (Levels 1 to 2) and psychological (Levels 3 through 8) levels of processes. Brief mention should be made of at least the first social level, so that the concept of biopsychosocial images becomes clear. Research indicates that social support and numerous other social variables alter physiological processes. The emerging interdisciplinary field of social psychophysiology recently has been reviewed in depth [18].

Since social factors can have a profound effect on physiological processes, it follows that imagery can be used to recreate these social situations internally. The more effective and elaborate the social imagery, the more comprehensive the physiological response patterns should be to this imagery. Creative social imagery should involve the making of new connections at the social level which, according to systems theory, should connect a combination of psychological, and therefore biological, processes as well. Social images have the potential to serve as meta images, integrating combinations of Level 1 to 8 processes. For example, if a patient imagines that the therapist is speaking to him/her in a reassuring manner, he/she may experience more psychological and physiological effects than if he/she simply imagines that he/she is feeling reassured. Numerous research and clinical questions are raised by this general hypothesis.

SUMMARY AND CONCLUSIONS

Systems theory is not a theory per se, but rather is a meta theory (or meta strategy) for conceptualizing and connecting diverse data and processes occurring across multiple levels. I have proposed that systems theory can be used to develop an integrative biopsychosocial framework for explaining how imagery can lead to changes in physiology and therefore affect health and illness. From the vantage point of systems theory, the nine levels of theories organized in Table 1 are not viewed as being alternative or competing theories of imagery, but rather are viewed as reflecting different levels of processes and theories layered hierarchically in conceptual/functional space (just as our nervous system is layered hierarchically in physiological/structural space).

The reason why I believe that systems theory is the most general and effective existing framework for understanding biopsychosocial interactions in general, and imagery/healing interactions in particular, is because it successfully meets three basic criteria for being an effective macro level theory (strategy).

1. The macro level theory should *integrate seemingly disparate* and/or *competing findings*. This includes the fact that data disregarded by more specific, micro level theories (e.g., findings that are viewed as anomalous findings that are not predicted and are not consistent with a given theory) should be viewed as being important and even essential from the perspective of the macro level theory.

2. The macro level theory should stimulate *new predictions* and *discoveries* that would not be derived from the more micro level theories. Hence, the effective macro level theory should not only integrate more data (criteria 1) but it also should uncover new data (criteria 2).

3. The macro level theory should be *friendly* to the micro level theories, illustrating how the *micro level theories are special cases* of the macro theory and are

appropriate to specific levels of processes. Hence, micro level theories should not be discarded because they appear wrong at certain levels. Rather, the micro level theories should be appreciated and incorporated to the extent that they reflect novel emergent processes occurring at specific levels.

I believe that a primary reason why imagery has been so confusing and has caused so much conflict (if not avoidance) in the scientific community is due to the fact that a rational approach to conceptualizing and organizing the seemingly confusing, contradictory and counterintuitive array of observations has been lacking. Systems theory has the potential to provide a general structure for organizing this information by incorporating disparate data (criteria 1), making new predictions (criteria 2), and integrating seemingly competing theories in a comprehensive and friendly manner (criteria 3).

This chapter has focused on the potential healing properties of imagery, emphasizing the systems concepts of connection and information interpretation as they influence self-regulation occurring at biological, psychological and social levels. This chapter has not discussed the opposite side of the coin, namely the disconnection/disregulation/disorder role that imagery can play in promoting disease [19]. However, the logic of how the theory can be applied to imagery that is disconnecting and therefore is psychophysiologically disordering should be self-evident. Also, this chapter has not discussed the applications of the theory to psychoneuroendocrinology and psychoneuroimmunology, two important new interdisciplinary fields within behavioral medicine. Again, the logic of how the theory can be applied to imagery/neural/immune connections that should promote self-regulation and healing at multiple levels in disorders such as cancer should be self-evident.

One challenge for the future is to bring conceptual and methodological rigor to the more macro levels of psychology and social relations that is comparable to the rigor found at the more micro levels of chemistry and physiology. I believe that systems theory is useful in this regard because it provides a *common* meta language reflecting structural and functional concepts that can be spoken in common by all disciplines (see [6, 8]). If this chapter has stimulated the reader's imagination to make new connections and interpretations (which theoretically should effect associated layers of the reader's physiological processes as well!) linking macro and micro levels of theory as applied to the imagery/healing question, then it will have achieved its primary goal.

REFERENCES

1. P. J. Lang, G. A. Miller, and D. N. Levin, Anxiety and Fear: Central Processing and Peripheral Physiology, in *Consciousness and Self-Regulation*, Vol. 3, R. L. Davidson, G. E. Schwartz and D. Shapiro (eds.), Plenum Press, New York, 1983.
2. L. von Bertalanffy, *General Systems Theory*, Braziller, New York, 1968.
3. J. G. Miller, *Living Systems*, McGraw Hill, New York, 1978.

4. G. E. Schwartz, The Brain as a Health Care System, in *Health Psychology*, G. E. Stone, N. Adler and F. Cohen (eds.), Jossey-Bass, San Francisco, 1979.

5. G. E. Schwartz, Behavioral Medicine and Systems Theory: A New Synthesis, *National Forum*, *4*, pp. 25-30, 1980.

6. G. E. Schwartz, A Systems Analysis of Psychobiology and Behavior Therapy: Implications for Behavioral Medicine, in Special issue on behavioral medicine of *Psychotherapy and Psychosomatics*, H. Leigh (ed.), *36*, pp. 159-184, 1981.

7. G. E. Schwartz, Testing the Biopsychosocial Model: The Major Challenge Facing Behavioral Medicine?, Special issue on behavioral medicine of *Journal of Consulting and Clinical Psychology*, E. Blanchard (ed.), *50*:6, pp. 1040-1053, 1982.

8. G. E. Schwartz, Biofeedback as a Paradigm for Health Enhancement and Disease Prevention: A Systems Perspective, in *Behavioral Health: A Handbook of Health Enhancement and Disease Prevention*, Matarazzo, Miller et al. (eds.), Wiley, New York, in press.

9. G. E. Schwartz, Biofeedback as Therapy: Some Theoretical and Clinical Issues, *American Psychologist*, *29*, pp. 666-673, 1973.

10. W. B. Cannon, *The Wisdom of the Body*, Norton, New York, 1932.

11. N. Weiner, *Cybernetics or Control and Communication in the Animal and Machine*, MIT Press, Cambridge, 1948.

12. G. E. Schwartz, Disregulation Theory and Disease: Applications to the Repression/Cerebral Disconnection/Cardiovascular Disorder Hypothesis, in Special issue on behavioral medicine of *International Review of Applied Psychology*, J. Matarazzo, N. Miller, and S. Weiss (eds.), *32*, pp. 95-118, 1983.

13. G. E. Schwartz, and K. Rennert, Effects of Attention and Sensory Feedback on Automatic Self-Regulation of Heart Rate Versus Respiration, manuscript in preparation.

14. R. J. Davidson, G. E. Schwartz, and L. P. Rothman, Attentional Style and the Self-Regulation of Mode-Specific Attention: An Electroencephalographic Study, *Journal of Abnormal Psychology*, *85*, pp. 611-612, 1976.

15. P. J. Lang, A Bio-Informational Theory of Emotional Imagery, *Psychophysiology*, *16*, pp. 495-512, 1979.

16. R. Abelson, Psychological Status of the Script Concept, *American Psychologist*, *37*, pp. 715-729, 1981.

17. G. E. Schwartz, D. A. Weinberger, and J. A. Singer, Cardiovascular Differentiation of Happiness, Sadness, Anger, and Fear Following Imagery and Exercise, *Psychosomatic Medicine*, *43*, pp. 343-364, 1981.

18. J. T. Cacioppo and R. E. Petty (eds.), *Social Psychophysiology*, Guilford Press, New York, 1983.

19. G. E. Schwartz, Social Psychophysiology and Behavioral Medicine: A Systems Perspective, in *Social Psychophysiology*, J. T. Cacioppo and R. E. Petty (eds.), Guilford Press, New York, 1983.

CHAPTER 3

Imagery, Cerebral Laterality, and the Healing Process

ROBERT G. LEY
AND RICHARD J. FREEMAN

The use of mental imagery as a healing technique is well established. Countless instances of the invocation of imagery to facilitate therapeutic change can be cited. Psychotherapists, nurses, thanatologists, neurologists, and hypnotists are among the modern-day healers who might employ imagery to alleviate the physical and psychological suffering of their patients. Currently, specific imagery techniques are used to promote weight control, to stop smoking, to ease post-surgical complications, to cure acne vulgaris, to assist in the removal of an abscessed tooth, or in the treatment of a sex offender. In fact, the practitioner's creative capacity imposes perhaps the only limitation on the number and nature of imagery procedures which can be deployed. Within the domain of behavior therapy alone, over twenty specific imagery strategies can be identified [1]. Given that a recent book on innovative psychotherapies identified over 250 non-traditional, therapeutic techniques [2], the mind reels in speculating about the number of imagery strategies employed in these approaches. However, despite the extensive clinical application of mental imagery, few theoretical models exist to account for the therapeutic effectiveness of imagery [3].

In this chapter, a rudimentary model is developed which proposes that the diversity of imagery-based therapeutic techniques share common cognitive, affective, neuroendocrine and immunologic mechanisms. Furthermore, the model to be advanced provides a novel formulation of the exquisite interdependency of mind and body, by integrating the differential functions of the left and right cerebral hemispheres with the cognitive, emotional, and ultimately, cellular events which constitute healing. This brain/immune theory potentially accounts for the effectiveness of imagery in both psychotherapy and behavioral medicine. Thus, it is hoped that this model will provide a conceptual framework for practitioners' understanding of imagery-based, therapeutic change, regardless of whether they are working with molars, moles, or molesters.

THE CONCEPT OF CEREBRAL LATERALITY

These days it is rare to pick up a magazine or newspaper without finding some reference to cerebral laterality. Hemispheric differences in function have been used to suggest explanations for behavior as varied as tennis playing [4], the seating arrangements in classrooms and auditoriums [5], vocational choice [6], and even winetasting and movie preferences. Left and right hemispheric cognitive styles also have been employed metaphorically to explain differences in religious and political philosophies [7], the development of civilizations [8] and educational practice [9]. This proliferation of public interest mirrors a spate of scientific activity: A ten-fold increase in studies of cerebral laterality occurred between 1960 and 1980.

Given the proliferation of interest in brain laterality, it is worth taking stock of what is and is not known about the cerebral hemispheres. This brief review of cerebral asymmetries generally, will provide a background for the more specific discussion of the relationship between laterality, imagery, and healing which follows.

THE "BASICS" OF LATERALITY

A variety of research strategies, ranging from clinical case descriptions of brain-injured patients to measurements of EEG alpha suppression, have confirmed that the two cerebral hemispheres are specialized for different cognitive functions. Additionally, it is known that each cerebral hemisphere controls movement in the opposite half of the body. This means that sounds coming to the left ear, images in the left visual field, and sensations in the left hand are transmitted largely to the right hemisphere. Conversely, stimuli and experiences from the right half of the body or space are projected to the left hemisphere. One dramatic example of this contralateral ennervation or "cross-wiring" is the occurrence of a left-side paralysis of the arm, leg, trunk, or facial musculature following right hemispheric injury [10].

In the mid-nineteenth century, the work of European neurologists, such as Paul Broca, showed that damage to certain portions of the left hemisphere resulted in speech aphasias. Aphasias were rarely observed to follow instances of right hemispheric damage, and consequently it was inferred that the left hemisphere was functionally specialized for most language and verbal processes. In contrast, the right hemisphere seems relatively dominant for visual spatial tasks [11], although no right hemispheric cognitive ability is as firmly established as the left hemisphere's predominance for language. The right hemisphere seems more involved in making fine sensory discriminations, such as detecting tactile patterns [12]. Also, the right hemisphere plays an important role in other nonverbal activities, such as music [13], face recognition [14], and emotional expression [15].

It is most appropriate to view the relative hemispheric advantages for verbal, as opposed to visual-spatial tasks, as reflecting the different cognitive "styles" of each hemisphere. It is not so much that each hemisphere is tooled to work with different stimuli—the left with words and the right with spatial patterns—but rather that each hemisphere is specialized to provide a distinctive mode of information processing. The styles are more or less proficient in operating on different stimuli. For example, the left hemisphere is characterized as a logical, analytic, and sequential processor for which words are most fitting; the right hemisphere is characterized as a holistic, gestalt, and simultaneous processor for which spatial relationships are most appropriate [7].

IMAGERY: ITS DEFINITION (!) AND RELATION TO THE RIGHT HEMISPHERE

Although the current popularity of imagery research has led to the identification of certain characteristics of imagery and imagers [16], a consensual definition of imagery has eluded many researchers. Most commonly, individuals describe images as being "pictures in the head": This metaphor treats images as mental photographs or snapshots [17]. However, recent reviews of the "image as picture" theories have found them lacking [18]. Alternatively, it has been proposed that images are best conceptualized as "propositional" constructs [19]. In other words, images are more accurately represented as symbolic descriptions and are conceptual, rather than pictorial, in nature.

Although the debate on images as pictures or propositions continues, a relatively unambiguous relationship between imagery and cerebral laterality has emerged. It seems that regardless of what imagery is, or does, it is most likely to be doing it in the right hemisphere of the brain. In short, clinical and experimental evidence indicates that the right hemisphere has a primary role in imagery processes [20]. A number of points regarding the relationship between the right hemisphere and imagery can be made.

Damage to the various parts of the right hemisphere frequently leads to loss of visualization, visual memory, visual dreaming, and vividness of imagery [21]. Such right-sided damage also typically impairs imagery-based learning and performance on spatial tasks with imageable components. Conversely, compensation for verbal-memory deficits due to left-hemisphere injury can be achieved by teaching patients to use imagery mnemonics which are mediated by the intact right hemisphere [22]. An example of such a visualization technique is the familiar "One is a bun, two is a shoe, three is a tree, etc." rhyme for remembering such things as a grocery list. Electrical stimulation of the right temporal lobe generally produces reports of rich images and other visual hallucinatory impressions similar to those occurring in night dreams and epileptic auras. Right hemispheric involvement in visual dreaming and in epileptic "dreamy states" also has been postulated [23]. Electrophysiological (EEG and GSR) studies of normal subjects have found that increased activation of the right hemisphere accompanies subjects' imagery experiences [24]. Conjugate lateral eye movement or CLEM research has found left CLEMs and theoretically a presumed right hemispheric activation to correlate with the preferred use and clarity of images as well as with performance on imagery tasks [25]. Visual-recognition studies of laterally presented abstract and concrete words have indicated a right hemispheric capacity to "read," store, or otherwise mediate the processing of high-imagery words [20].

In sum, the vast majority of research on imagery and brain functions identifies the role of the right hemisphere in imagery: Reports of left hemispheric participation in imagery processes are infrequent. That images can arouse strong emotions and vice versa is beyond question. One reason for this interdependence may be that the right cerebral hemisphere predominantly mediates both imagery and affect.

LATERALIZATION OF EMOTIONAL PROCESSES

Although some controversy exists as to the relative contribution of each hemisphere to the perception of emotion [26], the majority of experimental studies of normal subjects has found overall right hemispheric superiorities for processing a diversity of emotional stimuli, including speech, music, and facial expressions [27]. Right hemispheric superiorities have been found for recognizing nonverbal human sounds with affective components, such as laughing, crying and shrieking [28]. Right-hemisphere superiorities also exist for identifying the emotional tone of spoken passages [29]. That music arouses emotions is indisputable, and evidence now supports the likelihood of a right hemispheric superiority for such information processing. Tonal sequences evoking both positive and negative moods are rated more accurately and judged more emotional when listened to on the left ear [30]. Photographs and drawings of faces expressing different emotions seem to be more quickly and accurately identified when they are presented in the left visual field (LVF) and thus processed by the right hemisphere [15, 31].

The experimental studies mentioned here have investigated largely the lateralization of emotion *perception*. Evidence also exists that the right hemisphere may be disproportionately involved in emotion *expression*. For example, a number of experiments have found that emotions are expressed more intensely on the left side of the face [32]. Some clinical evidence also points to the special role of the right hemisphere in emotional expression: Studies of hysterical conversion symptoms [33, 34] and psychosomatic symptoms [35] have found sidedness differences in symptom manifestation which implicate the right hemisphere.

Clinical evidence also shows functional hemispheric differences in emotionally disturbed individuals. The results of neuropsychological studies of clinically depressed subjects are important for the case relating laterality, imagery, and healing. For example, a standard neuropsychological test battery [36] administered to a depressed psychiatric population revealed indications of right-hemisphere dysfunction. Yosawitz and Bruder also found that patients who have been diagnosed as having affective disorders show a test performance characteristic of right-hemisphere disability [37]. Similarly, Flor-Henry has shown degraded right-hemisphere test performance in an affective-disordered psychiatric population [38].

Electrophysiological studies of depressed psychiatric patients have produced results consistent with these findings. Studies of the EEG amplitude of depressed patients [39] indicate that the right hemisphere is less activated than the left. In short, the bulk of experimental investigations of depressed patients shows a pattern of right hemispheric disorganization.

IMAGERY, LATERALITY, AND HEALING IN PSYCHOTHERAPY AND SOMATIC DISEASE

To this point the case has been made that the right hemisphere mediates processes involving imagery and emotion. Additionally, it was indicated that some form of right hemispheric disorganization was implicated in depression. Elsewhere, Ley has written extensively on the implications of these findings for psychotherapy [40]. Ley's position has been that most psychotherapeutic strategies, whether psychoanalytic, behavioral, or gestalt, can be construed as attempts at decoding a right hemispheric repository of experience. Furthermore, he asserts that the affective and imagery mechanisms of the right hemisphere mediate much of the therapist/client process as well as more general therapeutic change. A diversity of psychotherapies can be construed as attempts at creating a therapeutic atmosphere that is congenial to right hemispheric mentation and facilitative of such a mode of experience. Ley describes the specific ways in which the therapeutic setting, the therapeutic "words," and the therapeutic task(s) contribute to the creation of a right hemispheric environment. For a detailed description of these relationships the interested reader is referred to the original source [40].

However, just as the relationship between laterality, imagery, and affect has relevance for explicating the process of psychotherapy, it is also plausible that this same tripartite association underpins somatic healing. The possibility that functional hemispheric differences are implicated in holistic healing is strengthened because of the seeming interdependence of imagery, affect, and disease in the field of behavioral medicine. This consideration first requires an examination of the relationship between affect and disease.

Affect and Disease

As long ago as the second century A.D., Galen reported that cancer was more frequent in depressed, melancholic women, than in women of cheery or sanguine temperament. Since that time, there has been an enduring interest in the relationship between affect and a wide variety of disease processes. For our present purposes, suffice it to say that various affective states have been linked to either exacerbation of existing illnesses or have been implicated as risk factors for the development of diseases, such as hay fever [41], asthma [42], hypertension [42], ulcerative colitis [43], and cancer [44].

Interpretation of the various findings on affect and disease is made difficult by the variability in the research undertaken, which ranges from archival studies based on hospital records to prospective studies of individuals at risk for disease. The methods employed have included interviews, self-reports, physician ratings, and laboratory tests, which measure attitudes, affects, life events, electrophysiologic responses, and endocrine metabolites. The constructs invoked to account for the relationship between emotion and illness have included such concepts as organ vulnerability, response specificity, and genetic risk combined with environmental insult. Despite the diversity of subjects, methods, and measures, a remarkable consistency emerges: A wide variety of diseases are linked with two particular affective patterns. Table 1 presents the conclusions of twenty-eight papers on affect and disease, representing more than fifty empirical studies of various diseases.

It can be seen in Table 1 that feelings of helplessness, hopelessness, and loss often manifested in an episode of clinical depression have been consistently linked to a number of diseases, particularly cancer. Less frequently, it has been suggested that the psychological defenses of repression and denial, particularly of anger, have been linked to disease. While many of the studies are retrospective in nature, and therefore invite the argument that individuals with serious illness are quite likely to become depressed, the small number of prospective studies available confirm the idea that individuals who feel a sense of helplessness are more likely to develop illnesses [68].

With reference to Table 1, the link between specific affective states and disease is strengthened further if one considers that helplessness, hopelessness, and depression may be manifestations of one phenomenon: The clinical syndrome of depression incorporates self-perceptions or cognitions of helplessness and an affective state of hopelessness and despair.

Varied evidence supports this conclusion. For example, Seligman and his co-workers have argued that depression develops as a result of repeated exposure to inescapable stressors, and that the consequences of such exposure is a sense of helplessness and the development of clinical depression [69]. Additionally, much animal experimentation has found a link between exposure to inescapable stressors and the development of disease. For example, Sklar and Anisman have

Table 1. The Relationship Between Affect and Disease

Investigator	Disease	Affective State
Guy [45]	Cancer	Depression
Evans [46]	Cancer	Loss of hope
Miller and Jones [47]	Leukemia	Depression, anxiety
Greene and Miller [48]	Leukemia	Loss of sig. other
LeShan [49]	Neoplasm	Hopelessness, despair
Booth [50]	Cancer	Self-directed aggression
Mezai and Nemeth [51]	Cancer	Depression
Schmale and Iker [52]	Cancer	Hopelessness
Bahnson and Bahnson [53]	Cancer	Depression, hostility
Brown et al. [54]	Lung Cancer	Rigidity, repression, hostility, despair
Thomas and Greenstreet [55]	Cancer	Decreased depression
Pauli and Schmidt [56]	Cancer	Lethargy, depression
Kerr, Schapira, and Roth [57]	Cancer	Affective disorder
Witlock and Siskind [58]	Cancer	Affective disorder
Thomas, Duszynski, and Schaffer [59]	Cancer	Affective disorder
Greer [60]	Cancer	Repression of anger
Lipowski [61]	"Physical Illness"	Depression
Lewin [62]	Pernicious Anemia	Depression
Holmes et al. [41]	Hay Fever	Helplessness
Grace and Graham [42]	Asthma	Helplessness
Holmes [63]	Tuberculosis	Poor coping with stress
Lipowski [64]	Coronary Heart Disease	High and frustrated aspiration
Kimball [65]	Coronary Bypass, Mortality	Hopelessness, depression
Luborsky, Docherty, and Pennick [66] (Review Paper)	Psychosomatic Illness	Hostility, depression, frustration, anxiety, helplessness
Parens, McConville and Kaplan [67]	Various Illnesses	Helplessness, hopelessness

demonstrated that it is the inescapability from a stressor, rather than the mere exposure to it, which is the critical component in the development of a disease [70]. This same experimental paradigm, which features repeated exposure to inescapable stress also has been used to induce an animal analog of human depression. This procedure for producing depression, whether in people or in pigeons, has led to the elaboration of the so-called learned-helplessness model of depression [69]. This relationship between helplessness and depression suggests that studies reporting links between helplessness and depression and disease may in fact be observations of a single phenomenon.

An association between a sense of helplessness and the development of disease is further strengthened by a series of studies examining the relationship between life events and the development of illness. Minter and Kimball have reviewed this research and have pointed out many of the methodological problems encountered therein [71]. From this review, it appears that an adequate model of the relationship between life events and illness requires consideration of the individual's ability to cope. Coping ability appears to determine the relationship between *stress*, the magnitude or severity of the environmental event, and what has been called *strain*, the impact the event has on the organism [72]. In general, however, the term stress continues to be used to describe both the environmental event as well as the individual's response to it. It seems probable that the failure of coping mechanisms would be functionally equivalent to an inability to escape the stressor, and consequently a sense of helplessness might ensue. The well-established finding that individuals are more prone to illness when exposed to life events beyond their coping ability, is further evidence for the proposed relationship between helplessness and disease.

HELPLESSNESS, DEPRESSION, AND THE IMMUNE SYSTEM

Efforts to understand the relationship between psychological and psychosocial variables, such as life stress or a sense of helplessness, and the development of somatic disease must deal with what Weiner has called the transduction problem [73], that is, the mechanism whereby the social, cognitive, or affective experience influences the cellular events we call illnesses. Recent transduction models of the relationship between psychological experiences and disease have focused largely on the immune system.

Recent theoretical reviews [72, 74, 75] have pointed out that various stressors can have a profound impact on immunocompetence, that is, on the vigor with which the immune system responds to disease agents. For example, it has been reported that, in humans, decreased T-cell activity follows bereavement, and that natural killer cell activity decreases following stress in individuals with poor coping ability [76]. This is significant, in that, both T-cells and natural killer cells are instrumental in maintaining health. T-cells, once sensitized to a particular disease organism or allergen, act to destroy that substance upon second exposure. The natural killer cell is a recently identified cell which acts in much the same way to destroy invading cells to which the organism may not have been previously exposed. In addition, T-cells also might have a special role in the surveillance function of the immune system, that is, in the ability to distinguish "self" from "not-self," which is believed to play a crucial role in the body's early response to neoplasms. In short, impairment of T-cell and killer cell functions is likely to increase the vulnerability of an organism to disease, and a few studies have implied that states of helplessness and hopelessness can lead to such impairment.

Similar effects have been demonstrated in animals [77]. For example, lymphocyte cytotoxicity and lymphocyte response to mitogens decreased in response to stress, and fewer numbers of lymphocytes were seen following inescapable shock [78]. In other words, stress and inescapable shock decreased the number of T-cells and other lymphocytes, impaired their ability to kill invading cells, and decreased their defensive response to substances which induce the rapid cell division characteristic of neoplasia. Again, such impairment in immune function seems likely to increase the organism's vulnerability to disease.

STRESS, COPING, AND DISEASE: TOWARD AN INTEGRATIVE MODEL

Recent reviews [74, 75] have suggested that the effect of stress on the immune system is probably mediated by neurohumoral and endocrine pathways. Evidence for this relationship is derived from studies such as those of Riley [79] which showed a strong correlation between stress-induced suppression of the immunological system and levels of corticosteroids. Corticosteroids are endocrine substances released under hypothalamic control in response to stress, which are employed clinically to dampen immune response to tissue transplants. In Riley's studies, the degree to which a stressor suppressed immune response was correlated with the degree to which that stressor elicited corticosteroid release. There is also direct evidence of neurohumoral influence on immune function. Receptors for neurohumors, particularly catecholamines, have been found both on the thymus (the organ of origin for T-cells) and on the lymphocytes themselves, implying that some aspect of lymphocyte function is responsive to neurohumoral regulation. Of particular interest is that Sklar and Anisman have noted that the effects of stress are parallel on neurohumoral, endocrine, and immunologic levels [76]. These researchers assert that it is the organism's ability to cope with the stress that determines the neurochemical (particularly catecholamine) and endocrine effects, and perhaps the immunologic consequences as well.

Another building block in our brain/immune model is that research shows that exposure to stress, particularly inescapable stress, increases the synthesis and excretion of dopamine (DA) and norepinephrine (NE) [80], and may eventually lead to a state of catecholamine depletion. Of interest here is that catecholamine depletion is a critical component of the most widely held biological model of depression [81]. Similarly, corticosteroids, such as ACTH, which can induce immunosuppression [82] are not produced to the same extent by avoidable stressors [83]. The two phenomena may be related, in that the release of ACTH is increased when the hypothalamic store of NE and DA is depleted [84].

Further evidence for a connection between depression and corticosteroids is suggested by recent efforts to find a biological marker to assist in the diagnosis of depression. Carroll and colleagues have reported the development of the so-called "dexamethasone suppression test" as a means of identifying certain subtypes of depression [85]. In normal individuals and in those with psychiatric disorders other than depression, administration of dexamethasone suppresses the release of cortisol for the succeeding 24 hours. This effect is much attenuated in depressed individuals, supporting the connection between depressive disorder and cortisol function. In any case, exposure to unavoidable stress depletes catecholamines, increases secretion of immunosuppressive corticosteroids, and leads to the development of learned helplessness. At this point, a number of parallel events exist, and the framework of a model begins to emerge. This model relates exposure to unavoidable stress, the experience of helplessness, the development of depression, the depletion of brain catecholamines, the release of corticosteroids, the suppression of immune function and ultimately, the development of disease.

Although the evidence is far from conclusive and involves attempts to generalize across species and levels of organization which range from the cellular to the social, it is possible to speculate about a model of the aforementioned relationships. As a first step, it seems that a connection between a sense of helplessness and disease has been found consistently despite enormous variation in experimental design. In this regard, although seemingly disparate, a number of findings can be requisitioned to act as conceptual stepping-stones, easing the theoretical crossing from states of helplessness to states of cellular illness:

1. Experimental manipulations that induce the so-called learned helplessness phenomenon [69] which has been implicated in depression, are similar to those which lead to catecholamine depletion in the brain.
2. The major biochemical theory of affective disorder [81] posits a similar catecholamine depletion.
3. Drugs used in the treatment of depression are thought to work by blocking the degradation of catecholamines.
4. Sachar reported hypersecretion of cortisol in depression [86].
5. When norepinephrine and dopamine are depleted in the hypothalamus, production of corticosteroids is increased [84] which may lead to suppression of immune responses [82].
6. It has likewise been reported [83] that the corticosteroid 17-hydroxycorticosteroid is released in dramatically greater amounts following exposure to inescapable as opposed to escapable shock.
7. Anisman and Sklar demonstrated more rapid tumor growth and decreased survival time in mice exposed to inescapable shock [87].

This set of observations suggests a possible mechanism whereby the experience of stresses that exceed the organism's ability to cope (for example, inescapable shock or irreversible loss) may induce an organismic state that can be described cognitively as a sense of helplessness, emotionally as despair or depression, neurochemically as catecholamine depletion, and endocrinologically as a surplus of corticosteroid secretion. Through the action of elevated corticosteroids on the thymus [88] and perhaps of catecholamines on the spleen, thymus, and even directly on lymphocytes, this hypothesized organismic state increases the risk of disease by interference with immune functioning. This provisional model admits the possibility of intervention on any level of organization and, in this sense, points towards the utility of holistic approaches. For example, "therapists" could attempt to modify the psychosocial status, coping ability or stress responses of a high-risk premorbid personality type; chemically alter the disease process itself, or assist the ill person in cognitively adjusting (perhaps via imagery) their self-perceptions or situational attributions.

IMAGERY, LATERALITY, AND HEALING

The model described above permits consideration of the mechanism by which imagery and laterality are implicated in the healing process. If we assume that something like the earlier described relationship between a sense of help-lessness, despair or depression, catecholamine depletion, corticosteroid over-secretion, and immunosuppression exists, the healing effect of imagery could be understood in a number of different ways. Perhaps the most direct explanation would be that engaging in "combative imagery" counteracts a sense of helpless-ness [89]. Simonton, for one, has strongly encouraged his patients with advanced malignancy to take an active stance in their treatment [89]. Simonton believes that the role of imagery is integral to his treatment process. Norman Cousins, the former editor of *Saturday Review*, has written a widely acclaimed account of his own efforts to combat a sense of helplessness and despair engendered by a serious collagen illness, a disease of the connective tissue. The model proposed in the present chapter could explain the effectiveness of such efforts. The role of expectancy effects is well-documented in both psychological and somatic thera-pies [90, 91]. Given the model we have proposed, the effectiveness of so-called "non-specific effects," such as faith in one's healer or the belief that a surgical procedure, hypnotic induction, or imagery technique will alleviate suffering, may be due to an alteration in the individual's sense of helplessness. Thus imagery would be thought of as a coping mechanism, mediating the relationship between stress and strain, or more specifically, as an "antidote" to feeling hope-less. To the degree to which a sense of hopelessness entrains the catecholamine and endocrine events discussed previously, engaging in coping imagery might derail the process leading to immunosuppression.

A consideration of the relationship between imagery, affect, and the right cerebral hemisphere suggests another possible mechanism by which imagery can effect healing and disease. We have discussed some of the evidence that imagery and affect, and perhaps especially depressive affect, are primarily right hemi-sphere phenomena. Engaging in imagery appears to activate the right hemisphere [24]. It has been shown that electrical activation of the right hemisphere, such as that produced by engaging in imagery, leads to elevations of cerebrospinal fluid levels of serotonin metabolites, while left hemisphere activation leads to increased levels of norepinephrine (NE) and dopamine (DA) metabolites. It will be recalled that depletion of NE and DA results from exposure to unavoidable stress, is associated with depression, and may be involved in immunosuppression. If the relationship between the cerebral hemispheres is one of reciprocal inhibi-tion, engaging in imagery could activate the right hemisphere and thereby rela-tively inhibit activation of the left hemisphere. In this fashion, engaging in right-hemisphere imagery may reduce the rate at which NE and DA are utilized in the left hemisphere, and thus conserve these substances, decreasing the probability of depression and illness. Thus, imagery might be involved in the disease/healing process by virtue of its activation of the right hemisphere and consequent protection of the left hemisphere from catecholamine depletion.

IMPLICATIONS FOR RESEARCH AND CLINICAL PRACTICE

Although the relationship we have suggested between imagery, affect, the right hemisphere, and disease is a conjectural one, it does suggest a number of potentially testable hypotheses. One might, for example, look for different patterns of hemispheric activation in healthy and diseased individuals. The model, which suggests a relationship between relative cerebral activation, depression and disease, would also predict different levels of immunocompetence in individuals suffering from unilateral lesions of the left and right hemispheres. For example, patients with lesions of the right hemipshere might suffer from a higher incidence of immune or allergic diseases; whereas, those with left-hemisphere damage actually might have hyperactive immune systems and perhaps suffer from an increase in autoimmune disorders, those wherein the immune system turns on the patient himself/herself. In this regard, Geschwind has recently reported an increased incidence of certain autoimmune diseases in left-handed individuals [92]. Similarly, our model would suggest that patients with lateralized focal epilepsies of the right hemisphere might actually have more immune disorders than those with left-sided foci, to the degree to which an epileptic focus reflects increased cortical activity.

The proposed model makes quite a specific prediction about the relationship between depression and immune function. While the relationship has been consistently found, it is true that not all depressed individuals develop disease. This model would predict that among depressed individuals, that subgroup in whom dexamethasone fails to suppress cortisol release would be particularly prone to disease. We are at present testing this hypothesis by examining T-cell activity, natural killer cell activity and response to mitogens in the blood of depressed patients undergoing the dexamethasone suppression test. These patients will be followed longitudinally to determine whether those with elevated cortisol escapement are more prone to illness.

To summarize, we are proposing that available evidence on the relationship between helplessness, depression and disease, the function of the cerebral hemispheres, and the reported role of imagery in healing can be understood in terms of a model of environment/brain/immune system interactions. The proposed model is admittedly conjectural and some of the experimental evidence may be viewed as circumstantial. Nevertheless, the aggregate divergent research on exposure to inescapable stress indicates that it appears to engender a sense of helplessness, which has cognitive, affective, neuroendocrine, and immunologic concomitants, which become manifest as depression and disease. Tests of this model may lead to a greater understanding of the link between affect and disease and to a more systematic integration of imagery into the healing process.

REFERENCES

1. D. Meichenbaum, Why Does Using Imagery in Psychotherapy Lead to Change?, in *The Power of Human Imagination*, J. L. Singer and K. Pope (eds.), Plenum Press, New York, 1978.
2. R. J. Corsini, *Handbook of Innovative Psychotherapies*, Wiley and Sons, New York, 1981.
3. D. Strosahl and J. C. Ascough, Clinical Uses of Mental Imagery: Experimental Foundations, Theoretical Misconceptions, and Research Issues, *Psychological Bulletin, 89*:3, pp. 422-438, 1981.
4. W. T. Gallwey, *The Inner Game*, Random House, New York, 1974.
5. R. C. Gur, H. S. Sackheim, and R. E. Gur, Classroom Seating and Psychopathology: Some Initial Data, *Journal of Abnormal Psychology, 85*, pp. 122-124, 1976.
6. P. Bakan, The Eyes Have It, *Psychology Today, 4*, pp. 65-67.
7. R. Ornstein, *The Psychology of Consciousness*, W. H. Freeman, San Francisco, 1972.
8. J. Jaynes, *The Origins of Consciousness in the Breakdown of Bicameral Mind*, Houghton-Mifflin, Boston, 1976.
9. M. McLuhan, *City as Classroom: Understanding Language and Media*, Book Society of Canada, Agincourt, Ontario, 1977.
10. M. P. Bryden, *Laterality: Functional Asymmetry in the Intact Brain*, Academic Press, New York, 1983.
11. R. Ornstein, H. Johnstone, J. Herron, and C. Swencionis, Differential Right Hemisphere Engagement in Visuospatial Tasks, *Neuropsychologia, 18*:1, pp. 49-64, 1980.
12. A. G. Dodds, Hemispheric Differences in Tactuo-Spatial Processing, *Neuropsychologia, 16*, pp. 247-254, 1978.
13. A. Gates and J. L. Bradshaw, The Role of the Cerebral Hemispheres in Music, *Brain and Language, 4*, pp. 403-431, 1977.
14. G. Geffen, J. Bradshaw, and G. Wallace, Interhemispheric Effects on Reaction Time to Verbal and Nonverbal Stimuli, *Journal of Experimental Psychology, 87*, pp. 415-422, 1971.
15. R. G. Ley and M. P. Bryden, Hemispheric Differences in Recognizing Faces and Emotions, *Brain and Language, 7*, pp. 127-138, 1979.
16. A. Sheikh, *Imagery: Current Theory, Research and Application*, Wiley and Sons, New York, 1983.
17. A. Paivio, Perceptual Comparisons Through The Mind's Eye, *Memory Cognition, 3*, pp. 635-647, 1975.

18. P. J. Lang, A Bio-Informational Theory of Emotional Imagery, *Psychophysiology*, *16*:6, pp. 495-506.
19. Z. W. Pylyshyn, What the Mind's Eye Tells the Mind's Brain: A Critique of Mental Imagery, *Psychological Bulletin*, *80*, pp. 1-24, 1978.
20. R. G. Ley, Cerebral Laterality and Imagery, in *Imagery: Current Theory, Research and Application*, A. A. Sheikh (ed.), Wiley and Sons, New York, 1983.
21. M. D. Humphrey and O. L. Zangwill, Cessation of Dreaming after Brain Injury, *Journal of Neurology, Neurosurgery, and Psychiatry*, *14*, pp. 322-325, 1951.
22. M. Jones-Gotman and B. Milner, Right Temporal Lobe Contribution to Image-Mediated Learning, *Neuropsychologia*, *16*, pp. 61-71, 1978.
23. W. Penfield and P. Perot, The Brain's Record of Auditory and Visual Experience, *Brain*, *86*, pp. 595-696, 1963.
24. K. Robbins and D. McAdams, Interhemispheric Alpha Asymmetry and Imagery Mode, *Brain and Language*, *1*, pp. 189-193, 1974.
25. P. Bakan, Imagery Raw and Cooked: A Hemispheric Recipe, in *Imagery: Its Many Dimensions and Applications*, J. E. Shorr, G. E. Sobel, P. Robin, and J. A. Connella (eds.), Plenum Press, New York, 1980.
26. D. Tucker, Lateral Brain Function, Emotion and Conceptualization, *Psychological Bulletin*, *89*, pp. 19-46, 1981.
27. M. P. Bryden and R. G. Ley, Right Hemispheric Involvement in the Perception and Expression of Emotion in Normal Humans, in *The Neuro-Psychology of Emotion*, K. Heilman and P. Satz (eds.), Academic Press, New York, 1983.
28. A. Carmon and I. Nachson, Ear Asymmetry in Perception of Emotional and Non-Verbal Stimuli, *Acta Psychologica*, *37*, pp. 352-357, 1973.
29. R. G. Ley and M. P. Bryden, A Dissociation of Right and Left Hemispheric Effects for Recognizing Emotional Tone and Verbal Content, *Brain and Cognition*, *1*, pp. 3-9, 1982.
30. M. P. Bryden, R. G. Ley, and J. H. Sugarman, A Left-Ear Advantage for Identifying the Emotional Quality of Tonal Sequences, *Neuropsychologia*, *20*:1, pp. 83-87, 1982.
31. M. A. Safer, Sex and Hemisphere Differences in Access to Codes for Processing Emotional Expressions and Faces, *Journal of Experimental Psychology: General*, *110*, pp. 86-100, 1981.
32. J. C. Borod and H. S. Caron, Facedness and Emotion Related to Lateral Dominance, Sex and Expression Type, *Neuropsychologia*, *18*, pp. 237-241, 1980.
33. D. Galen, R. Diamond, and D. Braff, Lateralization of Conversion Symptoms: More Frequent on the Left, *American Journal of Psychiatry*, *134*:5, pp. 578-580, 1977.
34. R. G. Ley, An Archival Examination of an Asymmetry of Hysterical Conversion Symptoms, *Journal of Clinical Neuropsychology*, *2*:1, pp. 1-9, 1980.
35. S. Axelrod, M. Noonan, and B. Atanacio, On the Laterality of Psychogenic Somatic Symptoms, *Journal of Nervous and Mental Disease*, *168*, pp. 517-525, 1980.

36. S. G. Goldstein, S. B. Filskov, L. A. Weaver, and J. Ives, Neuropsychological Effects of Electroconvulsive Therapy, *Journal of Clinical Psychology, 33*, pp. 798-806, 1977.

37. A. Yosawitz and G. Bruder, Dichotic Perception: Evidence for Right Hemispheric Dysfunction in Affective Psychosis, paper presented at the Annual Meeting of the American Psychological Association, Toronto, 1978.

38. P. Flor-Henry, Lateralized Temporal-Limbic Dysfunction and Psychopathology, *Annals of the New York Academy of Sciences, 280*, pp. 777-797, 1976.

39. G. D'Elia and C. Perris, Cerebral Functional Dominance and Memory Function: An Analysis of EEG Integrated Amplitude in Depressive Psychotics, *Acta Psychiatrica Scandinavica, 244*, pp. 143-157, 1974.

40. R. G. Ley, Cerebral Asymmetries, Emotional Experience and Imagery: Implications for Psychotherapy, in *The Potential of Fantasy and Imagination*, A. A. Sheikh and J. T. Shaffer (eds.), Brandon House, New York, 1979.

41. T. Holmes, H. Goodell, H. Wolff, and S. Wolf, *The Nose: An Experimental Study of Reaction Within the Nose in Human Subjects During Varying Life Experiences*, Charles C. Thomas, Springfield, 1950.

42. W. Grace and D. Graham, Relationship of Specific Attitudes and Emotions to Certain Bodily Diseases, *Psychosomatic Medicine, 14*, pp. 243-251, 1952.

43. W. Grace, S. Wolf, and H. Wolff, Life Situations, Emotions and Chronic Ulcerative Colitis, *Journal of the American Medical Association, 142*, pp. 1044-1048, 1950.

44. L. LeShan, An Emotional Life History Pattern Associated with Neoplastic Disease, *Annals of the New York Academy of Sciences, 125*, pp. 780-793, 1966.

45. R. Guy, *An Essay on Scirrous Tumours and Cancer*, Churchill, London, 1759.

46. E. Evans, *A Psychological Study of Cancer*, Dodd, Mead and Co., New York, 1926.

47. F. Miller and H. Jones, The Possibility of Precipitating the Leukemic State by Emotional Factors, *Blood, 3*, pp. 880, 1948.

48. W. Greene and G. Miller, Psychological Factors in Reticulo-endothelial Disease: IV Observations of Children and Adolescents with Leukemia. An Interpretation of Disease Development in Terms of the Mother-Child Unit, *Psychosomatic Medicine, 20*, pp. 124-144, 1958.

49. L. Leshan, Psychological States as Factors in the Development of Malignant Disease: A Critical Review, *Journal of the National Cancer Institute, 22*, pp. 1-18, 1959.

50. G. Booth, Lung Cancer and Personality, *Abstracts of the International Psychosomatic Study Group, 13*, pp. 568, 1960.

51. A. Mezai and G. Nemeth, Regression as an Intervening Mechanism: A System—Theoretical Approach, *Annals of the New York Academy of Medicine, 164*, pp. 560-567, 1969.

52. A. Schmale and J. Iker, The Psychological Setting of Uterine Cervical Cancer, *Annals of the New York Academy of Sciences, 125*, pp. 807-813, 1966.

53. C. Bahnson and M. Bahnson, Role of the Ego Defenses: Denial and Repression in the Etiology of Malignant Neoplasm, *Annals of the New York Academy of Sciences, 125*, pp. 824-845, 1969.

54. R. Brown, M. Wilkins, W. Buxton, and D. Abse, Psychological Factors in the Etiology of Lung Cancer, *Virginia Medical Monthly, 102*, pp. 935, 1975.

55. C. Thomas and R. Greenstreet, Psychobiological Characteristics in Youth as Predicators of Five Disease States: Suicide, Mental Illness, Hypertension, Coronary Heart Disease and Tumour, *John Hopkins Medical Journal, 132*, pp. 16-43, 1973.

56. H. Pauli and V. Schmid, Psychosomatische Aspekte bei der Kinischen Manifestation von 'Mammakarzinomen,' Ein Psychosomatiske untersuchung, *Zeitschrift fur Psychotherapie und Medizinische, 22*, pp. 76-80, 1972.

57. T. Kerr, K. Schapira, and M. Roth, The Relationship between Premature Death and Affective Disorders, *British Journal of Psychiatry, 115*, pp. 1277-1282, 1969.

58. F. Whitlock and M. Siskind, Depression and Cancer: A Follow-up Study, *Psychological Medicine, 9*, pp. 747-752, 1979.

59. C. Thomas, K. Duszynski, and J. Shaffer, Family Attitudes Reported in Youth as Potential Predicators of Cancer, *Psychosomatic Medicine, 41*, pp. 287-302, 1979.

60. S. Greer, Psychological Attributes of Women with Breast Cancer, *Cancer Detection and Prevention, 2*, pp. 289-294, 1979.

61. Z. Lipowski, Review of Consultation Psychiatry and Psychosomatic Medicine: II. Clinical Aspects, *Psychosomatic Medicine, 29*, pp. 201-224, 1967.

62. K. Lewin, Role of Depression in the Production of Illness in Pernicious Anemia, *Psychosomatic Medicine, 21*, pp. 23-27, 1959.

63. T. Holmes, Psychosocial and Psychophysiological Studies of Tuberculosis, in *Physiological Correlates of Psychological Disorders*, R. Roessler and N. Greenfield (eds.), University of Wisconsin Press, Madison, pp. 239-255, 1962.

64. Z. Lipowski, Psychophysiological Cardiovascular Disorders, in *Comprehensive Textbook of Psychiatry*, A. Freedman, H. Kaplan, and B. Sadock (eds.), Wilkins, Baltimore, pp. 1036-1089, 1974.

65. C. Kimball, A Predictive Study of Adjustment to Cardiac Surgery, *Journal of Cardiovascular Surgery, 58*, pp. 891-896, 1969.

66. L. Luborsky, J. Docherty, and S. Penick, Onset Conditions for Psychosomatic Symptoms: A Comparative Review of Immediate Observation with Retrospective Research, *Psychosomatic Medicine, 35*, pp. 187-204, 1973.

67. H. Parens, B. McConville, and S. Kaplan, The Prediction of Frequency of Illness from the Response to Separation, *Psychosomatic Medicine, 28*, pp. 162-176, 1966.

68. S. Greer and T. Morris, Psychological Attributes of Women who Develop Breast Cancer: A Controlled Study, *Journal of Psychosomatic Research, 19*, pp. 147-153, 1975.

69. S. Maier and M. Seligman, Learned Helplessness: Theory and Evidence, *Journal of Experimental Psychology: General, 105*, pp. 3-46, 1976.

70. L. Sklar and H. Anisman, Stress and Coping Factors Influence Tumor Growth, *Science, 205*, pp. 513-515, 1979.
71. R. Minter and C. Kimball, Life Events, Personality Traits and Illness, in *Handbook on Stress and Anxiety,* I. Kutash, L. Schlesinger and Associates (eds.), Jossey-Bass, San Francsico, pp. 189-206, 1980.
72. M. Rogers, D. Dubey, and P. Reich, The Influence of the Psyche and the Brain on Immunity and Disease Susceptibility: A Critical Review, *Psychosomatic Medicine, 41*, pp. 147-164, 1979.
73. H. Weiner, Some Comments on the Transduction of Experience by the Brain: Implications for our Understanding of the Relationship of Mind to Body, *Psychosomatic Medicine, 34*, pp. 355-380, 1972.
74. A. Amkraut and G. Solomon, From the Symbolic Stimulus to the Pathophysiologic Response: Immune Mechanisms, in *Psychosomatic Medicine: Current Trends and Clinical Applications*, Z. Lipowski, D. Lipsitt, and P. Whybrow (eds.), Oxford University Press, New York, pp. 228-250, 1977.
75. L. Sklar and H. Anisman, Stress and Cancer, *Psychological Bulletin, 89*, pp. 364-406, 1981.
76. R. Bartrop, E. Luckhurst, L. Lazarus, L. Kiloh, and R. Penney, Depressed Lymphocytic Function After Bereavement, *Lancet, I*, pp. 834-836, 1977.
77. A. Monjan and M. Collector, Stress-induced Modulation of the Immune Response, *Science, 196*, pp. 307-308, 1977.
78. H. Neibergs, The Role of Stress in Human and Experimental Oncogenesis, *Cancer Detection and Prevention, 2*, pp. 307-336, 1979.
79. V. Riley, Mouse Mammary Tumors: Alteration of Incidence as Apparent Function of Stress, *Science, 184*, pp. 465-467, 1975.
80. J. Weiss, H. Glazer, and L. Pohorecky, Coping Behavior and Neurochemical Changes: An Alternative for the Original "Learned Helplessness" Experiments, in *Animal Models in Human Psychobiology*, G. Serban and A. Kling (eds.), Plenum Press, New York, 1976.
81. H. Akiskal and W. McKinney, Depressive Disorders: Toward a Unified Hypothesis, *Science, 183*, pp. 20-29, 1973.
82. J. Balow and A. Rosenthal, Glucocorticoid Suppression of Macrophage Migration Inhibiting Factor, *Journal of Experimental Medicine, 137*, pp. 1031-1041, 1973.
83. J. Brady, Experimental Studies of Stress and Anxiety, in *Handbook on Stress and Anxiety*, I. Kutush, L. Schlesinger and Associates (eds.), Jossey-Bass, San Francisco, pp. 207-236, 1980.
84. W. Ganong, The Role of Catecholamines and Acetylcholine in the Regulation of Endocrine Function, *Life Sciences, 15*, pp. 1401-1414, 1976.
85. D. Carroll, M. Feinberg, and J. Greden, A Specific Laboratory Test for the Diagnosis of Melancholia: Standardization, Validation, and Clinical Utility, *Archives of General Psychiatry, 138*, pp. 15-22, 1981.
86. E. Sachar, J. McKenzie, W. Binstock, and J. Mach, Corticosteroid Responses to the Pharmacotherapy of Depression, *Archives of General Psychiatry, 16*, pp. 461-470, 1967.

87. H. Anisman and L. Sklar, Catecholamine Depletion in Mice upon Reexposure to Stress: Mediation of the Escape Deficits Produced by Inescapable Shock, *Journal of Comparative and Physiological Psychology*, *93*, pp. 610-625, 1979.
88. H. Selye, Stress and Disease, *Science*, *122*, 1955.
89. O. Simonton, S. Mathews, and T. Sparks (eds.), Psychological Intervention in the Treatment of Cancer, *Psychosomatics*, *21*, p. 226, 1976.
90. J. Frank, *Persuasion and Healing*, Schocken, New York, 1974.
91. A. Shapiro and L. Morris, Placebo Effects in Medical and Psychological Therapies, in *Handbook of Psychotherapy and Behavior Change*, S. Garfield and A. Bergin (eds.), John Wiley and Sons, New York, pp. 369-411, 1978.
92. N. Geschwind and P. Behan, Left-Handedness: Association with Immune Disease, Migraine and Developmental Learning Disorder, *Proceedings of the National Academy of Sciences*, *79*, pp. 5097-5100, 1982.

CHAPTER 4

Changing "Unchangeable" Bodily Processes by (Hypnotic) Suggestions: A New Look at Hypnosis, Cognitions, Imagining, and the Mind-Body Problem

THEODORE X. BARBER

In this chapter, I will describe and explain how "unchangeable" bodily structures and processes—for example, the size of a woman's breasts, warts that have been present for many years, and incurable congenital skin diseases—can be beneficially altered by suggestions in situations labeled as *hypnosis*. The fact that anatomical-physiological processes can be influenced by suggestions is very important for medicine, psychology, philosophy, and the other disciplines which deal with the mind-body problem. In this chapter, I shall attempt to thoroughly document these suggestion-induced body changes and try to explain how they occur.

To understand how suggestions given in situations labeled as *hypnosis* can change bodily structures and functions, it is necessary to view hypnosis in a new way; the laymen's or amateur's conception of hypnosis is misleading and simply does not help us understand how these phenomena occur. We can begin to see what is involved, however, if we view the term *hypnosis* as referring primarily to a situation in which individuals are purposefully guided by carefully chosen words and communications (suggestions) to "let go" of extraneous concerns and to feel-remember-think-imagine-experience ideas or events that they are rarely asked to experience. For instance, to feel-remember-think-imagine-experience the vibrating heat of the sun penetrating deep into the breasts and causing them to grow as they did at puberty, or to feel-remember-think-imagine that one is being burned and, concomitantly, to experience a blister forming at the "burned"

[1]This chapter is adapted in part from a lecture presented at the "Power of Imagination" conference held in San Francisco on April 1-4, 1982, and it updates some of the material that I have presented in a series of earlier publications [1-8].

area. From this viewpoint, the question at issue becomes more precise and also more answerable. Instead of asking the vague question, "How does hypnosis alter 'unchangeable' bodily functions and processes?" we can ask the more precise and more productive question, "How do suggestions to let go of extraneous concerns and to feel-remember-think-imagine in new or unusual ways lead to the cure of warts, the amelioration of incurable skin diseases, the production of skin inflammation and blisters, the inhibition of allergic responses, the growth of mammary glands during adulthood, etc.?"

Let us look at a representative series of relevant studies and then let us attempt to explain their dramatic results.

POISON IVY-LIKE CONTACT DERMATITIS PRODUCED AND INHIBITED BY BELIEVED-IN SUGGESTIONS

An experiment reported by two Japanese physicians, Drs. Ikemi and Nakagawa showed that "believed-in suggestions" can produce "amazing" effects on the skin [9]. They worked with thirteen individuals who were very sensitive to the leaves of a tree found in Japan that produces skin reactions similar to our poison ivy. When these individuals came in contact with the leaves of this Japanese tree, they reacted with the kind of marked skin changes (contact dermatitis) that are observed in people who are highly sensitive (allergic) to poison ivy; these reactions included itching, marked redness of the skin due to increased blood in the capillaries (erythema), small, solid, circumscribed skin elevations (papules), edema, and small blisters (vesicles).

The experiment was conducted at a prestigeful institution (Kyushu Medical University) by two highly respected physicians, and the thirteen subjects were high-school boys (15-17 years of age). Five of the young men were exposed first to a hypnotic induction procedure comprised presumably of repeated suggestions for relaxation and drowsiness; after completion of the induction procedure, they were told that they were being touched on one arm by leaves from the poison ivy-type tree while they were actually being touched by leaves from a harmless tree.

The remaining eight students were assigned to a suggestion-alone treatment which did not include the preliminary hypnotic induction procedure. When these suggestion-alone subjects' eyes were closed, they also were touched by harmless leaves while being told the leaves were from the poison ivy-type plant.

There is every reason to expect that both the hypnotic subjects and the suggestion-alone subjects would believe what was being suggested, namely, that they were being stimulated by the poison ivy-type plant. Both the hypnotic subjects and the suggestion-alone subjects had their eyes closed and could not distinguish what kinds of leaves were actually touching them. Both sets of subjects were told firmly by a prestigious physician in a very respected medical setting that he was touching them with the leaves of the poison ivy-type plant. There was no reason whatsoever for the young high-school students to disbelieve the respected physician's statement.

The deep acceptance of the physician's statement played an important role in producing the results which I shall describe in a moment. A second consideration also probably played an important role, namely, the suggestions aroused deep feelings and emotions in the subjects—these young people had suffered severely from their sensitivity (allergy) to the poison ivy-type plant and the statement that they were being touched by this plant could not fail to arouse fear and other negative emotions.

The results were dramatic: All five of the hypnotic subjects and all eight of the suggestion-alone subjects showed some degree of dermatitis as a result of the believed-in suggestions that they were being touched by the poison ivy-type leaves. This dermatitis (e.g., itching, erythema, papules, edema, and vesicles) was slight in some cases and amazingly strong in others. In twelve of the thirteen students, the dermatitis reaction began within 10 to 60 minutes after the suggestion was given and then became more severe over a period of hours or days; in the remaining subject, the dermatitis began six hours after the suggestions were given.

In the next part of the experiment, the procedure was reversed: Each student was told that the leaves of a harmless tree were being applied to the other arm, when actually the leaves of the poison ivy-type tree were applied. When thus led to believe that the poison ivy-type leaves were harmless, four of the five hypnotic subjects and seven of the eight suggestion-alone subjects did *not* react to the poison leaves with itching, erythema, papules, small blisters, or any other sign of contact dermatisis.

In summary, the impressive data presented by Ikemi and Nakagawa [9] indicate the following:

1. In sensitized individuals (who manifest a marked allergic dermatitis when exposed to a poison ivy-type plant): 1) some or all aspects of the dermatitis can be produced by a harmless plant if the individuals feel-think-imagine-believe it is the poison ivy-type plant and 2) the dermatitis can generally be inhibited if the individuals feel-think-imagine-believe that the poison ivy-type leaves are leaves from a harmless plant.

2. A hypnotic induction procedure, for example, repeated suggestions of deep relaxation or of eye-heaviness, eye-closure, and drowsiness, is definitely not necessary to produce these effects. At least in some situations, for example, when suggestions are given by a respected physician whose statements are accepted as true, a hypnotic induction procedure is irrelevant in producing these effects.

3. It appears that the critical variable in producing and inhibiting the skin changes is the subject's feeling-thinking-imagining-believing that a harmless substance is actually the dermatitis-producing substance and, vice versa, that the dermatitis-producing substance is actually a harmless substance. It also appears probable that the feeling-thinking-imagining-believing has to be at a level that is more than superficial. Since the subjects participating in the Ikemi and Nakagawa experiment had previously suffered deeply from the effects of the poison ivy-type plant, we can surmise that the suggestions that they were being touched by this plant aroused profound negative feelings, thoughts, and emotions.

4. These data also have important implications for understanding and controlling contact allergies and, possibly, other immunological responses. They indicate that when individuals have become sensitized (allergic) to contact on the skin by a specific substance (allergen), their hypersensitive response to the allergen is reduced when they are unaware that they are in contact with the allergen and, possibly, when they are aware of contact but are unconcerned (very calm) about it. This suggests, further, that sensitized individuals who believe that they have been exposed to a contact allergen, such as poison ivy, should give themselves suggestions for calmness and tranquility, that is, they should utilize calming self-suggestions (self-hypnosis). We can deduce from Ikemi and Nakagawa's data that clamness, which reduces anxiety about and attention to the allergen, will also reduce the skin reaction to it.
5. Ikemi and Nakagawa's data also showed that, once a hypersensitive response to a contact allergen has been firmly established, the response (dermatitis) can be reinstated in part and, at times, totally, by the feeling, thought, and emotional belief that one is being stimulated by the allergen (when one is not). This, of course, has vast implications for immunology, since it indicates that at least some immune responses, such as the T-cell mediated skin response to an allergen, may be much more influenced by emotionally tinged feelings-thoughts-imaginings-beliefs than has heretofore been supposed.

ALTERING OTHER ALLERGIC RESPONSES BY SUGGESTIONS

A large number of studies indicate many other kinds of allergic responses can be inhibited by communications that affect the allergic person's feelings, thoughts, emotions, or attitudes toward the allergen. A series of Russian studies, cited by Platonov [10], indicated that allergic skin responses, such as urticarial rashes developed after eating strawberries, lobsters, etc., can be inhibited by suggestions given during "suggested sleep." Although Platonov stated that sleep was suggested, he did not state what specific suggestions were given to the patients to inhibit their allergic responses.

Ikemi carried out a relevant experiment with five high-school students who developed various gastrointestinal symptoms after eating certain foods and also showed quasi positive (allergic) skin reactions (6 to 10 mm) to the foods [11]. When they ate the food in a disguised form, and thus did not know that they were eating it, they did not develop the gastrointestinal symptoms.

Mason and Black blocked an allergic reaction in a woman who had suffered from May to July yearly for the past twelve years with asthma and a severe hay fever reaction to pollen [12]. Previous medical treatments had been unsuccessful, and she was subject to prolonged attacks of respiratory distress and was practically an invalid each summer. After exposing her to a hypnotic procedure (and finding that she was an excellent subject), Mason suggested to her that this coming summer she would have no difficulty with her breathing and that she would not have a blocked nose, her eyes would not run, she would not itch around the eyes, and she would not have sneezing attacks. She was given these kinds of suggestions in weekly sessions for ten weeks. During this period, which was the height of the pollen season, she was completely free of all of the symptoms of asthma and hay fever for the first time in twelve years. Mason and Black's success with this patient prompted them to carry out additional work with her, and they came up with a striking finding.

While the patient was being treated as described above, pollen extracts were applied to her arms at intervals to monitor her skin reactivity to the allergen. As a control, the same pollen extracts were applied unexpectedly to the patient's legs. The skin reaction on her arms decreased steadily each week and reached zero by the seventh week, but the occasional unexpected test on her legs always produced large wheals. Thus, the suggestions had suppressed the reaction in one part of her body but not in another part. Next, the patient was given the direct suggestion that the skin over her entire body would be unresponsive to the pollen extracts; this suggestion was successful in inhibiting all skin reactions to the allergen. Nevertheless, although the patient now was free from both symptoms and skin reactions, her blood could still be shown (by the Prausnitz-Küstner reaction) to contain the antibodies which originally had given rise to the hypersensitivity to the pollen. Mason and Black concluded that the suggestions had established "an overriding psychic system of control" which could not only keep the patient well, but could also inhibit selectively the allergic reaction in different parts of her body.

Mason carried out another study, along the same lines as those described above, with a patient who showed an allergic skin response (a positive Mantoux reaction) when skin-pricked with old tuberculin [13]. The tuberculin was injected into both arms with the suggestion that one arm was receiving an injection of water and would react as it would to water. The positive Mantoux reaction was blocked in the suggested arm while it was maintained to its original degree in the other arm. In a later session, Mason performed the same test with the same patient and was successful in reversing, by suggestions, the arms which showed the inhibited and the allergic reaction to the tuberculin.

A similar but more extensive study was subsequently reported by Black, Humphrey, and Niven [14]. They worked with four (Mantoux-positive) highly selected good hypnotic individuals who were reactive to tuberculin injections. Daily for the next twelve days, they were exposed to a hypnotic induction procedure (suggestions of relaxation and drowsiness) and then to these suggestions (repeated no less than five times at each session): "You will no longer react to the injection as you did before. There will be no redness, no swelling, no heat, no itching, no pain—the skin will remain perfectly normal." After the twelfth day, three of the four subjects showed no reactions to the tuberculin injection and a slight response was observed in the fourth subject. There was no measureable swelling in the first three subjects and the area of swelling was markedly reduced in the fourth. The area of erythema was greatly reduced in all subjects. Further histological studies indicated that the exudation of fluid had been inhibited probably by blocking of a vascular constituent of the reaction.

In a related experiment, Black worked with twelve highly selected good hypnotic subjects who showed allergic responses to one or more common allergens and who had a history of psychosomatic disorders some of which were allergic [15]. The subjects were first tested on one arm for response to the selected allergen. Then they were skin tested again, after they had been exposed to a hypnotic induction procedure and to repeated suggestions that they would not react to their specific allergen: "You will have the same injection again, but this time there will be no response—there will be no heat, no redness, no swelling, no itching, no reaction. Your arm will no longer respond to the fluid as it did before. It will be just as if water had been pricked in." Eight of the twelve selected subjects manifested reduced response to the allergen on second testing, as indicated by an observable reduction in edema and by temperature measurements at the site of the injection. A control group apparently excluded the possibility that subjects who have not been exposed to suggestions show reduced response on second testing to the selected allergens used in this experiment. In a subsequent experiment carried out along similar lines, Black [16] found that, with selected good hypnotic subjects, suggestions not to react to a skin prick test, which were given after a hypnotic induction procedure, reduced and, at times, totally inhibited the Prausnitz-Küstner reaction, that is, the expected allergic skin reaction that is produced in previously nonallergic persons after they have received blood serum (containing skin-sensitizing antibodies) from an allergic person.

Fry, Mason, and Bruce-Pearson carried out a large-scale study to ascertain whether the results described above applied to subjects who were not preselected as superb hypnotic subjects [17]. They began with fifty unselected patients who had either or both asthma and hay fever and who showed skin reactions to pollen or house dust. Forty-seven of the patients, who were at least somewhat responsive to the hypnotic induction suggestions, were included in the studies, and the remaining three patients, who were not at all affected by the hypnotic induction suggestions, were not included.

In the first study, nine subjects were randomly assigned to a control group and were skin tested for response to their allergen on two occasions. Nine additional subjects were assigned to a hypnotic induction treatment, were given suggestions that their skin reactions would be abolished, and were skin tested on the same two occasions. Each subject was tested on four different spots on the skin with four different strengths of the allergen. Although the suggestions not to react—"there will be no reaction at all, no redness, no swelling, no itching, or burning"—were not effective at the two higher strengths of the allergen, they had a significant effect at the two lower strengths. Specifically, three of the nine subjects under the hypnosis suggestion treatment showed no reaction whatsoever to the two lower strengths of allergens (even though they had reacted to the same strengths prior to the hypnosis suggestion treatment).[2]

In brief, the above and other studies indicate that abnormally reactive (allergic) skin responses to pollen, house dust, tuberculin, and many other allergens can be reduced and at times totally blocked by suggestions not to react. It appears that the inhibition that is associated with the suggestions is much more readily obtained in individuals who are highly responsive to suggestions (superb hypnotic subjects). Mason [18] emphasized that all of the subjects who showed dramatic inhibition of allergic responses (in the studies he and/or Black had conducted) were not only exceptionally responsive to suggestions, but were also unusually responsive psychosomatically, had an especially close relationship with the physician-experimenter, and were "ultra-sensitive to secondary gain" which included obtaining more attention and positive regard from the physician.

We also might expect that suggestions are more potent when subjects are ready to accept them at a deep level; this may be more likely when subjects feel at ease and not distracted and also when they feel they are in a special kind of expectancy situation or in a situation (such as hypnosis) which they view as magic-like. Hypnotic inductions of the type used by Mason, Black, and their co-workers, which focused on suggestions of relaxation, eye-closure, and drowsiness, may have been helpful in removing distractions, enhancing expectancies, and preparing the subjects to respond to the suggestions, but the reader should not be misled into believing that they were necessary to produce the allergy-blocking effects. From everything that we know today about the effects of hypnotic inductions and suggestions, it is clear that when there is a close relationship beween the subjects and the suggestor, some subjects do not need any kind of preliminary procedure to become absorbed in the suggestions. Other subjects can be helped to become absorbed either 1) by talking to them about the power of their mind and about their ability to imagine [19], 2) by utilizing Erickson-like stories, parables, and metaphors [20], or 3) by administering traditional hypnotic induction procedures such as those used by Mason, Black, and their co-workers. Unfortunately, these researchers never tried any other kinds of preliminary procedures or any other kind of "inductions" to help their subjects become absorbed in the suggestions and readers of their papers could

---

[2]In a second study, Fry et al. [17] exposed all of the remaining twenty-nine subjects to a hypnotic induction procedure, comprised of suggestions of relaxation and sleepiness, and then gave them either 1) no suggestions, 2) suggestions that the right arm would not react to the skin tests, or 3) suggestions that neither arm would react. There was a similar small average decrease in the response to the prick-tests after the hypnotic induction in all three groups. Unfortunately, control subjects not exposed to the hypnotic induction, were not used, so that it was impossible to state whether the hypnotic induction procedure by itself reduced the allergic responses or whether the reduction would have occurred anyway on second testing without the hypnotic induction.

be misguided to believe that their specific induction (pivoting around suggestions of relaxation and drowsiness) was necessary or more important than it actually was. Mason himself very strongly emphasized that the highly selected subjects (used in the experiments conducted by himself, by Black, and by the two together) probably did not need hypnosis to actualize the suggestions to inhibit the allergic responses [18]. He predicted that further studies, which use subjects who are very responsive to suggestions, who manifest exceptional "psychosomatic plasticity," and who have a "special unconscious relationship" with the physician, will find that these individuals actualize suggestions to inhibit allergic responses when the suggestions are given without any kind of hypnotic induction procedure.

TREATING CONGENITAL SKIN DISEASES ("FISH-SKIN" DISEASE AND PACHYONYCHIA CONGENITA) BY SUGGESTIONS

Four amazing reports have demonstrated that a serious skin disease—congenital ichthyosiform erythrodermia or "fish-skin disease"—can be markedly altered by suggestions. The first case, reported by Mason involved a sixteen-year-old youth who had suffered with this disease since birth [21]. With the exception of his chest, neck, and face, his skin was thick, black, and covered with papillae. The skin was about as hard as normal fingernails, was numb for a depth of several millimeters, and was so inelastic that attempts at bending would produce cracks in the surface which would then ooze blood-stained serum. The patient's skin had been progressively thickening from birth. This horny layer of the epidermis provided a suitable medium for bacterial growth which caused a putrid odor of the scales [22]. His education had been interrupted because the teachers and students objected to the odor. The youth was shy and lonely and avoided people because of his distressing appearance and odor.

He had not been helped by medical treatments. In fact, dermatology texts state consistently that the cause of the disease is unknown and that it is incurable. Presumably, he believed that hypnosis could help him, because he went to see Dr. Mason who had written a well-known book on hypnosis and who had the reputation of being a successful hypnotherapist. Dr. Mason exposed the young man to a hypnotic induction procedure (presumably comprised of suggestions for relaxation and drowsiness); it was followed by suggestions to focus on the left arm and to feel the skin becoming normal. Although Mason's report does not state explicitly whether the young man continued practicing the suggestive procedure at home, it states that, within five days, the hard, horny layer of skin on the left arm softened and fell off. The new skin underneath was somewhat reddish at first, but within ten days the entire arm, from shoulder to wrist was normal in color and texture.

Over a series of hypnotic treatment sessions, Mason then suggested that the skin would become normal first in one specific part of the body and then in another. Rapid and dramatic results were obtained during the first few weeks. The right arm was cured. The skin on the palms became normal, the skin on the back was 90 percent cleared, and 50-70 percent of the buttocks, thighs, and legs showed the same amazing transformation.

In brief, during the first few weeks of treatment, dramatic skin changes were produced when they were suggested; however, there were some areas—for example, the fingers and parts of the buttocks, thighs, and feet—that did not change. During the next few months of treatment, there was no further improvement. The patient was then seen again by Dr. Mason four years later. The original improvement was still present, and the patient showed some additional improvement [23].

When I first read Mason's paper in the 1950's in the *British Medical Journal*, I found it difficult to believe; it was saying unequivocally that by guiding a person to feel-think-imagine in a new way about his/her abnormal skin, new normal skin forms step by step with the guided feeling-thinking-imagining. At the time I read Mason's report, I already was deeply involved in trying to understand the mind-body problem; Mason's report was the final, determining factor which led me to decide to devote my efforts to understanding hypnosis, since it indicated that the royal road to solving the mind-body problem involved unraveling the mystery of hypnosis.

Few people seem to be aware that Mason's "unbelievable" results were confirmed by three later investigators. Another English medical practitioner, Dr. Wink, had read Mason's report some years before he saw two sisters, ages eight and six, who also suffered from congenital ichthyosiform erythrodermia [24]. Wink followed Mason's procedures step by step—hypnotic-induction suggestions followed by suggestions that specific affected skin areas would soon start to grow soft and smooth and that the thick skin would fall off. Each girl was exposed to these procedures at weekly intervals for eight weeks, then biweekly for two months, and then monthly for a further two months. At the end of this period, the eight-year-old girl showed from 50 to 75 percent reduction in skin thickness in various areas of the body, and the six-year-old girl showed a 75 percent reduction in skin thickness on the face, and a 20 to 40 percent reduction in skin thickness on other parts of the body.

A few years later Dr. Kidd obtained striking results in Scotland with a thirty-four-year-old father (but not with his four-year-old son who was distractible and would not attend to the suggestions) [25]. The father's "fish-skin" became normal over 90 percent of his body after Dr. Kidd had worked with him almost daily over a five-week period.

Dr. Schneck saw a similar case in New York [26]. A twenty-year-old woman suffered from ichthyosiform dermatosis extending over virtually the entire body. A striking change occurred within a week of the first session during which she was given suggestions for deep relaxation and for skin normalization: 50 percent of the thickened skin sloughed off and new normal skin formed. During the next several months, the young woman continued to receive therapy, but there was little further improvement. (Schneck [27] previously had treated a similar ailment, ichthyosis simplex, in a thirty-three-year-old man and, over a period of time, had obtained a skin improvement assessed at between 40 and 45 percent.)

Not long after they had read Mason's [21] report pertaining to the healing of a congenital ichthyosiform dermatosis, Mullins, Murray, and Shapiro decided to try similar procedures with a patient who had another congenital skin disease which involved both the epidermis and the nails, namely, pachyonychia congenita [28]. The patient, an eleven-year-old boy, began to show a thickening of the skin on his palms and soles when he was around one year of age. By age two, his fingernails had thickened and had elevated from the matrix; he also developed large blisters on his palms and soles which would rupture and lead to the formation of a thick layer of hyperkeratotic epidermis.

When seen during his eleventh year, his condition was very painful; to avoid pressure on his tender soles, he walked only with crutches or crawled. Both the fingernails and toenails were markedly enlarged and extremely hard, the plantar and palmar surfaces were covered with thick hyperkeratotic material, and there were erythematous papules with central horny plugs on the elbows and knees. Many physicians had previously treated him without benefit with numerous topical and systemic agents.

The authors presented their treatment procedures and their results in an extremely succinct manner, as follows:

> On August 14, it was decided to try hypnotherapy. . . . All other local and systemic therapy was discontinued, and the patient was seen by one of us (N.M.) at one- to three-day intervals during the remainder of his hospital stay. During these sessions an attempt was made to investigate the patient's personality structure and to induce abreactive phenomena by means of hypnotic procedures. The patient was at the same time reassured, as well as encouraged to express and act out various aggressive and destructive traits which had been noted as being present by prior psychometric examination. Furthermore, posthypnotic suggestions were made to the effect that clearing of the lesions would take place, at first, in the left hand. Within three days, there was noticeable softening of the keratotic material on the left hand and considerable subjective improvement. By August 24, the tenth day of treatment, he was able to tolerate a pair of leather shoes. By August 27, he stood on his feet without pain for the first time in his life that he could remember, and by August 31, he was able to walk the length of the ward without pain. He was discharged on September 8, to attend school, and psychological therapy was continued at biweekly intervals. After two months, this therapy was discontinued. When he was last seen five months later, he was walking with only slight impairment [28, pp.

266-267]. The authors also presented photographs of the plantar surfaces before and after hypnotherapy which showed a dramatic improvement.

In brief, the data presented by Mullins et al. indicate that hypnotherapy had both subjective and objective ameliorative effects on a congenital skin disorder [28]. However, the hypnotherapy included at least two sets of procedures: 1) suggestions for clearing of the skin and 2) investigations of the patient's personality structure together with abreaction and expression of aggressive feelings—and we do not know which procedures were more important in producing the positive results.

The five studies discussed above appear to me to be sufficient to topple the dualistic dichotomy between mind and body which has prevailed in Western culture since Descartes. They show that, in at least some individuals, abnormally functioning skin cells begin to function normally when the individual is exposed to specific words or communications (suggestions). There is, of course, much to learn concerning when and how suggestions are associated with such dramatic effects. At the present time, hypotheses that can guide our thinking and research include the following: Suggestions are associated with dramatic skin changes when they are experienced and accepted at a deep emotional level, and the deep acceptance of suggestions is more likely in a close interpersonal relationship, when the individual has a passive-receptive attitude, and when the suggestions are given with deep feeling and emotion.

CURE OF WARTS BY BELIEVED-IN SUGGESTIONS

A number of investigators have reported that they have cured warts by suggestions given during hypnosis [29-32]. Also, textbooks which aspired to cover all facets of hypnosis typically included a section on the treatment of warts by hypnotic suggestions [33, 34]. These claims raise two important questions. First, is there truth in the contention that warts have been cured by suggestions given during hypnosis? Second, if the contention has validity, then which aspects of suggestions and which aspects of hypnosis were effective in producing the cures?

We can begin to answer the above questions by noting that 1) warts at times can be cured by suggestions that they will disappear, provided the suggestions are believed and have a powerful effect on the feelings-thoughts-imaginings-emotions of the subject, and 2) good hypnotic subjects are more prone than poor hypnotic subjects to be affected in a potent way by the suggestions. Let us begin by first summarizing studies indicating that believed-in suggestions are associated with the cure of warts.

Before mentioning more recent studies, I should emphasize that the cure of warts by emotion-arousing suggestions has a very long history. The most time-honored cure for warts, according to Tuke [35, p. 365], which goes back at least to ancient Rome, consisted of "stealing a piece of beef from a butcher's shop, rubbing your warts with it, then throwing it away or burying it; then as the beef rots, the warts decay." Tuke wisely added, "I daresay that the excitement of the theft was one element in the cure."

Some years ago, Dr. Bloch became famous throughout Zurich as the "wart doctor" because he was so successful in treating warts [36]. When an individual with warts entered his office, s/he was confronted with an impressive "wart-killing" machine that had a noisy motor, flashing lights, and "powerful X-rays." After the patient had placed the part of the body with warts on the machine, Dr. Bloch turned on the electricity and told the patient not to move until the warts were dead; however, no current reached the patient. In fact, nothing reached the patient physically from this suggestive or placebo machine.

After the machine had completed its suggestive effect, Dr. Bloch placed a dot of brightly colored innocuous dye on each wart and told the patient, now confronted with the luridly colored warts, that the dead warts must not be washed or touched until they had disappeared. Of the 179 patients thus treated and adequately followed up, 31 percent showed wart disappearance after the first session. This, of course, is far higher than the base-level expectations for wart disappearance within a brief time; for example, Surman et al. [31], reported that not one of the seven subjects in their control group showed loss of any of their warts during the three month control period, Memmesheimer and Eisenlohr [37] reported that less than 3 percent of their seventy control subjects showed wart resolution during a one-month period, and Rulison [38] reported that the average duration of warts in 921 cases that he followed was about two to three years. I interpret Bloch's report as indicating that in some individuals the involution of warts is associated with suggestions which arouse belief and an emotional response [36]. This interpretation derives from indications that at least some of Bloch's patients were impressed at deep emotional level by the "powerful" machine and by the strong suggestions "not to move until the machine kills the warts," "not to touch the dead warts until they fall off," etc.

Allington also reported impressive results with suggestions [39]: Thirty-five of eighty-four patients (42%) were cured of their long-enduring warts after only one (emotion-arousing, strongly suggestive) intragluteal placebo injection (comprised of distilled water). Using various types of placebo-suggestive procedures, for instance, suggesting that a placebo injection was a powerful cure or painting the warts with a brightly colored innocuous dye while suggesting firmly that the dye was a powerful wart-killing drug, Bonjour [40], Dudek [41], Grumach [42], Memmesheimer and Eisenlohr [36], Sulzberger and Wolf [43], Vollmer [44], and others reported success in a comparable percentage of cases with warts that usually had been present for many years. In general, these suggestive procedures were more effective when the patients were younger and when they had many warts rather than a single wart; also, this type of treatment tended to be more successful when the warts were more recent and were of the juvenile type rather than the common type.

If the suggestions are to lead to success, they should affect the patient deeply and should be believed. Since a prestigeful doctor was the experimenter in each of the studies cited above, the patients had every reason to accept as absolutely true his statement that he was injecting a powerful wart-killer, and they were very likely to be emotionally affected when he injected this "powerful drug" into their body. Another method that can make suggestions more potent, emotional, and believable is to call the situation *hypnosis* and to utilize the rituals that are associated by the layman with hypnosis. Let us look at a study which illustrates the effectiveness of "hypnosis" in making procedures more believable.

In an experiment carried out a few years ago by Dr. Johnson and me [45], we posted signs stating that warts would be treated free in the Research Building of our hospital. The twenty-two individuals who volunteered were assigned randomly to one of two treatments with half to each treatment. The one group of eleven subjects was told that their warts would be treated with hypnosis; each subject agreed to the treatment and each was exposed to a typical hypnotic induction procedure comprised primarily of suggestions for deep relaxation, deep calmness, and drowsiness. The eleven subjects assigned to the other treatment were told that their warts would be treated by *focused contemplation* and they were not exposed to the hypnotic induction. The two treatments thus differed in that one was called *hypnosis* and the other was called *focused contemplation*, and the former included a hypnotic induction procedure whereas the other did not. The remaining aspects of the two treatments were the same; all subjects were asked to focus on specific warts, they were given suggestions to feel the skin in and around the warts tingling, and it was implied that the tingling sensations were associated with healing processes. At the end of each session, each subject was instructed to practice the procedure every day for a few minutes—to focus on the warts and to feel them tingling—until the warts were gone. The subjects also were told firmly that, if they closely followed the directions, the warts soon would disappear. Two follow-up appointments were then made: The subjects were to return after about two weeks and again after an additional three weeks.

When seen at the follow-up appointment about two weeks later, three of the eleven subjects in the hypnotic treatment and none of the eleven in the focused-contemplation treatment showed a reduction in either or both the number and the size of their warts. When seen again at the second follow-up session, the three subjects in the hypnotic treatment and none in the focused-contemplation treatment, had lost all or virtually all of their warts. One woman had lost thirty-seven of the thirty-nine common warts that were observable on her hands, neck, and face. (The remaining two warts also disappeared within a few weeks.) One young man lost all thirteen filiform warts that were on his chin, and another young man was cured of all five large common warts that were present on two fingers. Although, as I mentioned previously, biometric studies [37, 46] demonstrate that warts usually go away by themselves sooner or later, the odds are very small that three of the eleven individuals randomly allocated to the hypnotic treatment (as compared to none in the focused-contemplation treatment) would begin losing their warts soon after they first received the suggestions and that the warts would continue to regress steadily during the practice period until they were gone.

Why did three of the eleven subjects in the hypnotic treatment and none in the control treatment lose their warts? All three hypnotic subjects who lost their warts believed that hypnosis was an effective treatment for warts, had positive attitudes, motivations, and expectancies. They apparently allowed themselves to "let go" and to become calm and noncritical when they received the hypnotic induction suggestions, then they focused on the warts and imagined and felt them tingling, and, finally, they continued practicing the tingling exercise each day at home. We did not collect sufficient data to be able to state to what extent the remaining hypnotic subjects practiced the tingling exercise at home. However, I am certain that the subjects in the comparison treatment seriously doubted that "focused contemplation," which they had never heard of before, could cure their warts and did not conscientiously practice the "imagined tingling" exercise at home. In summary, it appears that "believed-in efficacy" played an important role in the Johnson and Barber experiment [45]: Subjects who believed that hypnosis was efficacious in curing warts took the instructions seriously. The continual focusing on the warts could have affected the blood supply to this area and then led to wart regression. We will return to this consideration later.

In addition to helping make the possibility of healing believable, "hypnosis" can play a role in the cure of warts in at least two additional ways. First of all, good hypnotic subjects, that is, individuals who are very responsive to suggestions of the type used in hypnotic situations, are more likely than poor hypnotic subjects to be less critical of suggestions for wart healing, to become deeply absorbed in suggestions to feel-think-imagine that the warts are tingling and disappearing, and to practice at home experiencing changes in the warts. In fact, in a series of studies, suggestions for the cure of warts were generally ineffective with poor hypnotic subjects and were generally effective with good hypnotic subjects. For instance, Asher [29] reported that he cured warts by suggestions given after a hypnotic induction procedure in eleven of seventeen (65%) good hypnotic subjects, in four of eight (50%) fair hypnotic subjects, and in none of eight (0%) poor hypnotic subjects. Similarly, Sinclair Gieben and Chalmers [30] cured warts by suggestions in hypnosis sessions in nine of ten good hypnotic subjects and in none of four poor hypnotic subjects. Others [32] presented similar results.

The above data have interesting implications. First, as Bowers pointed out, the clear relationship between the effectiveness of the suggestive treatment and the subjects' hypnotic (suggestive) abilities makes it unlikely that the cures were due to spontaneous remission rather than to the suggestive procedures [47]. Secondly, the claim that "hypnosis is effective in curing warts" appears to derive from studies in which suggestions for wart remission were given after a hypnotic induction procedure and were found to be much more effective with good rather than poor hypnotic subjects. If these investigators had given believable suggestions for wart remission without a hypnotic induction procedure, for instance, if they had injected a placebo with the suggestion that it was a powerful wart-curing drug, they probably also would have found that good hypnotic subjects were more responsive to the suggestion than poor hypnotic subjects. Consequently, they may have concluded, as I am concluding, that 1) the effective factor in curing warts in these studies was not "hypnosis" in the way an amateur believes but suggestions given in a believable way that affected, at a deep level, the feelings-thoughts-imaginings-emotions of the subject, and 2) the suggestions had a more profound effect on the good rather than the poor hypnotic subjects regardless of whether they had or had not been exposed to a hypnotic induction procedure. One can, of course, predict from these considerations that good hypnotic subjects also will show a greater degree of wart remission when they are exposed to placebo-suggestive treatments, such as those used by Bloch [35], Allington [39], Grumach [42], Vollmer [44], Dudek [41], and others.

Another aspect of "hypnosis" also is relevant to the treatment of warts. A number of therapists who used suggestions for deep relaxation (and other hypnotic induction suggestions) together with suggestions to relive earlier life events have presented very interesting data indicating that warts can have psychodynamic implications and can at times be cured by psychological approaches. For instance, French reported the case of a twenty-nine-year-old married woman who developed numerous warts around the genital area (condyloma acuminatum) which were not helped at all by medical treatment [48]. In the course of two hypnotic sessions, material emerged which strongly indicated that the warts served the purpose of preventing her from continuing a secret sexual affair with a man she found exciting but also wished to discontinue seeing. During the second hypnosis session, the patient accepted the therapist's explicit suggestion that the genital warts were not needed since there were more appropriate means of dealing with her ambivalence over the sexual affair. Within two days, there was a dramatic regression of the warts which continued for a few weeks until they totally disappeared.

Surman, Gottlieb, and Hackett presented the case of a nine-year-old girl with multiple common warts who did not respond to conventional medical treatment but responded dramatically to hypnotherapy [49]. Other writers also have presented cases indicating that warts may have psychodynamic implications and can at times be cured by psychological approaches [50].

In brief, it appears that warts can be cured in at least some individuals by 1) direct believed-in suggestions that they will disappear and also by 2) psychodynamic approaches which resolve psychological problems associated with the warts.

The Cartesian dichotomy between mind and body, which is still strong in our culture, will make it difficult for some readers to accept these data. However, these data, together with other data presented in this chapter, should help move us away from the Cartesian dichotomy, and we should begin to view the organism as a unity. From this viewpoint, mental constructs, such as *thoughts* and *emotions*, will be seen to refer to some aspects of the total unity and anatomical or physiological constructs, such as warts and allergic responses, will be seen to refer to other aspects. An analogy which may help the reader move toward this viewpoint is to think of a person as analogous to a nation: Both the person and the nation are comprised of many individuals (e.g., 200 trillion cells in the person and 200 million people in a nation such as the U.S.A.) each performing a function in the total division of labor. The federal government and the communications systems (telephones, television, newspapers, transportation systems, etc.) integrate and coordinate all 200 million individuals in the U.S.A. into one nation, and, in the same way, the central nervous system, the autonomic nervous system, and the endocrine system integrate and coordinate all 200 trillion cells of the body into one individual. Each cell in the body does its specific job in a very complex division of labor just as each individual in the U.S.A. has a part in a complex division of labor. Just as the citizens of the U.S.A. all are affected by information and laws emanating from the federal government through the communication channels, so every cell in the organism is affected by the feelings-thoughts-imaginings that are closely intertwined with the nervous and hormonal systems viewed as executive or directive centers and also as communication channels. From this viewpoint, every cell in the organism can be affected by communications, which arrive via the integrating and communicating systems of the body, in much the same way as every individual in a nation can be affected by the communications from the federal government. If readers will keep this analogy firmly in mind, the data discussed above and the remaining data may be more understandable and acceptable.

EFFECTS OF SUGGESTIONS
ON THE MAMMARY GLANDS

In five published studies, women who desired larger breasts were treated by hypnosuggestive procedures. The hypnotherapist typically informed the women that they would participate in weekly hypnosis sessions at the office for about twelve weeks and that they would be taught self-hypnosis to practice daily at home. In the office sessions, the women first were taught hypnosis and autohypnosis procedures—that is, they were taught to let go of extraneous concerns, to relax deeply, and to experience a profound feeling of calmness. After they had attained a state of deep calmness, they typically were given suggestions along the following lines (and they also were instructed to give themselves the same suggestions when practicing self-hypnosis at home): "Imagine that the sun (or a heat lamp) is shining on the breasts or that wet, warm towels are on the breasts and feel the heat as it flows through the breasts; imagine the breasts growing, as they did during puberty, and experience feelings of tenderness, swelling, and tightness of the skin over the breasts; and imagine that the breasts are becoming warm, tingling, pulsating, sensitive, and that they are growing." Thus, hypnosis for breast enlargement involved procedures aimed at producing deep relaxation as well as suggestions to feel warmth and other sensations in the breast area and to feel the breasts growing.

About seventy women participated in five investigations which used procedures like those described above [51-55]. In all five studies, the average increase over the twelve-week period in the circumference of each breast was about 1¼ inches. In all but the earliest of these studies [52], the breast measurements apparently were performed with care and they took into consideration possible changes in breast size due to weight gain and menstrual cycle.

Since the above summary is in general terms, let us look more specifically at one of the studies. Willard [54] worked with twenty-two women of ages nineteen to fifty-four. Breast measurements—height, diameter, and circumference—were made by an independent physician. The women were given suggestions for deep relaxation and calmness and suggestions to imagine warm water flowing over the breasts, to imagine a heat lamp making the breasts warm, and to feel the breasts pulsating. Tape recordings were made of these office procedures, which the patients were to utilize when alone at home. Of these women, 85 percent showed some breast enlargement during the twelve-week period, and 46 percent required a larger bra. The average increase in breast size was 1.37 inches in circumference, over 1 inch horizontally, and 2/3 inch vertically. Weight gains were not correlated with the increase in breast size; in fact, 42 percent of the women lost 2 or more pounds during the twelve weeks.

Were these breast changes temporary or lasting? An attempt to follow-up after the twelve-week treatment period was made in only one study. In this investigation [53], the women were seen again three months later, and 81 percent of the breast gain was still present; it thus appears that the breast changes were not transient but generally endured afterwards.

What aspects of hypnosis were important in producing the breast changes? When we look carefully at the details of the five reports, it becomes increasingly clear that the effective factors were that the women participating in these studies 1) were in a high-expectancy situation (hypnosis or autohypnosis), 2) experienced the suggested relaxation, the letting go of extraneous concerns, and the deep calmness, and 3) took the suggestions to imagine the breast changes seriously and thus focused on the task of imagining. Calling the procedure "hypnosis" and "autohypnosis" (terms which have the connotation that this is a serious situation in which unusual things can occur) apparently was important in leading the women to take the suggestions seriously and to practice conscientiously at home; if the approach had been called as it could have been, "relaxation," or "self-suggestions" or "imagining," we can surmise that the women may not have viewed it so seriously and practiced so willingly. The suggestions for relaxation, letting go, and deep calmness apparently were important in helping define the situation as "hypnosis" (in which unusual events can occur) and also in helping the women reduce critical or distracting thoughts so that they could better focus on the task of imagining.

Another consideration pertaining to hypnosis also played a role in these investigations. As I have stated previously, good hypnotic subjects are generally responsive to suggestions regardless of whether or not they are exposed to hypnotic induction. There is some evidence that in these studies, as might be expected, the good hypnotic subjects had greater breast changes than the not-so-good subjects. For instance, Willard [54] reported that there was a clear relationship between the women's reports of how vividly they could imagine the warmth and other sensations in the breast and the amount of breast growth that was evident at the completion of the study. As has been noted previously [56-60], and as will be discussed in more detail later in this chapter, very good hypnotic subjects tend to be individuals who are able to fantasize and imagine vividly regardless of whether or not they have undergone hypnotic induction. In brief, in this study (and also in many other studies) ability to imagine played an important role in producing the effects attributed to hypnosis.[3]

Parenthetically, it would be useful in further studies on suggested breast changes to determine what role sexual arousal may play in producing the effects. When women are given suggestions by men to relax, let go, and imagine the breasts tingling, pulsating, and growing, they might recall or imagine sexual situations which could produce sexual arousal and bring more blood to the breasts. The enhanced blood supply, as will be discussed again later in this chapter, may play a role in stimulating growth in the breasts.

Before closing this section, I should mention another possibility that I believe should be taken seriously: Breast development may be inhibited during puberty by psychological factors, and breast growth associated with suggestions may be more likely in adult women who have overcome those inhibiting psychodynamic factors which were present during puberty. Erickson presented two cases which support this possibility [62]. The first case involved a twenty-year-old girl who was brought to him by her older sister for a single hypnotic session because of failure of breast development. The girl had been deeply religious since childhood,

---

[3] The close association between *hypnosis* and *fantasy* or *imagining* was noted at the beginning of the official history of hypnotism by the commission that was appointed by the King of France to report on Mesmer's procedures. The commission reported that the dramatic effects associated with mesmerism were due primarily to the patient's *imagination* and secondarily to social contagion (imitation of one patient by another) and to bodily contact. In fact, the Mesmerists, who were charismatic males, had prolonged contact with their patients, who were virtually always women, placing or "laying" their hands on the women's body for long periods of time and arousing sexually related effects [61, pp. 18-25].

and her religious convictions included elements of austerity and a rejection of the body. Following a hypnotic induction procedure, Erickson suggested to her that she carefully read the Song of Solomon which glorifies the female body in all its parts. He gave additional suggestions designed to change her attitude toward her body and especially to help her sense her breasts "as living structures of promise, and in which she would have an increasing sense of comfort and pride." Subsequent to this one hypnotic session (how soon afterwards is not clear from the report) the patient and her sister both told Erickson that significant breast development had occurred.

Erickson's second case involved a seventeen-year-old girl whose breasts had failed to develop despite the adequacy of her physical development otherwise. After hypnotic induction, Erickson gave her a variety of suggestions including suggestions to develop an itch around the breast area which would change to an undefined feeling which would render her continuously aware of her breasts. Some months later she reported to Erickson that her breasts had grown to a "large medium size." A complete physical examination by another physician confirmed her statement.

Before closing this section, it appears appropriate to call for much further research to answer an important question: Of the many tissues and organs in the human body, which can be altered in size by suggestive psychological approaches?

SKIN CHANGES, SUCH AS INFLAMMATION, WHEALS, AND BLISTERS, PRODUCED BY SUGGESTION

A number of investigators have reported that suggestions that the skin is being burned, when given to receptive subjects, at times gives rise to skin changes—for example, inflammation, wheals, and/or blisters—which also are observed naturally (without suggestions) when the skin is injured. As Lewis noted in his classical book on this topic [63], when the skin is injured, it typically manifests a "triple response" consisting of the release of a histamine like substance, a localized dilation and an increased permeability of the minute blood vessels, and a widespread arteriolar dilation. This reaction first produces erythema, and then dermographism and wheals, and if it is sufficiently intense, it leads to blisters. In fact, nearly every type of stimulus that produces wheals will lead to blisters if it is increased in intensity.

Suggestions that the skin is being burned have been reported to produce all gradations of the triple response of the skin to injury. Let us first look at an experiment and then at a case report in which suggestions gave rise to a limited skin change (erythema or inflammation) which did not develop into wheals or blisters.

Johnson and Barber conducted an experiment with forty unselected student nurses [64]. These students were told that an attempt would be made to produce a blister by hypnosis. After a formal hypnotic induction procedure (repeated suggestions of relaxation, drowsiness, and sleep) had been administered, each subject was given the suggestion that it was morning, she was in her kitchen, bacon was cooking in a red-hot frying pan, and she accidently touched the frying pan and was burned on the back of the hand: "The frying pan burns the back of your hand . . . you move away from the frying pan now . . . but you can still feel the burning sensation . . . soon a blister will form there . . . a blister is forming there."

In this experiment, only one of the forty subjects showed a skin change that was clearly associated with the suggestions. While receiving the suggestions that she was being burned, this subject developed a striking bright red inflammation on the back of her hand. The inflammation formed an irregular pattern, covering about 75 percent of the hand and part of the index finger. There was a very sharp boundary between the inflamed and uninflamed part of the hand. The inflammation appeared soon after the experimenter began giving the suggestions and continued for about three minutes.

Immediately upon completion of the experiment, the subject reported that six years previously she had been burned by hot grease on the very spot that now had become red. She also added that the previous burn she had experienced had been due to a kitchen cooking accident.

Thus, the suggestions that were used in this experiment closely resembled what actually had happened to the subject at an earlier time. These fortuitous events led her to relive the experience vividly; for example, she stated post-experimentally that when she received the suggestions she could feel the "burning" and the formation of the "blister." Apparently, the skin changes manifested by this subject were due, not to a global hypnosis factor, as the amateur might assume, but to very specific "microevents" and "microcognitions" such as the following: 1) The subject had positive attitudes towards the experimenter and toward the total experimental situation and was willing to relax, let go of extraneous concerns, and become absorbed in the specific suggestions. 2) The specific suggestion of being burned in the kitchen fortuitously revived vivid memories, feelings, and emotions associated with a previous burn. 3) The "microcognitions" (the specific moment-to-moment memories, feelings, thoughts, and images) related to the previous burn were interblended with "microphysiological" changes which were associated with the previous experience, namely, with increased blood supply to the area.

A case study presented by Bellis also showed that the skin has the potential to react to the vivid reliving of a previously experienced burn in virtually the same way as it had reacted to the actual burn [65]. Bellis stated that during a hypnotic induction procedure, he suggested to a patient that she imagine herself on the beach on a sunny day. The patient became very aroused and called out, "I feel like I'm on fire!" Her face, shoulders, and half of both arms were beet red. The hypnotist touched her skin and found that it felt very hot; he then gave suggestions of deep relaxation, coolness, and comfort. The patient relaxed and appeared comfortable, but her sunburnlike reaction, which was due to the suggestions, lasted eighteen hours. Later, Bellis learned that the patient previously had suffered an allergic-type sunburn reaction that was apparently related to a drug she was receiving as part of her psychiatric therapy. The erythema which was induced by the suggestions of being at a sunny beach was similar in the extent of area affected, in itching, and in intense heat to the previous allergic sunburn.

In a number of cases, suggestions of blister formation gave rise to wheals but not to blisters. For example, after hypnotic induction suggestions follwed by suggestions for blister formation, Doswald and Kreibich [66, case 2] observed a wheal form on a patient. Interestingly, the patient had a medical history of wheals which were associated with emotional arousal. Similarly, after administering a hypnotic induction, Borelli suggested to a patient with neurodermatitis that he was being burned at a spot on the skin where a coin had been placed and that, within a day, a blister would form in that area; when the patient returned the next day, he showed a sharply circumscribed and elevated area at the designated spot which had the characteristics of a wheal [67].

The wheals that are associated with suggestions for blister formation are more understandable in the light of studies which show that some individuals develop localized wheals when recalling former experiences in which wheals occurred. Moody presented two case studies along these lines [68, 69]. The first patient manifested marked aggressive behavior when he was asleep or seemingly asleep. On one occasion, during a hospitalization, the patient's hands had been tied behind his back during sleep, and wheals had formed in the traumatized area. At a later time, when the patient recalled this experience after hexobarbital administration, wheals appeared on both forearms in the area which previously had been tied. Moody's second patient, who was being treated for psychiatric problems, manifested swelling, bruising, and even bleeding in localized body areas on at least thirty occasions when she was vividly reliving previous experiences which involved injuries to the areas. For instance, when vividly recalling a former occasion when she had been struck across the dorsum of both hands with a cutting whip, she developed wheals on both hands in the respective areas.

Similar data were presented by Graff and Wallerstein [70]; they reported that during a therapeutic interview, a twenty-seven-year-old sailor, who had a tattoo of a dagger on his arm, suddenly showed a wheal reaction sharply limited to the outline of the dagger. The wheal subsided after this session but reappeared in the same way in a later interview. The authors presented indirect evidence, derived from the patient's free associations, that the tattoo and the wheal that developed on it, had deep meaning for the patient. Brandt also presented cases of patients showing sharply localized wheal reactions which appeared to be closely associated with recall of meaningful, emotional material [71].

The patients described above manifested wheals and other skin reactions when vividly reliving earlier events that had given rise to skin reactions. In a later study, Kaneko and Takaishi showed that similar cutaneous changes can be obtained by suggesting the reliving of earlier experiences to subjects who have been exposed to a traditional hypnotic induction. These investigators worked with four selected patients who often suffered from wheals on their skin (chronic urticaria). Two of the patients believed that their urticaral hives were due to heat, and the other two believed that their wheals appeared when they were anxious or depressed. The former two patients were exposed to a traditional hypnotic induction procedure and given suggestions that they were exposed to heat which would produce wheals; and the latter two were exposed to a hypnotic induction and given suggestions intended to produce emotional conflict. Kaneko and Takaishi reported that wheals developed in each of the four cases during or immediately after the hypnosis-suggestion sessions.

Cases have been reported in which suggestions for blister formation led to an extremely strong "triple reaction" of the skin to injury [63]; in these cases, the reaction apparently continued to its maximum extent and a blister was produced. For instance, after administering a hypnotic induction procedure to a selected subject, Hadfield gave vivid suggestions that a red-hot iron was being applied to a specific area of the arm (where he touched the subject) and that a blister would form in the "burned" area [73]. The arm was then bandaged and sealed, and the subject was observed continuously during the following twenty-four hours. At the end of this period, the bandage was opened in the presence of three physicians and, on the specified area, the beginning of a blister was noted which gradually during the day developed into a large blister.

After administering a hypnotic procedure, Ullman suggested to a soldier who recently had been in combat that he was on the battlefield again and that a small fragment of molten shell just had glanced off the top of his hand [74]. At this point in the procedure, Ullman brushed the soldier's hand with a small flat file to add emphasis to the suggestion. Pallor followed immediately in the circumscribed area, about 1 centimeter in diameter; after twenty minutes a narrow red margin was present about the area of pallor, and after one hour the beginning of a blister was observable. The soldier was then dismissed; he returned about four hours later, and at this time a blister about 1 centimeter in diameter was evident.[4]

In an experiment reported by Platonov [10], Dr. V. Finne suggested to a thirty-five-year-old woman that she was relaxing and falling deeply asleep; he

---

[4] A number of writers have noted a possible artifact in the above investigation. When Ullman brushed the subject's hand with a small flat file in order to emphasize the suggestion, he may have initiated processes which gave rise to a blister. This criticism derives primarily from the finding that some individuals with a history of urticaria develop wheals in the skin areas stimulated by metal, for example, around a wristwatch metal strap [34, p. 144; 75]. It seems unlikely, however, that the blister was due to the brushing with the file because of the following reasons: 1) There is no indication that the subject had a history of urticaria; 2) wheals are produced in individuals with urticaria, not by very brief stimulation by metal (as in the Ullman experiment) but by more prolonged stimulation (as by a wristwatch band); and 3) although metal stimulation does produce wheals in some individuals, it does not produce blisters.

then suggested that a copper coin, which he placed on her arm, was a hot, burning metal disc. This excellent hypnotic subject cried out as if she had been burned and and she clearly seemed to be suffering from severe pain. After arousal, the subject was watched continuously by a physician who observed the following sequence: The skin was red at the suggested burn area for fifty-five minutes; then a clear swelling was evident; two and one half hours after the suggestion, a white spot appeared at the center of the swelling, and after one more hour a clear blister was present.

Similarly, after a hypnotic induction, Weatherhead [76] touched the knee of his eighteen-year-old subject with a pencil while telling her that she was being burned with a red-hot iron. The knee was bound with a bandage and then sealed in the presence of medical witnesses. Within twenty hours, the subject developed a blister which was "puffed out with fluid" but was not especially painful. Weatherhead emphasized that this woman had been selected for the experiment because she was a superb hypnotic subject. (In previous studies, in which she had been given suggestions for temperature elevation and for heart rate change, she had been able to raise her oral temperature from $96°$ to $104°$ and to accelerate and decelerate her heart rate.)

In the experiments described above, and also in other studies reviewed by Pattie [77], Weitzenhoffer [34], Barber [1], Paul [78], and Chertok [78], some subjects manifested at least the early stages of a blister when they were being carefully monitored. Consequently, it is definite that a suggested burn can initiate the processes which lead to a blister. (Also, the Ikemi and Nakagawa [9] study, which I summarized earlier in this chapter, showed that individuals who are hypersensitive to a poison ivy-type plant respond with small blisters to the mere suggestion that they are being touched by this plant.)

In the above discussion, I focused on studies in which the designated skin area was bandaged and sealed or the subject was observed by the experimenter until some definite skin change was evident. Studies which did not include these kinds of careful controls are open to the following critical considerations: 1) The excellent hypnotic subjects who are selected for these experiments often are highly motivated to produce the phenomena suggested by the hypnotist [80-81]; 2) If they do not develop erythema, whealing, or blistering when given suggestions of being burned, they may try to "make the experiment succeed" by artifactually trying to produce the skin changes. Although this may be a rare occurrence, a case presented by Wolberg [82, p. 26] shows that it does occur. Wolberg suggested to an excellent hypnotic subject that wheals would develop on his forearm. Several days later, the subject showed a "markedly irritated skin" where the wheals were suggested. The subject denied that he had in any way irritated the skin. However, during a later hypnotic session, he admitted that he had taken a walk in the woods, "picked poison ivy and rubbed it vigorously on the inner surface of his arms."

A similar case was reported by Schrenck-Notzing [83, 84]. In this instance, the excellent hypnotic subject, who had been given suggestions intended to produce a blister, was observed scratching the designated skin area with a needle passed through the bandage on her arm. Although a number of investigators have interpreted this observation as an indication that the subject was artifactually trying to produce a blister on her arm, the data in the original report are open to an alternative explanation: The subject was itching unbearably at the spot where the blister was to form and tried to relieve the itch in the only way she could without removing the bandage.

The latter possibility is supported by data presented by Johnson and Barber [64]. An excellent hypnotic subject who was participating in their experiment had vividly experienced the suggested burn but did not manifest any noticeable skin change. However, when she returned to the laboratory the next day, the skin area where the blister was to develop was inflamed and swollen. She stated that, since the experiment, the designated area had been itching and she had been scratching it for relief.[5]

There is an important fact that needs to be further emphasized in regard to the results discussed above: All of the individuals who developed inflammation, wheals, or blisters in response to the suggestion that they were being burned were labeled in the earlier studies as "somnambules" and in the later studies as excellent hypnotic subjects. Since such superb hypnotic subjects can respond easily and profoundly to a wide variety of suggestions, including the suggestions to deeply relax and to let go of extraneous concerns (to go into "deep hypnosis or trance"), the amateur could easily misinterpret that the cutaneous alterations were due simply to deep hypnosis.

A more correct interpretation would emphasize the following: 1) The superb hypnotic subjects were able to let go of other concerns and to become involved deeply at an emotional level in the suggestion that they were being burned; consequently, they felt (experienced) the suggested burn in practically the same way as an actual burn. 2) When individuals experience (hallucinate) a suggested burn in virtually the same way as they experience an actual burn, the central nervous system can react in virtually the same way as it reacts to an actual burn—by releasing the triple response of the skin which can lead to erythema, wheals, and blisters.

According to this theory, the hallucination of a burn is an important mediating step in the production of the cutaneous changes. Since the ability to experience profoundly (to hallucinate) the suggested burn appears to be limited to only a small proportion of individuals (those labeled as *good* or *excellent hypnotic subjects*), we would expect such experiments to succeed only in rare cases.

However, even among selected good hypnotic subjects who *have* the ability to hallucinate, only a very small proportion manifested inflammation, wheals, or

---

[5] This case illustrates an important principle: Some individuals who are highly responsive to suggestions, at times continue to experience some of the suggested effects after the formal experiment is terminated [85, 86]. This is why suggestions that are meant to be experienced only during the experiment should be cancelled before the experiment is terminated.

blisters when it was suggested that they were being burned [64, 87-89]. Apparently, several other variables may be necessary; as Chertok [79] has suggested, these may include 1) a strong interpersonal or transference relationship between the subject and the experimenter, 2) an exceptional degree of psychosomatic "plasticity," especially skin reactivity, on the part of the subject, and 3) a previous, profound experience of being burned. With regard to the first of these three variables, Chertok found in his review of successful cases, that in *each* case a strong transference relationship appeared to exist between subject and hypnotist. Let us look at the other two variables in more detail.

Psychosomatic plasticity, as indicated by a history of conversion reactions, clearly characterized nearly half of the subjects who showed skin changes when given the suggestion of being burned; for example, they had manifested such conversion reactions as arm anesthesia, anesthesia of almost the entire body, skin gangrene of neurotic origin, hysterical mutism, hysterical ecchymoses, and hysterical blindness [79]. In addition to the conversionlike dermatological disorders mentioned in the preceding sentence (neurotic skin gangrene and hysterical ecchymoses), other types of cutaneous plasticity also were encountered; for instance, one subject had a history of wheals following emotional arousal [66, case 2], another showed demographia [90] and a third was afflicted with atopic dermatitis [67]. In brief, to produce skin changes by suggesting a burn, it would be wise to select excellent hypnotic subjects who form intense personal relations with hypnotists and who have previously shown conversionlike reactions or the kind of cutaneous lability that underlies dermographia, atopic dermatitis, and emotionally induced urticaria.

In addition, it also appears helpful if the subjects have had previous burn experiences that they can recall with profound emotion. In some of the successful cases, the suggestions of being burned produced a strong emotional effect because they revived vivid memories of a burn previously experienced in the same place as the suggested burn [64, 91], or they revived vivid memories of a battle that the soldier subject had recently experienced in a traumatic way [74].

The importance of previous experience is illustrated in a study carried out by Podyapolsky and reported by Vasiliev [92, pp. 75-76]. A selected good hypnotic subject on two occasions was given the suggestion that a mustard plaster had been applied to his skin, once before and once after he had experienced a mustard plaster. Erythema was observed in the designated area when the suggestions were given after he had experienced the mustard plaster but not before. In brief, it appears that subjects can more vividly hallucinate a suggested burn if they have had a previous profound experience of a burn similar to the one suggested. However, we would expect very few individuals who have had such previous profound burn experiences to manifest skin changes when given the suggestion of being burned [93]; as stated above, many other variables also seem to be needed.

STIGMATA, SPONTANEOUS BLEEDING, AND
SPONTANEOUS AND SUGGESTED BRUISES

The cutaneous alterations discussed above are related to a broad range of phenomena that have been labeled as stigmata. There are at least fifty well-documented cases of individuals who thought often about and identified with the suffering of Christ and who apparently bled spontaneously and developed skin alterations on their hands or feet which resembled Christ's wounds during his crucifixion [94]. One of the most famous stigmatics was St. Francis of Assisi. He had become obsessed with the crucifixion. Tuke [35, p. 82] observes, "One thought, one definite idea, henceforth occupied him—his Master's crucifixion. His imagination revelled, so to speak, in all His sufferings. He strove while fasting more and more, and praying more and more intensely, to realize them himself." As he became more and more immersed in the fantasy of the crucifixion, "He then suffered pain in his hands and feet (in the areas where he believed Christ had been nailed to the cross) and this was succeeded by inflammation so severe as to terminate in ulceration." [35, p. 82]

The many cases of stigmata are summarized by Summers [95] and Thurston [94]. Although some of these older cases—for example, that of Louise Lateau, Katherina Emmerich, and Therese Neumann [96]—appear relatively well-documented, a hard-nosed skeptic nevertheless could argue that the bleeding and the wounds might have been self-inflicted. In a more recent case, however, the bleeding was clearly observed to develop naturally without external stimulation. This case, presented by Early and Lifschutz [97], involved a ten-and-one-half-year-old black girl of fundamentalist religious background. Two weeks before Easter she read a book about Christ's crucifixion and was deeply affected emotionally; three days later she saw a television movie on the same topic and had a vivid dream about it that night. Within a few days she began to bleed from the left and right palms, the upper part of the right foot, the right side of the chest, and the middle of her forehead. This was seen by teachers, nurses, and others. A physician could clearly observe the blood increasing in volume on her palm. After wiping the wet palm, no lesions were observed. The bleeding stopped after Good Friday.

Two cases of blood extravating from the skin have been reported by psychoanalysts. The first patient bled in three psychoanalytic sessions from the pores of his hands; according to the analyst [98], each of these bleeding episodes was immediately preceded by the emotional recall of events that stirred up Oedipal strivings, fantasies, and guilt feelings. The second case, presented by Lifschutz [99], involved a woman who, when she was thirteen, had been scratched down her back by her angry and sadistic father with his long fingernails and had been left with three long scars. Years later, when she lived at a distance from her father, her scars would redden and bleed just prior to his contemplated visits.

These cases also remind us of patients described by Schindler who suffered from recurrent spontaneous ecchymoses (discoloration of the skin caused by extravasation of blood), and who also developed the same kinds of bruises after receiving hypnotic suggestions. More recently, Agle, Ratnoff, and Wasman conducted intensive studies with four women who developed such spontaneous bruises during periods of anxiety or stress [101]. Each of these women also showed hysterical character traits as well as a propensity to express psychological problems in psychophysiological responses and through conversion mechanisms. Three of these four women were superb hypnotic subjects; the fourth responded to some hypnotic suggestions but not to others and then seemed disoriented for several hours afterwards. Each of these patients was exposed to a hypnotic induction procedure and given suggestions, worded in emotional ways, to the effect that a bruise would form spontaneously. These kinds of suggestions were effective in giving rise to a bruise at least once with each woman. For instance, after a hypnotic induction, one of the women was given the suggestion that at the count of a specific number, she would feel as if her husband had struck her; at the end of the count, the suggested area was touched with the blunt end of a fountain pen. After an (unstated) period of time, a bruise developed at the designated area. To rule out the possibility that the bruise was self-induced, one of the four women was watched continuously for twenty-four hours. Since a bruise developed in this case also, we can conclude that at least in good hypnotic subjects who have a history of spontaneous ecchymoses, emotional suggestions can give rise to bruises in specifically suggested body areas. The authors of this report postulated that the bruise produced by emotional suggestions in these patients is due to the emotionally associated release of a vasodilator polypeptide which leads to vascular permeability sufficient to allow the leakage of blood.

SUGGESTED INHIBITION OF BLEEDING

The studies summarized above, which indicate that abnormal bleeding can be produced in some individuals by believed-in suggestions, are complemented by another set of studies which indicate the reverse—bleeding can be inhibited by appropriate suggestions. The latter contention received some support from studies carried out by Lucas with seventy-five hemophiliacs undergoing tooth extraction [102]; when given hypnotic suggestions focusing on tranquility, these patients did not show abnormal bleeding during the postoperative period and did not require transfusions of blood. Unfortunately, Lucas' investigations failed to demonstrate conclusively that bleeding after tooth extraction can be blocked simply by suggestions for deep relaxation, because he tried to control the bleeding also by packing the extraction sockets and also by covering the area with a splint.

More recently, in a better controlled experiment, Chaves [103] demonstrated that bleeding associated with tooth extraction can be controlled by (hypnotic) suggestions. He worked with nine volunteers who were to undergo bilateral symmetrical tooth extraction. Three sessions separated by at least two weeks were involved. In Session 1, the subjects were exposed to a hypnotic induction procedure and tested for response to the Barber Suggestibility Scale. One of the next two sessions (Session 2 or 3) was used as a control; a tooth (or teeth) was extracted with local anesthesia. In the other session (either Session 2 or 3), another tooth (or teeth) was extracted after subjects had been given a local anesthetic and exposed to tape-recorded suggestions for deep relaxation and for reduced pain sensitivity to be experienced during extraction and for reduced blood loss to occur during and after extraction. Under the hypnotic condition, the subjects were told to use one or more of Dubin and Shapiro's three methods to reduce the blood loss [104]; they were told that they could visualize the blood as water from a faucet that can be turned off, or they could imagine that they were suturing the wound so that it would not bleed, or they could willfully constrict the blood vessels in the area. The loss of blood, which was carefully observed and calculated, was reduced by 65 percent under the hypnotic-suggestions condition. This striking result confirmed the claim commonly proffered by dentists who use hypnosis [105] that hypnotic suggestions can reduce bleeding after extractions. Although Chaves' study indicated that these statements are valid, it did not delineate how the effect is produced: the reduction in bleeding may have been due to the suggestions for deep relaxation, or to the suggestions to use imagery (or willpower) to stop the bleeding, or to both. Further studies would be useful to ascertain whether one of these suggestions or both mediate the effect.

MINIMIZING THE EFFECTS OF BURNS BY SUGGESTION

Data reviewed above showed that some individuals, who vividly experience (hallucinate) the heat and the pain of a suggested burn, manifest the same kinds of skin changes which are associated with actual burns. Is it possible also to reduce or eliminate the skin changes produced by an actual burning stimulus if the subject is unaware of, does not attend to, or is unconcerned about the burn stimulus? Bramwell summarized Delboeuf's experiment, carried out around 1887, which attempted to answer this question [106, p. 84]. He worked with a young, healthy peasant girl who was a superb hypnotic subject. First he explained what he was going to do and obtained her consent. He then administered a hypnotic induction procedure, extended both her arms on a table, and suggested that the right arm was becoming anesthetized and would be insensitive to pain. Each arm was then burned to the same extent and for the same duration by a red-hot iron bar, 8 mm. in diameter. The subject appeared to experience pain when the left arm was burned but not when the right arm was burned. The burns were then carefully bandaged and the subject went to bed. The pain continued in the left arm throughout the night; the next morning there was a wound on the left arm, 3 cm. in diameter, with an outer circle of inflamed blisters. On the right arm there was a definite burned area which was the exact size of the iron (less than 1 cm. in diameter) without redness or inflammation. Hadfield later carried out a very similar experiment with a superb hypnotic subject and obtained the same results [73]. These experiments showed that the effects of a burn stimulus are only partly due to the stimulus per se; in part they are due to how individuals react to the burn stimulus. If they remain calm about, do not attend to, or are unaware of the burning stimulus, the skin may react minimally (manifesting a burn limited precisely to where the burn stimulus touched the skin); whereas, if they are especially anxious, concerned about, and focusing on the sensations of burning and pain, they can increase the extent and the depth of the skin damage produced by the burn stimulus.

Delboeuf's and Hadfield's experiments were replicated many years later by Chapman, Goodell, and Wolff [107]. In this investigation, thirteen subjects were exposed to suggestions of deep relaxation and hypnosis followed by suggestions that one arm was either normal or insensitive. A standardized heat stimulus, which produced very small burns, was then applied to three selected spots on the arm. (Specifically, 500 milicalories per second per square centimeter were applied for 3 seconds to each spot.) After an interval of 15 to 30 minutes, during which time the subjects received continuous suggestions for relaxation, calmness, and hypnosis, it was suggested that the other arm was very sensitive, tender, and painful and the same standardized burn stimulus was applied three times.

The results of forty trials with the thirteen subjects were as follows: In thirty trials, the extent of burn (the inflammatory reaction and tissue damage) left by the standardized burn stimulus was greater in the arm suggested to be sensitive, tender, and painful; in two trials, the extent of burn was greater in the normal or "insensitive" arm; and in eight trials, no difference was noted. Recordings of skin temperature and plethysmograph indicated that local vasodilation and elevation in skin temperature was larger in magnitude and persisted longer in the sensitive, tender, painful arm. Furthermore, perfusion of the area around the burn, showed that a potent vasodilator (a histamine like substance) was present to a greater degree in the sensitive, tender, painful arm. In brief, it appears that the physiological effects of an external stimulus can be altered by changing an individual's *reaction* to the stimulus; when an individual's reaction to a burning stimulus is enhanced by suggestions that the area to be burned is sensitive, tender, and painful, the individual's overreaction has both behavioral and physiological components—physiologically a vasodilator is produced in elevated quantities which allows more blood to escape from the minute blood vessels and which is associated with a greater degree of inflammation and tissue damage.

The data summarized above led Ewin to conjecture that real-life burn victims could be helped significantly (to manifest a minimum degree of inflammation and tissue damage) if they are seen soon after they are burned and are given suggestions for deep relaxation plus suggestions that the burned area is cool, comfortable, or insensitive [108]. Since he practiced medicine in downtown New Orleans, he made himself available quickly when called to aid a burn victim. In his first report [108] he stated that he was able to see, relatively soon after the accident, four individuals who had suffered severe burns on the face or extremities. One of these four scoffed at the hypnotic procedures and did not benefit from them; the procedures appeared to be strikingly effective with the remaining three subjects—each healed rapidly.

In a second report, Ewin presented the case of a man who had fallen into a pot of molten lead (950°C) up to his knee [109]. He was a good hypnotic subject, responding with profound involvement to the suggestions for deep relaxation and rapid healing. Instead of developing a third-degree burn requiring skin grafting as definitely would be expected from this type of burn, the patient developed only a second-degree burn and was out of the hospital in three weeks.

THE SECRET OF FIRE-WALKING

The data presented above remind us of the fact that a large number of individuals throughout the world have walked without harm over burning or very hot coals, ashes, charcoal, stones, etc. Writers who are unacquainted with the many thorough investigations of fire-walking [110, pp. 99-109] consider these feats to be a miracle that is simply unexplainable. However, investigators who have looked more closely have concluded that it simply is not what it at first appears to be. Although the pits include extremely hot material, they are (knowingly or unknowingly) constructed in such a way that if one walks through firmly and *without hesitation*, one simply does not burn. Calmness, confidence, and lack of anxiety are important because fire-walkers who lack these qualities tend to hesitate during their passage through the pit and even brief moments of hesitation are often enough to produce burns.

In an early experiment, Langley [111] showed that the volcanic basalt stones used in the Tahiti fire-walk were deceptive, because they were very poor conductors of heat and, although they were red-hot on one end, the surface that was touched by the fire-walker was comfortable. Later experimenters tried, as closely as possible, to model their experimental fire-pits on those observed in various parts of the world, and they thus constructed pits with different burning material and of various depths, widths, and lengths. They found that, if one does not hesitate, it is possible to walk without burning over extremely hot material. After observing in his carefully planned experiments that both professional fire-walkers and amateurs were able to walk in bare feet and with perfect safety across a twelve-foot trench with a surface temperature of 800°C, Price wrote as follows: "There was not the slightest trace of blistering . . . each foot was in contact with the embers for not more than about a third of a second [112]. This time factor (plus *confidence* and a steady, deliberate placing of the feet) is the secret of fire-walking. The low thermal conductivity of the wood ash may be a contributory factor .... Any person with the requisite determination, confidence, and steadiness, can walk unharmed over a fire as hot as 800° Centigrade. The experiments proved once and for all that no occult or psychic power, or a specially induced mental state, is necessary in a fire-walker." [113, p. 262]

Coe, an American chemist, confirmed Price's general conclusions [114]. With eight steps he crossed barefooted a fourteen-foot pit of red-hot coals without suffering pain or forming blisters. At first, he used the "spheroidal-state" theory to explain his success; he hypothesized that perspiration from his feet was converted by the heat into a cushion of vapor which acted as a buffer between the skin of his feet and the fiery surface. However, after thinking further about his accomplishment, Coe [115] concluded that he was able to walk successfully through the fiery pit because the necessary psychological factors were present—he was totally focused and absorbed in the task and thus was able to place each foot squarely and firmly on the bed of hot coals without any hesitation.

The experimental results presented by Price and by Coe were validated by Fonseka who built a variety of fire-pits in Ceylon [116]; he again found that confidence was all that was needed for five amateurs to walk safely across an eighteen-foot long pit with a surface temperature of 350-500°C.

Many other ordinary people also have been surprised to find that they could walk over extremely hot or burning material if they were calm and thus could step through without hesitation. For instance, McElroy [117] found that he could walk across a bed of coals (which originally seemed so hot that he could not stand nearby) after he had seen other bystanders walk across the coals without harm and after he had been told, 1) "make sure the feet are brushed free of grass and twigs, 2) place the feet firmly and with force, and 3) never hesitate and always keep moving." Similarly, Rosner observed that successful fire-walkers never showed fear and hesitation [118], and a young American Ph.D. candidate found that, when he had complete confidence in the leader who asked that he follow him across the pit, he was able to walk briskly dozens of times over a six-foot pit of flaming logs [119, p. 157].

In summary, the layman's assumption that individuals surely will be badly burned if they attempt to walk through a burning pit without some incomprehensible change in their being, is simply wrong. Fire-walking is within our capabilities provided we believe that we can do it and thus remain calm and walk without hestiation through the hot coals.

CONTROL OF BLOOD FLOW AS MEDIATOR

There is evidence to indicate that changes in blood supply to the skin may play an important role in producing some of the phenomena described above. For instance, enhanced blood flow to a localized area clearly played an important role in the Johnson and Barber experiment [64]: A subject was given the suggestion that she was being burned on the top of the hand, and she responded with an irregular inflammation of that part of the hand, which was primarily due to vasodilation or markedly increased blood supply to the area.

It also appears possible that when warts are cured by suggestive treatments, changes in blood supply to the warts may mediate the effect. Supporting data for this contention derive from a series of studies: It has been noted that, when warts are beginning to regress, an inflammatory reaction can be observed around the wart. Unna, quoted by Samek observed histologically that, during the spontaneous healing of warts, the skin immediately around the wart showed a distinctive reaction consisting of hyperemia (increased blood supply) and cell proliferation [120]. Several other investigators [43, 44, 121, 122] also observed a distinct hyperemia immediately preceding the spontaneous, suggestive or medical healing of warts. In important histological studies of warts undergoing remission in a patient treated by a suggestive procedure, Samek observed a distinct inflammatory reaction in the dermis, consisting of dilation of blood vessels, hyperemia, edema, and perivascular infiltration of white blood cells [120]. A number of earlier investigators [43, 123, 124] also had hypothesized that vasomotor changes are crucial factors in wart remission.

Alterations in blood supply to the skin also may play a role in the alleviation of "fish-skin" disease by suggestions. After successfully using hypnotic suggestions to cure a man with this disease, as discussed earlier in this chapter, Kidd [25] conjectured that the suggestions or idea of healing gave rise to nerve impulses which stimulated the vascular bed of the affected skin areas and influenced "the disturbed metabolism of affected areas."

A number of investigators who successfully used suggestions to enlarge the mammary glands in their clients hypothesized that the effect may have been produced by means of increased vascularity of the breasts. Willard, for instance, proposed that "the actual mechanism or reason for the growth" might have been delineated if he had been able to conduct actual blood flow studies or measure vascular dilation [54]. Staib and Logan also concluded that changes in blood supply to the breast may have played a role [53].

Vasodilation in localized areas appears to play a crucial role in producing some of the specific phenomena discussed in this chapter. For instance, the bruises which were produced by suggestions in appropriately predisposed individuals probably were mediated by the local release of a vasodilator substance in abnormally large quantities which produced such extensive vascular permeability as to allow the leakage of blood [101]. Similarly, when an individual reacts to a small burn with a high level of anxiety and fear, it appears that a vasodilator substance is produced around the area of burn in increased quantities, and the greater the amount of blood which thus escapes from the dilated minute blood vessels, the greater the degree of inflammation and tissue damage [107].

In brief, localized changes in blood flow and blood volume may play an important role in producing some of the striking phenomena I have discussed in this chapter, for example, cure of warts, production of inflammation, wheals, blisters, or ecchymoses, enlargement of mammary glands, and cure of congenital "fish-skin" disease. The possibility that phenomena of this type are associated with localized changes in blood flow is underscored by a series of studies which have shown that some individuals already know how to control and most individuals can easily learn to control blood flow to localized areas of the skin and thus also can control localized skin temperature.[6] In the next four sections of this chapter, I will quote from an earlier paper [5, pp. 21-25] in which I reviewed these studies.

COGNITIVE CONTROL OF BLOOD FLOW AND SKIN TEMPERATURE

Many individuals are aware from their own experience that strong feelings or emotions are associated with changes in blood supply to the skin; for instance, anger is associated with a red countenance (increased blood supply to the skin of the face), whereas fear is associated with a pale countenance. A series of studies extending over many years has demonstrated that some individuals voluntarily can shift more blood to a specific area of the skin and thus can make the area warmer. Interesting data along these lines were reported by Wenger and Bagchi, who had gone to India to study the psychophysiological effects of yoga training [125]. They found one yogi who voluntarily was able to raise the temperature of and to perspire from his forehead within 10 minutes after he began meditation. The yogi stated that he learned to increase his feeling of warmth and to perspire at will when he spent two winters in caves in the Himalayas. Since it was very cold in the mountains, his guru advised him to concentrate on warmth and to imagine and visualize himself in a very warm place, such as in the south of India. After about six months of practice, he found that he was able to make himself warm and even to perspire by allowing his cognitions— his imaginings, visualizings, and thoughts—to dwell on warm situations. Recently Benson showed that by imagining heat, some Tibetan lamas are able to produce sufficient heat to melt snow [126].

Another relevant study was carried out at the Menninger Clinic with Swami Rama [127]. During this investigation, the Swami stated that he was going to

---

[6]Although I shall refer simply to localized "blood flow" as a possible mediating variable in producing the effects mentioned above, many aspects of blood circulation are involved, for example, blood pressure, blood volume, heart rate, and resistance of the blood vessels.

make one part of his palm much warmer than another part. Temperature transducers which had been placed on two sides of his palm showed that within a few minutes there was a 9°F difference between the two sides of his palm. Apparently, he accomplished this feat by voluntarily increasing the blood supply to one side of the palm and reducing the blood supply to the other side.

A series of additional reports, reviewed elsewhere [128] showed that some individuals voluntarily can produce localized changes in blood flow and skin temperature. For instance, Luria presented a case study of an individual with very vivid imagery who was able to increase the temperature of one hand by 2 degrees while reducing the temperature of the other hand to the same degree by remembering-thinking about-imagining that one hand was on a hot stove and the other on a piece of ice [129]. Menzies also reported that three out of five subjects showed localized vasodilation on the hand (with a concomitant rise in skin temperature) when they imagined steam escaping from a valve onto the hand, and all five subjects showed localized vasoconstriction (with a concomitant drop in skin temperature) when they imagined extreme cold [130]. Similar changes in skin temperature associated with imagining were reported by Duggan and Sheridan [131], Erickson [132, p. 180], Jones [133], and Kunzendorf [134].

In an earlier study, Hadfield also found that localized changes in skin temperature could be produced by suggestions [87]. The subject participating in the investigation had exercised vigorously before the experiment and the temperature of both hands had reached 95°F. It was suggested to the subject that the right hand was becoming cold. Within half an hour, the temperature of the right palm fell to 68°F, while the temperature of the left palm remained at 94°. Next the subject was given the suggestion that the right hand was becoming warm; within 20 minutes, the temperature of the hand rose from 68° to 94°. Although sufficient data were not presented in the report to specify the mediating processes that were involved, I would hypothesize that when the subject was told that the hand was becoming cold or warm, the subject vividly visualized, imagined, and thought about previous cold or warm experiences and these microcognitions were associated with the change in skin temperature.

A more recent experiment [135, 136] similarly showed that some individuals can use self-suggestions to raise and also to lower their skin temperature. The three subjects who took part in this experiment had practice in hypnosis, that is, practice in relaxing, concentrating, imagining vividly, and dissociating themselves from specific events. In the experimental session, each subject was given suggestions for deep relaxation and then was asked to make one hand hot and the other hand cold. Several images were suggested that might be useful in changing the temperature of the hands, and each subject also was encouraged to use self-suggestions and his/her own imagery. All three subjects succeeded in lowering the temperature of one hand (by 2° to 7°C), and two of the three also were able to raise the temperature of the other hand (by 2°C). When the subjects increased and decreased blood flow to the hands and thus raised and lowered the hand temperature, they typically were thinking and imagining that one hand was becoming red with anger while the other was becoming white with fear or that one hand was under a heat lamp while the other was in a bucket of ice water [136]. Subjects in a control group did not succeed in changing the temperature of their hands.

There are at least two possible reasons why the hypnotic subjects in the above experiment were more successful at altering skin temperature than the control subjects. The hypnotic group apparently was comprised of good hypnotic subjects who had highly developed imaginative abilities and were highly motivated to succeed at the task. The control subjects were not selected as good hypnotic subjects and, apparently, they were neither especially proficient at imaging nor especially motivated. A second possibility is that the training the hypnotic subjects had received in relaxing, concentrating, imagining, and attending selectively (dissociating) was an important factor in enabling them to alter the flow of blood to the hands and thus alter the hand temperature. Of course, another possibility is that the better performance of the hypnotic subjects was due both to their special talents in imagining and also to the special training they had received in utilizing their talents.

BIOFEEDBACK AND SELF-REGULATION OF BLOOD FLOW

Important recent studies utilizing biofeedback suggest that everyone may have the potential ability to control voluntarily the flow of blood to specific areas of the skin. Before I describe these studies, I will explain briefly how biofeedback is used.

Biofeedback means simply that individuals are obtaining information pertaining to what is occurring inside or on the surface of their bodies. The simplest form of biofeedback is measuring the heart rate by placing the hand on the chest above the heart or by picking up the pulse near the wrist or above the carotid artery. During the past fifteen years, however, a large variety of electrical or electronic instruments have been utilized to feed back information to subjects about what is occurring on their skin or within their internal organs [4, 137-143]. For instance, temperature sensors attached to the skin can inform subjects that their skin temperature is rising or dropping, and electrode leads attached to the back of the scalp can inform them that certain "brain waves," such as the alpha rhythm, are increasing or decreasing. These and other instruments—for instance, heart monitors, monitors of the electrical conductance or resistance of the skin, and monitors of muscle activity—can provide information concerning what is happening in specific organs or parts of the body. This information typically is presented to the subjects by a tone that varies in pitch or by a visual display that varies in brightness as the function being monitored decreases or increases.

Using these types of biofeedback procedures, Taub and Emurian set out to train individuals to control voluntarily the flow of blood to (and thus the temperature of) an index finger [144]. Twenty subjects participated in four brief (15-minute) training sessions in which variations in finger temperature were indicated by variations in the brightness of a light. The subjects were told to try to make the light more intense or less intense, that is, to increase or decrease finger temperature and blood flow. To achieve the intended self-regulation of finger temperature, they were encouraged to imagine hot or cold stimuli imping-ing upon the finger. By the end of the four brief training sessions, nineteen of the twenty subjects had attained control of finger temperature; on the average, they voluntarily could raise and also lower the finger temperature by about 2.5°F. After additional training, they were able to raise and also to reduce the temperature of the finger as easily without biofeedback as with biofeedback, and when they were retested after an interval of four to five months, they demon-strated that they had retained the ability to vary the temperature.

Subsequent work by the same investigator [145] showed that, after receiving additional training, some subjects 1) could raise or lower the temperature on localized areas of the skin by as much as 8° to 15°F in 15 minutes, 2) could maintain a considerable increase in localized skin temperature for about 45 minutes while performing a concurrent task, and 3) could keep their skin warm when placed in very cold environments.

These studies have broad implications. They indicate that we can learn, within a reasonably brief period, to produce substantial changes in blood flow to the periphery of our body, to maintain this changed blood supply over substan-tial periods of time, and to use this skill for practical purposes, such as keeping warm in a cold environment. Taub [145] has pointed out that the self-regulation of temperature through control of blood flow also could be useful in 1) pro-tecting against cold injury, 2) producing temporary sterility in males by elevating the temperature of the scrotum [146], 3) treating ailments such as migraine headaches and Raynaud's disease which involve impaired circulation, 4) reducing edema and pain following tissue damage, 5) reducing the size of warts or tumors by influencing blood flow to the area of the tumors, and 6) promoting the healing of wounds by increasing blood supply to the affected area.

COGNITIVE CONTROL OF BLOOD SUPPLY TO SEXUAL ORGANS

Before concluding this discussion on the self-regulation of blood flow and temperature, let us consider briefly how normal individuals control the flow of blood to one specific part of the body, namely, to the genital organs. From a physiological viewpoint, sexual arousal is basically a blood flow phenomenon.

As a man becomes sexually aroused, more and more blood enters and remains in his penis. Similarly, as a woman becomes sexually aroused, more and more blood flows into the sexual organs and gives rise, for example, to enlargement of the breasts, erection of the nipples, erection of the clitoris, and engorgement of the labia.

The important point here is not just that sexual arousal is intimately related to blood flow and temperature change in the genital areas, but that normal men and women are able to self-regulate this blood flow by their cognitions—by their thoughts, images, imaginings, and feelings. A man does not become sexually aroused by a woman that he finds unappealing; he becomes aroused when he thinks or feels about the woman in a positive way. Similarly, arousal in a woman is related to how she perceives the man. In other words, thoughts, feelings, and imaginings (cognitions) affect the flow of blood to the sexual organs.

It needs to be underscored that blood flow to the genital organs can be controlled voluntarily. A series of studies [147-149] have demonstrated that most men are able to produce a small degree and some men are able to produce a large degree of penile erection when they simply are asked to do so. These studies also showed that "this normal ability to produce penile engorgement can be increased by biofeedback procedures" [149], but the important point here is not that biofeedback can improve the performance but that normal men voluntarily can control blood flow to the penis by controlling their cognitions. As Rosen et al. [149] pointed out, "It seems that subjects who are readily able to conjure up sexual images or fantasies are able to utilize these images to 'voluntarily' control the engorgement of the penile corpora." In other words, healthy men either are able to or potentially can control blood flow to the genital areas by deliberately focusing or shifting their thoughts and imaginings. For instance, they can produce an erection by turning their thoughts and visualizations to a woman they love and then focusing on those aspects of her being that they view as especially pleasing and desirable; and they then can lose the erection by turning their thoughts away from the beloved women to other extraneous concerns.

The way our cognitions affect blood supply to the genital areas is the most dramatic and clearest example of how our thoughts, images, and feelings, produce variations in the blood supply to various parts of our body. The data summarized in this chapter suggest the exciting possibility that blood flow not only to the genital areas, but also to other parts of the body, for example, to the skin, is continually affected to some degree by what we are thinking, feeling, and experiencing.

INTEGRATION OF BLOOD FLOW DATA

Let us now integrate the data pertaining to blood flow and relate them to some of the phenomena described earlier in this chapter.

1. Blood flow to the sexual organs is affected by cognitions, that is, by thoughts, feelings, and imaginings. This phenomenon occurs in all healthy

individuals regardless of whether or not they are aware of how their cognitions affect their sexual organs.

2. Many individuals are aware, and apparently all healthy individuals potentially can become aware, that they can increase blood flow to the sexual organs by thinking, fantasizing, or imagining arousing sexual situations.

3. Although there is little doubt that cognitions affect blood flow to the sexual organs, it is not as obvious that cognitions also affect blood flow to the skin (and other organs). Nevertheless, data, such as the following, indicate that our cognitions alter the blood supply to localized cutaneous areas: 1) Many individuals are aware experientially of changes in blood supply to the skin that are associated with strong feelings or emotions—the red face of anger, the pallor of fear, and the blush of shame. 2) Some individuals clearly can self-regulate blood flow to the hands or to localized cutaneous areas. In general, these individuals shift blood to specific areas by thinking or imagining that cold or warm objects are stimulating the area. 3) Recent data suggest that all healthy individuals can learn to increase and decrease blood flow to localized areas of the skin. The training that seems especially helpful involves biofeedback, that is, the individual tries to increase or decrease the temperature of (and thus the blood flow to) a specific area of the body while receiving continuous information pertaining to moment-by-moment variations in the temperature of the area.

4. We can begin to explain some of the phenomena discussed in this chapter if we accept the postulate that blood supply not only to the sexual organs but also to the skin (and possibly to other organs of the body) is affected by cognition, feelings, imaginings, and other cognitive processes. If we accept this postulate, then we can hypothesize that believed-in suggestions, which are incorporated into ongoing cognitions, affect blood supply in localized areas, and the altered blood flow, in turn, plays a role in producing some of the phenomena that were described in this chapter. Specifically, the altered blood flow may play an important role in 1) reducing the dermatitis produced by a poison ivy-like plant [9], 2) giving rise to a degree of dermatitis when the poisonous plant is not actually present [9], 3) producing a localized skin inflammation that has the specific pattern of a previously experienced burn [64], 4) curing warts that have been present for a long period of time [45], 5) ameliorating congenital ichthyosis [21, 24-26], 6) stimulating the enlargement of the mammary glands [53-55], 7) producing bruises by suggestions [101], 8) minimizing bleeding after exodontia, etc. [103], and 9) minimizing and also enlarging the effects of a burn [107]. Further research is needed to delineate more precisely how suggestions which are accepted and incorporated into ongoing cognitions are related to changes in blood flow and how these alterations, in turn, are related to the phenomena that have been described. Further studies also are needed to determine how local changes in blood supply are related to alterations in immunological functions, and how variations in the functions of the T-cells, the B-cells, the macrophages,

and other components of the immunological system are involved in the effects of suggestions on the phenomena discussed in this chapter.

THE FANTASY-PRONENESS AND PSYCHOSOMATIC PLASTICITY OF GOOD HYPNOTIC SUBJECTS

The phenomena discussed above can be elicited more readily in a good than in a poor hypnotic subject. Unfortuantely, the layman tends to believe that a good hypnotic subject is more likely to show the phenomena because s/he can be deeply hypnotized or can shift to a markedly altered state of consciousness. Although the good hypnotic subject can respond more easily to explicit or implicit suggestions to let go of extraneous concerns and to focus on the ideas that are suggested, this ability plays only a small role in curing warts, minimizing allergic responses, etc. Much more important in producing these kinds of effects is that the good hypnotic subject 1) is typically more cooperative and more motivated to do well and to please the hypnotist and 2) is better able to imagine or fantasize vividly and thus to experience in a fantasized reality those things that are suggested. The good hypnotic subject is able to imagine and fantasize so vividly that the imagined event is often difficult to distinguish from an actual event. These imaginative-fantasy skills, which have been developed over a lifetime as a result of a special life history, enable the good subject to respond positively to the large number of suggestions which involve imagining or fantasizing, for instance, to the suggestion to hear music (auditory hallucination), to see a person or object that is not actually present (visual hallucination), and to experience himself/herself in the future (age progression) or in the distant past (past-life regression). Of course, the good hypnotic subject also can respond easily to the type of suggestions used in traditional hypnotic inductions (e.g., suggestions of deep relaxation and drowsiness); however, this subject can respond well to the many other kinds of suggestions which utilize their ability to imagine, regardless of whether or not these suggestions have been preceded by a formal hypnotic induction procedure [3, 19, 150-152].

Good hypnotic subjects will manifest their profound ability to imagine and fantasize if the experimenter can elicit their maximal cooperation. To do so, the experimenter should remove their fears and misconceptions, help them feel at ease, untroubled, and relaxed in the situation, and help them feel that what is to be accomplished is good and useful [153, 154]. Traditional or formal hypnotic induction procedures are helpful with some good hypnotic subjects in eliciting their cooperation. However, in many instances, sincerely asking good hypnotic subjects to respond to the best of their ability is more effective than formal induction procedures in eliciting their best effort, especially when they and the hypnotist have a close relationship [19, 60].

In fact, if the good hypnotic subject has high respect for and wants to please the hypnotist and feels at ease and not threatened in the situation, s/he can experience a large number of suggested effects without any preliminaries; all that is necessary is for the hypnotist to give specific suggestions, for example, "Please look closely at your left hand and feel it beginning to get numb. Feel the numbness and insensitivity moving into the little finger."

The conclusion that good hypnotic subjects have developed special talents in imagining is supported by a large number of investigations. One set of studies, reviewed by Sheehan [155], generally found positive correlations between individuals' degree of responsiveness to hypnotic suggestions and their ability to form vivid images and to control their images [56, 156-160]. Three additional sets of studies related subjects' responsiveness to (hypnotic) suggestions to the degree of their involvement in imaginative activities outside of the hypnotic situation. Three types of approaches were used to measure the subjects' extent of involvement in activities involving imagining: 1) self-rating scales which assessed the extent to which the subjects felt they became involved in imagination-related activities, such as daydreaming and becoming absorbed in a novel [161-163], 2) measures of performance in skills that utilize imaginative ability, such as dramatic acting [164], and 3) interviews which assessed subjects' degree of involvement in activities which seem to pivot around imagining, such as having imaginative companions, reading imaginative fiction, and acting in dramatic productions [56]. These studies generally found positive correlations between the subjects' responsiveness to suggestions in a hypnotic situation and their degree of involvement in imagination-related activities [56, 58, 151, 161-172].

Of the many studies cited above, the most extensive one was conducted by Josephine Hilgard [56, 57]; she found that good hypnotic subjects are characterized by a lifetime history of involvement in imagination-related activities, such as daydreaming, reading or hearing imaginative stories, reading science fiction, and acting in plays. Sheryl Wilson and I confirmed and extended these earlier findings in a recent investigation [59, 60].

Our study utilized lengthy, in-depth interviews, focusing on childhood and adult memories, fantasies, and psychic experiences. The subjects were fifty-two women; twenty-seven of these consistently had been rated as superb or excellent hypnotic subjects, and twenty-five had been rated as less than excellent (medium good, medium, and poor) hypnotic subjects.

With one exception, all of the excellent hypnotic subjects, but not the comparison subjects, had a profound daydreaming-imagining-fantasy life, their daydreams or fantasies were often "as real as real" (hallucinatory), and their profound involvement in fantasy played an important role in producing their superb hypnotic performance. In addition to becoming involved in fantasy very deeply and very often, the excellent hypnotic subjects also reported that, since early childhood, they have been profoundly aware of sensory experiences involving touching, smelling, hearing, seeing, etc. (e.g., "the feel of my grandmother's skin . . . the smell outside after the rain"), they had vivid memories of their very early life (prior to age 2) and also of their subsequent life experiences, they had special abilities as "healers," and they had had numerous telepathic, precognitive, out-of-the-body, and other kinds of psychic, extrasensory, or paranormal experiences.

Wilson and Barber labeled excellent hypnotic subjects, who seem to constitute a small percentage (possibly around 4%) of the normal population, as *fantasy-prone personalities* [59, 60]. The crucial point here, however, appears to be that this fantasy-proneness also gives rise to a "psychosomatic plasticity" [79] and to a special ability to manifest the kinds of psychophysiological or psychosomatic effects discussed in this chapter, such as cure of warts or enlargement of mammary glands. Let us first look a little more closely at the fantasy abilities of these excellent hypnotic subjects and then relate this ability to their psychosomatic plasticity.

Wilson and Barber noted that, during childhood, the superb hypnotic subjects typically were involved in many activities that required imagining or fantasy [59, 60]. They played many pretend games or make-believe games. They saw their dolls, teddy bears, etc., as having distinct personalities, and they treated them as alive even when they were not playing with them. They commonly had imaginary playmates who they felt were "really there." They also believed that fairies, brownies, elves, leprechauns, and also bogeymen and monsters, were alive and real. Typically, they also heard or themselves read, at an early age, many stories which stimulate imagining; these stories had a wide range of characters extending from fear-inducing types to fair-maiden types such as Snow White. In brief, during childhood the superb hypnotic subjects lived much of the time in a kind of fantasy world.

As adults they still live in a fantasy world much of the time. They still spend a large part of the time daydreaming or fantasizing, and they view daydreaming, imagining, or fantasizing as central to their lives. As they grew older, they did not stop fantasizing, they just stopped talking about it. They are now "closet fantasizers" who keep this part of their life hidden not only from strangers but also from their parents, mates, children, and close friends. (In fact, with few exceptions, people who think they know them well do not know that they have special talents for fantasy and for hypnosis, and they see them as falling within the range of ordinary, normal individuals.) We were able to penetrate their secrets, after we learned how to obtain their confidence and deep trust and how to help them feel comfortable about their fantasy life and not fear reprisals for revealing it.

As implied above, they typically fantasize vividly throughout much of the day—while performing routine tasks at work or at home, during leisure time, during special periods set off just for daydreaming or fantasizing, and before they fall asleep at night. The depth of their fantasies can be illustrated quickly by mentioning the impressiveness of their sexual fantasies. Although practically all of the excellent hypnotic subjects interviewed by Wilson and Barber [59, 60] were married or had boyfriends, they typically also had fantasied lovers who were "as real as real"—who could be seen, heard, smelt, and touched. The fantasied lover was better than their husband or boyfriend because he always did exactly what he should. In fact, in these fantasied sexual situations, most of the superb hypnotic subjects have orgasms that are triggered by the imagining itself, apparently without tactile sexual stimulation. In brief, their sexual fantasies and also their many other fantasies often become hallucinatory in all senses; it can be said that, for a time, they create for themselves another world which is as real to them as the actual world.

A striking characteristic shared by all but two of the twenty-seven superb hypnotic subjects interviewed in depth by Wilson and Barber [59, 60] is that their vivid fantasies and memories at times are associated with physiological or bodily reactions.[7] As mentioned above, their sexual fantasies are often so realistic, complete with all the sights, sounds, smells, sensations, feelings, and emotions, that they lead to orgasms. The majority of these subjects stated spontaneously, without being asked directly, that imagined heat and cold affect them in the same way as actual heat and cold. A typical report was given by Emma D. who reported that she was freezing as she sat bundled up in a blanket in a warm living room watching on television the part of *Dr. Zhivago* that took place in Siberia. (Hilgard [57], reported the same kind of reaction to *Dr. Zhivago* by good hypnotic subjects.)

Five of Barber and Wilson's superb hypnotic subjects reported that they had participated in one or more experimental or clinical biofeedback sessions. All five of these subjects added that those who were to administer the biofeedback to them consistently were impressed by their talent, manifested *prior* to the biofeedback training, for controlling psychophysiological processes, such as accelerating and decelerating their heart rate, raising and lowering their blood pressure, or increasing and decreasing their skin termperature.

About 70 percent of the excellent hypnotic subjects (as compared to 8 percent in the comparison group) reported having had illnesses or physical symptoms that seemed to be directly related to their imaginings. For instance, they became ill when they imagined (incorrectly) that food they had eaten was spoiled. A representative report was given by one of the superb hypnotic subjects; she had developed a wheal at the site of an imagined injection and she also had inhibited expected skin changes at the site of an actual injection. Let us look at this case more closely.

The subject works at a hospital as a nurses' aide. A few days prior to receiving

---

[7]In the remainder of this paper, in which I discuss the "psychosomatic plasticity" of excellent hypnotic subjects, I am including data obtained in the interviews conducted by Sheryl Wilson and myself but which have not been included in the papers we have published to date [59, 60]. I am deeply indebted to Sheryl Wilson for her invaluable assistance in writing this part of the chapter.

a routine Mantoux test (a skin prick test utilizing old tuberculin for determining the possible presence of tuberculosis), she was told by a co-worker, "It's really awful. They stick you with a needle a bunch of times, it really hurts terribly. . . ." Our subject said that, while her co-worker was describing the skin prick test, she clearly could feel the pain of the (imagined) needle puncturing her arm in a specific spot. She further related that she was later surprised to discover a skin reaction, a wheal, on the exact spot on her arm where she had imagined the skin pricks. The next day, she showed me the wheal, and it remained on her arm for almost a week.

A few days after she had developed the wheal by imagining the skin prick test, she was given an actual Mantoux test on her other arm. She explained that since she had reacted to an imagined test, she was sure that she also would react markedly to the actual test and consequently would be required to have a chest X-ray to determine whether or not she had tuberculosis. Not wanting to be unnecessarily exposed to X-rays, she constructively utilized her ability to imagine during the actual skin prick test; she fantasized herself in a beautiful meadow during the actual test, and thus, she stated, she felt absolutely no sensations and her skin did not react at all.

I later conducted a test with this excellent hypnotic subject: I simply told her to close her eyes and relax, and then I said I was going to give her an injection at a specific spot on her lower arm; I then touched the spot quickly with my finger. Her skin reacted immediately: A bright red circle (about 5 mm. in diameter) appeared at the spot I had touched, and within a few minutes a wheal was evident which resembled the one she previously had developed apparently due to the imagined skin pricks.

In brief, this subject felt and physiologically reacted to (as shown by her wheals) imagined skin pricks and a suggested injection but did not feel or react to the actual skin pricks. This illustrates the importance of feelings (or unconscious sensations or perceptions) in producing bodily changes. The realistically experienced painful feelings of an imagined or suggested needle produced a physiological effect, while the same effect was inhibited when an actual needle was purposively not felt.

As stated earlier, the great majority of the superb hypnotic subjects (and only a small number in the comparison group) reported having had physical symptoms or illnesses that seemed to have been directly related to their imaginings or thoughts. For instance, it was not uncommon for them to develop an uncomfortable and continuous itch when they (incorrectly) believed that they had been contaminated with lice. An illustrative report was given by a subject who stated that some years earlier she had recaptured a neighboring child's pet frog that had escaped; she had been told that frogs cause warts, and soon she developed a wart on her hand that was highly resistant to treatment. Another excellent hypnotic subject reported that she had literally fainted when she was forced to make an "impossible" decision—whatever she would have decided would have aroused the wrath of one or the other of her divorced parents. Another superb hypnotic subject, who always had perfect teeth, related how she developed severe and increasing pain in her teeth and gums during the six months between teeth-cleaning appointments with a dentist who had told her, "You have the mouth of a seven- or eight-year-old. That's when teeth begin to decay." Consequently, she believed her teeth were decaying, and she was in continual pain until her next dental examination when she was told her teeth were in perfect condition. The pain vanished immediately when she heard the good news. Another excellent hypnotic subject described how she was initially unable to breast-feed her second child. She had nursed her firstborn, a daughter, with no difficulty, and she had planned to nurse the second also. However, her second child, a boy, looked so much like his father, from whom she had a very emotional and conflictual separation, that she produced no milk until a knowledgeable physician told her, "You know he is not his father. He is a separate individual." From that moment on she was able to breast-feed him without difficulty.

A surprisingly large number of Wilson and Barber's [59, 60] excellent hypnotic subjects (60% of those asked) stated that they had experienced one or more false pregnancies (pseudocyesis). They had believed they were pregnant and they had had many of the symptoms. In addition to the cessation of menstruation (amenorrhea), they typically had experienced at least four of the following five symptoms: abdominal enlargement, morning sickness, breast changes, cravings for specific foods, and "fetal" movements. Two of these women had gone for abortions following which they had been told that no fetus had been found. All of the other false pregnancies terminated quickly when negative results were received from pregnancy tests. (In the comparison group of not-so-good hypnotic subjects, 16% had failed to menstruate at least one time previously and had believed they were pregnant. However, with the exception of one subject, who had had many of the symptoms of pregnancy, they had experienced only one symptom, namely, morning sickness.)

The psychosomatic plasticity of superb hypnotic subjects can be illustrated also by their tendency to experience specific physical symptoms or illnesses in certain kinds of situations. These recurrent episodes seem to be directly related to their thoughts or imaginings. For instance, Becky R. told us of a time when she was diagnosed by a physician as having rheumatic fever the day following a traumatic episode with her older brother. She was sixteen and was returning home very late from a date. Her father recently had died and her older brother, who was home on leave from the army, took the role of her father and beat her severely. The next day, she was delirious with a high fever. The doctor was called and he diagnosed her as having rheumatic fever. (Diagnostic tests revealed an elevated sedimentation rate.) She remained ill during the remainder of her brother's leave. Two years later her brother returned home once more on army leave; she was again stricken with a diagnosed rheumatic fever, complete with febrile temperature and elevated sedimentation rate, and she had to stay in bed throughout the period her brother was at home on leave.

The same excellent hypnotic subject, Becky R., told us that she had suffered from severe reoccurring neck pain since age nine. During the in-depth interviews, we learned that at age nine, she had tried unsuccessfully to save her dog from being "put to sleep." She was running across a field trying to carry her dog to safety when her mother called the dog; the dog obeyed the mother's call, jumped from Becky's arms, and ran home to his death. Becky's mother threatened to punish her severely if she cried for the dog. The next day, Becky had a very painful stiff neck, and since then she repeatedly has experienced a stiff and painful neck whenever she was in a situation in which she felt angry and helpless.

The psychosomatic lability of superb hypnotic subjects is illustrated also by their "vicarious symptoms." They typically state that they experience another person's symptoms when they hear or read about them. More than half of the excellent hypnotic subjects reported, without being asked, that they become seriously affected or even sick when they see violence on the screen. Furthermore, they reported that they cannot let themselves fantasize anything with violence because they are certain to become sick. They tended to become very emotional when they were asked how they responded to violent scenes on the screen. Most often they stated that they developed headaches or became nauseous, but some reported that they have vomited during or after the bothersome scene. Although they try to avoid viewing violence whenever possible, violent scenes sometimes appear without prior warning. Jane G. described her reaction to such unexpected scenes as follows: "I plug my ears and try to close off things. I'll talk to myself and do whatever I have to do to avoid incorporating the scene . . . I feel a lot of hatred towards the filmmaker when I see a violent scene and I wasn't expecting it." These extreme reactions to violence seem to be due to their absorption in the movie or television show and to their identifying with one or more of the characters.

The superb hypnotic subjects interviewed by Wilson and Barber can become ill while watching certain kinds of nonviolent scenes also. Barbara S. stated that she becomes ill and vomits whenever she sees someone else vomit. Another subject reported that she recently became ill and vomited in the movie theater because she identified with a character who was drinking beer while riding in the back of a truck over a bumpy road. She said she feels ill if she tastes beer, and while watching the movie she could smell and taste the beer. Also, her head ached and she became dizzy from the bumpy truck ride she also was experiencing. She was unable to leave the threater before she vomited. To prevent such incidents, she often tries to prevent herself from becoming involved in movies or television shows by deliberately "distancing" herself from them.

Over the years, many of the superb hypnotic subjects have developed an awareness of their ability to influence their body both negatively and positively by their thoughts, emotions, and fantasies. For instance, Ruth T. became aware that the headaches she had been experiencing daily for several months, which she attributed to various supposed physical problems, vanished immediately after her physician gave her a complete physical examination and stated emphatically that she was in perfect health. She explained, "That's what my imagination does to me sometimes. It can really cause me trouble." Similarly, after explaining how she always feels the pains of others when they are described to her, Ginger S. remarked, "If I wonder whether or not there is a pain in my knee, there will be a pain in my knee." She also worries that her thoughts or imaginings might lead her to become seriously ill. Thus, after reading a certain book, she decided to have amnesia for it ("to block herself from remembering it") because she was certain that she would have breast cancer if she remembered and accepted what the book said. Another excellent hypnotic subject, Jennifer T., explained how she had learned to control her psychosomatic plasticity: "If someone told me falsely that I was in poison ivy, I'd break out. But now I've learned to reverse that. Even if I have been in poison ivy, if I can convince myself that I haven't, I won't break out."

The recognition that they have the ability to influence their bodies both negatively and positively is usually beneficial for these individuals. However, their awareness that they can make themselves sick by their emotions and imaginings can be dangerous when they have a physical ailment. For instance, Emma D. recalled how she thought she was having a negative emotional reaction to the birth of her first child when actually she was dying of peritonitis because the doctor had failed to remove the afterbirth and it was decaying inside her.

Another excellent hypnotic subject, Carol Ann B., was told by her family doctor that she should have an inflamed mole surgically removed immediately. This large mole on her back had been highly irritable for five years, making it necessary for her to keep an adhesive bandage over it to prevent it from becoming red and painful. However, she had been sick in bed for several days with influenza, had failed to place the adhesive bandage over the mole, and it had become very painful and inflamed. She immediately made an appointment with a surgeon; however, she had a profound phobia of surgery, so she cancelled the appointment and determined to use hypnosis to remove the mole. "I gave myself a month [to remove it by hypnosis] and decided that if it was still there, I'd have to have it out. I was really determined, because, boy, I didn't want to have that cut off. I just didn't want to have surgery at all. I didn't like the idea at all and the whole thing scared me anyway because they always say, 'Look out for moles that are changing.' I gave myself a deadline with terrible consequences [surgery] if it didn't work." She believed she could use hypnosis to remove the mole because she had heard of hypnosis curing warts and she felt, "I'm good at that kind of thing," that is, good at hypnosis and the ability to change her body. She replaced the adhesive bandage on the mole and kept her thoughts and imagery focused on the feeling that the mole was becoming flatter and was going away. At the end of the month, she removed the bandage and the mole was perfectly flat; now five years later, the mole is still perfectly flat. During the past five years, she has never worn a bandage on it, and it has never been a problem.

Later, the same subject, Carol Ann B., heard me talk about increasing breast size by hypnosis. Encouraged by her success with her mole, she was certain she could do this also. I described to her the types of suggestions that have been successfully used for breast enlargement—suggestions to feel the warm sun or warm, wet towels bringing deep heat into the breasts and to feel tingling, pulsating, growing sensations in the breasts, etc. I also told her to place herself in self-hypnosis daily and to practice the suggestions at home for three months. Three months later she informed me that she had practiced the self-hypnosis and suggestions "every spare moment," and she also had added suggestions of liking her breasts, feeling good about them, and having intense sexual feelings in them—"I'd think of my breasts and how good they feel when my husband touches them. It was more like feeling sexually aroused, and a feeling of swelling in my breasts." She also reported that her breasts had grown and she had to use a new bra, a cup size larger. She stated that she had never previously changed her bra size from age thirteen to age thirty-one (her age at that time).

Carol Ann proffered several reasons why she may have inhibited the growth of her breasts during purberty. "When my breasts should have been growing, I was dancing [professionally] with girls who were older and had breasts already, so I had to wear artificial ones. Because of that, I had the image that I was way too small and would never be any good and always would have to be artificial and phony. Besides, I felt intimidated by my mother who was very large breasted and who always shopped with me when I bought a bra. So I had a real negative thing and maybe that prevented them from growing—the expectation that they were never going to grow. Also, my mother told me they wouldn't grow because as a child I had always insisted on sleeping on my stomach and girls who did that never had breasts. Anyway, I never changed bra size and I didn't like to think about my breasts. So I think I blocked them."

Carol Ann added that in recent years she had felt good about her breasts because she knew her husband liked them. Apparently, her breast growth was related to this new viewpoint working in conjunction with (a) her belief that she was able to change her body by her thoughts and imaginings and (b) her ability to imagine vividly the feelings in her breast I had suggested as well as the imagery she herself added.

COMMENT

The data presented in this chapter should, once and for all, topple the dualistic dichotomy between mind and body which has strongly dominated Western thought since Descartes. The meanings or ideas imbedded in words which are spoken by one person and deeply accepted by another can be communicated to the cells of the body (and to the chemicals within the cells); the cells then can change their activities in order to conform to the meanings or ideas which have been transmitted to them. The believed-in (suggested) idea of being stimulated by a poison ivy-type plant, transmitted to a person who is normally hypersensitive to this type of plant, can affect specific cells (probably in the immunological and vascular systems) so that they produce the same type of dermatitis which results when the person actually is stimulated by a poison ivy-type plant. Similarly, individuals who are viewed as allergic to pollen or house dust may not manifest the allergic reaction when they believe (falsely) that they have not been exposed to the allergic substance.

Congenital abnormalities of the skin, such as congenital erythrodermia and pachyonychia congenita, can be markedly ameliorated by ideas (suggestions) which alter the subject's thoughts-feelings-emotions which in turn affect the skin cells. Similarly, specific kinds of communications, which are deeply accepted or believed by the recipient, can alter microphysiological processes and can lead to the reduction of warts, to the reduction of bleeding, to the minimization of the effects of a burn, and to the production of erythema, wheals, blisters, and ecchymoses. Also, appropriate suggestions can enlarge female breasts, and self-suggestions which produce confidence and lack of anxiety are associated with the ability to walk through fire pits.

Believed-in suggestions can affect specific parts of the body in very specific ways. Suggestions of being burned can give rise to a very specific irregular pattern of inflammation on the hand that closely follows the pattern of a previously experienced actual burn in the same place. Suggestions that a congenital skin disorder will ameliorate step by step first in one area of the body, then in another, can be actualized exactly as suggested. At least one set of investigators found that suggestions that specific warts will regress can be effective in removing just those warts and not others.

It appears that it is possible to elicit some of the effects discussed in this chapter in a relatively large proportion of individuals, whereas others can be elicited in very few. Potentially every individual can fire-walk; even though this possibility is open to everyone, it is by no means easy to convince most individuals that they have nothing to fear and that they simply should remain calm and focused on the task as they walk briskly through the hot material. Similarly, although it is within everyone's capability to remain calm when they are burned and thus to minimize the effects of a burn, actualization of this potential is difficult. At best, we can expect the great majority of individuals to remain more calm than they usually do and to reduce the effects of a burn only to a small degree. Similarly, we would expect most individuals to be able to reduce bleeding from exodontia after receiving appropriate suggestions only slightly, but we would expect a small number to show an extreme reduction in bleeding.

It seems that some of the pneomena can be produced in a substantial proportion of *physiologically predisposed individuals*. For instance, a substantial proportion of individuals who exhibit spontaneous ecchymoses may be expected to manifest the same type of bruises when given (believed-in) suggestions to reexperience situations in which spontaneous bruising occurred. Apparently, a substantial number of individuals who are hypersensitive to a chemical found in poison ivy-type plants will manifest some degree of dermatitis when they are convinced that they have been in contact with the plant even though they actually have not touched it. It also appears that a substantial proportion of women who focus for several months on self-suggestions for breast growth may be expected to show an increase in breast size, especially if they held negative attitudes toward their breasts during puberty which may have inhibited their breast development.

Other effects discussed in this chapter appear increasingly more difficult to produce. For instance, although suggestions were associated with an amelioration of fish-skin disease in four cases, in a much larger number of cases suggestions did not lead to a noticeable effect [173]. Similarly, suggestions can be expected to result in the cure of warts only in a small proportion of cases [174-176]. Although suggestions of being burned can be expected to produce noticeable erythema in a small proportion of individuals, only an infinitesimally small proportion of the population can be expected to develop a blister following such suggestions.

Why are some subjects much more prone than others to manifest the suggested bodily alterations? The suggested effects discussed in this chapter are more likely to be manifested when subject variables and situational variables are as follows: Subjects and experimenter have a close personal relationship or a positive transference and countertransference relationship. The experimenter has elicited the subjects' maximum cooperation, has enhanced their expectancies that they are in a situation in which unusual effects can occur, has helped them reduce distracting thoughts and extraneous concerns, and has helped them become ready to be absorbed in and to feel-imagine-think those things that will be suggested. Traditional hypnotic induction procedures often are useful in maximizing the interpersonal relationship, eliciting maximum cooperation at a high level of expectancy, reducing distracting thoughts, etc. However, extensive research over the past 25 years has shown that very informal induction procedures, and even simply talking to subjects in a very meaningful way, can be as effective and, at times, more effective in eliciting the subjects' maximum responsiveness to the suggestions [3, 132, 150].

Although the relationship between subjects and experimenter and the experimenter's manner of communicating to the subjects are important, the personal characteristics of the subjects also play a very important role. A small proportion of individuals, who are commonly labeled as excellent hypnotic subjects, are much more likely than others to form a close relationship with the experimenter, to cooperate fully, and to try to do well. Also, these same individuals are more likely than others to experience the suggested effects at a deep emotional level, and since they are aware to a certain extent of their own "psychosomatic plasticity," they are prone to believe that they actually *can* manifest the suggested physiological alterations.

In addition, these excellent hypnotic subjects have a special life history which makes it easier for them to imagine and fantasize so vividly that the fantasized event becomes difficult to distinguish from the actual event. Most of the effects discussed in this chapter appear to be closely dependent on this ability, possessed by a small proportion of individuals, to experience in a fantasized reality those things that are suggested to them.

By becoming deeply absorbed in imagining a physiological change, excellent hypnotic subjects can reinstate the same feelings that are present when the actual physiological change occurs, *and the reinstated feelings can stimulate the cells to produce the physiological change.* By becoming deeply absorbed in a fantasized sexual situation these individuals can reinstate the same sexual feelings which are found in the actual sexual situation, and these feelings then can result in an orgasm. Similarly, by becoming deeply absorbed in imagining, fantasizing, "hallucinating" that they are being burned, that warts are tingling and receding, that mammary glands are growing, etc., they reinstate the feeling of being burned, the tingling feeling in the warts indicating that they are receding, and sensations associated with growth in the breasts; then the cells in the skin, in the mammary glands, etc., react to the messages communicated by the feelings—messages which instruct the cells to behave the way they would if a burn was occurring, warts were regressing, or mammary glands were growing.

REFERENCES

1. T. X. Barber, Physiological Effects of "Hypnosis," *Psychological Bulletin*, *58*, pp. 390-419, 1961.
2. T. X. Barber, Physiological Effects of "Hypnotic Suggestions": A Critical Review of Recent Research (1960-64), *Pschological Bulletin*, *63*, pp. 201-222, 1965.
3. T. X. Barber, *LSD, Marijuana, Yoga, and Hypnosis*, Aldine Publishing Co., Chicago, 1970.
4. T. X. Barber, Self-control: Temperature Biofeedback, Hypnosis, Yoga, and Relaxation, in *Biofeedback and Self-Control: 1975/76*, T. X. Barber et al. (eds.), Aldine Publishing Co., Chicago, pp. xiii-xxix, 1976b.
5. T. X. Barber, "Hypnosis," Suggestions, and Psychosomatic Phenomena: A New Look from the Standpoint of Recent Experimental Studies, *American Journal of Clinical Hypnosis*, *21*, pp. 13-27, 1978.
6. T. X. Barber, Medicine, Suggestive Therapy, and Healing, in *Old, Sick, and Helpless: Where Therapy Begins*, R. J. Kastenbaum, T. X. Barber, S. C. Wilson, B. L. Ryder, and L. B. Hathaway (eds.), Ballinger Publishing Company, Cambridge, Massachusetts, pp. 7-56, 1981.

7. A. S. Dalal and T. X. Barber, Yoga, "Yoga Feats" and Hypnosis in the Light of Empirical Research, *American Journal of Clinical Hypnosis*, *11*, pp. 155-166, 1969.

8. A. N. D. Frederick and T. X. Barber, Yoga, Hypnosis, and Self-Control of Cardiovascular Functions, *Proceedings, 80th Annual Convention, APA*, pp. 859-860, 1972.

9. Y. Ikemi and S. Nakagawa, A Psychosomatic Study of Contagious Dermatitis, *Kyushu Journal of Medical Science*, *13*, pp. 335-350, 1962.

10. K. Platonov, *The Word as a Psychological and Therapeutic Factor*, Foreign Language Publishing House, Moscow, 1959.

11. Y. Ikemi, Psychological Desensitization in Allergic Disorders, in *Hypnosis and Psychosomatic Medicine*, J. Lassner (ed.), Springer-Verlag, New York, pp. 160-165, 1967.

12. A. A. Mason and S. Black, Allergic Skin Responses Abolished under Treatment of Asthma and Hay Fever by Hypnosis, *Lancet*, *1*, pp. 877-880, April 26, 1958.

13. A. A. Mason, Hypnosis and Suggestion in the Treatment of Allergic Phenomena, *Acta Allergologica*, *15*, Supplement VII, pp. 332-338, 1960.

14. S. Black, J. H. Humphrey, and J. S. F. Niven, Inhibition of Mantoux Reaction by Direct Suggestion under Hypnosis, *British Medical Journal*, *1*, pp. 1649-1652, 1963.

15. S. Black, Inhibition of Immediate-Type Hypersensitivity Response by Direct Suggestion under Hypnosis, *British Medical Journal*, *1*, pp. 925-929, 1963a.

16. S. Black, Shift in Dose-Response Curve of Prausnitz-Küstner Reaction by Direct Suggestion under Hypnosis, *British Medical Journal*, *1*, pp. 990-992, 1963b.

17. L. Fry, A. A. Mason, and R. S. Bruce-Pearson, Effect of Hypnosis on Allergic Skin Responses in Asthma and Hay Fever, *British Medical Journal*, *1*, pp. 1145-1148, 1964.

18. A. A. Mason, Hypnosis and Allergy, *British Medical Journal*, *1*, pp. 1675-1676, 1963.

19. T. X. Barber and S. C. Wilson, Hypnosis, Suggestions and Altered States of Consciousness: Experimental Evaluation of the New Cognitive-Behavioral Theory and the Traditional Trance State Theory of "Hypnosis," *Annals of the New York Academy of Sciences*, *296*, pp. 34-47, 1977.

20. J. F. Zeig, *Teaching Seminar with Milton H. Erickson, M.D.*, Brunner/Mazel, New York, 1980.

21. A. A. Mason, A Case of Congenital Ichthyosiform Erythrodermia of Brocq Treated by Hypnosis, *British Medical Journal*, *2*, pp. 422-423, 1952.

22. P. Frost and G. D. Weinstein, Ichthyosiform Dermatoses, in *Dermatology in General Medicine*, T. B. Fitzpatrick (ed.), McGraw-Hill, New York, pp. 249-265, 1971.

23. A. A. Mason, Ichthyosis and Hypnosis, *British Medical Journal*, *2*, p. 57, 1955.

24. C. A. S. Wink, Congenital Ichthyosiform Erythrodermia Treated by Hypnosis: Report of Two Cases, *British Medical Journal*, *2*, pp. 741-743, 1961.

25. C. B. Kidd, Congenital Ichthyosiform Erythrodermia Treated by Hypnosis, *British Journal of Dermatology*, *78*, pp. 101-105, 1966.
26. J. M. Schneck, Hypnotherapy for Ichythyosis, *Psychosomatics*, *7*, pp. 233-235, 1966.
27. J. M. Schneck, Ichthyosis (Simplex) Treated with Hypnosis, *Diseases of the Nervous System*, *15*, pp. 211-214, 1954.
28. J. F. Mullins, N. Murray, and E. M. Shapiro, Pachyonychia Congenita: A Review and New Approach to Treatment, *A.M.A. Archives of Dermatology*, *71*, pp. 265-268, 1955.
29. R. Asher, Respectable Hypnosis, *British Medical Journal*, *1*, pp. 309-313, 1956.
30. A. H. C. Sinclair-Geiben and D. Chalmers, Evaluation of Treatment of Warts by Hypnosis, *Lancet*, *2*, pp. 480-482, 1959.
31. O. S. Surman, S. K. Gottlieb, T. P. Hackett, and E. L. Silverberg, Hypnosis in the Treatment of Warts, *Archives of General Psychiatry*, *28*, pp. 439-441, 1973.
32. M. Ullman and S. Dudek, On the Psyche and Warts: II. Hypnotic Suggestion and Warts, *Psychosomatic Medicine*, *22*, pp. 68-76, 1960.
33. W. S. Kroger, *Clinical and Experimental Hypnosis*, J.B. Lippincott Company, Philadelphia, 1963.
34. A. M. Weitzenhoffer, *Hypnotism: An Objective Study in Suggestibility*, John Wiley, New York, 1953.
35. D. H. Tuke, *Illustrations of the Influence of the Mind Upon the Body in Health and Disease Designed to Elucidate the Action of the Imagination*, J & A., Churchill, London, 1872.
36. B. Bloch, Ueber die Heilung der Warzen durch Suggestion, *Klinische Wochenschrift*, *6*, pp. 2271-2275, and pp. 2320-2325, 1927.
37. A. M. Memmesheimer and E. Eisenlohr, Untersuchungen ueber die Suggestivebehandlung der Warzen, *Dermatologie Zeitschrift*, *62*, pp. 63-68, 1931.
38. R. H. Rulison, Warts: A Statistical Study of Nine Hundred and Twenty-One Cases, *Archives of Dermatology and Syphilology*, *46*, pp. 66-81, 1942.
39. H. V. Allington, Sulpharsphenamine in the Treatment of Warts, *Archives of Dermatology and Syphilology*, *29*, pp. 687-690, 1934.
40. J. Bonjour, Influence of the Mind on the Skin, *British Journal of Dermatology*, *41*, pp. 324-326, 1929.
41. S. Z. Dudek, Suggestion and Play Therapy in the Cure of Warts in Children: A Pilot Study, *Journal of Nervous and Mental Disease*, *145*, pp. 37-42, 1967.
42. L. Grumach, Ueber Suggestivebehandlung von Warzen, *Muenchener Medizinische Wochenschrift*, *74*, pp. 1093-1094, 1927.
43. M. B. Sulzberger and J. Wolf, The Treatment of Warts by Suggestion, *Medical Record*, *140*, pp. 552-557, 1934.
44. H. Vollmer, Treatment of Warts by Suggestion, *Psychosomatic Medicine*, *8*, pp. 138-142, 1946.
45. R. F. Q. Johnson and T. X. Barber, Hypnosis, Suggestions, and Warts: An Experimental Investigation Implicating the Importance of "Believed-in Efficacy," *American Journal of Clinical Hypnosis*, *20*, pp. 165-174, 1978.

46. A. M. Massing and W. L. Epstein, Natural History of Warts: A Two-Year Study, *Archives of Dermatology*, *87*, pp. 306-310, 1963.

47. K. S. Bowers, Hypnosis: An Informational Approach, in *Conceptual and Investigative Approaches to Hypnosis and Hypnotic Phenomena*, W. E. Edmonston, Jr. (ed.), *Annals of the New York Academy of Sciences*, *296*, pp. 222-237, 1977.

48. A. P. French, The Treatment of Warts by Hypnosis, *American Journal of Obstetrics and Gynecology*, *116*, pp. 887-888, 1973.

49. O. S. Surman, S. K. Gottlieb, and T. P. Hackett, Hypnotic Treatment of a Child with Warts, *American Journal of Clinical Hypnosis*, *15*, pp. 12-14, 1972.

50. I. D. Yalom, Plantar Warts: A Case Study, *Journal of Nervous and Mental Disease*, *138*, pp. 163-171, 1964.

51. G. J. Honiotes, Hypnosis and Breast Enlargement—A Pilot Study, *Journal of the International Society for Professional Hypnosis*, 6:4, pp. 8-12, 1977.

52. L. M. LeCron, Breast Development Through Hypnotic Suggestion, *Journal of the American Society of Psychosomatic Dentistry and Medicine*, *16*, pp. 58-61, 1969.

53. A. R. Staib and D. R. Logan, Hypnotic Stimulation of Breast Growth, *American Journal of Clinical Hypnosis*, *19*, pp. 201-208, 1977.

54. R. D. Willard, Breast Enlargement Through Visual Imagery and Hypnosis, *American Journal of Clinical Hypnosis*, *19*, pp. 195-200, 1977.

55. J. E. Williams, Stimulation of Breast Growth by Hypnosis, *Journal of Sex Research*, *10*, pp. 316-326, 1974.

56. J. R. Hilgard, *Personality and Hypnosis: A Study of Imaginative Involvement*, University of Chicago Press, Chicago, 1970.

57. J. R. Hilgard, Imaginative and Sensory-Affective Involvement: In Everyday Life and in Hypnosis, in *Hypnosis: Developments in Research and New Perspectives*, (New and Revised Second Edition), E. Fromm and R. E. Shor (eds.), Aldine Publishing Company, Hawthorne, New York, pp. 483-517, 1979.

58. A. Tellegen and G. Atkinson, Openness to Absorbing and Self-Altering Experiences ("Absorption"), A Trait Related to Hypnotic Susceptibility, *Journal of Abnormal Psychology*, *83*, pp. 268-277, 1974.

59. S. C. Wilson and T. X. Barber, Vivid Fantasy and Hallucinatory Abilities in the Life Histories of Excellent Hypnotic Subjects ("Somnambules"): Preliminary Report with Female Subjects, in *Imagery. Volume 2, Concepts, Results, and Applications*, E. Klinger (ed.), Plenum Press, New York, pp. 133-149, 1981.

60. S. C. Wilson and T. X. Barber, The Fantasy-Prone Personality: Implications for Understanding Imagery, Hypnosis, and Parapsychological Phenomena, in *Imagery: Current Theory, Research, and Application*, A. A. Sheikh (ed.), John Wiley, New York, 1983.

61. A. Binet and C. Féré, *Animal Magnetism*, D. Appleton and Co., New York, 1888.

62. M. H. Erickson, Breast Development Possibly Influenced by Hypnosis, *American Journal of Clinical Hypnosis*, *2*, pp. 157-159, 1960.

63. T. Lewis, *The Blood Vessels of the Human Skin and Their Responses*, Shaw, London, 1927.

64. R. F. Q. Johnson and T. X. Barber, Hypnotic Suggestions for Blister Formation: Subjective and Physiological Effects, *American Journal of Clinical Hypnosis, 18*, pp. 172-181, 1976.

65. J. M. Bellis, Hypnotic Pseudo-Sunburn, *American Journal of Clinical Hypnosis, 8*:4, pp. 310-312, 1966.

66. D. C. Doswald and K. Kreibich, Zur Frage der Posthypnotischen Hautphanomene, *Monatshefte Praktik Dermatologie, 43*, pp. 634-640, 1906.

67. S. Borelli, Psychische Einflusse and Reactive Hauterscheinungen, *Muenchener Medizinische Wochenschrift, 95*, pp. 1078-1082, 1953.

68. R. L. Moody, Bodily Changes During Abreaction, *Lancet, 2*, pp. 934-935, 1946.

69. R. L. Moody, Bodily Changes During Abreaction, *Lancet, 1*, p. 964, 1948.

70. N. I. Graff and R. S. Wallerstein, Unusual Wheal Reaction in a Tattoo, *Psychosomatic Medicine, 16*, pp. 505-515, 1954.

71. R. Brandt, A Tentative Classification of Psychological Factors in the Etiology of Skin Diseases, *Journal of Investigative Dermatology, 14*, pp. 81-90, 1950.

72. Z. Kaneko and N. Takaishi, Psychosomatic Studies on Chronic Urticaria, *Folia Psychiatrica Neurologica Japonica, 17*, pp. 16-24, 1963.

73. J. A. Hadfield, The Influence of Hypnotic Suggestion on Inflammatory Conditions, *Lancet, 2*, pp. 678-679, 1917.

74. M. Ullman, Herpes Simplex and Second Degree Burn Induced Under Hypnosis, *American Journal of Psychiatry, 103*, pp. 828-830, 1947.

75. D. T. Graham and S. Wolf, Pathogenesis of Urticaria: Experimental Study of Life Situations, Emotions, and Cutaneous Vascular Reactions, *Journal of American Medical Association, 143*, pp. 1396-1402, 1950.

76. L. D. Weatherhead, *Psychology, Religion and Healing*, Abington Press, Nashville, Tenn., 1952.

77. F. A. Pattie, The Production of Blisters by Hypnotic Suggestions: A Review, *Journal of Abnormal and Social Psychology, 36*, pp. 62-72, 1941.

78. G. L. Paul, The Production of Blisters by Hypnotic Suggestion: Another Look, *Psychosomatic Medicine, 25*, pp. 233-244, 1963.

79. L. Chertok, *Sense and Nonsense in Psychotherapy: The Challenge of Hypnosis*, Pergamon Press, Elmsford, New York, 1981.

80. F. A. Pattie, A Report of Attempts to Produce Uniocular Blindness by Hypnotic Suggestion, *British Journal of Medical Psychology, 15*, pp. 230-241, 1935.

81. M. T. Orne, The Nature of Hypnosis: Artifact and Essence, *Journal of Abnormal and Social Psychology, 58*, pp. 277-299, 1959.

82. L. R. Wolberg, *Hypnosis: Is It For You?* Harcourt, Brace, Jovanovich, New York, 1972.

83. A. F. von Schrenck-Notzing, Ein experimenteller und kritischer Beitrag zur Frage der Suggestiven Hervorrufung Circumscripter Vasomotorischer Veranderungen auf der Ausseran Haut, *Zeitschrift Hypnotismus, 4*, pp. 209-228, 1896.

85. S. Fisher, The Role of Expectancy in the Performance of Posthypnotic Behavior, *Journal of Abnormal and Social Psychology*, *49*, pp. 503-507, 1954.
86. M. T. Orne, P. W. Sheehan, and F. J. Evans, Occurrence of Posthypnotic Behavior Outside the Experimental Setting, *Journal of Personality and Social Psychology*, *9*, pp. 189-196, 1968.
87. J. A. Hadfield, The Influence of Suggestion on Body Temperature, *Lancet*, *2*, pp. 68-69, 1920.
88. T. R. Sarbin, Physiological Effects of Hypnotic Stimulation, in *Hypnosis and its Therapeutic Applications*, R. M. Dorcus (ed.), McGraw-Hill, New York, Ch. 4, 1956.
89. W. R. Wells, The Hypnotic Treatment of the Major Symptoms of Hysteria: A Case Study, *Journal of Psychology*, *77*, pp. 269-297, 1944.
90. F. Heller and J. H. Schultz, Ueber einen Fall Hypnotisch Erzeugter Blasenbildung, *Muenchner Medizinische Wochenschrift*, *56*, p. 2112, 1909.
91. D. Smirnoff, Zur Frage der Durch Hypnotische Suggestion Hervorgerufenen Vasomotorischen Stoerungen, *Zeitschrift Psychotherapie Medizinische Psychologie*, *4*, pp. 171-175, 1912.
92. L. L. Vasiliev, *Mysterious Phenomena of the Human Psyche*, University Books, New Hyde Park, New York, 1965.
93. N. P. Spanos, C. McNeil, and H. J. Stam, Hypnotically "Reliving" a Prior Burn: Effects on Blister Formation and Localized Skin Temperature, *Journal of Abnormal Psychology*, *91*:4, pp. 303-305, 1982.
94. H. Thurston, *The Physical Phenomena of Mysticism*, Henry Regnery Co., Chicago, 1952.
95. M. Summers, *The Physical Phenomena of Mysticism*, Barnes and Noble, New York, 1950.
96. J. V. Klauder, Stigmatization, *Archives of Dermatology and Syphilology*, *37*, pp. 650-659, 1938.
97. L. F. Early and J. E. Lifschutz, A Case of Stigmata, *Archives of General Psychiatry*, *30*, pp. 197-200, 1974.
98. W. Needles, Stigmata Occurring in the Course of Psychoanalysis, *Psychoanalytic Quarterly*, *12*, pp, 23-27, 1943.
99. J. E. Lifschutz, Hysterical Stigmatization, *American Journal of Psychiatry*, *114*, pp. 526-531, 1957.
100. R. Schindler, *Nervensystem und Spontane Blutunge*, Karger, Berlin, 1927.
101. D. P. Agle, O. D. Ratnoff, and M. Wasman, Studies in Autoerythrocyte Sensitization: The Induction of Purpuric Lesions by Hypnotic Suggestions, *Psychosomatic Medicine*, *29*:5, pp. 491-503, 1967.
102. O. N. Lucas, Dental Extractions in the Hemophiliac: Control of the Emotional Factors by Hypnosis, *American Journal of Clinical Hypnosis*, *7*:4, pp. 301-307, 1965.
103. J. F. Chaves, Hypnotic Control of Surgical Bleeding, paper presented at Annual Meeting of the American Psychological Association, Montreal, September, 1980.
104. L. L. Dubin and S. S. Shapiro, Use of Hypnosis to Facilitate Dental Extraction and Hemostasis in a Classic Hemophiliac with a High Antibody Titer to Factor VIII, *American Journal of Clinical Hypnosis*, *17*, pp. 79-83, 1974.

105. M. Newman, Hypnotic Handling of the Chronic Bleeder in Extraction: A Case Report, *American Journal of Clinical Hypnosis, 14*, pp. 126-127, 1971.

106. J. M. Bramwell, *Hypnotism: Its History, Practice and Theory*, Grant Richards, London, 1903.

107. L. F. Chapman, H. Goodell, and H. G. Wolff, Increased Inflammatory Reaction Induced by Central Nervous System Activity, *Transactions Association of American Physicians, 72*, pp. 84-109, 1959.

108. D. M. Ewin, Hypnosis in Burn Therapy, in *Hypnosis 1979*, G. D. Burrows, D. R. Collison, and L. Dennerstein (eds.), Elsevier/North-Holland Biomedical Press, New York, pp. 269-275, 1979.

109. D. M. Ewin, Clinical Use of Hypnosis for Attenuation of Burn Depth, in *Hypnosis at its Bicentennial: Selected Papers*, F. H. Frankel and H. S. Zamansky (eds.), Plenum Press, New York, pp. 155-162, 1978.

110. J. C. Pearce, *The Crack in the Cosmic Egg*, The Julian Press, New York, 1971.

111. S. P. Langley, The Fire Walk Ceremony in Tahiti, *Journal of the Society for Psychical Research, 10*, pp. 116-121, 1901.

112. H. Price, Kuda Bux, *Spectator, 158*, p. 808, 1937.

113. H. Price, *Fifty Years of Psychical Research*, Longmans, Green & Co., London, 1939.

114. M. R. Coe, Jr., Fire-walking and Related Behaviors, *Psychological Record, 7*, pp. 101-110, 1957.

115. M. R. Coe, Safely Across the Fiery Pit, *Fate, 31*:6, pp. 84-86, 1978.

116. C. Fonseka, *Experiments in Fire-Walking*, Privately Printed, Colombo, Sri Lanka (Ceylon), 1969.

117. J. H. McElroy, Firewalking, *Folklore, 89*, pp. 113-115, 1978.

118. V. Rosner, Fire-Walking the Tribal Way, *Anthropos, 61*, pp. 177-190, 1966.

119. J. Mishlove, *The Roots of Consciousness*, Random House, New York, 1975.

120. J. Samek, Zum Wesen der Suggestiven Warzenheilung, *Dermatologische Wochenschrift, 93*, pp. 1853-1857, 1931.

121. H. V. Allington, Review of Psychotherapy of Warts, *Archives of Dermatology and Syphilology, 29*, pp. 687-690, 1934.

122. H. Biberstein, Immunization Therapy of Warts, *Archives of Dermatology and Syphilology, 50*, pp. 12-22, 1944.

123. M. Ullman, On the Psyche and Warts: I. Suggestions and Warts: A Review and Comment, *Psychosomatic Medicine, 21*, pp. 473-488, 1959.

124. C. G. Zwick, Hygiogenesis of Warts Disappearing Without Topical Medication, *Archives of Dermatology and Syphilology, 25*, pp. 508-521, 1932.

125. M. A. Wenger and B. K. Bagchi, Studies of Autonomic Functions in Practitioners of Yoga in India, *Behavioral Science, 6*, pp. 312-323, 1961.

126. H. Benson, Body Temperature Changes During Practice of g'Tum-mo Yoga, *Nature, 295*, pp. 234-236, Jan. 23, 1982.

127. E. E. Green, D. W. Ferguson, A. M. Green, and E. D. Walters, *Preliminary Report on Voluntary Controls Project: Swami Rama*, Research Department, Menninger Foundation, Topeka, Kansas, 1970.

128. T. X. Barber, N. P. Spanos, and J. F. Chaves, *Hypnosis, Imagination, and Human Potentialities*, Pergamon Press, Elmsford, New York, 1974.

129. A. R. Luria, *The Mind of a Mnemonist*, Basic Books, New York, 1968.

130. R. Menzies, Further Studies of Conditioned Vasomotor Responses in Human Subjects, *Journal of Experimental Psychology*, *29*, pp. 456-482, 1941.

131. M. Dugan and C. Sheridan, Effects of Instructed Imagery on Temperature of Hands, *Perceptual and Motor Skills*, *42*, p. 14, 1976.

132. M. H. Erickson, *The Collected Papers of Milton H. Erickson on Hypnosis*, in *Hypnotic Alterations of Sensory, Perceptual and Psychophysical Processes*, E. L. Rossi (ed.), Irvington Publishers, New York, 1980.

133. M. A. Jones, Locus of Control of Visual Imagery in Skin Temperature Control, doctoral dissertation, California School of Professional Psychology, 1976, *Dissertation Abstracts*, *37*, p. 4651B, 1977.

134. R. G. Kunzendorf, Individual Differences in Imagery and Autonomic Control, *Journal of Mental Imagery*, *5*, pp. 47-60, 1981.

135. C. Maslach, G. Marshall, and P. Zimbardo, Hypnotic Control of Peripheral Skin Temperature, *Psychophysiology*, *9*, pp. 600-605, 1972.

136. P. G. Zimbardo, C. Maslach, and G. Marshall, *Hypnosis and the Psychology of Cognitive and Behavioral Control*, Department of Psychology, Stanford University, 1970.

137. T. X. Barber (ed.), *Advances in Altered States of Consciousness and Human Potentialities*, Psychological Dimensions, New York, 1976a.

138. T. X. Barber, Tape Review. Brown, Barbara, B. *EEG Biofeedback: Clinical Applications and Research Frontiers*; Love, William A., Jr., *EMG Biofeedback: Therapeutic Applications*; Adler, Charles S., and Adler, Sheila Morrissey, *Biofeedback in Psychotherapy*, *Behavior Therapy*, *7*, pp. 716-718, 1976c.

139. T. X. Barber, Forward, in *Clinical Applications of Biofeedback: Appraisal and Status*, R. J. Gatchel and K. P. Price (eds.), Pergamon Press, Elmsford, New York, p. ix, 1979.

140. T. X. Barber, L. V. DiCara, J. Kamiya, N. E. Miller, D. Shapiro, and J. Stoyva (eds.), *Biofeedback and Self-Control 1970*, Aldine-Atherton, Chicago, 1971a.

141. T. X. Barber, L. V. DiCara, J. Kamiya, N. E. Miller, D. Shapiro, and J. Stoyva (eds.), *Biofeedback and Self-Control: An Aldine Reader on the Regulation of Bodily Processes and Consciousness*, Aldine-Atherton, Chicago, 1971b.

142. T. X. Barber, L. V. DiCara, J. Kamiya, N. E. Miller, D. Shapiro, and J. Stoyva (eds.), *Biofeedback and Self-Control: 1975/76*, Aldine Publishing Co., Chicago, 1976.

143. M. W. Ham and T. X. Barber, Biofeedback Techniques and their Clinical Applications, in *Current Psychiatric Therapies*, Vol. 14, J. H. Masserman (ed.), Grune and Stratton, New York, pp. 67-75, 1974.

144. E. Taub and C. S. Emurian, Self-Regulation of Skin Temperature Using a Variable Intensity Light, in *Biofeedback and Self-Control: 1972*, J. Stoyva, T. X. Barber, L. V. DiCara, J. Kamiya, N. E. Miller, and D. Shapiro (eds.), Aldine Publishing Co., Chicago, p. 504, 1973.

145. E. Taub, Self-Regulation of Human Tissue Temperature, in *Biofeedback: Theory and Research*, G. E. Schwartz and J. Beatty (eds.), Academic Press, New York, 1977.

146. D. French, C. Leeb, and S. Fahrion, Self-Induced Scrotal Hypothermia: An Extension, paper presented at Meeting of Biofeedback Research Society, Colorado Springs, 1974.

147. D. R. Laws and H. B. Rubin, Instructional Control of an Autonomic Sexual Response, *Applied Behavioral Analysis*, 2, pp. 93-99, 1969.

148. D. E. Henson and H. B. Rubin, Voluntary Control of Eroticism, *Applied Behavioral Analysis*, 4, pp. 37-44, 1971.

149. R. C. Rosen, D. Shapiro, and G. E. Schwartz, Voluntary Control of Penile Tumescence, *Psychosomatic Medicine*, 37, pp. 479-483, 1975.

150. T. X. Barber, *Hypnosis: A Scientific Approach*, Van Nostrand Reinhold, New York, 1969.

151. T. X. Barber and S. C. Wilson, Guided Imagining and Hypnosis: Theoretical and Empirical Overlap and Convergence in a New Creative Imagination Scale, in *The Potential of Fantasy and Imagination*, A. A. Sheikh and J. T. Shaffer (eds.), Brandon House, New York, pp. 67-88, 1979.

152. S. C. Wilson and T. X. Barber, The Creative Imagination Scale as a Measure of Hypnotic Responsiveness: Applications to Experimental and Clinical Hypnosis, *American Journal of Clinical Hypnosis*, 20, pp. 235-249, 1978.

153. T. X. Barber, and W. DeMoor, A Theory of Hypnotic Induction Procedures, *American Journal of Clinical Hypnosis*, 15, pp. 112-135, 1972.

154. D. M. Cronin, N. P. Spanos, and T. X. Barber, Augmenting Hypnotic Suggestibility by Providing Favorable Information About Hypnosis, *American Journal of Clinical Hypnosis*, 13, pp. 259-264, 1971.

155. P. W. Sheehan, Hypnosis and the Process of Imagination, in *Hypnosis: Developments in Research and New Perspectives*, E. Fromm and R. E. Shor (eds.), Aldine Publishing Company, New York, pp. 381-411, 1979.

156. C. Perry, Imagery, Fantasy and Hypnotic Susceptibility: A Multidimensional Approach, *Journal of Personality and Social Psychology*, 26, pp. 217-221, 1973.

157. R. E. Shor, M. T. Orne, and D. N. O'Connell, Psychological Correlates of Plateau Hypnotizability in a Special Volunteer Sample, *Journal of Personality and Social Psychology*, 3, pp. 80-95, 1966.

158. N. P. Spanos, R. Valois, M. W. Ham, and M. L. Ham, Suggestibility, and Vividness and Control of Imagery, *International Journal of Clinical and Experimental Hypnosis*, 21, pp. 305-311, 1973.

159. J. P. Sutcliffe, Hypnotic Behaviour: Fantasy or Simulation?, unpublished Doctoral Dissertation, University of Sydney, Australia, 1958.

160. J. P. Sutcliffe, C. W. Perry, and P. W. Sheehan, The Relation of Some Aspects of Imagery and Fantasy to Hypnotizability, *Journal of Abnormal Psychology*, 76, pp. 279-287, 1970.

161. A. As, Non-Hypnotic Experiences Related to Hypnotizability in Male and Female College Students, *Scandinavian Journal of Psychology*, 3, pp. 112-121, 1962.

162. T. X. Barber and L. B. Glass, Significant Factors in Hypnotic Behavior, *Journal of Abnormal and Social Psychology*, *64*, pp. 222-228, 1962.

163. R. E. Shor, M. T. Orne, and D. N. O'Connell, Validation and Cross-Validation of a Scale of Self-Reported Personal Experiences which Predicts Hypnotizability, *Journal of Psychology*, *53*, pp. 55-75, 1962.

164. W. C. Coe and T. R. Sarbin, An Experimental Demonstration of Hypnosis as Role Enactment, *Journal of Abnormal Psychology*, *71*, pp. 400-405, 1966.

165. M. Andersen, Correlates of Hypnotic Performance: An Historical and Role-Theoretical Analysis, unpublished Doctoral Dissertation, University of California, Berkeley, 1963.

166. A. As, J. W. O'Hara, and M. P. Munger, The Measurement of Subjective Experiences Presumably Related to Hypnotic Susceptibility, *Scandinavian Journal of Psychology*, *3*, pp. 47-64, 1962.

167. G. A. Atkinson, Personality and Hypnotic Cognition, unpublished Doctoral Dissertation, University of Minnesota, 1971.

168. W. C. Coe, The Hueristic Value of Role Theory and Hypnosis, unpublished Doctoral Dissertation, University of California, Berkeley, 1964.

169. E. Lee-Teng, Trance-Susceptibility, Induction Susceptibility, and Acquiescence as Factors in Hypnotic Performance, *Journal of Abnormal Psychology*, *70*, pp. 383-389, 1965.

170. T. R. Sarbin and D. T. Lim, Some Evidence in Support of the Role-Taking Hypothesis in Hypnosis, *International Journal of Clinical and Experimental Hypnosis*, *11*, pp. 98-103, 1963.

171. N. P. Spanos and J. D. McPeake, The Effects of Involvement in Everyday Imaginative Activities and Attitudes Toward Hypnosis on Hypnotic Susceptibility, *Journal of Personality and Social Psychology*, *31*, pp. 594-598, 1975a.

172. N. P. Spanos and J. D. McPeake, The Interaction of Attitudes Toward Hypnosis and Involvement in Everyday Imaginative Activities on Hypnotic Susceptibility, *American Journal of Clinical Hypnosis*, *17*, pp. 247-252, 1975b.

173. K. S. Bowers, Hypnosis and Healing, *Australian Journal of Clinical and Experimental Hypnosis*, *7*:3, pp. 261-277, 1979.

174. G. H. V. Clarke, The Charming of Warts, *Journal of Investigative Dermatology*, *45*:1, pp. 15-21, 1965.

175. L. Stankler, A Critical Assessment of the Cure of Warts by Suggestion, *The Practitioner*, *198*, pp. 690-694, 1967.

176. J. H. Tenzel and R. L. Taylor, An Evaluation of Hypnosis and Suggestion as Treatment for Warts, *Psychosomatics*, *10*, pp. 252-257, 1969.

CHAPTER 5
The Use of Imagery in Alleviating Depression
K. DAVID SCHULTZ

INTRODUCTION

In spite of William James's [1] challenge to study ongoing thought in all its richness, diversity, and complexity, a review of much of the literature in psychology, psychiatry, and psychotherapy during the last seventy-five years indicates little serious interest in the study of our ever-changing stream of consciousness [2]. Although Freud and other psychoanalysts drew our attention to primary process thinking, they were primarily interested in uncovering the ways in which nonverbal, irrational, wishful, childlike, fantasy-laden material intrudes into adult mental life to bring about maladaptive, self-defeating behavior and other aspects of psychopathology. Freud and many other psychoanalysts appeared to be saying that a well-analyzed adult would rely primarily on secondary process thinking and avoid primary process thinking as much as possible. Within such a framework, there was little room for the adaptive, pleasurable, creative, and therapeutic qualities of imagery-laden mentation. Instead, the value of goal-directed logical thinking was greatly underscored; and psychologists, psychiatrists, and psychotherapists developed a bias toward the use of verbal, directed thought and this bias still persists.

Fortunately, this onesidedness is gradually being counterbalanced. Aspects of the stream of consciousness have become legitimate areas of scientific research [3]. A new appreciation for the role of imaginal processes in learning [4], memory [4], and perception [5] has developed. The clinical implications of imaginal processes have become increasingly recognized [2, 6, 7], and numerous imagery techniques now are being used in the treatment of various medical and psychiatric disorders [2, 7-10].

In this paper, the major scientific models of depression and their respective treatment approaches are examined. Then an in-depth review of systematic research regarding the psychotherapeutic use of imagery in alleviating depression is presented, and the author offers some suggestions for future research in this area. He then turns to a brief review of related research on depression and imagery and concludes with a theoretical discussion of the cognitive-affective aspects of a biopsychosocial model of depression.

DEPRESSION

Depression is a negative affective state which is an almost universal human phenomenon. It is characterized by feelings of despondency, despair, disinterest, and boredom and by attitudes of remorse, regret, self-blame, hopelessness, and helplessness [11]. However, due in part to its common and frequent occurrence, a variety of definitions of depression have been proposed; and the concept has been applied to a wide range of phenomena including: 1) a temporary mood state experienced by all individuals, 2) an acute psychological disorder, and 3) a chronic character disorder. While similar in some ways, these three phenomena vary along dimensions of intensity, duration, and degree of reality distortion. Therefore, to avoid confusion, depression is herein defined as a negative affective state which can vary in intensity from relatively mild to severe and from a subtle, transitory experience to a profoundly disabling psychiatric syndrome [12]. Furthermore, depression can represent a relatively appropriate response to an accurate appraisal of reality or it can be based on marked distortions of reality.

Theories of Depression

Widespread differences in the classification of depressive disorders may reflect the fact that psychiatric syndromes have been conceptualized historically according to "specialized frames of reference that largely depend on the training and indoctrination of the clinician or researcher." [13, p. 285] Although the development and use of the Diagnostic and Statistical Manual III (DSM-III) [14] criteria for classifying psychiatric dysfunction are positive steps toward unifying clinical and research efforts nationally and internationally, different theories of depression (and of other psychiatric disorders) are likely to prevail until clinicians and researchers develop a more comprehensive, interdisciplinary approach to the study of well-defined psychiatric phenomena.

Currently, there are several major theories of depression: biological (physiological factors), biochemical (changes in neurotransmitters), psychoanalytic (traumatic early life experiences), cognitive (cognitive distortions of self and others), behavioral (learned helplessness), and existential (current loss of meaning). Akiskal and McKinney [13] focused on ten different models of depression which they considered to reflect five dominant "schools of thought" as indicated in Table 1.

Akiskal and McKinney recognized the importance of striving toward a more unified theory of depression and, therefore, developed an hypothesis which

Table 1. TEN MODELS OF DEPRESSION[a]

School	Model	Mechanism
Psychoanalytic	Aggression-turned-inward	Conversion of aggression instinct into depressive affect.
	Object loss	Separation: Disruption of an attachment bond.
	Loss of self-esteem	Helplessness in attaining goals of ego-ideal.
	Negative cognitive set	Hopelessness.
Behavioral	Learned helplessness	Uncontrollable aversive stimulation.
	Loss of reinforcement	Rewards of "sick role" substitute for lost sources of reinforcement.
Sociological	Sociological	Loss of role status.
Existential	Existential	Loss of meaning of existence.
Biological	Biogenic amine	Impaired monaminergic transmission.
	Neurophysiological	Hyperarousal secondary to intraneuronal sodium accumulation; Cholinergic dominance; Reversible functional derangement of diencephalic mechanism of reinforcement.

[a]Akiskal and McKinney [13, p. 296]

integrates more fully these various clinical models [13, 15]. Briefly, the depressive syndrome is viewed as the psychobiological common pathway of various social, psychological, and biological processes which result in reversible dysfunction of the diencephalic mechanisms of reinforcement. The major advance introduced by Akiskal and McKinney's approach is the conceptualization of depression at several different levels simultaneously, which replaces the focus on a one-to-one relationship with a single event on a biological, a psychological, or a social level. Perhaps without fully recognizing it, Akiskal and McKinney took a major step toward a biopsychosocial model of depression implicitly based upon

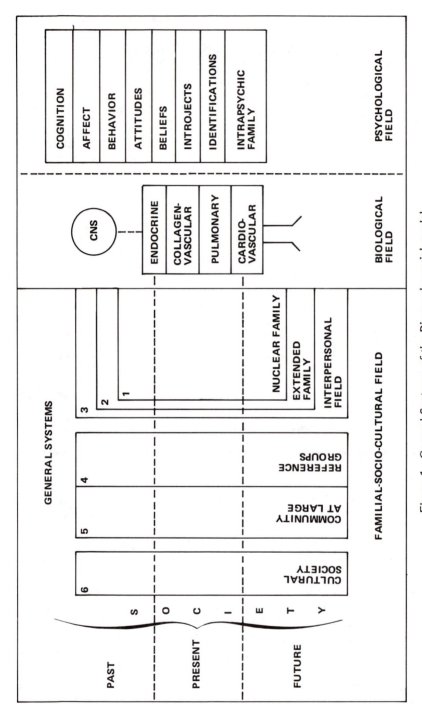

Figure 1. General Systems of the Biopsychosocial model.
(Figure represents modifications of Greenberg's basic model [16].)

General Systems Theory [13]. It is just such a biopsychosocial model of psychiatric disorder based explicitly on General Systems Theory which Greenberg [16], Gross [17], and Schultz [18] have found particularly useful in the diagnosis and treatment of a broad spectrum of psychiatric disorders (See Figure 1.).

Treatment of Depression

Consonant with the various theories of depression are the different approaches in the treatment of depression. Each theoretical framework has given rise to its own therapeutic modalities which unfortunately have tended to be competitive rather than complementary. Treatments range from psychoanalysis to behavior therapy and from sociopolitical activism to pharmacotherapy and electroconvulsive therapy (ECT). Since psychotherapeutic interventions represent the major focus of this paper, only a very brief review of these other treatment approaches will be presented here. A more detailed discussion is available elsewhere [11, 19, 20].

Biological and biochemical theories of depression have contributed to the development of various *somatic treatments*, including insulin shock therapy, ECT, and pharmacotherapy. The effectiveness of the major antidepressant medications, particularly the tricyclics and the monoamine oxidase (MAO) inhibitors, has become so well-established that insulin shock therapy is no longer used and ECT has become the last treatment of choice among biological psychiatrists. In addition, the value of activity therapy such as regular exercise and running as a way of alleviating as well as preventing depression is being stressed more and more. While clinical experience supports the usefulness of these approaches, systematic research remains to be done in this promising therapeutic area.

Sociological and interpersonal theories of depression have contributed to *sociopolitical activism*. It aims at rectifying inequities in the social system which contribute to depression by depriving various individuals (e.g., blacks, women, Hispanics, and other minorities) of certain roles and/or of control over their destinies. Other major *interpersonal interventions* in the treatment of depression include group therapy, marital and family therapy, and family group therapy. While group therapy and family group therapy clearly have an interpersonal component, they originally arose due to a shortage of clinicians and have only gradually developed their potential along with marital and family systems therapy, as relationship and social system therapies. Furthermore, although considerable clinical information is available regarding the usefulness of group therapy, marital therapy, family therapy, and family group therapy in the treatment of depression and other psychiatric disorders [21-24], little systematic research exists which focuses on reducing depression by resolving interpersonal conflict through either group, marital, family, or family group therapy.

Psychological theories of depression have contributed to the development of various *psychotherapeutic approaches* toward the treatment of depression.

Psychotherapeutic treatment of depression ranges from minimal, once-a-month *supportive psychotherapy* to intensive, five-times-a-week *psychoanalysis*. Such treatments can range in duration from brief, time-limited psychotherapy lasting two or three months to long-term psychoanalytic psychotherapy and psychoanalysis lasting five to ten years or more. While supportive therapy aims at maintaining the patient's level of functioning and preventing further relapse, psychoanalytic treatment is geared toward major personality reorganization. The former often focuses upon crisis intervention and upon helping the individual to develop improved coping mechanisms, while the latter usually holds out the hope of "total cure."

Dynamic, Insight-Oriented Psychotherapy. This therapy offers a more moderate alternative to both brief supportive psychotherapy and intensive psychoanalytic treatment. Like psychoanalysis, it usually involves the exploration of complex historical patterns of behavior stemming from early life experiences and it emphasizes the usefulness of insight to improvement. While there is considerable controversy regarding the efficacy of insight and the usefulness of traditional psychotherapy regardless of orientation, the fact that most traditional dynamic psychotherapies are limited to those who are wealthy, intelligent, relatively stable, and able to tolerate considerable frustration for extended periods of time lead many clinicians to explore other types of psychotherapeutic treatment for patients suffering from depression as well as other psychiatric disorders.

Behavior Therapy. This treatment of depression is based upon the theory that specific maladaptive behaviors need to be altered to restore the depressed person to a healthier level of functioning. Such interventions as assertiveness training, skills acquisition training, social skills training, parent effectiveness training, sex therapy, marital therapy, role modeling, and psychodrama have been utilized in various behavioral therapy approaches to the treatment of depression with reasonably good results [25-27].

Cognitive Psychotherapy. This psychotherapy combines the specificity of behavior therapy with the dynamic aspects of more traditional psychotherapies. Cognitive psychotherapy as a treatment of depression is based upon the theory that the depressed or depression-prone individual maintains certain unconscious idiosyncratic cognitive patterns which may become activated and/or intensified by specific stresses impinging on specific areas of vulnerability or by overwhelming, nonspecific stresses [11, 28-30]. Beck hypothesized the use of a cognitive psychotherapeutic approach geared toward helping the patient to gain "objectivity toward his automatic reactions and counteract them." [11] The patient's cognitive patterns (whether they are verbal or pictoral "events" in his/her stream of consciousness) are conceptualized as being based upon attitudes and assumptions (cognitive schemas) developed from previous experiences [28]. Beck regards the therapy as designed to modify these idiosyncratic cognitive patterns, thereby reducing the patient's vulnerability to further depressions. Briefly, the major aspects of this approach include: 1) delineating the major maladaptive depressive patterns; 2) pinpointing the depressive cognitions; 3) examining, reality testing, and neutralizing "automatic" thoughts and images; 4) identifying idiosyncratic content; 5) distinguishing "ideas" from "facts"; and 6) weighing alternative explanations. Thus, cognitive psychotherapy of depression provides an active, directive, structured treatment approach which is time limited.

Beck reported that he has found cognitive psychotherapy to be effective during the depressed phase in mild reactive depressions, but he recommended that its major application occur during the postdepressed period, particularly for endogenous depressions and reactive depressions of a moderate to severe degree [11]. Beck emphasized that during the postdepressed period, although the patient may be feeling "blue," he/she is functioning well enough to examine objectively his/her life patterns, his/her automatic thoughts and images, and his/her basic misconceptions. Thus, implicit in Beck's thinking is the importance of avoiding a one-sided unidimensional approach to the treatment of depression. The reader is, therefore, once again reminded not only of the value of the multidimensional general systems approach [16-18] to the diagnosis and treatment of dysfunction but also of the importance of integrating various treatment approaches, especially complementing the more verbal aspects of the various psychotherapies with nonverbal imagery techniques [2].

IMAGERY AND FANTASY TECHNIQUES IN PSYCHOTHERAPY

Historical Review

The psychotherapeutic uses of imagery can be divided according to several "schools of thought" (see Singer's review [31]). The use of imagery techniques in *classical psychoanalysis* dates back to Freud's [32] initial reliance on induced imagery in hypnotic abreaction with hysterical patients. However, after Freud abandoned induced imagery for an increased focus on verbal free associations, imagery remained important in psychoanalysis only in the reexperiencing of dream material and in the emergence of transference phenomena. More recently, however, Reyher has emphasized the usefulness of an imagery free association method in enhancing affective expression [33, 34]. In contrast to the implicit utilization of imagery in classical psychoanalytic work, the non-Freudial *European school of psychoanalysis* was greatly influenced by Jung and his explicit emphasis on "active imagination" in dream interpretation [35]. After Jung, the development of mental imagery techniques in Europe was furthered by Desoille's [36] guided daydream technique, Frétigny and Virel's [37] "oneirodrama," and Leuner's [38] "guided affective imagery technique." The *nonpsychoanalytic psychotherapeutic* uses of imagery in the United States include psychodrama [39], transactional analysis [40], Gestalt therapy [41], the personal growth movement [42], and psychosynthesis [43, 44]. Finally, the psychotherapeutic use of imagery has become an integral part of various *behavior modification techniques* including systematic desensitization [45], positive imagery in the treatment of peptic ulcer patients [46], noxious imagery in covert aversive therapy [47], symbolic modeling [48], Meichenbaum's [49] self-regulatory techniques, and Stampfl's [50] implosive therapy.

There currently exists, then, a growing body of literature with a lengthy historical tradition indicating that induced imagery techniques play an important role in behavioral change [31]. Visual imagery has been utilized in relaxation techniques for childbirth [51], in the voluntary control of heart rate [7], in improving athletic performance, in the treatment of cancer [8], in a group-oriented psychiatric treatment program [54], in the treatment of parent-child conflict [9], and in the treatment of serious child abuse [10].

Although Beck [11, 28] and Lazarus [53, 54] have used both spontaneous and directed imagery in the treatment of various clinical disorders including depression, until recently little systematic effort had been made to evaluate the effects of particular imagery techniques on the mood and general clinical condition of patients representative of a specific psychiatric syndrome.

Current Uses of Imagery in Alleviating Depression

Increasing evidence indicates that different affective states can be induced systematically [55-57] and altered through various imagery procedures [11, 28, 53-57]. Schultz decided to narrow the field of investigation to a specific affective disorder, depression, and he reviewed the use of imagery in its treatment [58, 59]. He suggested that directed imagery might either distract the depressed person from his/her depressed affective state and/or help him/her to contact and discharge suppressed affect, which would lead to a reduction in underlying conflict and a corresponding decrease in level of depression. In view of the fact that the study of imaginal processes previously had focused primarily on nonpatient populations and that the use of imagery in the treatment of depression had not yet been systematically evaluated, Schultz designed and conducted a study to investigate the immediate changes in the affective state of depressed psychiatric patients in response to specific imagery content [58, 59]. The short-term and long-term changes in level of depression as a result of imagery therapy recently have been investigated and will be discussed later.

Immediate Changes. Schultz studied the immediate changes in level of depression of sixty depressed male psychiatric patients who experienced a brief induction procedure of either aggressive, socially gratifying, positive or free imagery [58, 59]. Each patient was seen individually within the first week after the beginning of psychiatric treatment and was encouraged to regard the use of imagery as a skill which can be learned. After being instructed to get as comfortable as possible, he was asked to close his eyes or to focus his gaze at a point. The patient was then instructed to follow one of the four imagery procedures by visualizing the entire experience in his "mind's eye" in as much detail as possible. The *aggressive imagery procedure* directed the patient to recall someone saying or doing something which angered him. In the *socially gratifying imagery procedure* the patient was instructed to recall someone saying or doing something which made him feel very pleased. The *positive imagery procedure* requested the patient to recall a place in nature he used to visit in order to relax. In the *free imagery procedure* the patient was instructed to report all images, thoughts, fantasies and ideas which occurred to him without consciously trying to direct his stream of consciousness. After participating in the imagery induction procedure which lasted about 10 minutes, each patient was instructed to complete a series of cognitive, affective, and perceptual measures which have been shown to be related to one's level of depression.

Findings indicated that: 1) directed imagery (aggressive, socially gratifying, and positive) produced significantly lower levels of depression than free imagery, and 2) more socially oriented imagery (aggressive highest, socially gratifying second, positive third, and free lowest[1]) produced significantly lower levels of depression than less socially oriented imagery. Furthermore, particular types of depressives responded differently to the various imagery contents: 1) those patients whose depression was characterized by themes of dependency achieved lower levels of depression after aggressive and socially gratifying imagery; 2) those patients whose depression centered around self-criticism attained lower levels of depression after socially gratifying and positive imagery; 3) those depressives whose daydreaming was positively oriented showed lower levels of depression after socially gratifying and positive imagery; and 4) those depressives who experienced considerable guilty dysphoric themes in their daydreaming showed more signs of depression after positive imagery. Clearly, not only did directed and socially oriented imagery serve to reduce the level of depression, but also different types of depressed patients improved more after some directed imagery contents than after others.

In a somewhat related study, Burtle investigated the immediate changes in level of depression of eight depressed patients (with psychomotor retardation) who experienced either *positive imagery training* or *relaxation training* [60]. Those depressives in the positive imagery training experienced a three-stage procedure which included perceptual training using Thematic Apperception Test (TAT) cards, relaxation training with practice in imaging TAT cards, and a period of making self-generated positive changes in the TAT images. Those depressives who experienced positive imagery training showed lower levels of depression than those who experienced relaxation training only and a considerable increase in imagery production.

The findings from these two studies indicated that different types of directed imagery can help seriously depressed people to reduce their level of depression

---

[1] This ordering along a continuum of social involvement was determined on the basis of the patients' behavior during the various imagery sessions [58, 59].

for a brief period of time and that different types of depressives are likely to improve more after experiencing some directed imagery contents than after others. However, the question whether directed imagery could produce positive changes in level of depression which would persist for a more extended period of time required further investigation.

Immediate and Long-Term Changes.   Extending the work of Schultz [58, 59], Jarvinen and Gold [61] studied the immediate and long-term changes in level of depression of fifty-three mildly to moderately depressed female undergraduate students who practiced either neutral, positive, or self-generated positive imagery or who were assigned to a no treatment control condition. Those students in the *neutral* or *positive imagery group* were given five neutral scenes and five positive scenes, respectively, which they were asked to visualize throughout the day and to picture at least twice daily. Each student in the *self-generated positive imagery* condition generated five positive scenes (which matched the scenes in the positive imagery condition) and these students were asked to visualize these five scenes throughout the day and to picture them at least twice daily. The students in the *no treatment control condition* were given no scenes to practice. All students were asked to make daily mood ratings for a two week period.

After two weeks, the students in the three imagery conditions reported lower levels of depression (as measured by the Beck Depressive Inventory [11]) than the students in the no treatment condition. They also reported lower levels of depression on the Zung Self-Rating Depression Scale [62] and higher mood ratings, but these findings did not reach significance. Six months later, the thirty-one students who responded to a follow-up questionnaire reported no significant differences in level of depression. Nevertheless, of the twenty-one students in the three imagery conditions, 57 percent reported noticing a change in mood as a result of the study; whereas, of the eight students in the no treatment condition, only 13 percent reported noticing such a change. Sixty-two percent of the students in the imagery conditions also reported that they were applying what they had learned through the study, but only 38 percent of those in the no treatment condition reported so doing. Thus, while the initial changes in level of depression as a result of practicing directed imagery for a two week period are quite promising, the degree of benefit does appear to diminish gradually over time. Such a finding in a six month follow-up study is not surprising. What is indeed impressive and encouraging, however, is that mildly depressed students are likely to report noticing a change in mood even six months after experiencing a two week directed imagery practice period.

Propst studied the immediate and intermediate changes in level of depression of thirty-three female and eleven male mildly depressed undergraduate students who scored moderately high on a religiosity scale [63, 64]. Interested in systematically investigating the use of religious imagery reported in the Bible [65] and by various Christian counsellors [66-68], Propst assigned each depressed religious student to one of the four following treatment conditions: nonreligious imagery, religious imagery, self-monitoring plus nondirective discussion, and self-monitoring only. Each student showed a mildly depressed mood for a baseline period of two weeks and then experienced two one-hour group therapy sessions per week for a four-week period (for a total of eight group therapy sessions).[2] Those students in the *nonreligious imagery group* were asked to relive their depressive episodes, to describe their accompanying images, and to develop an awareness of their depression-engendering images. They also were instructed to record their moods and accompanying mental images five times daily between sessions as added self-awareness practice. Usually in Session 3, students were given a list of coping statements and images directed toward modifying the three components of Beck's [69] cognitive triad of depression (negative self, environment, and future), and they were instructed to select statements and images from this list to reduce their depression. The students then relived their depressive images and attempted to modify them using their selected coping imagery and statements. Students in the *religious imagery group* followed an identical procedure except that a list of religious images and coping statements were used in modifying their depressive images (e.g., "I can visualize Christ going with me into that difficult situation in the future as I try to cope"). Students in the *self-monitoring plus nondirective discussion group* were permitted to discuss whatever they wanted with little therapist intervention, were asked to keep track of their daily mood, and were given homework which consisted of recording items for group discussion on their mood cards. Students in the *self-monitoring only condition* were informed that they were in a control condition, a very important part of the project, and were asked to fill out daily mood cards.

Findings indicated that: 1) students who experienced either religious imagery or self-monitoring plus nondirective discussion reduced their level of depression as compared to those who experienced self-monitoring only; 2) only 14 percent of the students who had experienced religious imagery still scored in the depressed range as compared with 60 percent of the nonreligious imagery group and 60 percent of the self-monitoring only condition[3]; and 3) students who experienced religious imagery also showed a greater increase in group interaction than the students in the other conditions. Furthermore, a six-week follow-up study indicated that students who had experienced religious imagery continued to show a trend ($p < .10$) toward decreased global psychopathology and decreased depression as compared to students in the other conditions. Unfortunately, there was no longer any significant difference among the four conditions in the proportion of students who still scored in the depressed range or in degree of group interaction.

---

[2] Therapists were one first- and one second-year graduate students. Neither was religious and both reported feeling less comfortable though not antagonistic to the religious treatment.

[3] Twenty-seven percent of those students in the self-monitoring plus nondirective discussion group still scored in the depressed range.

Thus, similar to the findings reported by Jarvinen and Gold [61], mildly depressed students are able to reduce their level of depression through participating in an eight-session directed imagery therapy group of four weeks' duration, but the degree of benefit appears to diminish gradually over a six-week period following the end of treatment. Of particular interest in the Propst [63, 64] study are two additional factors. First, the reduction in level of depression as a result of directed imagery therapy was indicated by behavioral as well as self-report indices of depression, thus minimizing the likelihood that demand characteristics produced the decrease in depression. Second, and even more important, is the fact that Propst demonstrated the increased therapeutic efficacy of imagery which is geared specifically to the individual's value system.

Interested in the differential effectiveness of various aspects of Rational Emotive Therapy (RET) [70], Lipsky, Kassinove, and Miller investigated the immediate posttreatment changes in level of anxiety, depression, hostility, and neuroticism among thirty-seven female and thirteen male mental health clinic patients [71]. All patients were diagnosed as neurotic or suffering from adjustment reaction of adulthood, and they were assigned to one of five treatment conditions which were then divided into high and low IQ groups. Patients in the *Rational Emotive Therapy (RET)* condition were taught the basic principles of RET and how to use these principles to cope with the emotional upsets which brought about the need for treatment. These patients also were given a minimum of twelve ABC statements to analyze, were taught the eleven irrational ideas postulated by Ellis [70], and were given bibliotherapy and behavioral homework assignments when appropriate. Patients in the *RET plus Rational Role Reversal (RRR)* condition were treated similarly to those in the RET condition but they also were given one RRR exercise per therapy session beginning with the third treatment session. Each RRR exercise consisted of the therapist and patient reversing roles for 15 minutes. At the end of the twelve-week treatment period, each patient had participated in ten RRR's. Patients in the *RET plus Rational-Emotive Imagery (REI)* condition were treated similarly to those in the RET condition, but they also were given one REI scene per therapy session. Each REI scene lasted approximately 15 minutes; during this period the patient imagined a disturbing event to which he/she usually responded with an irrational thought and excessive emotion. He/she then imagined responding with rational thoughts which led to the experience of a new feeling which was less negative, excessive, and counterproductive. At the end of the twelve-week treatment period, each patient had participated in ten REI scenes. Patients in the *alternate treatment (AT)* control condition received a combination of supportive therapy and deep muscle relaxation training. Relaxation training exercises began with the third treatment session and lasted for approximately 20 minutes each session. At the end of the twelve-week treatment period, each patient had received two sessions of supportive therapy and ten sessions of combined supportive therapy and relaxation training. Patients in the *no contact (NC)* control condition were informed that they had been placed on a treatment waiting list. Patients in the three RET conditions and the AT condition met individually with one of two experienced therapists[4] for a 45-minute therapy session once per week for a total of twelve weeks. Patients in all five conditions were administered the dependent measures immediately before and after the twelve-week period. Both therapists were blind to the patients' pretreatment scores and remained so throughout the entire study.

Findings indicated that: 1) patients who participated in any of the three RET treatment conditions reported more RET content acquisition, less depression, and less neuroticism than those in the AT and NC conditions; and 2) patients in the RET plus RRR and RET plus REI conditions reported lower state anxiety than those in the AT and NC conditions and lower trait anxiety than those in the RET, AT, and NC conditions. Also, of particular interest is the finding that although high and low IQ patients acquired the principles and concepts of RET equally well, they responded differently to some of the treatment conditions: 1) low IQ patients reported lower depression than high IQ patients regardless of treatment modality, 2) high IQ patients in the RET plus REI condition reported less trait anxiety than low IQ patients in the same condition, and 3) low IQ patients in the AT condition reported less trait anxiety than high IQ patients in the same condition. Thus, once again, the use of directed imagery in therapy is demonstrated not only to be very effective in reducing depression but also to be particularly helpful in enhancing the therapeutic benefit of more purely verbal psychotherapeutic approaches. Also, of particular interest is the fact that although IQ does not seem to be a major factor affecting therapeutic benefit in this study, there is sufficient evidence to indicate the importance of balancing IQ across different treatment conditions.

A related study by Reardon and Tosi [72] investigated the immediate post-treatment effects and intermediate follow-up changes in self-concept and level of depression of thirty-two adolescent delinquent females who had experienced one of the following five conditions: 1) *Rational Stage Directed Imagery (RSDI)*[5], 2) a *cognitive behavioral treatment* approach which utilized vivid emotive imagery and intensive muscle relaxation, 3) a *cognitive treatment* utilizing rational restructuring, 4) a *placebo treatment*, or 5) *no treatment*. All patients in the four treatment conditions met one hour per week in their respective groups for six consecutive weeks during which time homework assignments also were utilized. At the end of six weeks, self report measures of self-concept and level of depression were obtained for patients in all five conditions.

---

[4] Each therapist had more than two years of training and supervised clinical experience in RET and behavior therapy. Both reported being equally committed to behavior therapy and RET.

[5] RSDI is a synthesis of sensory imagery, deep relaxation or hypnosis, and rational or cognitive restructuring which also includes the use of directed imagery to bring the patient through various developmental states (e.g., increased awareness of self and enviornment, re-experiencing through imagery of real life situations, etc.). It, therefore, has much in common with the previous RET plus REI condition [71].

Findings indicated that: 1) patients who had participated in the RSDI group reported a higher self-concept and a lower level of depression than patients in the remaining four conditions, and 2) patients who had participated in the cognitive rational restructuring group reported somewhat similar improvement. A two-month follow-up study, however, indicated that only those patients in the RSDI group still reported higher self-concept and lower depression. Thus, directed-imagery therapy can be useful not only in reducing level of depression but also in improving deficiencies in more global aspects of personality, such as self-concept and self-esteem, which are often characteristic of more chronic depressive disorders. Furthermore, it is encouraging that such gains can be maintained for at least two months after the cessation of a relatively brief six-week treatment period.

Taken together, the studies by Lipsky et al. [71] and Reardon and Tosi [72] offer encouraging evidence for the usefulness of imagery therapy in the treatment of patients whose difficulties include but are not limited to symptoms of depression. Of particular interest is the finding that therapeutic modalities which integrate nonverbal imagery techniques with verbal approaches appear to produce more extensive and long-lasting improvements, including lowered depression, less neuroticism, and improved self-concept.

Summary. The six studies reviewed above [58-61, 63, 64, 71, 72] provide the only evidence the author was able to obtain[6] which is directly relevant to the systematic use of imagery in alleviating depression. The fact that there have been relatively few studies of this nature is not very surprising, since such studies are particularly challenging endeavors which ideally require the collaborative efforts of several researchers and clinicians. It is, therefore, especially interesting that most of these studies were originally conducted as dissertation research projects.

Of these six studies only four [58-60, 71, 72] utilized patient populations; and only two [58-60] of these four studies utilized moderately to severely depressed psychiatric patients. Nevertheless, the findings from these six studies offer clear evidence that various types of directed imagery procedures, either alone or in combination with other cognitive and behavioral approaches, can reduce both self-report and behavioral indices of depression for mild to moderately depressed college undergraduate students [61, 63, 64], mental health center patients whose symptoms included depression [71], adolescent delinquent females whose symptoms included depression [72], and moderately to severely depressed psychiatric patients [58-60]. Furthermore, three studies [61, 63, 64, 72] provide evidence that, although the initial improvement in level of depression gradually diminishes over time, there are still some indications of continued improvement in level of depression for six weeks [63, 64], two months [72], and even

[6] Several other articles relevant to the therapeutic use of imagery were not obtainable [73, 74].

six months [61] after the cessation of relatively brief therapeutic interventions. Finally, it is particularly unfortunate that no outcome or follow-up study of the use of imagery in alleviating depression has yet utilized senior level clinicians to provide the treatment; and only a few outcome studies [58-60] and no follow-up studies have utilized moderately to severely depressed psychiatric patients. While such studies are clearly needed to determine the stability of therapeutic benefit for more seriously depressed populations, there is now considerable evidence indicating immediate, intermediate, and relatively long-term improvement in level of depression after relatively minimal directed-imagery therapy interventions lasting for as little as two to six weeks but no longer than twelve weeks. In addition, of particular interest is the finding that therapeutic interventions which integrate nonverbal imagery techniques with verbal approaches appear to produce more extensive and long-lasting improvements.

Implications for Future Research. The current findings offer considerable encouragement for further systematic study of the use of imagery in alleviating depression. Of particular clinical relevance would be the development of a comprehensive interdisciplinary research project geared toward investigating the integration of directed imagery techniques with more verbal approaches as well as the integration of interpersonal and psychopharmacological interventions. Such an endeavor represents a monumental undertaking and is, therefore, not likely to come about in the foreseeable future. In any case, collaborative investigators and independent researchers are recommended to consider the following suggestions in designing and conducting future research.

Population. It is particularly important that future research in this area utilize depressed psychiatric patients. With the recent development of the DSM-III [14], greater uniformity in diagnostic criteria is readily available nationally and internationally. Depressed psychiatric patients[7] who meet the DSM-III diagnostic criteria for major unipolar depressive disorder and those who meet the criteria for dysthymic disorder could be studied by researchers nationally and internationally thereby not only facilitating the possibility of establishing a comprehensive research network but also fostering the comparison of studies among different researchers. Furthermore, depressed psychiatric patients who meet various DSM-III criteria should be further subdivided according to current level of depression as measured by the Beck Depressive Inventory [11] or the Zung Self-Rating Depression Scale [62]. One could thereby determine whether depressed psychiatric patients differ in their response to the various imagery procedures according to their current level of depression [11].

In addition, various researchers already have indicated a number of other population variables which may affect therapeutic outcome and which, therefore,

---

[7]It is particularly important to be certain that there are no undiagnosed and/or untreated medical illnesses which could contribute to depression, and, therefore, could diminish the likelihood of clinical improvement regardless of the therapeutic intervention(s) employed.

are worthy of further investigation. Such population variables include IQ [71], sex [75], types of depression [58, 59], daydreaming patterns [58, 59], and attitudes toward various imagery procedures [63, 64].

Therapists. Another crucial variable which requires greater attention in future research concerns the level of experience and training of the therapists who provide treatment. The minimal criteria for therapist inclusion should be at least two to four years of experience in the particular cognitive, behavioral, or imagery modality, and in lieu of the foregoing, clearly demonstrable competence. The inclusion of even more experienced therapists would be still better.

The attitude of therapists toward a particular treatment modality is also a crucial variable. Propst was interested in controlling for therapist expectancies and therefore chose therapists who were not committed to the use of religious imagery [63, 64]. However, generally it is advisable to utilize therapists who are not only experienced in a particular modality but also convinced of its therapeutic efficacy. It is the author's contention that in actual practice, therapists cannot hope to be truly neutral and objective in providing treatment and that more naturalistic research should be conducted. Such research should take into consideration the fact that therapists generally become committed to a limited number of therapeutic modalities and develop their skills in these modalities to the exclusion of others; and that, where choice is available, patients often seek out a particular therapist because he/she is known to be committed to a particular point of view.

Finally, therapeutic differences which may arise secondary to the sex of the therapist also should be given greater attention in future research.

Cognitive, Behavioral, and Imagery Modalities. A major factor in future research concerns the types of therapeutic modalities which will be compared and contrasted with each other. Currently, there is sufficient evidence to indicate that most types of therapeutic interventions, including cognitive, behavioral, and directed imagery modalities, have been useful in alleviating depression in some instances. But the question that requires further investigation is whether a particular cognitive, behavioral, or imagery approach is better, either singly or in combination, than another for a particular type of depressed individual (depending upon, for instance, sex, age, IQ, severity of depression, type of depression, attitude about treatment, etc.). Another question that needs to be addressed is: What should be the minimal length of a therapeutic intervention to bring about meaningful and enduring improvement? Furthermore, will a particular cognitive, behavioral, or directed-imagery approach be more or less effective if antidepressant medications also are prescribed or if increased exercise and activity therapy are also a focus of treatment? Will differences arise if antidepressant medications or increased exercise and activity therapy are prescribed before or after the beginning of a particular cognitive, behavioral, or directed-imagery intervention?

It is also important to determine whether certain cognitive, behavioral, and directed imagery approaches produce better results through individual therapy, group therapy, or a combination of the two.

Furthermore, there is some evidence to suggest that the therapeutic efficacy of various directed imagery approaches may be improved if relaxation training and/or hypnotic procedures are utilized to enhance the imagery experience. Therefore, future research should take into consideration the importance of comparing the use of various directed imagery approaches with and without the use of relaxation training and with and without the use of hypnotic procedures.

Finally, while directed imagery clearly seems to be consistently more effective in alleviating depression than nondirected imagery approaches, there is considerable work to be done in determining the particular imagery content (e.g., aggressive, socially gratifying, positive, socially oriented, religious, neutral, etc.) which is more suitable for alleviating depression in a particular group of depressed people.

Control Groups. Future research not only should include more comparable treatment groups as outlined above, but also should include at least two treatment control conditions. One control condition should be a no treatment waiting list condition. The second control condition should consist of patients who are seen individually or as a group in consonance with the main treatment conditions but not exposed to a particular cognitive, behavioral, or directed imagery intervention.

Indices of Depression. Considerable evidence indicates that future therapy outcome depression research should utilize behavioral indices of depression as well as self-report measures. Of particular interest is the work of Schwartz and his colleagues [7, 56, 57, 75] who have utilized changes in facial electromiography (EMG) activity as a measure of current affective state. Research in the future should be conducted utilizing such behavioral indices of level of depression as: facial EMG activity, localization of gaze [58, 59], time productions [58, 59], verbal productions (e.g., creating a dream [58, 59]), mirth response [58, 59], and/or level of interpersonal interaction [63, 64]. In addition, future research may benefit from the use of weekly observational checklists for the presence or absence of various neurovegetative signs of depression as another behavioral index of degree of clinical improvement.

Although there are numerous self-report measures of affective state and trait, the most promising and widely used measures of level of depression include the Beck Depressive Inventory [11], the Zung Self-Rating Depression Scale (ZSDS) [62], the MMPI-D Scale [76], the Multiple Affect Adjective Checklist (MAACL) [77], and the Differential Emotions Scale (DES) [78]. The ZSDS offers the rater flexibility in stating on a 4-point scale the degree to which twenty particular statements are presently true for him/her. Thus, it is the author's contention that the ZSDS has particular advantages over the other self-rating depression scales. The DES also offers the rater flexibility in stating on a 5-point scale the degree to which thirty emotions are presently true for him/her. As such the DES has particular advantages over the MAACL which contains 132 adjectives which the rater must check or not depending on whether the adjective currently applies to him/her.

Other Issues Relevant to Research Design. It is particularly important to establish a similar level of expectancy and mental set among subjects across all treatment conditions. All subjects initially should be informed that one of the major purposes of the research project is to determine which individuals are more likely to show greater improvement in level of depression in the various treatment categories. Since many facilities have treatment waiting lists, subjects who are placed on a waiting list can be given the same initial expectancy and then later provided with a particular treatment approach as openings arise.

Furthermore, it is crucial that all subjects who participate in any research project be informed that they will be expected to complete various questionnaires and participate in various tasks to assess systematically the degree and rate of improvement attained; and that they will be asked to do so at three-month, six-month, and one-year follow-up intervals as well. Of course any subject who later decides not to do so should complete the therapy without interruption. However, in all research of this nature, the attempt should be made to minimize subject attrition as much as possible. Therefore, paying subjects to complete the questionnaires and to participate in the tasks (or reducing their therapy charges, in some instances) may help to reduce attrition. Finally, since follow-up studies are essential, paying subjects to complete questionnaires and/or to participate in tasks at three-month, six-month, and one-year follow-up intervals may help to reduce attrition in follow-up studies as well.

This leads to another crucial issue in clinical treatment and research design. The importance of follow-up contact in clinical care now is becoming increasingly recognized. Therefore, the need for follow-up studies in clinical research parallels the clinical needs of many populations served. Perhaps follow-up research studies could divide subjects into two groups: those who complete follow-up measures without additional review of previous therapeutic interventions and those who complete follow-up measures but with additional review and rehearsal of the previous therapeutic interventions (e.g., the particular cognitive, behavioral, or imagery approach previously employed).

Summary. Clearly, although the suggested future imagery therapy research would provide necessary information, many of the suggestions are difficult to bring into practice unless a comprehensive, multidisciplinary clinical research project were designed and conducted with the collaboration and commitment of numerous researchers and clinicians. From a General Systems Theory perspective[8], it is just such a research project which would provide the most fruitful information [18]. Since it is unlikely that such a collaborative project will arise in the near future, individual researchers at least can contribute

---

[8] For example, a biopsychosocial model of dysfunction postulates that all areas of an individual's life must be considered when attempting to resolve dysfunction and to maximize personal growth. (See Figure 1.)

to comparability across various research studies by endeavoring to follow many of the present suggestions as well as establishing additional common guidelines in the future.

Depressive Affect and Imaginal Processes

Although the following research does not investigate the systematic use of imagery to alleviate depression, the findings are particularly relevant to theoretical considerations regarding the relationship between depressive affect and imaginal processes.

Daydreaming Patterns. Much of the work on daydreaming patterns and imaginal processes accomplished thus far has been concerned with establishing normative data on nonpatient samples [79-81]. Work relating specific daydreaming patterns to aspects of psychopathology is sparse [82, 83]. Recently, however, Starker and Singer found the daydreaming of psychiatric patients to be less positive and less vivid with greater emphasis on fear of failure than the daydreams of college students [84]. Streissguth, Wagner, and Weschler also reported more dysphoric daydreaming among psychiatric patients than among nonpsychiatric medical patients and normals [83]. Another study by Starker and Singer found that psychiatric patients whose presenting symptoms included signs of depression reported fewer positive daydreams and fewer guilt daydreams as compared with psychiatric patients having few or no signs of depression [85]. Level of depression now has been found to relate positively to dysphoric daydreaming patterns and negatively to positive daydreaming patterns in college students [86], male prisoners [86], and depressed psychiatric patients [58]. Taken together, these findings are clearly consistent with clinical evidence of the presence of anhedonia and ruminative doubt in depression. Of particular interest is the fact that moderate to severe levels of depression appear to result in an inability to experience positive daydreams and memories spontaneously. This inability indicates the importance of induced directed imagery training in disrupting negative introspection and thereby reducing painful inner experience.

Neuropsychological Functioning and Imagery Capacity. Research conducted by Schwartz and his colleagues has focused on the study of involuntary facial muscle patterning in response to various types of affective imagery [56, 57, 75]. One study compared the changes in electromyography (EMG) activity from selected regions of the face of twelve nondepressed nonpatient females, six depressed nonpatient females, and six depressed female patients when asked to imagine happy, sad, and angry situations which had strongly evoked these emotions in the past [56]. Each person was asked to imagine each emotional situation for 3 minutes with the instruction to attempt to reexperience the feelings associated with the imagery. Also included as a nonspecific emotional control condition was the instruction to think for 3 minutes about the activities in a typical day with no requirement to experience any particular emotion. As might be expected, findings indicated that: 1) Each discrete emotional imagery period produced a different facial EMG activity pattern and 2) depressed subjects showed an attenuated EMG pattern for happiness as compared to normals. In addition, whereas nondepressed subjects more reliably generated a happy EMG pattern, depressed subjects more reliably generated the sad EMG pattern. Of particular interest is the finding that the typical day EMG pattern for nondepressed subjects is similar to the happy EMG pattern, while the typical day EMG pattern for depressed subjects is similar to the sad EMG pattern. Finally, subjective reports of experienced emotion generally mirror the differences found in facial EMG activity; nondepressed subjects report more happiness during happy imagery and typical day mentation than do depressed subjects. These findings were later replicated by Schwartz and his colleagues who also found that depressed patients who showed decreases in resting corrugator muscle tension (an EMG indicator of decreased level of depression) after two weeks of antidepressant treatment, showed corresponding improvements in clinical symptoms [87]. Taken together, these findings not only underscore the importance of facial EMG activity as an indicator of current affective state but also stress the importance of utilizing directed imagery and other structured cognitive techniques to disrupt typical daily patterns of negative introspection among depressives.

Additional studies by these researchers have indicated that: 1) Females show greater affective response to imagery and elicit greater facial EMG activity changes [88]; 2) females show greater laterality in zygomatic facial activity for positive versus negative emotions [88]; and 3) right-handed females show greater zygomatic activity on the right side of their faces for positive emotions [56, 75, 88]. One of the major implications of such findings is the hypothesis that the left cerebral hemisphere in right-handed subjects may play a special role in positive emotions.

Similarly, several studies by Tucker and his associates indicated that [89]: 1) College students who reported greater levels of depression also had less vivid visual imagery; 2) right-handed college students who experienced hypnotic induction of depressed mood as compared to hypnotic induction of euphoric mood reported a right-ear attentional bias and poorer visual imagery but no difference in arithmetical calculation ability; and 3) right-handed college students who experienced an induced depressed mood as compared to an induced euphoric mood showed less EEG activation of the left frontal hemisphere and greater activation of the right frontal hemisphere. Taken together, these studies indicate that depression may coincide with a decrement in the information processing capacity of the right hemisphere. Such findings parallel the evidence of right hemisphere dysfunction in depressed psychiatric patients in visuospatial task performance [90-92] and dichotic listening [93]. These studies also suggest that "there may be a functional and transient relationship between depressive affect and decreased information processing capacity of the right hemisphere." [89, p. 173] This possibility is consistent with another study which found that patients who showed alleviation of depressed mood after ECT also showed improvement in right hemisphere task performance [92].

Thus, mounting evidence indicates that the left cerebral hemisphere may play a special role in positive emotions [56, 75, 88]; whereas, the right frontal cerebral hemisphere may play a special role in negative emotions [89-93]. Of particular interest as well is the finding in several different kinds of studies [84, 89] that depressives have a decreased imagery capacity, suggesting that the effectiveness of imagery approaches in alleviating severe levels of depression may be enhanced with specific imagery training procedures. Furthermore, the finding that improvement in right hemispheric functioning corresponded with alleviation of depressed mood suggests that imagery approaches may be more effective in reducing depression when utilized in consonance with other treatment interventions [11].

Depressive Affect, Memory, and Attributions of Life Events.   Several studies have reported that memories which are inconsistent with induced mood are retrieved more slowly than memories which are consistent with induced mood [94, 95]. In addition, Clark and Teasdale found that depressed patients were more likely to recall memories of unhappy experiences on occasions when they were more depressed than on less depressed occasions [96]. Furthermore, they noted that depressed patients rated the current pleasantness of a recalled experience more negatively than the original level of pleasantness depending upon the current level of depression. Another study reported that when unipolar depressed patients were asked to imagine vividly six good and six bad events, they were more likely to attribute bad events to internal, stable, and global causes than were nondepressed medical patients [97]. A related study found that depressed patients showed greater depressive attributions in response to their most stressful life events than did nondepressed psychiatric patients, but there was no difference in their attributions in response to either hypothetical or experimental tasks [98]. These findings are consistent with clinical evidence that depressed patients are characterized by a negative attributional style in which bad outcomes are attributed to self-deficiencies which are chronic and pervasive whereas good outcomes are more likely to be related to external circumstances which are unstable and likely to be limited to a specific situation. Furthermore, Schwartz has reported the interesting finding that for nondepressed normal females, EMG zygomatic activity increases immediately during elation and then decreases over time, whereas facial EMG corrugator activity grows over time in response to depressive statements [57]. Thus, it may well be that the subjective and physiological experience of happiness as an emotion peaks and diminishes over time while depression as an emotion gradually builds over time. In the case of depressed patients, however, their experience of the depressive emotion persists and perhaps grows so pervasively over time that their feeling state stands in marked contrast to that of others around them who are experiencing normal fluctuations in their emotional life. Thus, depressed patients may be unable to find any suitable explanation for this contrast other than causes which reflect chronic, pervasive, self-deficiencies.

THE COGNITIVE-AFFECTIVE ASPECTS OF A BIOPSYCHOSOCIAL MODEL OF DEPRESSION

The reader will recall an earlier discussion in this chapter of some of the major theories and models of depression. While a comprehensive consideration of the many models of depression is beyond the scope of this paper, a brief discussion of some of the implications of imagery research for current theories and models of depression will be pursued. The reader is already somewhat acquainted with the author's present commitment [18] to a General Systems Theory biopsychosocial model of dysfunction (see Figure 1). Since an adequate discussion of the biopsychosocial model is available elsewhere [16-18] and in forthcoming articles, the following remarks will primarily be confined to a specific aspect of the biopsychosocial model—that is, the interaction between what happens intrapsychically on a cognitive and affective level in the depressed individual and what takes place externally.

Considerable research has underscored a cognitive-affective circular feedback model of depression [11, 58], and some evidence suggests that individuals may rehearse certain attitudes, beliefs, and themes (e.g., life scripts) in their fantasy life and thereby make them integrated aspects of their reality. Some researchers have emphasized the role of undesirable recent life events in the onset of depression [30] while other theorists have emphasized the role of previous losses and past traumatic life events in the development of depressive disorders. Incorporating many of the findings from cognitive, behavioral, and imagery approaches to the treatment of depression, Schultz suggested that undesirable recent life events may serve as cues to memories of more traumatic life events in the individual's past [58]. Such memories (whether verbal or visual-pictorial in nature) may then further exacerbate negative affect and further confirm the enduring aspects of the negative self-image, leading eventually to increased belief in the "reality" of the negative cognition. Figure 2 illustrates this process pictorially.

While the etiology of depression may continue to provoke controversy, there is considerable evidence that the conceptualization represented in Figure 2 is a useful and accurate model of the maintenance of depressive affect in seriously depressed individuals. Furthermore, this model is supported by more recent research regarding the chronic, pervasive self-deprecatory attributional style of depressives [96-98], their increased retrieval of negative experiences with increased depression [96], and the rating of recalled experiences as more negative at times of increased depression [96]. Additional research relevant to the neuropsychology of emotions, suggests that the left cerebral hemisphere may play a special role in positive emotions [57]; whereas, the right frontal hemisphere may

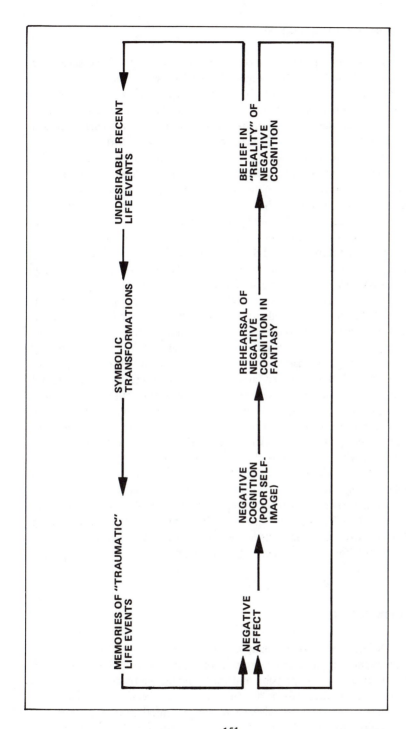

Figure 2. The cognitive-affective aspects of a biopsychosocial model of depression.

play a special role in negative emotions [89-93]. Further evidence suggests a possible transient functional relationship between depressive affect and decreased information-processing capacity of the right hemisphere [89, 92]. Thus, one implication of various treatment interventions, such as anti-depressant medication, ECT, increased exercise and activity therapy, and cognitive, behavioral, and imagery approaches, is that they all may serve eventually to disrupt the biopsychosocial final common pathway [13, 15] of the cognitive-affective circular feedback cycle, perhaps even at a metabolic or biochemical level in various cortical and/or subcortical areas of the brain. Whether various psychological treatment strategies may be useful only for less severe levels of depression [11] and more biological-biochemical interventions may be necessary initially in the treatment of more severe levels of depression remains to be established by further research.

If one were to develop a General Systems Theory approach with a biopsychosocial model of dysfunction, the various biological, psychological, and social interventions would not need to be seen as competitive but as complementary, with each serving a useful purpose. Perhaps it eventually will become well-established that severe levels of depression initially require a more biological-biochemical intervention. Nevertheless, current clinical experience as well as various research findings clearly indicate that various psychological (especially cognitive, behavioral, and imagery approaches) and social interventions are absolutely necessary in reducing other factors which contribute to depression and also are important in helping those who have resolved the acute phase of their depressive disorder to maintain their present level of functioning and lessen the likelihood of a relapse. Also, if further research regarding the use of imagery in alleviating depression can establish which types of depressed individuals respond better to which types of imagery contents and procedures as well as to other cognitive and behavioral approaches (either singly or in combination), clinicians will be able to assign more individuals to the best-suited psychological intervention, just as biological psychiatrists are now somewhat better able to determine which individuals will respond better to different types of antidepressant medications. Clearly, this is an exciting field of research with scientific and practical implications for improvement of the quality of life of many people throughout the world.

CONCLUSION

Considerable attention already has been focused upon the use of various imagery approaches in alleviating depression and upon the different theories and models of the etiology of depression and the maintenance of depressive affect. Such concerns are the major focus of this chapter but it would be deficient if it did not include some remarks relevant to the potential role of imagery approaches in health care regardless of one's particular theoretical orientation.

Those who seek psychotherapy are likely to vary not only in their current awareness of the effects of verbal and imagery experience on affective state but also in their current ability to utilize imagery as a cognitive coping device. Thus, the practitioner's initial step in using imagery in therapy is drawing attention to inner experience and verbal-imaginal processes and emphasizing the possibility of utilizing imagery as a resource in treatment. Also, the emphasis on imagery and stream of consciousness encourages the individual to become more aware of the many thoughts, fantasies, expectations, and judgments about people and situations which represent distorted and poorly integrated childhood experiences that no longer correspond appropriately to current life circumstances. Furthermore, imagery approaches in psychotherapy can serve to augment rather than replace more traditional verbal approaches. Of particular importance to the person seeking help, however, is not only the discovery of a new capacity to use imagery in generating positive affect and/or in shifting away from certain negative affective patterns, but also the realization that such a capacity is a skill which can be learned and perfected.

REFERENCES

1. W. James, *The Principles of Psychology:* Volume I and Volume II, Dover Publishing Company, New York, 1950.
2. J. L. Singer and K. S. Pope, The Use of Imagery and Fantasy Techniques in Psychotherapy, in *The Power of Human Imagination: New Methods in Psychotherapy*, J. L. Singer and K. S. Pope (eds.), Plenum Press, New York, pp. 3-34, 1978.
3. J. L. Singer, *Daydreaming*, Random House, New York, 1966.
4. A. Paivio, *Imagery and Verbal Processes*, Holt, Rinehart, and Winston, New York, 1971.
5. S. J. Segal (ed.), *Imagery: Current Cognitive Approaches*, Academic Press, New York, 1971.
6. J. L. Singer, Imagery and Daydream Techniques Employed in Psychotherapy: Some Practical and Theoretical Implications, in *Current Topics in Clinical and Community Psychology*, C. Spielberger (ed.), Academic Press, 1971.
7. G. E. Schwartz, Biofeedback as Therapy: Some Theoretical and Practical Issues, *American Psychologist, 28*, pp. 666-673, 1973.
8. O. C. Simonton and S. S. Simonton, Belief Systems and Management of the Emotional Aspects of Malignancy, *Journal of Transpersonal Psychology, 7*, pp. 29-47, 1975.
9. R. J. Green, Visual Imagery and Behavior Prescription in the Treatment of Parent-Child Conflict, in *Questions and Answers in the Practice of Family Therapy*, A. S. Gurman (ed.), Brunner/Mazel, Inc., New York, pp. 426-430, 1981.
10. J. Grinder and R. Bandler, *The Structure of Magic II*, Science and Behavior Books, Inc., Palo Alto, CA, 1976.

11. A. T. Beck, *Depression: Causes and Treatment*, University of Pennsylvania Press, Philadelphia, 1967.

12. S. J. Blatt, Levels of Object Representation in Anaclitic and Introjective Depression, *Psychoanalytic Study of the Child, 29*, pp. 107-157, 1974.

13. H. S. Akiskal and W. J. McKinney, Overview of Recent Research in Depression: Integration of Ten Conceptual Models into a Comprehensive Clinical Frame, *Archives of General Psychiatry, 32*, pp. 285-305, 1975.

14. ———, *Diagnostic and Statistical Manual of Mental Disorders:* 3rd Edition, American Psychiatric Association, Washington, D.C., 1980.

15. H. S. Akiskal and W. J. McKinney, Depressive Disorders, *Science, 182*, pp. 20-29, 1973.

16. I. M. Greenberg, General Systems: Social and Biological Interactions, unpublished manuscript, 1979.

17. D. A. Gross, Medical Origins of Psychiatric Emergencies: The Systems Approach, *International Journal of Psychiatry in Medicine, 11*:1, pp. 1-24, 1981.

18. K. D. Schultz, Humanistic Psychology and General Systems Theory: Toward a Humanistic General Systems Model of Mental Health Care, *Division of Humanistic Psychology, APA-Division 32 Newsletter, 10*:2, 1982.

19. D. M. Gallant and G. M. Simpson, *Depression: Behavioral, Biochemical, Diagnostic, and Treatment Concepts*, Spectrum Publications, New York, 1975.

20. E. E. Levitt and B. Lubin, *Depression: Concepts, Controversies, and Some New Facts*, Springer Publishing Co., New York, 1975.

21. A. S. Gurman (ed.), *Questions and Answers in the Practice of Family Therapy*, Brunner/Mazel, Inc., New York, 1981.

22. N. S. Jacobson and G. Margolin, *Marital Therapy*, Brunner/Mazel Publishers, New York, 1979.

23. L. R. Wolberg and M. L. Aronson (eds.), *Group and Family Therapy 1980*, Brunner/Mazel Publishers, New York, 1980.

24. L. R. Wolberg and M. L. Aronson (eds.), *Group and Family Therapy 1981*, Brunner/Mazel Publishers, New York, 1981.

25. P. D. McLean and A. R. Hakstian, Clinical Depression: Comparative Efficacy of Outpatient Treatments, *Journal of Consulting and Clinical Psychology, 47*:5, pp. 818-836, 1979.

26. M. Kovacs, Treating Depressive Disorders: Efficacy of Behavior and Cognitive Therapies, *Behavior Modification, 3*:4, pp. 496-517, 1979.

27. L. P. Rehm (ed.), *Behavior Therapy for Depression: Present Status and Future Directions*, Academic Press, New York, 1981.

28. A. T. Beck, A. J. Rush, B. F. Shaw, and G. Emery, *Cognitive Therapy of Depression*, Guilford Press, New York, 1979.

29. I. W. Miller, S. H. Klee, and W. H. Norman, Depressed and Nondepressed Inpatients' Cognitions of Hypothetical Events, Experimental Tasks, and Stressful Life Events, *Journal of Abnormal Psychology, 91*:1, pp. 78-81, 1982.

30. E. S. Paykel, J. K. Myers, M. N. Dienelt, G. L. Klerman, J. J. Lindenthal, and M. P. Pepper, Life Events and Depression: A Controlled Study, *Archives of General Psychiatry, 21*, pp. 753-760, 1969.

31. J. L. Singer, *Imagery and Daydream Methods in Psychotherapy and Behavior Modification*, Academic Press, New York, 1974.
32. J. Breuer and S. Freud, Studies in Hysteria, in *The Standard Edition*, Vol. 2, J. Strachey (ed.), Hogarth, London, 1955.
33. J. Reyher, Free Imagery: An Uncovering Procedure, *Journal of Clinical Psychology*, *19*, pp. 454-459, 1963.
34. J. Reyher, Emergent Uncovering Psychotherapy: The Use of Imagoic and Linguistic Vehicles in Objectifying Psychodynamic Processes, in *The Power of Human Imagination*, J. L. Singer and K. S. Pope (eds.), Plenum Press, New York, pp. 51-93, 1978.
35. C. G. Jung, *Analytical Psychology: Its Theory and Practice*, Vintage Books, New York, 1968.
36. R. Desoille, *Exploration de l'affectivité subconsciente par la méthode du rêve éveillé*, D'Autry, Paris, 1938.
37. R. Fretigny and A. Virel, *L'imagerie mentale*, Mont-Blanc, Geneva, 1968.
38. H. Leuner, Guided Affective Imagery (GAI): A Method of Intensive Psychotherapy, *American Journal of Psychotherapy*, *23*, pp. 4-22, 1969.
39. J. L. Moreno, Reflections on My Method of Group Psychotherapy and Psychodrama, in *Active Psychotherapy*, H. Grunwald (ed.), Atherton, New York, 1967.
40. E. Berne, *Games People Play*, Grove, New York, 1964.
41. F. Perls, *Gestalt Therapy Verbatim*, Bantam, New York, 1970.
42. H. R. Lewis and S. Streitfield, *Growth Games*, Harcourt, New York, 1971.
43. R. Assagioli, *Psychosynthesis: A Manual of Principles and Techniques*, Hobbs, Dorman, New York, 1965.
44. R. Gerard, Psychosynthesis: A Psychotherapy for the Whole Man, *Psychosynthesis Research Foundation*, *14*, 1964.
45. J. Wolpe and A. A. Lazarus, *Behavior Therapy Techniques: A Guide To the Treatment of Neuroses*, Pergamon Press, New York, 1966.
46. M. N. Chappell and T. I. Stevenson, Group Psychological Training in Some Organic Conditions, *Mental Hygiene of New York*, *20*, pp. 588-597, 1936.
47. J. R. Cautela and L. McCullough, Covert Conditioning: A Learning-Theory Perspective on Imagery, in *The Power of Human Imagination*, J. L. Singer and K. S. Pope (eds.), Plenum Press, New York, pp. 227-254, 1978.
48. A. Bandura, *Psychological Modeling*, Atherton, New York, 1971.
49. D. Meichenbaum, Toward a Cognitive Theory of Self-Control, in *Consciousness and Self-Regulation: Advances in Research*, G. Schwartz and D. Shapiro (eds.), Plenum Press, New York, 1975.
50. T. G. Stampfl and D. J. Levis, Essentials of Implosive Therapy: A Learning Theory Based Psychodynamic Behavior Therapy, *Journal of Abnormal Psychology*, *72*, pp. 496-503, 1967.
51. G. D. Read, *Childbirth Without Fear*, Harper, New York, 1953.
52. S. Starker, I. R. Levine, and G. J. Watstein, The Subjective Focus in a Group Oriented Treatment Program: A Preliminary Report, unpublished manuscript, 1974.
53. A. A. Lazarus, Learning Theory and the Treatment of Depression, *Behavior Research and Therapy*, *6*, pp. 83-89, 1968.

54. A. A. Lazarus, *In the Mind's Eye*, Rawson, New York, 1977.
55. E. Velton, A Laboratory Task for Induction of Mood States, *Behavior Research and Therapy*, 6, pp. 473-482, 1968.
56. G. E. Schwartz, P. L. Fair, P. Salt, M. R. Mandel, and G. L. Klerman, Facial Muscle Patterning to Affective Imagery in Depressed and Nondepressed Subjects, *Science, 192*, pp. 489-491, 1976.
57. A. D. Sirota and G. E. Schwartz, Facial Muscle Patterning and Lateralization During Elation and Depresion Imagery, *Journal of Abnormal Psychology, 91*:1, pp. 25-34, 1982.
58. K. D. Schultz, Fantasy Stimulation in Depression: Direct Intervention and Correlational Studies, unpublished doctoral dissertation, Yale University, 1976.
59. K. D. Schultz, Imagery and the Control of Depression, in *The Power of Human Imagination*, J. L. Singer and K. S. Pope (eds.), Plenum Press, New York, pp. 281-307, 1978.
60. V. Burtle, Learning in the Appositional Mind: Imagery in the Treatment of Depression, *Dissertation Abstracts International, 36*:11-B, p. 5781, 1976.
61. P. J. Jarvinen and S. R. Gold, Imagery as an Aid in Reducing Depression, *Journal of Clinical Psychology, 37*:3, pp. 523-529, 1981.
62. W. W. K. Zung, A Self-Rating Depression Scale, *Archives of General Psychiatry, 12*, pp. 63-70, 1965.
63. L. R. Propst, A Comparison of the Cognitive Restructuring Psychotherapy Paradigm and Several Spiritual Approaches to Mental Health, *Journal of Psychology and Theology, 8*:2, pp. 107-114, 1980.
64. L. R. Propst, The Comparative Efficacy of Religious and Nonreligious Imagery for the Treatment of Mild Depression in Religious Individuals, *Cognitive Therapy and Research, 4*:2, pp. 167-178, 1980.
65. ——, *The Holy Bible*, Thomas Nelson and Sons, New York, 1953.
66. F. McNutt, *Healing*, Ave Maria, Notre Dame, 1974.
67. M. Scanlon, *Inner Healing*, Paulist, New York, 1974.
68. N. V. Peale, *Dynamic Imaging*, Fleming Revell, Old Jappan, N.J., 1982.
69. A. T. Beck, *Cognitive Therapy and Emotional Disorders*, International Universities Press, New York, 1976.
70. A. Ellis, *Humanistic Psychotherapy: The Rational Emotive Approach*, Julian Press, New York, 1973.
71. M. J. Lipsky, H. Kassinove, and N. J. Miller, Effects of Rational-Emotive Therapy, Rational Role Reversal, and Rational-Emotive Imagery on the Emotional Adjustment of Community Mental Health Center Patients, *Journal of Consulting and Clinical Psychology, 48*:3, pp. 366-374, 1980.
72. J. P. Reardon and D. J. Tosi, The Effects of Rational Stage Directed Imagery on Self-Concept and Reduction of Psychological Stress in Adolescent Delinquent Females, *Journal of Clinical Psychology, 33*:4, pp. 1084-1092, 1977.
73. J. K. Morrison, Successful Grieving: Changing Personal Constructs Through Imagery, *Journal of Mental Imagery, 2*:1, pp. 63-68, 1978.
74. J. K. Morrison and M. S. Cometal, A Cognitive Reconstructive Approach to the Psychotherapeutic Use of Imagery, *Journal of Mental Imagery, 94*:1, pp. 35-42, 1980.

75. G. E. Schwartz, S. L. Brown, and L. Ahern, Facial Muscle Patterning and Subjective Experience During Affective Imagery: Sex Differences, *Psychophysiology*, *17*, pp. 75-82, 1980.
76. J. Overall, J. Butcher, and S. Hunter, Validity of the MMPI-168 for Psychiatric Screening, *Educational and Psychological Measurement*, *35*, pp. 393-400, 1975.
77. M. Zuckerman, B. Lubin, and S. Robins, Validation of the Multiple Affect Adjective Check List in Clinical Situations, *Journal of Consulting Psychology*, *29*, p. 594, 1965.
78. C. E. Izard, *The Face of Emotions*, Appleton-Century-Crofts, New York, 1971.
79. J. L. Singer and J. S. Antrobus, *Imaginal Processes Inventory: Revised*, Authors, New York, 1970.
80. J. L. Singer, *Daydreaming*, Random House, New York, 1966.
81. S. Starker, Aspects of Inner Experience: Autokinesis, Daydreaming, Dream Recall, and Cognitive Style, *Perceptual and Motor Skills*, *36*, pp. 663-673, 1973.
82. J. Cazeralon and S. Epstein, Daydreams of Female Paranoid Schizophrenics, *Journal of Clinical Psychology*, *22*:1, pp. 27-32, 1966.
83. A. P. Streissguth, N. Wagner, and J. Weschler, Effects of Sex, Illness, and Hospitalization on Daydreaming, *Journal of Consulting and Clinical Psychology*, *33*:2, pp. 218-225, 1969.
84. S. Starker and J. L. Singer, Daydreaming and Symptom Patterns of Psychiatric Patients: A Factor Analytic Study, *Journal of Abnormal Psychology*, pp. 567-570, 1975.
85. S. Starker and J. L. Singer, Daydreaming Patterns of Self-Awareness in Psychiatric Patients, *Journal of Nervous and Mental Disease*, pp. 313-317, 1975.
86. J. D. Traynor, Patterns of Daydreaming and Their Relationship to Depressive Affect, unpublished masters thesis, Miami University, Oxford, Ohio, 1974.
87. G. E. Schwartz, M. R. Mandel, P. L. Fair, P. Salt, M. Mieske, and G. L. Klerman, Facial Electromiography in the Assessment of Improvement in Depression, *Psychosomatic Medicine*, *40*, pp. 355-360, 1978.
88. G. E. Schwartz, G. L. Ahern, and S. L. Brown, Lateralized Facial Muscle Response to Positive Versus Negative Emotional Stimuli, *Psychophysiology*, *16*, pp. 561-571, 1979.
89. D. M. Tucker, C. E. Stenslie, R. S. Roth, and S. L. Shearer, Right Frontal Lobe Activation and Right Hemisphere Performance Decrement During Depressed Mood, *Archives of General Psychiatry*, *38*, pp. 169-174, 1981.
90. P. Flor-Henry, Lateralized Temporal-Limbic Dysfunction and Psychopathology, *Annual of the New York Academy of Science*, *280*, pp. 777-797, 1976.
91. S. G. Goldstein, S. B. Filskov, L. A. Weaver, et al., Neuropsychological Effects of Electroconvulsive Therapy, *Journal of Clinical Psychology*, *33*, pp. 798-806, 1977.

92. Z. Kronfol, K. Hamsher, K. Digire, et al., Depression and Hemispheric Functions: Changes Associated with Unilateral ECT, *British Journal of Psychiatry*, *132*, pp. 560-567, 1978.
93. A. Yozawitz and G. E. Bruder, Dichotic Listening Assymmetries and Lateralization Deficits in Affective Psychosis, presented at the American Psychological Association Annual Convention, Toronto, August 29, 1978.
94. R. O. Frost, M. Graf, and J. Becker, Self Devaluation and Depressed Mood, *Journal of Consulting and Clinical Psychology*, *47*:5, pp. 958-962, 1979.
95. J. D. Teasdale, R. Taylor, and S. T. Fogarty, Effects of Induced Elation-Depression on the Accessibility of Memories of Happy and Unhappy Experiences, *Behavior Research and Therapy*, *18*, pp. 339-346, 1980.
96. D. M. Clark and J. D. Teasdale, Diurnal Variation in Clinical Depression and Accessibility of Memories of Positive and Negative Experiences, *Journal of Abnormal Psychology*, *91*:2, pp. 87-95, 1982.
97. C. S. Raps, C. Peterson, K. E. Reinhard, L. Y. Abramson, and M. E. P. Seligman, Attributional Style Among Depressed Patients, *Journal of Abnormal Psychology*, *91*:2, pp. 102-108, 1982.
98. I. W. Miller, S. H. Klee, W. H. Norman, Depressed and Nondepressed Inpatients' Cognitions of Hypothetical Events, Experimental Tasks, and Stressful Life Events, *Journal of Abnormal Psychology*, *91*:1, pp. 78-81, 1982.

CHAPTER 6
Imagery and Cancer
HOWARD HALL

Imagery techniques were one of the earliest means of treating physical diseases. There is evidence that such procedures were employed in ancient Babylonia and Summaria [1]. It was as late as the 1960's however, that these imagery techniques began to receive serious scientific scrutiny [2]. Now, roughly twenty years later, imagery is being examined vigorously from a multitude of angles. It is interesting to note that Norman Vincent Peale recently published a book on imagery [3] and devoted several chapters to health-related uses of this technique. Imagery procedures also have been incorporated extensively into cognitive behavior therapy [4, 5].

Another relatively recent development is the use of imagery in facilitating physiological change with such techniques as autogenic training [6], hypnosis, biofeedback, relaxation procedures, and meditation [7]. These techniques are employed for what might be termed "stress-related illnesses." [8] A growing body of literature suggests a relationship between cancer and psychological factors such as stress [9-12]. After Achterberg and Lawlis [13] had reviewed about fifty studies in this area, they summarized them by stating that:

> There are two general conclusions that are evident from this research. First, regardless of instrumentation, there are enough replications to formalize the notion that a relationship does exist between the course of the disease and the psychological dimensions. Second, several premorbid psychological factors consistently appear. For example, the memory of an early home life inadequate to needs of support and security, a pre-disease event of an emotional loss, and

*This research was supported in part by grants from the Pennsylvania State University, Liberal Arts Research Office. The author wishes to express his deep appreciation to John Davis, JoAnn Gasporovic, Xyna Bell, Peter VanOot (Penn State), and Dr. Jeanne Achterberg (the University of Texas Health Science Center at Dallas), Dr. Patricia Norris (the Menninger Foundation) and Dr. Bernauer Newton (the Newton Center for Clinical Hypnosis). This chapter is dedicated to the memory of Dr. Carolyn Wood Sherif (1922-1982) of the Pennsylvania State University, who died of cancer before its completion.

feelings described as helplessness or hopelessness all emerged in several independent investigations [13, p. 19-22].

THE SIMONTONS' EARLY IMAGERY WORK

On the basis of the relationship between psychological factors and cancer, Carl Simonton, a radiation oncologist, and Stephanie Matthews-Simonton, a psychotherapist, developed a comprehensive treatment approach to cancer. Included within this package was one of the first reported uses of imagery and relaxation in the treatment of cancer. In addition to imagery exercises and the patient's regular cancer medication, the Simontons also conducted intensive psychotherapy to explore emotional issues surrounding the onset and course of the disease. This chapter will focus on the imagery component of the Simontons' program, which, of course, does not mean that it is the most important aspect of the treatment. It should be pointed out that their approach has continued to evolve [14] since the publication of their book, *Getting Well Again* [15].

The Simontons first employed imagery and relaxation in 1971 with a sixty-one year old man whose diagnosis was cancer of the throat [15]. The man's physical condition was very poor and his weight had dropped from 130 to 98 pounds. He also had difficulty breathing and swallowing his saliva. When the Simontons saw this patient his prognosis was that he had less than a 5 percent chance of surviving five years.

A program of imagery and relaxation was developed for this patient to practice three times a day. He was instructed to first concentrate on relaxing his muscles from his head down to his feet. Next he was to visualize being in a calm, pleasant place, such as the woods. Then he was to vividly picture the cancer in his body and to visualize his radiation treatment as "millions of tiny bullets of energy" striking all the cells in his body, both the normal and the cancerous cells. The cancer cells were seen as being "weaker and more confused" than normal cells, and thus they would die from the radiation; whereas, the healthy cells would be capable of repairing the damage. Then, the patient was asked to imagine his white blood cells carrying away the dead cancer cells through his kidneys and liver. Finally, he was able to picture his body as healthy and normal with the cancer tumors decreasing in size.

The results of this first case were remarkable. Halfway through the treatment, the cancer began to disappear and the patient started to eat and gain weight. Additionally, there were few negative side effects from the radiation treatment. After two months of continued improvement, there were no signs of cancer. It is interesting to note that this man successfully employed imagery on his own to decrease his arthritis symptoms and to restore full sexual activity after a twenty-year problem of impotence.

After this phenomenal case, the Simontons clinically tested this imagery/relaxation procedure with 159 highly selected patients diagnosed to have medically incurable cancer and given one year to live. Again, their results were quite remarkable. Of the original 159, sixty-three patients were alive two years after their diagnosis, that is, one year beyond their original prognosis. Furthermore, of those sixty-three patients who had practiced the imagery/relaxation technique and had survived beyond their prognosis, 22.2 percent demonstrated no evidence of cancer, 19.1 percent showed tumor regression, while 27.1 percent had stabilized. There was some new tumor growth for 31.8 percent of this group. This study had no untreated control groups, nonetheless the outcome was quite impressive.

The Simontons have argued that their approach to cancer treatment provides a means of actively involving patients in their own treatment. Even more interesting, they suggested that the imagery/relaxation component of their program leads to an enhancement of the patients' immune system. This intriguing hypothesis, however, was never directly tested as no blood measures of immune functioning were taken during the course of this initial study.

After extensive work with imagery in the treatment of cancer, the Simontons have identified eight features that they felt were important in altering the course of cancer. They noted that patients who did not do well often lacked one or more of these features.

1. The cancer cells are imagined as weak, confused, soft, and easily broken down. It is encouraging when the cancer cells are imagined to resemble hamburger meat or fish eggs, for example. On the other hand, ants or crabs, for example, are regarded as poor images, since they are quite tenacious.
2. The treatment is viewed as "strong and powerful" and able to interact with and destroy the cancer.
3. In the imagery, the healthy cells easily repair any treatment-related damage. The cancer cells, on the other hand, being "weak and confused," are not able to recover and consequently are destroyed.
4. The body's immune system or army of white blood cells are imagined to greatly outnumber and overwhelm the cancer cells.
5. Along the same lines, the white blood cells are viewed as aggressive and eager to destroy the cancer cells, and their victory seems inevitable.
6. It was important to visualize the dead cancer cells being flushed out of the body in a biologically natural way.
7. Patients should see themselves as healthy and disease free.
8. Finally, patients are to imagine themselves fulfilling their life's goals.

The Simontons recognized the importance of monitoring the contents of their patients' imagery after one individual's medical condition continued to deteriorate even though he was practicing imagery three times a day. It turned out that many of the above eight features were absent from his visualizations. For one, this patient described his cancer as a "big black rat." Clearly this rat was neither weak nor confused. His treatment, however, was viewed as "small yellow pills." The patient reported that occasionally the rat would eat one of these pills and become sick for a while but then recover and bite him even harder. In other words the cancer was visualized as stronger than the medical treatment. In addition, the white blood cells were described as eggs in an incubator waiting to be hatched. The Simontons pointed out that this patient had, in essence, visualized total suppression of his immune system. Thus, if a patient practices imagery regularly yet medically regresses, the content of the imagery may provide a key to understanding the lack of improvement.

THE IMAGE-CA TECHNIQUE
AND CANCER PREDICTIONS

Achterberg and Lawlis have extended the Simonton work on the content analysis of imagery, with the development of the Image-Ca technique [13]. This psychological instrument is employed to evaluate the effectiveness of the patient's imagery and also to predict the future development of the disease.

The Image-Ca has fourteen dimensions that are rated on a 5-point scale. The first three dimensions assess the imagery in terms of the (1) vividness, (2) activity, and (3) strength of the cancer cells. The more vivid, less active, and weaker these cells are imagined to be, the higher the person's score. Dimensions (4) through (8) measure the imagery for the white blood cells (i.e., the immune system). Specifically, they assess the (4) vividness, (5) activity, (6) proportions of white blood cells to cancer cells, (7) the size, and (8) strength of the white blood cells. The white blood cells should be seen vividly, they should appear active, larger and stronger than the cancer cells, and they should outnumber the enemy. Dimensions (9) and (10) evaluate the imagery of the medical treatment in terms of its (9) vividness and (10) effectiveness. Again, the more vividly the treatment is imagined and the more effective it is seen to be, the higher the score.

Imagery also is assessed along the dimension of (11) concrete or symbolic. The more symbolic the imagery is, the higher the score. For example, visualizing the white blood cells as white knights would be considered highly symbolic. Dimension (12) evaluates the overall strength of the imagery on a scale ranging from very weak to very strong. Dimension (13) deals with the patient's regularity in practicing imagery or thinking about his/her disease. This scale ranges from not imaging to imaging extremely frequently.

Finally, the last dimension (14) is the examiner's prognosis on a scale ranging from a continued active disease state to rapid remission. This last dimension requires a certain degree of clinical judgment, and it may be omitted for inexperienced examiners. With all fourteen dimensions, a total score can range from 247 or greater to 109 or less. With only the thirteen dimensions, the range is from 165 or greater to 86 or less.

The administration of the Image-Ca initially involves tape-recorded relaxation exercises, followed by instructions to visualize the white blood cells, cancer cells, and medical treatment. Unlike the Simontons' approach, however, the Image-Ca evaluation does not provide any suggestions concerning the form the images should take. As you will recall, the Simontons at times suggested that the cancer be visualized as hamburger meat and the radiation as bullets of energy [13].

Achterberg and Lawlis have their patients draw their images of their tumors, white blood cells, and medical treatment [13]. Subsequently, a structured interview is given so that the fourteen dimensions can be scored on the 5-point scale with 1 representing "weak or ineffective" visualization and 5 indicating "strong or most desirable" imagery [13].

The reliability and validity of the Image-Ca was examined within two normalization studies [13] employing samples from two different populations of cancer patients. The first study employed a group of fifty-eight patients having metastasized cancer with roughly a 0.05 chance of surviving five years. This group was composed of mostly white, middle class, highly educated individuals. The second study involved a group of twenty-one racially mixed cancer patients from a low socioeconomic level.

When the Image-Ca was administered to these two different populations, good intercorrelational and interrater reliability for both groups were obtained. Of greater interest, however, was the validity data from these two studies. In the first study an attempt was made to predict the patient's health status with the Image-Ca at a two-month follow-up. When a multiple regression analysis was performed on all fourteen dimensions of the Image-Ca scale, it made correct predictions for 93 percent of the patients that showed a favorable prognosis at a two-month follow-up. The individuals in this category scored 198 or above on the Image-Ca. This instrument also predicted correctly for 100 percent of the patients who showed an unfavorable prognosis at the follow-up period. In this group, all subjects who score 150 or below on the Image-Ca demonstrated new cancer growth or died. The middle range of the Image-Ca (i.e., 198-150) was not reliably predictive.

When the clinical opinion dimension was omitted from the total score [14], the predictive validity of the tool was still good for the uppermost and lowermost range of the Image-Ca scale, but it was more powerful when the full assessment was used.

In the second study, concurrent validation was attempted by correlating the Image-Ca with social workers ratings of the patients' general activity, working ability, and social adjustment. A Patient Status Form was employed to obtain these ratings. The results of the second study revealed significant concurrent validity between the Image-Ca and these ratings.

Achterberg and Lawlis [13] employ imagery not only for assessment purposes but also for the treatment of cancer and other diseases [14]. They, like the Simontons, feel that imagery provides patients the opportunity to participate in their rehabilitation process [15]. Also, they state that counterproductive imagery can be altered, although sometimes with difficulty [13].

The observation that the Image-Ca predicts future disease conditions was supported by findings from an earlier study by these same authors [16] that demonstrated that psychological instruments, including the Image-Ca, accurately predict the follow-up disease status; whereas, the blood chemistry data only provide information about the current disease state and are not predictive of later disease conditions. The other psychological tests employed within this battery were the Minnesota Multiphasic Personality Inventory, Locus of Control Scales, Fundamental Interpersonal Relations Orientation Test, Bem's Sex Role Inventory, and the Profile of Mood States. The blood chemistry data included measurements of complete blood count: free fatty acids, cortisol, cholesterol, acid phosphatase, lacticdehydrosenase, and alkaline phosphatase.

Achterberg and Lawlis's research on employing psychological instruments, such as the Image-Ca, to predict the outcome of cancer is a very exciting area of investigation. However, the question still remains: How can imagery have an impact on a physiological disease process? The Simontons argued that imagery can enhance general immune functioning [15], and Achterberg and Lawlis also maintained that the imagery of the white blood cells in particular, their vividness, activity, size, and strength, is more important in determining a short-term prognosis of the disease than other dimensions on the Image-Ca [13]. There is much suggestive evidence that imagery can influence the immune system. But, this interesting hypothesis has never been directly tested: The Simontons never took direct measures of immune system change in their clinical study, and Achterberg and Lawlis also did not observe functional changes in immune response, resulting from particular types of images.

The present author, along with two medical colleagues [17] (Hall, Longo, and Dixon, in preparation), conducted a study to examine the effects of imagery and hypnosis on immune responses, as assessed by traditional measures of lymphocyte function. Hypnosis, instead of relaxation, was employed for several reasons. For one, it is very similar to the relaxation technique used by the Simontons and Creighton [15, 18]. Secondly, the present author is experienced in the use of hypnosis for pain reduction with cancer patients. Also there is both clinical and experimental evidence in the literature which suggests that hypnosis can result in an inhibition of immune reactions [19]. In addition, Bowers and Kelly argued that the patients who improved in the Simonton study may have been highly hypnotizable individuals [18]. This may be so for only 5 percent of Simonton's private practice patients elected to participate in a hypnoticlike treatment approach, and 5 percent is close to the proportion of the general population that is highly hypnotizable. Thus, the Simontons may have inadvertently selected for such subjects [18]. However, they did not assess for hypnotizability, to determine the importance of this factor. Given the above factors, an experiment was designed to examine the effects of hypnosis and imagery on T and B cell immune functions.

EXPERIMENTAL STUDIES ON
IMAGERY AND BLOOD MEASURES
OF IMMUNE RESPONSES

Hall, Longo, and Dixon investigated the use of hypnosis to increase immunity function in twenty healthy individuals, ages twenty-two to eighty-five [17]. This broad age range was employed because research has shown that increasing age appears to decrease immune functioning. Also as one grows older, there is an increase in the production of cancer cells, possibly due to an immune deficiency [20].

The first step involved taking a 25cc sample of blood from each subject to provide prehypnosis baseline data of lymphocyte function. Subsequently, subjects were hypnotized with a relaxation induction. During hypnosis they were asked to imagine their white blood cells as "strong," "powerful" sharks with teeth that attacked and destroyed "weak," "confused" germ cells that caused colds and the flu. Following hypnosis subjects were given written and verbal instructions in self-hypnosis and asked to practice twice each day until the second session one week later. One hour after the end of hypnosis, another 25cc posthypnosis blood sample was taken. One week later, subjects returned for their second session during which hypnosis and imagery exercises were repeated and a third blood sample was drawn. The purpose of this second session was to determine the effects of practice on hypnosis and immune function. After completing both hypnosis sessions, each subject was individually assessed on hypnotizability with the Stanford Hypnotic Susceptibility Scale, Form C [21].

Two major findings emerged from this study. First, when subjects were divided into a young and an old group by median split at age fifty, the younger group had an overall higher level of immune functioning when in vitro mitogen analysis of the blood was done using pokeweed. This result was expected; but more interesting was the finding which emerged from a comparison between baseline data, the data collected one hour post hypnosis, and that gathered one week post hypnosis. When this was examined, only the younger group demonstrated a statistically significant increase following hypnosis one week later.

Of greatest interest, however, were the data on hypnotizability. For analysis purposes a median split divided subjects into a high and low hypnotizable group. Hypnotizability ranged from 3 to 11 with 7 as the median score. When lymphocyte count was examined there was a significant increase from baseline to one hour post hypnosis for only the high hypnotic subjects. For this group, the increase in lymphocyte count one week later was not maintained at the one hour level. The decrease was not to the baseline level but did approach statistical significance. The low hypnotizable subjects, on the other hand, did not show any significant changes across the three blood measures.

Thus, this study indicates that hypnosis and imagery may result in an increase in immune function for certain individuals. Further research is required to determine what component of this procedure was responsible for the observed increases. Goldwyn found that hypnosis with only suggestions of relaxation does not result in any significant changes in the number of white blood cells or lymphocytes [22]. Thus, the relaxation aspect of hypnosis may not have been solely responsible for the observed increases in immune functioning.

Our findings of alterations in lymphocyte function with hypnosis and imagery have been supported by research by Smith, Schneider, and Whitcher [23], who examined the effects of imagery and relaxation on a class of white blood cells called neutrophils. These authors found selected changes in the number, adherence, and shape of neutrophils as a function of the type of imagery used. In one study subjects were asked to imagine their white blood cells (i.e., neutrophils) leaving the area of venepuncture, becoming "sticky" and changing shape. Blood samples were drawn before and after the imagery/relaxation procedure.

The blood tests revealed a statistically significant drop in the number of neutrophils from 8,200 (preimagery) to 6,400 (postimagery). The adherence measure showed an unexpected decrease from baseline after imagery, in spite of the instructions to imagine the white blood cells becoming "sticky." There were no significant changes in the shape of the cells from preimagery to postimagery.

Thus, Smith, Schneider, and Whitcher were able to demonstrate a change in the number of white blood cells with their imagery/relaxation technique but failed to find a change on adherence [23]. They suggested that this negative finding may have resulted because there was not the necessary number of white blood cells present in order to demonstrate a reliable effect. In order to test that hypothesis, they conducted another study: Subjects were instructed to imagine their white blood cells not leaving the area of venepuncture but becoming "sticky" and changing shape.

The results from this study were even more interesting. They found no significant changes in the number of neutrophils from preimagery to postimagery. However, there was a significant increase in adherence. These directional changes in blood chemistry resulting from imagery, indicate that the basis of these effects is not simply relaxation. Such selected alterations suggest more higher-level central nervous system mechanisms [19].

CONCLUDING REMARKS

Imagery approaches to cancer have generated a great deal of controversy. A recent *Psychology Today* article by Maggie Scarf was entitled: "Images that Heal: A doubtful idea whose time has come." [24] This article attacked the underlying assumptions of the Simonton approach, particularly the relationship of stress, the immune system, and human cancers. She and others [17] also criticized the methodology employed by the Simontons in their clinical study.

Susan Sontag also has criticized psychological approaches to cancer, such as the use of imagery, on the grounds that they place blame on the patient for the development of his / her illness [25]. One of the major problems with this type of argument is that it assumes that imagery/relaxation techniques have no effect on cancer, and this has not been demonstrated. Also, this kind of criticism confounds psychological causality with treatment. That is to say, cancer may be treated with psychological procedures although it may not have been caused by such variables.

My reading of the literature in this area does not permit me to reach any strong conclusions at this point. It can safely be said, however, that imagery is far from being a "doubtful idea whose time has come." On the contrary, it promises to be a viable adjunct to traditional cancer treatment as well as a means of determining the prognosis of the disease. Also, imagery may provide a means of altering blood function, which has tremendous implications for a variety of medical disorders. Further research, of course, is needed to clarify many of these issues.

It is apparent that we are far from an understanding of the underlying mechanisms by which imagery can alter cancer or immune function. For example, it has been argued that the positive treatment effects observed when imagery techniques were employed, may have nothing to do with underlying immunological changes [17, 24]. Thus, these clinical improvements in cancer may have resulted from some other unknown process. It should be pointed out that there are reports in the literature of cancer regression due to procedures that do not employ imagery, such as intensive nonfocused meditation [26-28] and an imageless type of deep hypnotic inductions [29]. These types of relaxation procedures are apparently very different from those employed in the imagery/relaxation techniques reviewed in this chapter. They are also quite different from the progressive relaxation variety employed in behavior therapy programs [30]. The question of how these nonimagery procedures work or how they are similar to imagery techniques, cannot be answered at this time.

After reviewing the literature on imagery and cancer, it is quite apparent that fewer polemics and more hard scientific data are needed. The current studies being done in this area are quite promising. It must be kept in mind that this is not just a philosophical issue but, more importantly, an empirical one that potentially can be answered.

Finally, the question of the use of these imagery procedures as an adjunct to cancer treatment, given our current level of understanding, should be addressed. This issue was carefully considered by Achterberg and Lawlis [14]. They stated that:

> Our bias is that treatment must be as well grounded in a data base as possible but that to withhold psychological intervention until 'all the facts are in' is unethical. The facts may never be 'all in.' However, there are sufficient data currently available to warrant pursuing a psychological approach, together with medical treatment, in the best interests of patients with malignancy." [14, p. 129]

REFERENCES

1. M. Samuels and N. Samuels, *Seeing With the Mind's Eye: The History, Techniques and Uses of Visualization*, Random House, New York, p. 28, 1975.
2. R. R. Holt, Imagery: The Return of the Ostracized, *American Psychologist*, *19*, pp. 254-264, 1964.
3. N. V. Peale, *Imaging: The Powerful Way to Change Your Life*, Guidepost, Carmel, New York, p. 92, 1982.
4. W. E. Craighead, A. E. Kazdin, and M. J. Mahoney, *Behavior Modification: Principles, Issues, and Applications*, Houghton Mifflin Company, Boston, p. 153, 1981.
5. A. Lazarus, *In the Mind's Eye: The Power of Imagery for Personal Enrichment*, Rawson Associates Publishers, Inc., New York, p. 146, 1978.
6. J. H. Schultz and W. Luthe, *Autogenic Therapy Volume 1 Autogenic Methods*, Grune and Stratton, New York, p. 159, 1969.
7. K. R. Pelletier, *Mind as Healer Mind as Slayer: A Holistic Approach to Preventing Stress Disorders*, A Delta Book, New York, p. 191, 1979.
8. H. Selye, *Stress Without Distress*, A Signet Book, New York, p. 6, 1974.
9. R. Ader (ed.), *Psychoneuroimmunology*, Academic Press, New York, p. 31, 1981.
10. K. Bammer and B. H. Newberry (eds.), *Stress and Cancer*, C. J. Hogrefe, Inc., Toronto, p. 137, 1981.
11. C. Holden, Cancer and the Mind: How are They Connected?, *Science*, *200*: 23, pp. 1363-1369, 1978.
12. J. Tache, H. Selye, and S. B. Day (eds.), *Cancer, Stress, and Death*, Plenum Publishing Corporation, New York, p. 11, 1979.
13. J. Achterberg and G. F. Lawlis, *Imagery of Cancer*, Institute for Personality and Ability Testing, Champaign, Illinois, p. 19, 1978.
14. J. Achterberg and G. F. Lawlis, *Bridges of the Bodymind: Behavioral Approaches to Health Care*, Institute for Personality and Ability Testing, Inc., Champaign, Illinois, p. 42, 1980.
15. O. C. Simonton, S. Matthews-Simonton, and J. L. Creighton, *Getting Well Again: A Step-by-Step, Self-Help Guide to Overcoming Cancer for Patients and Their Families*, Bantam Books, New York, p. 114, 1978.
16. J. Achterberg, G. F. Lawlis, O. C. Simonton, and S. Matthews-Simonton, Psychological Factors and Blood Chemistries as Disease Outcome Predictors for Cancer Patients, *Multivariate Experimental Clinical Research*, *3*:3, pp. 107-122, 1977.
17. H. R. Hall, S. Longo, and R. H. Dixon, Hypnosis and the Immune System: The Effect of Hypnosis on T and B Cell Function, in preparation, 1982.
18. K. S. Bowers and P. Kelly, Stress, Disease, Psychotherapy, and Hypnosis, *Journal of Abnormal Psychology*, *85*:5, pp. 490-505, 1979.
19. H. R. Hall, Hypnosis and the Immune System: A Review with Implications for Cancer and the Psychology of Healing, *American Journal of Clinical Hypnosis*, *25*, pp. 92-103, 1983.
20. M. E. Weksler and T. H. Hutteroth, Impaired Lymphocyte Function in Aged Humans, *Journal of Clinical Investigations*, *53*, pp. 99-104, 1974.

21. A. M. Weitzenhoffer and E. R. Hilgard, *Stanford Hypnotic Susceptibility Scale, Form C*, Consulting Psychologists Press, Palo Alto, California, 1962.
22. J. Goldwyn, The Effect of Hypnosis on Basal Metabolism, *Archives of Internal Medicine, 45*, pp. 109-114, 1930.
23. C. W. Smith, J. Schneider, and S. Whitcher, personal communication, July 16, 1982.
24. M. Scarf, Images that Heal: A Doubtful Idea Whose Time Has Come, *Psychology Today*, pp. 32-46, September 1980.
25. S. Sontag, *Illness as Metaphor*, Vintage Books, New York, p. 55, 1978.
26. A. Meares, Regression of Osteogenic Sarcoma Metastases Associated with Intensive Meditation, *The Medical Journal of Australia, 2*, pp. 433, 1978.
27. A. Meares, Regression of Cancer of the Rectum After Intensive Meditation, *The Medical Journal of Australia, 2*, pp. 539-540, 1979.
28. A. Meares, A Form of Intensive Meditation Associated with the Regression of Cancer, *American Journal of Clinical Hypnosis, 25*, pp. 114-121, 1983.
29. B. W. Newton, The Use of Hypnosis in the Treatment of Cancer Patients, *American Journal of Clinical Hypnosis, 25*, pp. 104-113, 1983.
30. D. A. Bernstein and T. D. Borkovec, *Progressive Relaxation: A Manual for Therapists*, Research Press, Champaign, Illinois, 1973.

CHAPTER 7

Imagery and the Treatment of Phobic Disorders

BEVERLY K. HABECK
AND ANEES A. SHEIKH

Although semanticists may be reluctant to renounce their allegiance to Whorf's hypothesis [1], overwhelming evidence exists to dispute the notion that language is the limit of one's world. Imagistic thought integrates and processes experience. It also prompts new solutions to problems which eluded prior lexical resolution. Currently, imagistic thought is regarded to be equal in importance to man's enactive and lexical modalities [2]. Hence, despite Watson's [3] efforts to purge empirical inquiry of all things cognitive, imagery is enjoying an experimental, theoretical, and clinical resurrection [4, 5].

A diversity of psychotherapeutic techniques which use imagery prominently have become well-accepted and have served to prompt new clinical uses of imagery. Cohen observes that therapeutic ingenuity is seen perhaps with the greatest frequency in the clinical treatment of phobic disorders [6]. Therefore, it is not surprising that the power of human imagination has been used differentially by a wide range of therapists to relieve the anxiety or fears of their phobic patients.

THE FRIGHTENING PROPERTIES OF FEAR

Fear is acknowledged universally as one of man's primary motivating drives. Although fear often serves an essential function to protect the individual and preserve the species, it has an equally powerful potential to disrupt or destroy the quality of its victims' lives.

The ultimately debilitating dimensions of fear are illustrated dramatically in Huyghe's account [7]:

In the 1930's one celebrated doctor in India demonstrated the power of the mind and imagination in an astonishing and deadly experiment he performed on a criminal who had been condemned to death. The doctor wanted to learn whether the human imagination could kill. The convict was an assassin of distinguished rank and court permission had been obtained to bleed him to death inside the prison so that his family might be spared the disgrace of a public hanging. When the time came, the condemned man was blindfolded, led into a room, and strapped to a table. Under it a container was set up to drip water gently into a basin on the floor. The doctor pricked the skin of the man's arms and legs near his veins as if to bleed him and at the same time started the water dripping. The convict believed that the dripping he heard was his blood flowing out, and when the sound of the dripping water at length stopped, he passed out and died—without actually losing one drop of blood [7, p. 20].

Hence, one deduces that fear is a formidable adversary, whether the danger is real or whether it is imaginary.

THE NATURE OF PHOBIC DISORDERS

Errera provides a historical perspective, noting that the term *phobia* is derived from the name of the Greek god, Phobos, who had the ability to terrorize the enemy [8]. Nearly 2,000 years ago, Celsus first used the term "hydrophobia" to describe the primary symptoms of rabies. In Western Europe, until the seventeenth century, the treatment of phobias, regarded either as demonphobias, or theophobias, was relegated exclusively to theologians and philosophers. It was not until 1801 that the word *phobia* appeared as a generic term in the psychiatric literature. From that point forward, voluminous amounts of material documenting a wide spectrum of unreasonable fears have accumulated. Most of the early descriptions of patients' symptoms, the frequency of their occurrence, and the nature of the fears are consonant with today's clinical observations. The American Psychiatric Association estimates that 2 to 4 percent of the population has, at some time, been subject to an anxiety disorder [9]. According to the DSM III, phobic disorders fall into one of three major categories.

Agoraphobia is typified by an increasingly irrational fear and subsequent avoidance of being alone. This disturbance also engenders a fear of being powerless or incapacitated in public places, where escape would be impossible or help would be unavailable. Hence, these individuals avoid crowded settings, such as theaters and stores as well as public transportation or elevators. Agoraphobia, more frequently found among women, may progressively delimit normal activities. In the most severe occurrences of this illness, individuals may choose to remain housebound rather than to confront external, anxiety-producing situations.

Social phobias constitute the second category, the rarest of the three major phobic disorders. The prominent characteristic of this phobia is an irrational fear of being vulnerable to the scrutiny of others. Individuals will avoid those situations wherein others are likely to observe them behaving in an embarrassing fashion. Another dimension of the disorder is the fear that others will notice the anxiety. Although the individuals reason that the fear response is inappropriate, they nevertheless change their life style in order to avoid the phobic situation. Some of the more frequently diagnosed social phobias include: eating in public, using public lavatories, public speaking, or, writing in a situation where others might observe hand tremors.

Simple phobias comprise the third category and are the most common ones. A simple phobia is evidenced by an irrational fear and avoidance of a specific stimulus object or situation (exclusive of situations defined above). The level of impairment is dependent upon the frequency with which the phobic object or situation is confronted. Specific animal phobias (fear of rats, dogs, and insects), as well as a fear of heights and small places are among the most common of the simple phobias.

There are at least seventy-six discrete phobias, yet all share four characteristics [10]. Any phobia is a particular occurrence of fear which "1) is out of proportion to the demands of the situation, 2) cannot be explained or reasoned away, 3) is beyond voluntary control, 4) leads to avoidance of the feared situation." [11, p. 3]

Acquisition of Phobias

Early theorists claimed that phobic behavior was the result of maladaptive remnants of ancestral experience [12] or evidence of the nervous system's degeneration [13, 14].

Marks acknowledged that fear of certain stimuli is evident at birth, independent of experience [11]. An infant's startle reflex occurs commonly in response to novel, unexpected, or powerful stimuli. Marks suggests that the child's experience influences the manifestation of this innate fear response, that is, learning often diminishes its impact. That innate fear mechanism, however, provides a predisposition for the formation of phobias.

The paradigm provided by learning theory affords the most precise explanation of the acquisition of simple phobias. Summarized briefly, avoidance behavior is motivated by a classically conditioned fear; the avoidance behavior helps to reduce the level of fear, and it simultaneously becomes a negative reinforcement, strengthening the avoidance behavior [15-17]. From this perspective, neurotic symptoms may be understood as maladaptive habits that have been learned [18]. Marks notes that vicarious conditioning of a phobia (observing a model's response to noxious stimuli) is a variation of the simple learning paradigm [11]. The learning-theory paradigm, however, cannot explain the more gradual acquisition of a phobia, particularly those instances when a patient is unable to remember a single traumatic event [19]. Nor has learning theory explained those cases when abreaction recalls the generative trauma to awareness and relieves the patient of phobic symptoms [11].

In contrast, the psychodynamic interpretation of phobia relies upon the controversial constructs of repression and displacement to explain the origin of the fear reaction [20]. Psychoanalytic theory presumes that the presence of a phobia prevents the patient from understanding the true unconscious source of his/her anxiety. That is, the phobia is regarded as a set of symbols in which the genuine source of fear remains hidden from the conscious mind.

Personality Characteristics of Phobic Individuals

Most phobias appear to be much more common among women than among men. Animal phobias (which are often treated as a separate category) almost invariably have their onset in childhood [21]. All other phobias typically begin during young adulthood. About two-thirds of the phobics seeking treatment can vividly recall and describe the first phobic experience [21]. As DuPont points out, there are several personality characteristics associated with phobic people [21]:

1. Generally, they have been, since childhood, hyperreactive to a variety of stimuli, expressing their emotions in an excessive manner.
2. Already as youngsters, they have been obsessional and perfectionistic. They carry out a task either perfectly or terribly, never passably.
3. From an early age, they generally have found it difficult to cope with the unpleasant facets of life, such as suffering and death. Although they seldom are overcome by the events of the present, they suffer acutely from fears of what the future may hold.
4. Since future thinking is an essential ingredient of intelligence, it is not surprising to find that most phobic people are intelligent.
5. They are keenly sensitive to their own feelings and also to those of others, and they assume that others are equally aware. Often phobic people suffer because they feel that they have made a fool of themselves, while others did not even notice anything unusual in their behavior. Related to phobic persons' keen awareness of others is their strong need to please others and also their overwhelming concern with avoiding embarrassment.

Seeking Treatment for Phobias

Individuals suffering from simple phobias rarely seek treatment because they suffer no serious impairment in the management of their daily lives. Yet, experimental groups frequently include volunteers with simple phobias for purposes of research. Social phobias are uncommon in clinical practice, while agoraphobia is treated with the greatest frequency. Cohen observes that individuals seeking treatment often suffer from a variety of emotional disorders, of which phobic anxiety is only one component [6].

Paul and Bernstein have identified five prominent reasons why individuals suffering from phobia are motivated to seek treatment [22]: 1) they experience frequent or extreme distress as the result of irrational fear; 2) the physiological response to anxiety prompts psychosomatic disorders, such as peptic ulcers, migraine headaches, or high blood pressure; 3) anxiety interferes with efficient cognitive and/or motor functioning; 4) the severity of the inhibitory behavior reduces nearly all external reinforcement, resulting in depressive reactions; or, 5) individuals have adopted bizarre or socially unacceptable avoidance behaviors to reduce their anxiety reactions.

A phobia, then, refers to an intricate network of affective, cognitive, behavioral, and physiological reactions which is elicited by the phobic situation or object. Given the complexity of the symptoms' configuration, it is understandable that a variety of treatment techniques has been proven to be effective. Cohen asserts that no single treatment technique has been demonstrated to be superior to all other techniques; hence, the therapist is encouraged to "match the method to the malady." [6, p. 229]

CHARACTERISTICS OF IMAGERY PERTINENT TO TREATMENT OF PHOBIC DISORDERS

As suggested earlier, imagery is a universal human phenomenon which allows individuals to adapt to their experience in an autonomous fashion [23]. Imagery has progressively supplanted verbal, diagnostic, and therapeutic procedures in the treatment of phobic disorders. The superiority of imagistic thought to verbal processing has been documented in a variety of dimensions.

Imagery as Access to Right Hemispheric Functioning

Little doubt remains that the left hemisphere of the brain processes information differently than does the right hemisphere [24-26]. The left hemisphere functions in a logical, linear, and semantic mode; whereas, the right hemisphere processes information wholistically, simultaneously, and spatially.

Therapeutic intervention is most commonly directed at right-hemisphere consciousness, whether the therapist is grounded in psychoanalytic, gestalt-experiential, or behavioral theory [27]. The right hemisphere, for example, processes autonomic sensations from one's own body [28]. Furthermore, the right hemisphere is responsible for processing emotionally laden stimuli [29]. Perhaps of greatest importance to this discussion is the fact that the use and control of imagery is associated closely with right-hemisphere functioning [30, 31]. Galin has claimed that the right hemisphere is responsible for the control of unconscious processes which affect normal behavior [32]. Singer stresses the crucial role of right-hemisphere functioning in therapeutic settings [33]:

> The specific events of our life, the scenes witnessed, the early childhood fantasies associated with terrors and experiences of the uncanny often have not been classified under some general category and labeled verbally. Thus, they cannot easily be retrieved on demand and may influence us without our ability to connect their occurrence with particular verbal systems [33, p. 33].

Successful therapy with a phobic patient depends upon change of autonomic and affective behavior in the presence of a phobic situation or object. Inasmuch as imagery, affect, and autonomic control are right-hemisphere functions, an imagistic therapy allows for a type of processing not readily available to verbal approaches [34]. Imagery, consequently, is often interpreted as the language of the unconscious [35, 36].

Imagistic Thought Vivifies Recreation of Immediate Experience

It has been pointed out that words are not equivalent to experience; rather, words may be used to obfuscate experience or simply may abstract from experience to facilitate one's communication with another [33]. Conversely, the use of mental imagery allows the patient to plunge fully into the therapeutic experience.

If the therapist desires to create within the patient an autonomic and affective response, a mental picture of the phobic stimulus will prove to be as effective as the real phobic stimulus would be [37-40]. Mental pictures and physical objects are scanned [39, 40] and rotated [41] in an identical fashion. This functional equivalence between imagery and actual stimuli is crucial to the understanding of imagery's capacity to create therapeutic change [42].

Not only does imagery allow for the guided or spontaneous creation of experience, it also facilitates vivid storage and recall of significant events. When the patient has a mental image available for repeated reference, he/she speculates less, concentrates better, and is more likely to maintain an intense affective response [33]. The visual experience is simultaneous, like the real experience, and mental images elicit a depth of emotion with greater ease than does a verbally censored recital of affect.

BEHAVIORISTIC AND COGNITIVE USES OF IMAGERY

Systematic Desensitization

A critical feature of desensitization therapy, as adopted first by Salter [43] and popularized by Wolpe [15, 44], is the patient's reliance upon imagery rather than upon the phobic object. The technique, grounded in the classical conditioning paradigm, rests on the assumption that if a "response inhibitory of anxiety can be made to occur in the presence of anxiety-evoking stimuli it will weaken the bond between these stimuli and anxiety." [44, p. 14] The goal of therapy is the treatment of symptomatic behavior through reciprocal inhibition.

Deep muscle relaxation training is the preliminary goal in this therapy. The need for relaxation rests upon the premise that the autonomic and muscular response of imagining a phobic stimulus is similar to the effect produced by the real phobic stimulus. Consequently, reciprocal inhibition which succeeds in imagery will transfer and influence autonomic responses in the presence of the actual phobic stimulus [45].

Typically, training involves some variation of Jacobsen's progressive relaxation exercises, sensing and relaxing muscle groups in response to verbal instruction [46]. Relaxation also may be induced imagistically with Schultz's autogenic training procedure [47]. The therapist asks the patient to visualize a particular part of his/her body, to see vividly its shape, color, and texture, as he/she simultaneously relaxes the real musculature.

Alternate means of facilitating or supplementing relaxation include administration of drugs, such as methoxyflurane [48], anxiolytic drugs [49], or thiopental [50]. Such drugs may be classified into categories of antidepressants, sedatives, and beta blockers. Antidepressants have been shown to be most helpful initially; yet, their use often is followed by a high relapse rate after treatment [51].

Relaxation also may be induced through hypnotic suggestion. Phobics have demonstrated a relatively high hypnotic responsivity [52], and hypnosis generally induces superior relaxation and increased vividness of imagery [53-55].

Another prominent means of assisting relaxation are biofeedback processes. The physiological correlates of anxiety are well-known and easily measured [56]. Using feedback displays based on electrical activity of striated muscles (EMG), of the skin (GSR), or of the brain (EEG), the therapist and patient are able to assess the level of anxiety or relaxation present [57]. Biofeedback procedures are particularly useful in helping the patient to identify and control the internal cues that are most effective in creating a relaxation response. The technique is consonant with Wolpe's objective that systematic desensitization modify both behavioral and autonomic fear responses. In fact, Wolpe was one of the early behaviorists to use biofeedback with desensitization treatment [15]. A review of recent studies, however, indicates that biofeedback does not significantly enhance or retard the effectiveness of systematic desensitization [58].

The creation of a hierarchy is the next major component of desensitization therapy. The patient is encouraged to describe precisely the phobic stimulus. The therapist and patient work together to identify the smallest details of the phobic stimulus as well as the wide variety of settings in which it may occur. The patient then translates the phobic situation into a variety of visual images, and they are labeled for convenient referencing. Those visual images are then arranged hierarchically: The image eliciting the least anxiety is presented to the patient first, and it is followed by images which elicit progressively greater anxiety. Although some therapists prefer to use carefully constructed personal hierarchies, standardized hierarchies using common images for all individuals with the same simple phobia (e.g., fear of snakes or insects) have been found equally effective and less time consuming [59, 60].

In the final step of the desensitization process, *the hierarchy is presented* to the patient. The patient is asked to relax, and then the therapist determines, either by electronic measures or by visual detection of body stillness, of breathing pattern, and of muscle tension, if the patient is prepared. Upon reaching relaxation, the patient is asked to visualize as vividly as possible the least anxiety-producing image of the hierarchy, while remaining fully relaxed. If the patient experiences any anxiety, he/she signals the therapist and is instructed to stop visualizing and to return to full relaxation. Each image in the hierarchy must be visualized without anxiety before the next image is attempted.

Wolpe's desensitization procedure is a theoretical nucleus around which divergent techniques have massed. Desensitization, which was envisioned initially as a one-to-one treatment, was first used in group therapy by Lazarus [61]. The use of self-administered procedures was reported in 1967 by Mingler and Wolpe [62], and soon a variety of self-teaching kits and manuals appeared on the market. By 1969, desensitization had been automated by Lang [63], with a computer program of exercises and instructions which he assessed to be equal in effectiveness to human therapy.

At no point in the desensitization procedure is the therapist concerned with the nature of the imagery used by the client. No effort is made to investigate the symbolism or the underlying etiology of the phobia. Wolpe is emphatic in his disregard of patients' "dynamic" ideas or attempts to interpret symbolism present in their spontaneous imagery. Wolpe remarked in regard to a client, "Even if she has got hold of some "dynamic" ideas, since I can't see any use for them, I'm certainly not going to encourage them." [64, p. 144]

Efficacy of desensitization treatment for many phobic disorders is claimed widely. But there is considerably less consensus in explaining how features of the treatment process result ultimately in anxiety reduction.

> This phenomenon of response decrement could equally well be labeled adaption, habituation, extinction, inhibition, satiation, exhaustion, boredom, coping or merely getting used to it. Our learned labels won't get us far until we define more precisely those conditions which decide whether exposure will lead to the response decrement usually seen in therapy, or instead to the response increment seen during acquisition and incubation. We are empirically able to treat most phobias and ritualizers by exposure methods without knowing how exposure works [65, p. 74].

Despite Wolpe's preference for a learning or cognitive theoretical framework, the fundamental mechanism in his procedure is the vivid imagining of anxiety-producing scenes [31, 66].

McLemore hypothesized that the patient's skill in manipulating imagery and treatment effectiveness were likely to be related [67]. Wolpe acknowledged that approximately 15 percent of all subjects are unable to experience anxiety in response to an imagined stimulus and, thus, are unable to benefit from desensitization [64]. In an investigation of imaging vividness, Dyckman and Cowan found imaging ability to be directly related to the success of desensitization [68]. They determined that although pretherapy measures of vividness (such as those taken by the Betts questionnaire) are probably of limited value in predicting therapy outcome, they are useful in identifying very low imagers who then can be marked for *in vivo* treatment. Their investigation did confirm that imaging vividness during therapy correlated highly with symptom abatement.

Emotive Imagery

Whereas some patients have difficulty in projecting images, others are likely to experience difficulty in achieving a state of relaxation, perhaps due to a feeling of increased vulnerability [69], and still others, particularly children, are unable to follow sequential instructions. In such instances, the use of emotive imagery for counterconditioning anxiety is successful [70].

Guidelines for the usage of emotive imagery with children have been proposed by Rosentiel and Scott [71]. They suggest that to inhibit anxiety, emotive images be offered to the child's imagination, but these images should be tailored to fit the experience and understanding of the child. They recommend incorporating fantasy-mediated imagery, already used by Lazarus [61]. The child's most potent fantasies and cognitions, often descriptive of his/her heroes and wish fulfillment, are valuable tools. The therapist should be familiar with them, so that he/she can, for example, direct the child to call upon special heroes to help combat anxiety. Finally, Rosentiel and Scott advise that the therapist should rely heavily on the child's nonverbal cues to supplement verbal reports.

Hence, emotive imagery often relies upon idiosyncratic and perhaps bizarre creations of the patient's imagination. The objective of evoking such imagery is to create a flood of positive feelings to counter the patient's feelings of anxiety. As in systematic desensitization, the therapist is not interested in any symbolic or diagnostic features which may be present in the patient's imagery.

Covert Reinforcement

Some therapists prefer to work with operant shaping techniques. The framework of such procedures resembles that of systematic desensitization. The operant technique, however, provides the patient with a systematic reward for approaching the feared situation. That is, when the patient has imagined an approach behavior, he/she then is instructed to imagine a very pleasant contingent situation [72].

Cautela has used covert reinforcement successfully to direct patients' approach behavior in a wide range of phobias [73]. This technique is based upon the premise that imaginal stimuli and responses and overt stimuli and responses can be manipulated in an analogous fashion. Consequently, in covert reinforcement, Cautela instructs the patient to associate, in imagination, mental pictures of confronting the phobic situation with images of pleasurable situations. Cautela does not employ relaxation training in his technique, nor does he construct a hierarchy of progressively more threatening images. Instead, the therapist defines the logical sequence of approach responses needed to behave adaptively.

An example of Cautela's therapeutic process involves a capable doctoral student complaining of intense test anxiety and inability to concentrate while studying . After failing his qualifying exams, the student sought treatment. He was instructed to identify a reinforcing image (he chose the image of skiing with exhilaration) and to practice calling that image to mind. The therapist then began:

> Close your eyes and try to relax. I want you to imagine you are sitting down to study and you feel fine. You are confident and you are relaxed. I know you may be anxious here but try to imagine that when you are about to study you are calm and relaxed, as if you were acting a part. Start. (When the S raises his finger, the therapist delivers the word, "Reinforcement" which in this case signals the image of skiing down a mountain feeling exhilarated.) Practice this twice a day and just before you study. Now let's work on the examination situation. It is the day of the examination and you feel confident. ("Reinforcement.") You are entering the building in which the exam is going to be given. ("Reinforcement.") You remember that in all these scenes you are to try to feel confident. Now you enter the building and go into the classroom. ("Reinforcement.") You sit down and kid around with another student who is taking the exam. ("Reinforcement.") The proctor comes in with the exam. You feel good; you know you are ready. ("Reinforcement.") The proctor hands out the exam. ("Reinforcement.") You read the questions and you feel you can answer all of them. ("Reinforcement.") Now let's do that again. This time you look the questions over and you are not sure about one question, but you say, "Oh well, I can still pass the exam if I flunk this one question." ("Reinforcement.") All right, this time you look over the exam, and you can see two questions about which you are in doubt, and you say, "Well, I can still pass this exam if I take my time and relax." ("Reinforcement.") [73, p. 37]

The student passed his doctoral examination after ten sessions, and he reported that he had felt confident and relaxed while taking it.

Implosive Therapy

Implosive therapy, developed by Stampfl [74], may be regarded as material evidence for Singer's [31] and Wilkins' [66] contention that imagery is the crucial element of change in desensitization. In implosive therapy, or flooding, relaxation is not utilized [75]. In fact, in imagination, the patient evokes and confronts the fear-arousing stimulus without the possibility of escape, thereby extinguishing the avoidance response to that stimulus.

The mental usage of intense-fear stimuli may be understood within the learning-theory paradigm, which holds that neurotic behavior is comprised of learned and sustained avoidance responses which decrease anxiety [76]. The patient is asked to imagine circumstances involving the phobic object which create the greatest degree of tension and discomfort. Typically, the anxiety produced by the stimulus image exceeds the anxiety that would be confronted in the real-life situation. For example, a client with a fear of insects may visualize an attack by a 6-foot wasp whose buzz resonates throughout the room. The therapist instructs the patient to surrender to the imagery, to focus carefully on the selected scene without seeking escape from the rush of anxious feelings by adopting a less threatening image. Ultimately, that patient experiences no primary reinforcement (real aversive consequences), and anxiety decrements are often followed by extinction.

The therapeutic effectiveness of flooding also could be explained as the reduction of fear by an unusual form of abreaction [77]. It is not uncommon for psychiatric symptoms to remit as the patient experiences heightened affect. Therapists who adopt this understanding of Stampfl's technique are likely to introduce into the patient's imagery, material which they suspect has been repressed. Sheikh and Panagiotou observe that the precise mechanism accounting for change also could be attributed to nonconscious transformations or personal defenses due to the likelihood of symbolic content in the image [5]. Although some patients are able to acquire insight as a result of undergoing implosion, insight is not considered to be an essential objective of treatment.

An important dimension of implosion therapy is the length of time the patient remains exposed to the imagined fear stimulus. Continuous exposure during flooding has garnered more support than distributed exposure [78]. In a literature review, Levis and Hare found that flooding for at least 100-minute intervals is characteristically found in reports of successful implosion therapy [79]. One might reason that short and distributed exposure trials interrupt the intensity of the patient's imagery and subsequently interfere with his/her therapeutic immersion into affect [80].

The relative efficacy of implosion as compared to desensitization is uncertain. Mealiea and Nawas, working with snake phobia patients, concluded that implosive therapy should be used only if desensitization techniques have been unsuccessful [81]. They found that patients treated with flooding were at greater risk of relapse than were the desensitized patients. Nevertheless, in a study by Boulougouris et al. [77], flooding was found to be significantly superior to desensitization on GSR measures during phobic imagery, on patients' subjective assessment of anxiety, and on therapists' ratings of patients.

Covert Modeling

Bandura's theoretical and experimental work [82-86] has demonstrated convincingly that "virtually all learning phenomena that result from direct experiences can occur vicariously as a function of observing other people's behavior and its consequences for them." [83, p. 426] In Bandura's system, phobic patients repeatedly observe models completing tasks deemed fear provoking. The models provide the phobics with repeated performance trials which are not followed by aversive consequences. The modeling may be effected either through *in vivo* methods or *in vitro*, using pictures, slides, films, or video tapes.

Covert modeling, as discussed in Cautela's work [73, 87-91], has its origin in Bandura's assumptions concerning the efficacy of vicarious conditioning. Cautela's procedure was developed to assist those patients who reported difficulty imagining themselves interacting with the phobic stimuli. Cautela discovered that these phobics were, nevertheless, able to imagine vividly a surrogate performing the fear-provoking task.

The patient is encouraged to incorporate as many sensory modalities as possible when he/she imagines the scene suggested by the therapist. Also, the therapist may suggest that the patient imagine multiple models to reduce avoidance behavior, such as coping models and mastery models [92]. Kazdin has observed that the greater the degree of similarity between the patient and the imagined model, the greater the degree of patient imitation and of reduction of anxiety. The use of coping models, who are depicted as anxious at the outset but fearless by the end of the scene, leads to greater avoidance reduction than the use of mastery models who perform confidently and without fear throughout the imagined scene.

Cautela [88] advises that in order to determine the feelings evoked during a scene, the therapist must rely upon the patient's feedback: the vividness of the scene and the rate at which the scene is presented. The therapist may need to shape the patient's imagery if it begins to reflect negative outcomes [90]. Ultimately, covert modeling is as effective as overt modeling in reducing avoidance behavior [89].

One might observe that the imagery generated during conventional desensitization represents a parallel modeling process. Desensitization does not rely upon an image of the phobic object per se; rather, the images allow the patient to imagine his/her behaviors as he/she confronts the feared object. Wilkins suggests that in desensitization the patient is "'modeling' after his own imagined behavior." [66, p. 315]

Mariner found that self-modeling is particularly helpful in assisting a patient who becomes fixed at some point in the desensitization hierarchy [93]. When this occurs, Mariner instructs him/her to visualize himself/herself as a character in a film strip. The patient assumes the identity of a "disembodied observer" and visualizes a caricature of himself/herself perform the next scene in the hierarchy; thus, the anxiety he/she experiences is much attenuated. By observing this self-model engage in the scenes, the patient becomes able to imagine himself/herself participate in the scene. Mariner seems to rely on a dissociation of affect from performance to resolve this impasse in therapy.

Related Conditioning Therapies

Implosion and desensitization techniques inspired many adaptations. Prominent among the variations is Wolpin's *guided imagining* [94]. Unlike Wolpe [15, 44], Wolpin chooses not to introduce any relaxation training exercises; and, instead of guiding his client through a hierarchical series of incremental images, he encourages him/her to visualize the fear-arousing scene in its entirety. No provisions are made for him/her to relax or to reduce anxiety during the imagining. Instead, the patient is advised to experience whatever rush of affect may be produced by visualizing the performance of the target behavior. In contrast to the client undergoing implosion therapy, this patient is not expected to cope in imagination with levels of anxiety which exceed those produced by the actual performance.

The therapist leads the client through the imagined scene, and after each visualization of the entire scene, he/she conducts a systematic inquiry. The therapist determines what images were created by the patient during the scene. Although the therapist suggests the images for visualization, a client's idiosyncrasies may lead to meaningful variation or to absolute noncompliance. If the latter occurs, the therapist must attempt to encourage the patient to shape future images in conformity with the instructions. Of equal importance during the therapist's inquiry is an examination of the feelings generated during the visualization. Wolpin reports a uniform decrement of patient anxiety after repeated visualizations [94].

Brown asserts that Wolpe's technique would be more effective if the therapist knew what the client actually was imagining during desensitization [95]. Brown hypothesizes that the patient's fear of an object or situation might be related to his/her conceptualization of the phobic setting. When a patient reports feeling anxious, Brown asks him/her to convert his/her feelings into a mental image, perhaps a fantasy or a cartoon. When a client reported anxiety about giving a speech, he was instructed to create an image of his feelings. "He imagined an audience of straight-laced, critical women with peering eyes that extended a foot out of their heads toward him." [95, p. 120] Brown reports that when the patient is given an opportunity to examine such images, he/she is able to identify his/her idiosyncratic distortions with little or no coaching. Desensitization generally is successful after repetition of the imagery. Hence, Brown moves the client toward a clearer and more rational view of the feared setting by exposing his/her inaccurate conceptions of that setting.

Paradoxical Intention

Frankl's paradoxical technique is another short-term treatment for phobia [96]. Frankl's phobia management consists of advising the patient to intentionally amplify the feared symptoms to levels of behavioral extravagance.

In some instances, the behavior cannot be produced; for example, a person with a fear of heights would not be expected to jump from a skyscraper window and crash to the ground only to be ticketed for landing in a no-parking zone. When the symptoms cannot be produced, the client is encouraged to *wish* that the feared events would happen. The object of the paradoxical wish is to introduce the element of humor as a distancing phenomenon between the self and the external source of anxiety.

Frankl accounts for the efficacy of the technique in terms of a reduction of the client's anticipatory anxiety. When the fear of fear is eliminated, the client is able to free himself/herself from the cycle wherein "a symptom evokes a phobia and the phobia provokes the symptom. The recurrence of the symptom then reinforces the phobia." [97, p. 452]

Frankl admits, however, that the technique does not have universal applicability simply because not all individuals are capable of self-detachment and humor appreciation. He offers an example:

> I had a man in my Department, a guard in a museum who could not stay on his job because he suffered from deadly fears that someone would steal a painting. During a round I made with my staff, I tried paradoxical intention with him: "Tell yourself they stole a Rembrandt yesterday and today they would steal a Rembrandt and a Van Gogh." He just stared at me and said, "But Herr Professor, that's against the law!" This man was too feeble-minded to understand the meaning of paradoxical intention [97, p. 455].

Rational Emotive Therapy (RET)

RET, originated by Ellis, is a hybrid technique merging behavioristic methods and cognitive analysis [98]. Typically, RET is an *in vivo* form of desensitization which is grounded in the theory that irrational beliefs contribute to maladaptive emotions [99]. Rational emotive imagery (REI) is conceptualized as a component of RET [100].

The REI sessions begin with relaxation: The client takes several minutes to close his/her eyes, relax, and breathe as if he/she were trying to fall asleep. The procedure followed in REI therapy is described by Maultsby and Ellis [101] as a process wherein the patient learns to extinguish irrational fear responses, as he/she simultaneously conditions a rational response to the phobic situation or object. The mental imagery employed in this technique is evoked initially to allow the patient an opportunity to fantasize the anxiety-producing situation. The negative imagery is to be absorbed by the client until he/she feels the maladaptive emotion. The patient is then instructed, "Change this feeling in your gut, so that instead you *only* feel keenly disappointed, regretful, annoyed, or irritated NOT anxious." [101, p. 90]

Once the client has been able to transform his/her emotional response from debilitating anxiety to annoyance or irritation, he/she then must determine how that transformation was accomplished. That is, the therapist teaches the client to observe how he/she manipulated and controlled his/her affect. The negative fantasy situation is repeated in therapy and at home until the client can respond by producing automatically the more adaptive responses. Maultsby and Ellis encourage him/her to fantasize how it would feel if he/she *did not* hold irrational fears. The patient must then vividly picture himself/herself rejecting the irrational fears and accepting rational ideas.

Maultsby proposes that three psychotherapeutic objectives are realized through the use of REI [102]: 1) The patient deconditions himself/herself to the situation which usually elicited a response of fear. 2) The patient practices and learns to make adaptive and rational responses while visualizing the phobic situation. 3) The patient responds to the actual phobic situation automatically with a rational instead of an irrational response.

The efficacy of REI has been challenged experimentally [103]. The REI technique was found to be not as effective in reducing test anxiety as the RET technique which relies primarily on *in vivo* verbalizations and self-talk [103].

The cognitive and behavioral therapists using mental imagery to treat phobic disorders typically share a fundamental assumption: Either imagined or real external stimuli can evoke neurophysiological patterns which are qualitatively and quantitatively the same [104]. Thus imagery is an exposure stimulus which can be manipulated by the patient or therapist; and, unlike exposure *in vivo*, the imagery process is cost efficient and can be practiced at home.

Although the cognitive and behavioral approaches have documented success in treating a wide range of phobias, they have been the object of considerable criticism. The behaviorists have concerned themselves exclusively with symptom management. They have chosen not to muddy their theoretical waters with any exploration of the symbolic content which may be present in clients' imagery. Disciples of the behavioral modification strategies reject the medical model and therefore disavow the notion that a symptom may emerge as the result of an underlying disease process.

SYMBOLIC ANALYSIS OF IMAGERY IN PHOBIC DISORDERS

Psychoanalytic Approach

Logical, orderly, secondary-process thought traditionally has been more highly esteemed than fantasy and imagery. Imagery has acquired the unflattering characterization as regressive and narcissistically cathected, serving id and super-ego drives [105]. The presence of spontaneous imagery in psychoanalysis is interpreted, as are symptoms, to represent defenses which provide distance from an underlying impulse which receives resultant, indirect gratification.

The psychoanalytic treatment of phobia is but a narrow dimension of the analyst's broader task: major personality integration and change. In fact, the customary procedure of disclosing the origin of the symptom has not led to uniform success. Frazer and Carr note:

> Freud himself saw a necessity for the modification of psycho-analysis in the treatment of phobias, stressing the need for the psychoanalyst to intervene and insist that patients attempt to brave the anxiety-provoking situation . . . and to struggle with their anxiety while they make the attempt (quoted in [106, p. 402]).

At the appropriate stage of transference, the patient is encouraged to undergo a desensitization experience with the help of a trusted and supportive figure. Frazer and Carr suggest that, although the process utilized casts long Wolpean shadows, its theoretical affiliation is discussed rarely.

Hence, despite Freud's early endorsement of imagery analysis as a means through which the unconscious could be excavated and accepted, the role of free association in facilitating abreaction and catharsis ultimately was accented.

Eidetic Therapy Approach

Ahsen is regarded as the first theorist to explore systematically the psychotherapeutic usefulness of eidetics [107, 108]. Unlike the behavioral therapist, the eidetic counterpart is not content with simple redress of symptomatic complaints; and, unlike the psychoanalyst, the eidetic therapist is not compelled to explore analytically the full spectrum of the client's life experience to come to an understanding of the origin of symptoms.

Eidetic therapy relies on the elicitation and manipulation of eidetic images. Eidetic psychotherapists, in contrast to most experimental researchers in the area of eidetic imagery, view the eidetic as a semipermanent representation that has been figuratively impressed on the memory in response to the formative events in the past. Every significant event in one's developmental course is purported to implant an eidetic in the system. The visual part, the *image*, is considered to be accompanied always by a *somatic pattern*—a set of bodily feelings and tension, including somatic correlates of emotion—and a cognitive or experiential *meaning*. This tridimensional unity, the eidetic, displays certain lawful tendencies toward change and has specific meaningful relations to psychological processes. This description coincides to a great extent with Jung's conception of the image as an integrated unity with a life and purpose of its own [42].

Eidetics are observed to be bipolarly configured and involve ego-positive and ego-negative elements of the experience. It is believed that, among other factors, a quasi-separation of the visual part from other components, a fixation on the negative pole, or repression of a significant experience can lead to a variety of problems, including phobias. Eidetic therapists aim primarily at reviving the tridimensional unity, shifting attention to the positive pole, and uncovering appropriate healthful experiences through eidetic progression. Eidetic therapy includes a number of procedures designed to elicit the relevant eidetics.

Dolan and Sheikh report an adaptation of a specific eidetic procedure, the Age Projection Test, for use with patients suffering from phobic disorders [109]. In this procedure the therapist obtains all the names by which the patient has been called since childhood; these names are assumed to refer to the individual's various identities and therefore are used interchangeably throughout the procedure. The therapist instructs the patient to relax and listen carefully. Then he/she repeats the psychological and physical features of the symptom, discovered during an initial interview, thus eliciting the symptom in its most acute form. A 5-second silence ensues. "Suddenly the therapist starts talking about the times when the patient was healthy and happy. As the therapist talks about health in the areas in which the symptom now exists, the patient spontaneously forms a self-image and is asked to describe the following: 1) the self-image itself; 2) the clothing on the self-image; 3) the place where it appears; 4) the events occurring during the age projected in the self-image; 5) the events of the year prior to the age projected; 6) the events of the year following the projected age." [109, p. 599]

The above technique generally uncovers an event that precipitated the symptom or started a series of occurrences that ultimately resulted in symptom formation. After the self-image pertaining to this event is formed, the client is asked to project it again and again until it becomes clear, and then he/she is questioned further about that critical period. On the basis of information gathered through the test, a therapeutic image is constructed and the patient is asked to project it repeatedly [110, 111].

It should be noted that the above procedure is used to uncover the precipitating event of a phobia of long standing. To treat a symptom which has its origin in a recent event, one which occurred less than a year previously, it is not necessary to use the Age Projection Test. The therapist begins directly with an inquiry into the experiences during the year prior to the onset of the symptom. The following case history, described by Dolan and Sheikh, illustrates the use of the Age Projection Test in the treatment of phobias [109].

A Case History

A thirty-five-year-old woman, Regina, had been suffering from a phobia of thunderstorms for the past ten years. She reported that her fears were severely limiting her activities, especially, during the summer when electrical storms were more frequent. During a storm, she would hide in the basement, where she saw and heard less of it; nevertheless, she experienced sweating, palpitation, mild diarrhea, and acute dread that lightning would strike her.

The Age Projection Test revealed a healthy self-image at the age of twenty-four. Further inquiry uncovered that during the summer vacation in the mountains of the previous year, she had been on the front porch during a thunderstorm and had seen lightning strike nearby. At that time, she was afraid that she too would be struck by lightning and killed instantly.

Further investigation revealed that prior to this event, Regina had been in the mountains recuperating from a lobectomy to remove a benign lung cyst. The surgery had left her weak and nervous, and she had felt very vulnerable during thunderstorms.

At this point, the focus shifted from the phobia to the illness that preceded its onset. When she was told that she had a cyst that had to be surgically removed, she became very anxious. She feared that she had lung cancer and that she would not recover from the operation; therefore, she refused surgery. These feelings climaxed one evening when she became hysterical. Regina vividly saw herself sitting on her bed, with her mother and husband nearby, crying hysterically, "I'm not going to sign. I'm not going to sign." She heard her mother telling her that this hysterical behavior would only harm her and that she would benefit from the operation. The following day she signed the operative permit and underwent surgery the same day. She suffered no complications subsequently; however, she remained anxious nevertheless.

Regina's phobia was interpreted in the following manner: Since she was of the hysterical type, the prospect of having surgery had filled her with acute anxiety and fear of death. This anxiety stayed with her during her convalescence and then became displaced at the time of the thunderstorm.

Regina was asked to visualize again her mother at her bedside, telling her that the hysterical behavior would only harm her and that the surgery would help. As she did so, she gradually felt her entire body relax, in fact she almost fell asleep in her chair. Everytime she focused on the positive elements of the bipolar configuration, she felt relief. Then she was encouraged to again imagine herself crying hysterically due to the prospect of surgery. She again reported a fear of death and the anxiety connected with the thunderstorm. This procedure made Regina aware of the structure of her phobia and of her ability to recreate both sides of the phobic event. This awareness was vitally important. Over the next few days, Regina repeatedly projected the positive image, and her anxiety subsided. Her fear of death, which was the root of her fear of thunderstorms, was relieved and with it her phobia. A follow-up indicated no recurrence of her symptoms.

Death Imagery Approach

Several researchers have proposed that the fear of death may lie at the root of many phobic disorders. For example, Eugene Shea [112] claims that "it is our fear of death which accounts for the great majority of all the phobias with which humans are afflicted: acrophobia, claustrophobia, agoraphobia, etc. But these are only the symptoms of our 'Dis-ease', our fear of death; dealing with them does not remove the cause of phobias. Someday we must learn to deal with the cause of ALL our phobias, our fear of death, instead of just dealing with each specific phobia" (p. 46). Seligman [113] notes that "human phobias are largely restricted to objects that have threatened survival." Selan emphasizes the issue of death in the lives of many phobics [114]. Seven of the twenty-five phobics that she treated reported confrontation with death that had occurred during their childhood or adolescence. Most of them "also revealed a great preoccupation with death, saying they dream about it often and vividly." [114, p. 135] Also, it is noteworthy that some evidence exists in the literature that both phobias and death anxiety are more common among females than among males [21].

In the light of the forementioned indications, it seems desirable to explore and to attempt to resolve the phobic patients' anxiety concerning death. A death imagery technique, developed by Sheikh, Twente, and Turner may be helpful in this undertaking [115]. In this procedure, the client is asked to relax, confront his/her death in imagination, let go to the natural flow, and be willing to accept responsibility for whatever arises. The technique is based on the premise that purposeful life is possible only through an unflinching acceptance of death as an integral constituent of life: Confronting death draws one to the threshold of life. Several other related techniques, whose aim is to assist the individual in coming to terms with the idea of his/her own death and the death of significant others, have appeared in the literature. The precursors of these approaches include Buddhist and Sufi meditation on death, Plato's "practicing of death," and the ideas concerning "living toward death" presented in *The Tibetan Book of the Dead* (see [115] for a review of the literature).

CONCLUDING REMARKS

Treatment of phobic disorders generally is successful with patients who report that a single phobia has caused them to become aware of increasing disease within their environment. Cohen observes that these individuals, otherwise stable, reality-centered, and functioning competently, are likely to improve with *any* kind of therapy [6]. On the other hand, patients whose phobia is one element of a larger configuration of symptoms are less likely to respond successfully to phobia therapies.

For the past several years, an abundance of research has been carried out to determine the relative efficacy of therapeutic techniques in abating clinical phobias. The results are equivocal, but some conservative conclusions may be offered. In his review of fear-reduction research, Matthews reveals that generalization of results from one population to another is inappropriate simply because the variables of motivational state intensity of the presenting symptom, stimulus intensity, and duration of exposure have no consistent properties among research groups [116]. Furthermore, the effect of the subjects' type of phobia is becoming better understood. For example, small-animal phobics and public-speaking phobics differ significantly in the vividness and intensity of their imagery [117, 118].

Researchers have consistently found that although desensitization in fantasy is effective, exposure *in vivo* produces better immediate and delayed results [65]. One must observe, however, that the investigation of desensitization in fantasy focused exclusively on behavioral and cognitive phobia therapies. The empirical efficacy of "depth-imagery" approaches has yet to be studied systematically. Nevertheless, clinical case reports, using, for example, the eidetic approach, foreshadow empirical analyses which probably will support the continued use and development of such therapeutic techniques.

One is prompted to argue vigorously in support of mental-imagery techniques for a host of therapeutic reasons [2]. Looming large among those reasons is that a patient, introduced to the dramatic qualities of the human imagination, begins to acquire control over one of his/her innate abilities. The client in imagery therapy is likely not only to experience relief from his/her symptoms, but also enhance his/her self-esteem [31], and to learn to live more imaginatively, thereby increasing his/her ultimate human potential [23].

REFERENCES

1. B. L. Whorf, *Language, Thought and Reality: Selected Writings*, Cambridge Technology Press of Massachusetts Institute of Technology, Cambridge, 1956.
2. J. L. Singer and K. S. Pope (eds.), *The Power of Human Imagination: New Methods in Psychotherapy*, Plenum Press, New York, 1978.
3. J. B. Watson, Psychology as the Behaviorist Views It, *Psychological Review*, *20*, pp. 158-177, 1913.
4. A. A. Sheikh, Mental Images: Ghosts of Sensations?, *Journal of Mental Imagery*, *1*, pp. 1-4, 1977.
5. A. A. Sheikh and N. Panagiotou, Use of Mental Imagery in Psychotherapy: A Critical Review, *Perceptual and Motor Skills*, *41*, pp. 555-585, 1975.
6. S. B. Cohen, Editorial: Phobias, *The American Journal of Clinical Hypnosis*, *23*, pp. 227-229, 1981.
7. P. Huyghe, Mind, *Omni*, p. 20, August, 1982.
8. P. Errera, Some Historical Aspects of the Concept of Phobia, *The Psychiatric Quarterly*, *36*, pp. 325-336, 1962.
9. American Psychiatric Association, *Diagnostic and Statistical Manual of Mental Disorders*, 3rd edition, APA, Washington D.C., 1980.
10. H. P. Laughlin, *The Neuroses*, Reese Press, Baltimore, 1967.
11. I. M. Marks, *Fears and Phobias*, Academic Press, New York, 1975.
12. G. S. Hall, A Study of Fears, *American Journal of Psychology*, *8*, pp. 147-249, 1897.
13. E. Kraeplin, *Lehrbuch der Psychiatrie*, Barth, Leipzig, 1903.
14. H. Oppenheim, *Textbook of Nervous Diseases for Physicians and Students*, Stechert, New York, 1911.

15. J. Wolpe, *Psychotherapy by Reciprocal Inhibition*, Stanford University Press, Stanford, 1958.
16. O. Mowrer, *Learning Theory and Behavior*, Wiley, New York, 1960.
17. S. Rachman, *Phobias: Their Nature and Control*, Charles C. Thomas, Publisher, Springfield, Illinois, 1968.
18. H. J. Eysenck and S. Rachman, *The Causes and Cures of Neurosis*, Routledge and Kegan, Paul, London, 1965.
19. P. M. G. Emmelkamp, The Behavioral Study of Clinical Phobias, *Progress in Behavior Modification, 8*, pp. 55-125, 1979.
20. K. A. Brehony and S. Geller, Agoraphobia: Appraisal of Research and a Proposal for an Integrative Model, in *Progress in Behavior Modification*, Vol. 12, M. Hersen, R. Eisler and P. Miller (eds.), Academic Press, New York, 1981.
21. R. L. DuPont (ed.), *Phobia: A Comprehensive Summary of Modern Treatments*, Bruner Mazel, New York, 1982.
22. G. L. Paul and D. A. Bernstein, Anxiety and Systematic Desensitization, in *Psychopathology Today*, W. S. Sahakian (ed.), F. E. Peacock Publishers, Itasca, Illinois, 1979.
23. J. E. Shorr, *Psychotherapy through Imagery*, Intercontinental Medical Book Corporation, New York, 1974.
24. M. S. Gazzaniga, *The Bisected Brain*, Appleton-Century-Crofts, New York, 1970.
25. M. S. Gazzaniga and J. E. Ledoux, *The Integrated Mind*, Plenum Press, New York, 1978.
26. R. E. Ornstein, *The Psychology of Consciousness*, Freeman, San Francisco, 1972.
27. R. G. Ley, Cerebral Asymmetries, Emotional Experience and Imagery: Implications for Psychotherapy, in *The Potential of Fantasy and Imagination*, A. A. Sheikh and J. T. Shaffer (eds.), Brandon House, New York, 1979.
28. R. Davidson and G. Schwartz, Patterns of Cerebral Lateralization during Cardiac Biofeedback versus the Self-Regulation of Emotion: Sex Differences, *Psychophysiology, 13*, pp. 62-74, 1976.
29. L. Morrow, B. Vrtunski, Y. Kim, and F. Boller, Arousal Responses to Emotional Stimuli and Laterality of Lesion, *Neuropsychologia, 19*, pp. 65-71, 1981.
30. A. Paivio, *Imagery and Verbal Processes*, Holt, New York, 1971.
31. J. L. Singer, *Imagery and Daydreaming Methods in Psychotherapy and Behavior Modification*, Academic Press, New York, 1974.
32. D. Galin, Implications for Psychiatry of Left and Right Cerebral Specialization, *Archives of General Psychiatry, 31*, pp. 572-583, 1974.
33. J. L. Singer, Imagery and Affect in Psychotherapy, in *The Potential of Fantasy and Imagination*, A. A. Sheikh and J. T. Shaffer (eds.), Brandon House, New York, 1979.
34. M. J. Horowitz, Visual Thought Images in Psychotherapy, *American Journal of Psychotherapy, 22*, pp. 55-57, 1968.
35. R. Desoille, *The Directed Daydream*, Psychosynthesis Research Foundation, New York, 1965.

36. H. Leuner, Guided Affective Imagery: A Method of Intensive Psychotherapy, *American Journal of Psychotherapy*, *23*, pp. 4-22, 1969.
37. J. R. May and H. J. Johnson, Physiological Activity to Internally Elicited Arousal and Inhibitory Thoughts, *Journal of Abnormal Psychology*, *82*, pp. 239-245, 1973.
38. L. F. Van Egeren, B. W. Feather, and P. L. Hein, Desensitization of Phobias: Some Psychophysiological Propositions, *Psychophysiology*, *8*, pp. 213-228, 1971.
39. S. Kosslyn, Can Imagery Be Distinguished from Other Forms of Internal Representation?, Evidence from Studies of Information Retrieval Time, *Memory and Cognition*, *4*, pp. 291-297, 1976.
40. S. Kosslyn, T. Ball, and B. Reiser, Visual Images Preserve Metric Spatial Information: Evidence from Studies of Imagery Scanning, *Journal of Experimental Psychology: Human Perception and Performance*, pp. 47-60, 1978.
41. L. Cooper and R. Shepard, Transformations on Representations of Objects in Space, in *Handbook of Perception*, E. C. Carterette and M. Friedman (eds.), Academic Press, New York, 1978.
42. N. C. Panagiotou and A. A. Sheikh, The Image and the Unconscious, *International Journal of Social Psychiatry*, *23*, pp. 169-186, 1977.
43. A. Salter, *Conditioned Reflex Therapy*, Farrar, Strauss, New York, 1949.
44. J. Wolpe, *The Practice of Behavior Therapy*, Pergamon Press, New York, 1969.
45. A. M. Mathews, Psychophysiological Approaches to the Investigation of Desensitization and Related Procedures, *Psychological Bulletin*, *76*, pp. 73-91, 1971.
46. E. Jacobsen, *Progressive Relaxation*, University of Chicago Press, Chicago, 1938.
47. J. H. Schultz and W. Luth, *Autogenic Training*, Grune and Stratton, New York, 1959.
48. M. Meldman, Penthranization: An Adjuvant in Behavior Therapy, *Behavior Research and Therapy*, *7*, pp. 211-212, 1969.
49. R. Abrams, Psychopharmacology and Convulsive Therapy, in *The Therapist's Handbook: Treatment Methods of Mental Disorders*, B. Wolman (ed.), Van Nostrand Reinholt Co., New York, 1976.
50. T. Pearlman, Behavioral Desensitization of Phobic Anxiety Using Thiopental Sodium, *American Journal of Psychiatry*, *137*, pp. 1580-1582, 1980.
51. I. M. Marks, Behavioral Psychotherapy of Adult Neuroses, in *Handbook of Psychotherapy and Behavior Change*, S. L. Garfield and A. E. Bergin (eds.), John Wiley and Sons, New York, 1978.
52. F. H. Frankel, Trance Capacity and the Genesis of Phobic Behavior, *Archives of General Psychiatry*, *31*, pp. 261-263, 1974.
53. L. K. Daniels, Rapid In-Office and *In-Vivo* Desensitization of an Injection Phobia Using Hypnosis, *American Journal of Clinical Hypnosis*, *18*, pp. 200-203, 1976.
54. T. E. Deiker and D. H. Pollack, Integration of Hypnotic and Systematic Desensitization Techniques in Treatment of Phobias: A Case Report, *American Journal of Clinical Hypnosis*, *23*, pp. 15-27, 1975.

55. J. L. Gustavson and D. G. Weight, Hypnotherapy for a Phobia of Slugs: A Case Report, *American Journal of Clinical Hypnosis*, *23*, pp. 258-262, 1981.
56. L. F. Van Egeren, Psychophysiological Aspects of Systematic Desensitization: Some Outstanding Issues, *Behavior Research and Therapy*, *9*, pp. 65-77, 1971.
57. M. R. Werbach, Biofeedback and Psychotherapy, *American Journal of Psychotherapy*, *31*, pp. 376-382, 1977.
58. W. H. Rickles, L. Onoda, and C. Doyle, Task Force Study Section Report: Biofeedback as an Adjunct to Psychotherapy, *Behavioral Analysis and Modification*, *7*, pp. 1-34, 1982.
59. J. R. Emery and J. D. Krumboltz, Standard vs. Individualized Hierarchies in Desensitization to Reduce Test Anxiety, *Journal of Counseling Psychology*, *14*, pp. 204-209, 1967.
60. F. D. McGlynn, Individual versus Standardized Hierarchies in the Systematic Desensitization of Snake-Avoidance, *Behavior Research and Therapy*, *9*, pp. 1-5, 1971.
61. A. A. Lazarus, Group Therapy of Phobic Disorders by Systematic Desensitization, *Journal of Abnormal Social Psychology*, *63*, pp. 504-510, 1961.
62. B. Mingler and J. Wolpe, Automated Self-desensitization: A Case Report, *Behavior Research and Therapy*, *5*, pp. 133-135.
63. P. J. Lang, The On-Line Computer in Behavior Therapy Research, *American Psychologist*, *24*, pp. 236-239, 1969.
64. J. Wolpe, *Theme and Variations: A Behavior Therapy Casebook*, Pergamon Press, New York, 1976.
65. I. M. Marks. Toward an Empirical Clinical Science: Behavioral Psychotherapy of the 1980s, *Behavior Therapy*, *13*, pp. 63-81, 1982.
66. W. Wilkins, Desensitization: Social and Cognitive Factors Underlying the Effectiveness of Wolpe's Procedure, *Psychological Bulletin*, *76*, pp. 311-317, 1971.
67. C. W. McLemore, Imagery in Desensitization, *Behavior Research and Therapy*, *10*, pp. 51-57, 1972.
68. J. M. Dyckman and P. A. Cowan, Imaging Vividness and the Outcome of In Vivo and Imagined Scene Desensitization, *Journal of Consulting and Clinical Psychology*, *46*:5, pp. 1155-1156, 1978.
69. J. Wolpe, J. P. Brady, and M. Serber, The Current Status of Systematic Desensitization, *American Journal of Psychiatry*, *130*, pp. 961-965, 1973.
70. A. A. Lazarus and A. Abramovitz, The Use of "Emotive Imagery" in the Treatment of Children's Phobias, *Journal of Mental Science*, *108*, pp. 191-195, 1962.
71. A. K. Rosentiel and D. S. Scott, Four Considerations in Using Imagery Techniques with Children, *Journal of Behavior Theory and Experimental Psychiatry*, *8*, pp. 287-290, 1977.
72. M. J. Crowe, I. Marks, W. S. Agras, and H. Leitenberg, Time Limited Desensitization, Implosion and Shaping for Phobic Patients: A Crossover Study, *Behavior Research and Therapy*, *10*, pp. 319-328, 1972.
73. J. R. Cautela, Covert Reinforcement, *Behavior Therapy*, *1*, pp. 35-50, 1970.

74. T. G. Stampfl, Implosive Therapy: A Learning Theory Derived Psychodynamic Therapeutic Technique, in *Critical Issues in Clinical Psychology*, LeBarba and Dent (eds.), Academic Press, New York, 1961.

75. T. W. Vodde and F. H. Gilner, The Effects of Exposure to Fear Stimuli on Fear Reduction, *Behavior Research and Therapy, 9*, pp. 169-175, 1971.

76. R. A. Harper, *The New Psychotherapies*, Prentice-Hall, Englewood Cliffs, New Jersey, 1975.

77. J. Boulougouris, I. Marks, and P. Marset, Superiority of Flooding (Implosion) to Desensitization for Reducing Pathological Fear, *Behavior Research and Therapy, 9*, pp. 7-16, 1971.

78. R. Stern and I. M. Marks, Brief and Prolonged Flooding: A Comparison in Agoraphobic Patients, *Archives of General Psychiatry, 28*, pp. 270-276, 1973.

79. D. J. Levis and N. Hare, A Review of the Theoretical Rationale and Empirical Support for the Extinction Approach of Implosive (Flooding) Therapy, in *Progress in Behavior Modification*, M. Hersen, R. M. Eisler, and P. M. Miller (eds.), Academic Press, New York, 1977.

80. E. Foa and D. Chambless, Habituation of Subjective Anxiety during Flooding in Imagery, *Behavior Research and Therapy, 16*, pp. 391-399, 1978.

81. W. L. Mealiea and M. M. Nawas, The Comparative Effectiveness of Systematic Desensitization and Implosive Therapy in the Treatment of Snake Phobia, *Journal of Behavior Therapy and Experimental Psychiatry, 2*, pp. 85-94, 1971.

82. A. Bandura, Modeling Approaches to the Modification of Phobic Disorders, *The Role of Learning in Psychotherapy*, R. Porter (ed.), J. and A. Churchill, London, 1968.

83. A. Bandura, Factors Determining Vicarious Extinction of Avoidance Behavior through Symbolic Modeling, *Journal of Personality and Social Psychology, 8*, pp. 99-108, 1979.

84. A. Bandura, Modeling Theory, in *Psychology of Learning: Systems, Models, and Theories*, W. S. Sahakian (ed.), Marham, Chicago, 1970.

85. A. Bandura, Psychotherapy Based on Modeling Principles, in *Handbook of Psychotherapy and Behavior Change*, A. E. Bergen and S. L. Garfield (eds.), Wiley, New York, 1971.

86. A. Bandura and P. Barab, Processes Governing Disinhibitory Effects through Symbolic Modeling, *Journal of Abnormal Psychology, 82*, pp. 1-9, 1973.

87. J. R. Cautela, *Covert Modeling*, paper presented to the Association for the Advancement of Behavior Therapy, 1972.

88. J. R. Cautela, The Present Status of Covert Modeling, *Journal of Behavior Therapy and Experimental Psychiatry, 7*, pp. 324-326, 1976.

89. J. Cautela, R. Flannery, and E. Hanley, Covert Modeling: An Experimental Test, *Behavior Therapy, 5*, pp. 494-502, 1974.

90. J. R. Cautela and L. McCullough, Covert Conditioning: A Learning Theory Perspective on Imagery, in *The Power of Human Imagination*, J. L. Singer and K. S. Pope (eds.), Plenum Press, New York, 1978.

91. D. Upper and J. R. Cautela (eds.), *Covert Conditioning*, Pergamon Press, New York, 1979.

92. A. E. Kazdin, Covert Modeling and the Reduction of Avoidance Behavior, *Journal of Abnormal Psychology, 81*, pp. 78-95, 1973.

93. A. S. Mariner, Resolving an Impasse in Systematic Desensitization, *Psychotherapy: Theory, Research and Practice, 6*, p. 119, 1969.

94. M. Wolpin, Guided Imagining to Reduce Avoidance Behavior, *Psychotherapy: Theory, Research and Practice, 6*, pp. 122-124, 1969.

95. B. Brown, The Use of Induced Imagery in Psychotherapy, *Psychotherapy: Theory, Research and Practice, 6*, pp. 120-121, 1969.

96. V. E. Frankl, *Psychotherapy and Existentialism: Selected Papers on Logotherapy*, Washington Square Press, New York, 1967.

97. V. E. Frankl, Logotherapy, in *Psychopathology Today*, W. S. Sahakian (ed.), F. E. Peacock Publishers, Itasca, Illinois, 1979.

98. A. Ellis, *Reason and Emotion in Psychotherapy*, Lyce-Stuart Press, New York, 1962.

99. A. Ellis, *Humanistic Psychotherapy: The Rational-Emotive Approach*, Julian Press, New York, 1973.

100. A. Ellis and R. Harper, *A New Guide to Rational Living*, Prentice-Hall, Englewood Cliffs, New Jersey, 1975.

101. M. Maultsby and A. Ellis, *Techniques for Using Rational Emotive Imagery*, Institute for Rational Living, New York, 1974.

102. M. Maultsby, Rational Emotive Imagery, *Rational Living, 6*, pp. 24-27, 1971.

103. S. P. Hymen and R. Warren, An Evaluation of Rational−Emotive Imagery as a Component of Rational-Emotive Therapy in the Treatment of Test Anxiety, *Perceptual and Motor Skills, 46*, pp. 847-853, 1978.

104. J. C. Eccles, *The Physiology of Nerve Cells*, Johns-Hopkins Press, Baltimore, 1957.

105. D. L. Shapiro, The Significance of the Visual Image in Psychotherapy, *Psychotherapy: Theory, Research and Practice, 7*, pp. 209-212, 1970.

106. R. D. Chessick, The Treatment of Neuroses and Borderline Cases, in *The Therapist's Handbook: Treatment Methods of Mental Disorders*, B. Wolman (ed.), Van Nostrand Reinholt, New York, 1976.

107. A. Ahsen, *Basic Concepts in Eidetic Psychotherapy*, Brandon House, New York, 1968.

108. A. Ahsen, *Psycheye: Self-Analytic Consciousness*, Brandon House, New York, 1977.

109. A. T. Dolan and A. A. Sheikh, Short-Term Treatment of Phobia through Eidetic Imagery, *American Journal of Psychotherapy, 31*, pp. 595-604, 1977.

110. A. A. Sheikh and C. S. Jordan, Clinical Uses of Mental Imagery, in *Imagery: Current Theory, Research, and Application*, A. A. Sheikh (ed.), Wiley, New York, 1983.

111. A. A. Sheikh and C. S. Jordan, Eidetic Psychotherapy, in *Handbook of Innovative Psychotherapies*, R. J. Corsini (ed.), Wiley, New York, 1981.

112. E. B. Shea, *The Immortal "I."*, The Unprofitable Servants, Illinois, 1978.

113. M. Seligman, Phobias and Preparedness, *Behavior Therapy, 2*, pp. 307-320, 1971.

114. B. H. Selan, Phobias, Death, and Depression, in *Phobia: A Comprehensive Summary of Modern Treatments*, R. L. DuPont (ed.), Bruner Mazel, New York, 1982.

115. A. A. Sheikh, G. E. Twente, and D. Turner, Death Imagery: Therapeutic Uses, in *The Potential of Fantasy and Imagination*, A. A. Sheikh and J. T. Shaffer (eds.), Brandon House, New York, 1979.

116. A. M. Mathews, Fear Reduction Research and Clinical Phobias, *Annual Review Behavior Therapy, Theory, and Practice*, pp. 59-82, 1979.

117. P. J. Lang, B. G. Melamed and J. D. Hart, A Psychophysiological Analysis of Fear Modification Using an Automated Desensitization Procedure, *Journal of Abnormal Psychology*, 76, pp. 220-234, 1970.

118. T. C. Weerts and P. J. Lang, Psychophysiology of Fear Imagery: Differences Between Focal Phobia and Social Performance Anxiety, *Journal of Consulting and Clinical Psychology*, 46, pp. 1157-1159, 1978.

CHAPTER 8

Sex, Fantasy and Imagination: Scientific Research and Clinical Applications

KENNETH S. POPE, JEROME L. SINGER, AND LAWRENCE C. ROSENBERG

THE DISTRUST OF SEXUAL FANTASY

Mental health professionals and the public alike have been generally suspicious of sexual fantasies—and no wonder. Do we really want to admit the possibility that: 1) the last person we spent time with today is right now spinning out an elaborate private fantasy involving us in group sex, 2) the last person we made love with was, without our knowledge, thinking of someone else the whole time, and 3) our parents and our children occasionally spend time fantasizing sexual experiences involving extramarital sex, exhibitionism, and incest? It is disconcerting for many of us even to imagine such possibilities.

Sexual fantasies tend not only to disconcert us but also to strike us as somewhat objectionable, obnoxious, or downright disgusting. People become wary of acknowledging the private fantasies which genuinely express their sexuality or the imaginative scenes which they find arousing. As Woody Allen replied when asked if he thought sex was dirty: "Only if it's done right."

Our tendency to deny, or discount, sexual fantasies has led to an odd result. Until recently, texts and popular books on sexuality made no mention of sexual fantasies, and the topic is still virtually absent from works on romantic love, attraction, and intimate behavior. Yet more and more, sexual fantasy is emerging as a complex, widespread, and important aspect of human experience.

The Variety of Sexual Fantasy

Sexual fantasies may be erotic, romantic, or pornographic. They may be remembered, anticipated, imagined, read, viewed, shared, or acted out. They may be sudden, one-time, fragmentary images, or elaborate, detailed narratives to which we return again and again. They may be highly valued imaginative events which we voluntarily create for the mind's eye (and other senses), or they may be unwanted, distracting, "unbidden images" of which we would like to rid ourselves.

Sexual fantasy includes at least three kinds of imaginative activity. First, there are the images, daydreams, and other fantasies we have during sexual behavior. These fantasies need not have explicit sexual content, nor even be arousing. It is important to note that such fantasies may even diminish or prevent sexual arousal, functioning, or enjoyment. The variety of such distressing images which people report experiencing during sex is astounding. Imagine the difficulty of enjoying intercourse if one or more of the following fantasies comes into your mind:

1. The person I'm with right now is really in love with someone else.
2. When I take my clothes off, this person is going to feel either like laughing or crying.
3. I bet this time I'll catch herpes.
4. I'm sure the phone is going to ring any minute now and I'll have to answer it.
5. Tomorrow when I go to work, I can just see myself getting fired.
6. The kids are going to be home from school any minute now, and I forgot to fix the lock on our bedroom door.
7. I'll bet this person is going to ask me to do something I really don't want to do, and I'll be afraid to say no.
8. I remember what a disaster my last attempt at intercourse was—I can just see that happening again now.
9. I wonder what my parents would think of me, if they could see me right now.
10. We'd better be a little quieter—I can just imagine the neighbors calling the police.
11. Maybe I've already got herpes and don't know about it yet.
12. These contraceptives are never 100 percent safe. What if all this leads to another baby?
13. What if my partner wants to do all this again 5 minutes after we're through?

But fantasies during sexual activity also can increase sexual arousal and enjoyment and, when shared between lovers, can deepen and enrich the experience of intimacy, excitement, and communication.

Second, there are the images, daydreams, and other fantasies we have *about* sex. These need not occur during sexual behavior. During the most seemingly *un*-sexual times—a job interview, doing the laundry, jogging, or sitting in the doctor's waiting room—we may find ourselves remembering the last time we made love, imagining what it would be like to have intercourse with the person closest to us, or privately spinning out a new variation on a longtime favorite sexual theme.

Third, there are images, daydreams, and other fantasies which are sexually arousing for us, regardless of whether they have explicit sexual content or whether we are currently engaged in sexual behavior. Imagining the sound of a voice or special music, the look in someone's eye or a certain setting, a line of poetry or a simple object given as a gift by a lover long ago—these may initiate and serve as the subject of our fantasy, arousing us to a state of vague or intense sexual excitement. Such fantasies are extremely personal and idiosyncratic, having no real meaning or sexual associations to anyone else.

AN INCREASED ACCEPTANCE
OF SEXUAL FANTASY

Popular culture has recently become more able to acknowledge and accept sexual fantasy as an important part of human experience. "Men's magazines" devote increasing space to such fantasies. *Penthouse* (March, 1983), for instance, published eleven letters from readers describing such fantasies as sex with a stranger, group sex, spanking, and sex with inlaws. Stereotypically defined "real men," then, while they "don't eat quiche" and are not allowed to engage in numerous other activities, nonetheless *are* acknowleged to engage in sexual fantasies. At the other end of the spectrum, feminist literature explores sexual fantasies in the lives of women. Erica Jong, for example, describes in vivid detail the idealized fantasy of the "zipperless fuck." [1] Perhaps the most popular presentation of the fantasies of both men and women has occurred in the books of Nancy Friday, who describes sexual imagination among "normal" people in the realms of anonymous sex, exhibitionism, forced sex, masochism, domination, incest, fetishes, lesbianism, and prostitution [2, 3].

Evidence of the growing public acceptance of sexual fantasies is not limited to the written word. The *Los Angeles Free Press* (Feburary 10, 1983) lists seventeen separate organizations providing "Fantasy Hotlines" (a relatively new phenomenon). Such organizations invite the public to call in to explore their "most intimate fantasies." Many permit unlimited calling and accept Visa, MasterCard, and American Express. For those who want to listen repeatedly to a particular fantasy, another organization makes this offer: "Write me and tell me your fantasy, and I will send you a cassette tailor-made to suit your every desire." For those who prefer to act out their sexual fantasies in elaborate settings, there are eleven listings of such "parlors" as "Fantasy Playhouse," "Fantasy Retreat," and "Capricious, Inc."

Public acceptance of sexual fantasy, however, is less than whole-hearted. When Jimmy Carter confessed that he had lusted in his heart after women other than his wife, he found no shortage of people ready to condemn him for these fantasies. Some of the most controversial and troublesome questions are these: 1) What, if any, is the difference between erotic and pornographic fantasy?; and 2) What, if any, aspects of sexual fantasy should be considered immoral, unethical, or illegal? The questions are endlessly, often heatedly, argued, with few people changing their minds. A comprehensive discussion of these issues is beyond the scope of this chapter, but a few ideas are worth noting briefly. Regarding the first question, the poet Audre Lorde suggested the following distinction: "We have often turned away from the exploration and consideration of the erotic as a source of power and information, confusing it with its opposite, the pornographic. But pornography is a direct denial of the power of the erotic, for it represents the suppression of true feeling. Pornography emphasizes sensation without feeling." [5, p. 2] Regarding the second question, it is worth noting that although in Public Law 90-100, Congress claimed that pornography and obscenity were "a matter of national concern," nonetheless after the prestigious National Commission on Obscenity and Pornography had researched the subject, the U.S. Senate voted sixty to five against the report before they had laid eyes on it. Feminist Gloria Steinhem argues that "the long history of anti-obscenity laws makes it clear that such laws are most often invoked against political and life style dissidents." [6, p. 191] Andrea Dworkin, author of *Pornography: Men Possessing Women*, disagrees: "We will know that we are free when pornography no longer exists." [6, p. 191] She endorses laws banning pornography but recommends going beyond the law when necessary, to destroy the pornographic presses. The Reverend Tom Michel, leader of the Moral Majority in New England, welcomed Dworkin to his crusade to eliminate pornography but also pointed out that he would outlaw Dworkin's book: "We would most certainly ban such ungodly writings." [6, p. 191]

Like the general public, behavioral scientists and mental health professionals are increasingly able to recognize and acknowledge the importance of sexual fantasy in human experience. We are beginning to gain some understanding of the conditions under which it occurs and of the ways in which it contributes to enjoyment and fulfillment, as well as to dissatisfaction and dysfunction. This chapter will highlight some of the important research findings in the area of sexual fantasy.

NORMS, GENDER, AND THE LIFE SPAN

The idea that sexual fantasizing is atypical has been discredited by research. It is not uncommon for people to have sexual fantasies during nonsexual activities, while masturbating, or while engaging in sexual intercourse.

Daydreaming

Davidson found that 80 percent of 202 undergraduate women reported moderate to high frequencies of sexual daydreaming, and 100 percent acknowledged at least some sexual fantasizing [7]. Giambra, in a sample of 1,200 well educated, middle- and upper-class whites, aged seventeen to ninety-two years, found sexual daydreams to be common [8]. In fact, for males aged seventeen to twenty-nine, sexual daydreams were the most common fantasy activity.

Masturbation

In pioneering studies, Kinsey and his associates found that 72 percent of the males and 50 percent of the females who masturbated almost always fantasized during this activity, while 17 percent of the males and 14 percent of the females sometimes did [9, 10]. In a more recent study, Zeiss and Lentz found that 54 percent of the female college students in their sample reported fantasizing while masturbating [11]. Rosenberg, in a study of forty-five heterosexual, bisexual, and homosexual male college students, found that 95 percent reported at least occasionally fantasizing while masturbating, 81 percent reported more frequent fantasies, and 62 percent said that they fantasized every time [12].

Intercourse

Hariton and Singer, in a study of 141 suburban housewives, found that 65 percent reported some sexual fantasies during intercourse with their husbands, and 37 percent reported that such fantasies occurred with great frequency [13]. About 71 percent of the college women in the Zeiss and Lentz study reported fantasizing during foreplay, while 68 percent fantasized during intercourse [11]. In Rosenberg's sample of college men, 76 percent reported having at least occasional fantasies during sexual intercourse, while 30 percent reported more frequent fantasies [12].

Gender Differences

Kinsey and his associates presented evidence that women were less aroused than men by psychosexual stimuli, such as books or films [10]. A review of the accumulated subsequent research however, indicates that such difference in arousal level is unlikely [11].

Yet there may be a difference in the *ways* in which women and men respond to such psychosexual stimuli. As John Money writes:

> If a woman sees a sexy picture, for instance even an advertisement for Coca-Cola, she tends to project herself up onto the screen, onto the picture, and to imagine what it would be like to be that woman. Or, if she's seeing a sexy film, or a romantic film, to project herself into the story and perhaps change it a little to suit certain circumstances of her own existence, and also to feel that she's learning a few good lessons from the woman up there. She will then be able to put the lessons into practice in her own romantic and sexual life.
>
> As for the male viewer, his reaction is rather different, for he does not project himself up into the picture of a male on the screen and imagine what it would be like to be that lucky one with that good looking girl. He objectifies. He takes the girl down off the screen and has sex with her on the spot [14, p. 431].

There is evidence that while females report *higher* general levels of daydreaming frequency than males, they report *lower* levels of daydreams of a sexual nature [8].

Life Span

Sexual-daydreaming frequency, like general-daydreaming frequency, steadily decreases with increasing age. For females in the Giambra study sexual daydreams were the second most frequent type of fantasy ("problem solving" was the most frequent) in the age interval from seventeen to forty-nine years, third most frequent from fifty to fifty-nine years, fourth most frequent from sixty to sixty-nine years, and sixth most frequent from seventy to ninety-two years [8]. For males, sexual daydreams are the most frequent for the seventeen to twenty-three-year-olds and tied for first (with "problem solving") with the twenty-four to twenty-nine-year-olds. The drop to third most frequent is delayed to age sixty, while the drop to fourth most frequent is delayed to age seventy-five. However, sexual fantasies largely disappear after the 75th year.

PATHOLOGY

At least since Freud's statement that only discontent people fantasize, fantasies have been linked in some way to neurotic behavior or other psychopathology [15]. Sexual fantasies in particular have been viewed as representing the expression of or compensation for psychosexual deficiencies, distress, or dysfunction.

This sweeping generalization has not been supported by research, though certain kinds of sexual fantasies do appear to be associated quite frequently with psychological or sexual problems.

Hariton and Singer, for example, found that women frequently engaged in fantasy during intercourse with their husbands [13]. The most common fantasies involved a man other than her husband, submission fantasies, and making love in a different place (in a car, at the beach, etc.). Yet the frequency of these fantasies was not associated with any pathology in the woman nor indicative of problems within the marital relationship.

Campagna explored the masturbation fantasies of male college students and found essentially four patterns [16]. The first was a simple, common heterosexual scene, generally involving intercourse. The second involved a much more elaborate story line, as well as a plot which was not particularly realistic. For example, the student imagined himself to be a director of a movie and interviewed movie stars in which is called the "casting couch" tradition. Or the student imagined that he was a sultan in a harem. The third pattern involved off-beat fantasy of a kind often termed kinky or bizarre. It tended to involve discipline, bondage, and similar themes. None of these first three patterns is associated with pathology. The fourth, however, is often indicative of emotional disturbance. This scene did not contain a full-fledged sexual relationship; only one or two parts of the woman's body appeared, and she is always faceless.

FREQUENCY OF INTERCOURSE AND
OF ORGASM DURING INTERCOURSE

There is evidence that sexual fantasy is related to the frequency of intercourse for men and to the frequency of orgasm during intercourse for women.

Giambra and Martin write:

> Three behavioral attributes of sexual life history, developed from personal interviews with male respondents, were found to be directly related to current levels of daydreaming. Thus, on a comparable basis, men aged twenty-four to sixty-four years with more coital partners and/or greater customary coital frequency in the first two years of marriage were found to currently have higher levels of sexual daydreaming. Also, on a comparable basis, men forty-five to sixty-four years of age who had greater overall levels of sexual activity from age twenty to forty years were found to have more sexual daydreaming at time of report [17, p. 504].

Zeiss and Lentz discovered that for women the presence of intercourse fantasies during masturbation was positively correlated with attaining orgasms during intercourse [11].

RACE AND RELIGION

Robinson and Calhoun studied sexual attitudes and fantasies among four groups: 1) black males, 2) black females, 3) white males, and 4) white females [18]. Whites tended to be much more unrestrained, unconventional, and liberal than blacks in their sexual fantasies. Moreover, males tended to be more liberal in their attitudes to sexual fantasies than females. Finally, low church attenders tended to be more sexually permissive in their fantasies.

ROMANTIC AND EROTIC SEXUAL FANTASIES

In an ingenious study, Zeiss and Lentz explored women's sexual fantasies during daydreaming, masturbating, foreplay, or intercourse, as well as their reaction to reading sexual fantasies [11]. Of particular interest was the degree to which the sexual fantasies were romantic (emphasizing relationship factors which indicated that the people involved cared for each other and were having fun, and giving no details concerning the sexual interlude which followed) or erotic (emphasizing the sexual relationship and explicitly describing all sexual activity).

Reliance upon either romantic or erotic material for sexual fantasies seems partially determined by the situation or activity. That is to say, daydreaming is usually associated with romantic (or mixed, romantic and erotic) fantasies, while masturbation is associated with erotic (or mixed) fantasies. During intercourse, either type of fantasy is equally likely.

But individuals also seem to have a preferred type. A heavy use of romantic fantasies was related to a lack of arousal in response to stories with erotic elements. On the other hand, a high ratio of erotic fantasies in masturbation was related to a lack of arousal in response to stories with a romantic element.

SEXUAL ORIENTATION

Carefully designed, controlled, systematic studies of the relationship between sexual orientation and sexual fantasies so far have been undertaken only in regard to male masturbation fantasies. Guido analyzed the masturbation fantasies of 104 heterosexual and homosexual cohabitating and single males who were matched according to age, marital status, race, religion, education, income, and pathology [19]. Virtually no differences in the fantasy activities emerged aside from the sex objects. "Unknown people or situations" and "past sexual experience" were the most frequent themes. Consistent with the Giambra and Martin findings, high frequencies of sexual fantasies were positively related to high frequencies of sexual behavior [17].

In Rosenberg's study of forty-five heterosexual, bisexual, and homosexual college men, there were some themes associated primarily with sexual orientation (e.g., bisexual men more frequently imagined meeting a partner in a bar and spending a great night together than did homosexual men), but many fantasies were shared by all three groups [12]. Among themes occurring at least half the time for all three groups were: "I am having sex with a good-looking person I saw that day;" "I imagine the great sex experience I once had;" "I am caressing a nude woman's/man's body;" "A woman/man is committing fellatio on me;" "I imagine a long scenario evolving into sex;" "I am having sex with my lover;" "I picture a person I know naked;" and "I am deeply kissing a woman/man."

TELEVISION

Television provides a public expression of some of our fantasies about sex, and it also furnishes us with material for, and thus helps to shape, our private sexual fantasies. Most television sex (whether expressed through dialogue or implied by the plot) consists of extramarital affairs. Extramarital sex occurs five times as often as marital sex. Second to the extramarital affair is sex with prostitutes. Extramarital affairs and intercourse with prostitutes constitute about 70 percent of the portrayals of sex on television. "Sex is commonly linked with violence. On dramatic and action shows, discussions of sex are often in the context of rape and other sex crimes. Erotic relationships are seldom seen as warm, loving, or stable." [20, p. 55]

ROMANCE NOVELS AND ADULT BOOKS

Sexual fantasies also are given public expression in literature, which, like television, in turn helps to shape our private fantasies. Two genres which devote themselves almost exclusively to such fantasies are the romance novel and the adult book (the kind bought almost exclusively in adult book stores and often classified as pornography).

The February 1983 issue of *Ms.* expored the world of romance novels under the heading "Can Romance Novels Improve Your Sex Life?" [21, 22] Now a $250-million industry provides dozens of new books each month for 20 million loyal readers. The new form of this genre includes "realistic and detailed love scenes" and has become what critic Ann Douglas calls "soft-core pornography." [21, p. 97] Essential characteristics of these stories are:

> Sex, like love . . . , is an idealized, driving hunger of two perfectly matched souls. Birth control is never mentioned; sexual problems don't exist; and pregnancy is always welcomed and revered [21, p. 98].

The Council on Interracial Books is concerned that such stories not only are sexist but also often have overtones of racism [22, p. 99].

Whereas romance novels are overwhelmingly consumed by women, adult books are overwhelmingly consumed by men. The two genres have some distinct similarities as well as differences. A systematic study of a large number of adult books carried out by Pope found that such books, like the romance novels, carried themes of racism and made no mention of birth control [23]. But unlike romance novels, they contained no mention of pregnancy and little mention of affection or relatedness (other than sexual) between people. Furthermore, there were substantial differences in the speech and other activities of men and women during sex. Men tended not to say anything during intercourse, and if they did talk, it was only very briefly and in response to their partner. Women, on the other hand, frequently talked or made noises of excitement and ecstasy during sex. Contrary to the research suggesting that men masturbate more frequently than women, adult books portray women masturbating five times as often as men.

RAPE AND OTHER VIOLENCE

There is evidence that portrayals of violence not only have become more common in popular books, films, and television, but also have increased specifically in media presentations of sex [24]. And, once again, this phenomenon may be not only a public expression of our sexual fantasies but also a shaping influence upon our subsequent private fantasies (and, perhaps, behavior).

Malamuth, Heim, and Feshbach explored the factors which made violence more sexually arousing in fantasies [25]. They presented stories portraying either sexual assaults or mutually consenting sex. In the assault portrayals, the female victim either did or did not experience pain, and either did or did not experience orgasm. In general, both male and female subjects were less aroused by the assault than by the mutually consenting sex. However, pain and orgasm served to "disinhibit" the sexual responsiveness of the subjects to the assaults. More specifically, women became sexually aroused while reading about a rape in which the victim experienced an orgasm but no pain. Men, however, became sexually aroused while reading about a rape in which the victim experienced both orgasm and pain.

Malamuth furthermore demonstrated the ways in which such "externally directed" fantasies affected future "internally generated" fantasies [26]. He presented slide-audio shows depicting either rape or mutually consenting sex. His sample of male college students later created more violent sexual fantasies if they had seen the rape version than if they had seen the mutual-consent version.

SEXUAL FANTASIES
AND THE PSYCHOTHERAPIST

A discussion of the numerous and varied techniques for exploring or utilizing sexual fantasies in psychotherapy, sex therapy, and behavior modification is beyond the scope of this chapter. However, most clients (as well as most therapists) experience sexual fantasies, and such material is not unlikely to arise in the course of many clinical procedures. Consequently, there are some important ideas which may be of use to all psychotherapists in situations where sexual fantasies are part of the client's problem, become a topic of discussion or a focus of treatment, or seem to be influencing the course of therapy.

First, it is important to recognize and to communicate to the client that sexual fantasies are a common phenomenon, are a natural part of human experience, and are not inherently connected to pathology. So many clients are shocked, frightened, or ashamed of their fantasies. They feel isolated and "different," as if they alone were capable of such bizarre, monstrous, or totally unacceptable thoughts. Acceptance, education, and reassurance can be enormously helpful to these clients.

Second, it is important for the clinician to appreciate and to communicate to the client the substantial differences between fantasy and reality. We may experience and even cultivate and enjoy sexual fantasies which we would never want to put into practice. In marriage counseling, for example, a wife may feel ashamed that she has secret sexual fantasies about men other than her husband.

And it is easy to make the unfounded and potentially very damaging inference that *simply* because she has this fantasy, she must secretly or unconsciously desire an affair, or be discontent with her husband, or feel something is missing in her sex life. Such fantasies can be openly explored but without rushing to judgment. It is quite possible not only that this fantasy is simply part of her sexual repertoire, one that she will always enjoy (and come to share with her husband), but also that she is happy in a monogamous relationship with her husband.

Third, it is important for therapists to be comfortable with their own fantasy life and with the sexual fantasies created by their client. This is not that easy. Many of us are unfamiliar or uncomfortable with sexual fantasies, especially in their more unpredictable and unorthodox forms. If the client's sexual fantasy involves us, we may become anxious, guilty, or otherwise uncomfortable and defensive. Similarly, if we begin experiencing sexual fantasies about our client, we may become alarmed and less capable of functioning therapeutically. A study by Schover suggests that male therapists, in particular, have difficulty dealing appropriately with the sexual materials presented by female clients [27].

Fourth, it is important that therapy be a safe and open context for clients' sexual fantasies. Sexual fantasies tend to be arousing, and clients and therapists who are discussing such material (even if the fantasies do not explicitly involve both parties) may find it easy to become carried away. Sexual intimacies between therapist and client are unethical, illegal, and constitute extremely damaging clinical practice. Fortunately, clients are gaining increasing safeguards against exploitation and are becoming increasingly aware that such conduct is prohibited. Clients currently have three main avenues for seeking redress for such behavior: 1) filing a civil suit charging malpractice (note: malpractice insurance does *not* cover such damages); 2) filing a complaint with the state licensing board (to revoke the clinician's license); and 3) filing a complaint with the appropriate professional ethics board (e.g., American Psychological Association, American Psychiatric Association, National Association of Social Workers, American Association for Marriage and Family Therapy). In all cases, it is the therapist's responsibility to see that such intimacies do not occur.

Fifth and finally, it is important to recognize that sexual fantasy is no longer a forbidden, ignored, nor completely mysterious area. Clinicians have a responsibility, when approaching such material, to be well prepared and informed. To function in this area without adequate knowledge of the accumulating research and theory is to practice carelessly and is inexcusable. Sexual fantasies are emerging as an important aspect of human life, and in a clinical setting they deserve a careful, informed approach. In this chapter, we have attempted to highlight a few of the research findings which inform our increasing understanding of sexual fantasies and of the role they play in human behavior and experience.

REFERENCES

1. E. Jong, *Fear of Flying*, Holt, Rinehart, and Winston, New York, New York, 1973.
2. N. Friday, *My Secret Garden*, Pocket Books, New York, New York, 1973.
3. N. Friday, *Forbidden Flowers*, Pocket Books, New York, New York, 1975.
4. N. Friday, *Men in Love*, Del Publishing Company, New York, New York, 1980.
5. A. Lorde, *Uses of the Erotic: The Erotic as Power*, The Crossing Press, Trumansburg, New York, 1978.
6. A. M. Dershowitz, *The Best Defense*, Random House, New York, New York, 1982.
7. A. D. Davidson, The Relationship of Reported Sexual Daydreaming to Sexual Attitude, Sexual Knowledge, and Reported Sexual Experience in College Women, unpublished doctoral dissertation, University of Cincinnati, 1974.
8. L. M. Giambra, Sex Differences in Daydreaming and Related Mental Activity from the Late Teens to the Early Nineties, *International Journal of Aging and Human Development*, *10*, pp. 1-34, 1979-80.
9. A. C. Kinsey, W. B. Pomeroy, C. E. Martin, and P. H. Gebbard, *Sexual Behavior in the Human Female*, Saunders, Philadelphia, Pennsylvania, 1953.
10. A. C. Kinsey, W. B. Pomeroy, and C. E. Martin, *Sexual Behavior in the Human Male*, Saunders, Philadelphia, Pennsylvania, 1948.
11. A. M. Zeiss and S. L. Lentz, An Empirical Investigation of the Relationship Between Fantasy and Arousal in College Women, *Journal of Imagination, Cognition, and Personality*, in press.
12. L. G. Rosenberg, Sex-Role Identification, Erotic Fantasy and Sexual Behavior: A Study of Heterosexual, Bisexual, and Homosexual College Men, unpublished Masters Thesis, Yale University, 1983.
13. E. B. Hariton and J. L. Singer, Women's Fantasies during Sexual Intercourse: Normative and Theoretical Implications, *Journal of Consulting and Clinical Psychology*, *42*, pp. 313-322, 1974.
14. J. Money, Pornography in the Home: A Topic in Medical Education, in *Contemporary Sexual Behavior*, J. Zubin and J. Money (eds.), Johns-Hopkins University Press, Baltimore, Maryland, 1973.
15. S. Frued, Creative Writers and Daydreaming, in *The Standard Edition of the Complete Psychological Works of Sigmund Freud*, J. Strachey (ed.), Hogarth, London, England, 1972.
16. A. Campagna, Masturbation Fantasies in Male College Freshmen, unpublished doctoral dissertation, Yale University, 1975.
17. L. M. Giambra and C. E. Martin, Sexual Daydreams and Quantitative Aspects of Sexual Activity: Some Relations for Males Across Adulthood, *Archives of Sexual Behavior*, *6*, pp. 497-505, 1977.
18. W. L. Robinson and K. S. Calhoun, Sexual Fantasies, Attitudes and Behavior as a Function of Race, Gender, and Religiosity, *Imagination, Cognition and Personality*, *2*, pp. 281-290, 1982-83.

19. P. A. Guido, A Comparison of Heterosexual and Homosexual Single and Cohabitating Male Masturbation Fantasies, unpublished doctoral dissertation, California School of Professional Psychology, 1981.

20. National Institute of Mental Health, *Television and Behavior: Ten Years of Scientific Progress and Implications for the Eighties, Volume 1, Summary Report*, U.S. Department of Health and Human Services, Rockville, Maryland, 1982.

21. M. Nelson, Sweet Bondage: You and Your Romance Habit, *Ms.*, *9*:8, pp. 97-98, 1983.

22. K. L. Campion, Intimate Strangers: The Readers, the Writers, and the Experts, *Ms.*, *9*:8, pp. 98-99, 1983.

23. K. S. Pope, Pornographic Literature, unpublished paper, Harvard University, 1972.

24. N. M. Malamuth and B. Spinner, A Longitudinal Content Analysis of Sexual Violence in the Best-Selling Erotic Magazines, *Journal of Sex Research*, *16*:3, pp. 226-237, 1980.

25. N. M. Malamuth, M. Heim, and S. Freshbach, Sexual Responsiveness of College Students to Rape Depictions: Inhibitory and Disinhibitory Effects, *Journal of Personality and Social Psychology*, *38*:3, pp. 399-408, 1980.

26. N. M. Malamuth, Rape Fantasies as a Function of Exposure to Violent Sexual Stimuli, *Archives of Sexual Behavior*, *10*:1, pp. 33-47, 1981.

27. L. R. Schover, Male and Female Therapists' Responses to Male and Female Client Sexual Material: An Analogue Study, *Archives of Sexual Behavior*, *10*:6, pp. 477-492, 1981.

CHAPTER 9

Mind-Controlled Analgesia: The Inner Way to Pain Control

DAVID BRESLER

"Imagination is more important than knowledge" . . .
Albert Einstein

THE PAIN EPIDEMIC

Chronic pain has become the nation's most expensive, disabling, and common disorder. An estimated 8-10 percent of the population of most Western countries suffer from some form of migraine headache. Arthritis alone afflicts over 50 million Americans, of whom 20 million require medical care [1, 2]. Each year, arthritis claims 600,000 new victims, and its cost to the national economy is estimated to be nearly $13 billion.

Low back pain—another of the most common pain complaints—has disabled seven million Americans and, according to the National Center for Health Statistics, generates nearly 19 million visits to doctors annually. Add to these the many other pain-related disorders—facial and dental pain, neuralgia and neuritis, cancer, aching necks and shoulders, tennis elbow, muscle spasms and others—and it is understandable how chronic pain can cost the nation's economy an estimated $60 billion annually. Its cost in terms of human suffering is incalculable.

These statistics are shocking to me. If a mysterious new flu virus were expected to infect tens of millions of Americans and cost our country billions of dollars in lost wages, a national campaign immediately would be launched to mobilize our scientific resources for battle. Chronic pain runs rampant in our land, inflicting severe physical, emotional, intellectual, social, and economic damage upon its victims, their families, and society as a whole. But America has only now begun to respond to the problem.

We live in a time of medical miracles. With the development of immunizations, antibiotics, and improved health conditions, we have witnessed the virtual elimination of infectious diseases that once decimated entire civilizations. Infant mortality has dropped significantly, and, almost daily, we read of astounding medical advances that would have been unthinkable only a few years ago.

Yet there is still no single form of therapy that is completely safe and effective for the treatment of pain. Many of the most frequently used contemporary techniques were developed by ancient civilizations, not modern man, and they have remained fundamentally unchanged over thousands of years.

Morphine, modern medicine's most effective pain reliever, is derived from opium, which was widely used as an analgesic forty centuries ago by the Egyptians. The ancient Romans relied on a combination of opium and wine. Primitive tribes of India and South Africa employed willow leaves, which are rich in salicylic acid (an ingredient of aspirin), to ease joint discomfort as well as the pain of childbirth.

The Incas chewed on the leaves of the coca plant centuries before cocaine was isolated by a German scientist in 1860. Transcutaneous electrical stimulation—a technique for controlling pain by applying small amounts of electricity—was utilized by Pedanius Discordides, a surgeon with Nero's armies, who applied a torpedo fish as a source of electricity. Even before that, Plato and Aristotle had written about the numbing effects of the electric fish to treat gout and headaches. However, the mortality rate associated with this procedure was often greater than 50 percent, so understandably, it did not achieve great public acceptance.

Acupuncture, herbs, and various physical therapies (heat, cold, and massage) have been an integral part of Chinese medicine for at least 5,000 years. Acupuncture needles carved from stone have been found in China and have been dated back to the Stone Age.

Acute Versus Chronic Pain

By refining and expanding the insights of ancient civilizations, modern technology has created an almost endless variety of pharmaceutic products, many of which are available over the counter. For management of acute or self-limiting pain, these agents are usually highly effective, for they provide temporary relief while the body heals itself. With the development of neural blockade and other modern anesthetic techniques, patients who undergo operative procedures are generally spared even the slightest degree of surgical discomfort.

Yet the sophisticated pharmacologic approaches which have been proven so successful in the management of acute pain are often ineffective for controlling *chronic* or long-term pain. Although acute pain will usually get better by itself as the body heals, chronic pain often becomes worse with time. As a rough rule of thumb, chronic pain refers to any pain problem that lasts longer than six months. Its victims are referred endlessly from doctor to doctor; for even if temporary relief can be obtained, the pain frequently returns with time.

When medications fail, patients often are told, "Nothing more can be done. You'll have to learn to live with it." But in my opinion, there is always hope for someone in pain. Until *every* conceivable therapeutic approach has been attempted, no one should be told, "Nothing can be done."

Recently, a variety of new approaches have been developed that utilize the enormous healing power of the mind. These include hypnosis, suggestion, conditioned relaxation, guided imagery and biofeedback training. This chapter provides a brief overview of one particularly effective alternative for control and management of chronic pain: guided imagery.

The Pain Experience

It is important to distinguish between a painful *sensation* (mental awareness of an unpleasant stimulus) and the pain *experience* (the total subjective experience of suffering due to pain). Furthermore, it is important to recognize that there is not necessarily any direct relationship between the sensation and the experience of pain. For example, Beecher found that soldiers seriously wounded in battle reported only mild discomfort; for, they were elated to learn that they were to be sent home for the duration of the war [3]. In contrast, phantom limb pain often produces agonizing discomfort even while the entire stump is anesthetized [4].

Many individuals think of pain as a *thing*, much like a splinter is a thing—that is, an object or substance from the outside that infiltrates the body. Thus, if you accidentally strike your thumb with a hammer, you might say you have "pain in the thumb."

Such a notion is inaccurate, for there is not pain *in* your thumb. When you injure it, you stimulate neural receptors that send a barrage of electrical and chemical messages up through the nerves in your hand and arm to your spinal cord and brain. *Whether or not a given sensation becomes painful depends upon the way it is interpreted by the nervous system.* If the nervous system decides that the messages from the thumb are urgent, it may create an experience of pain that is identified with the thumb. However, the main pain receptor is between the ears, for that is really where pain resides.

It is easy to see that pain is not a "thing" when we consider its complement, the phenomenon of pleasure. If you eat food that tastes delicious, you probably would not say, "Boy, do I have a lot of pleasure in my mouth! My mouth is just filled with pleasure." Clearly, both pleasure and pain reflect a sophisticated interpretation of a complex series of events.

Pain is well known to be influenced by learning and early developmental predispositions. For example, animals raised in a pain-free environment show insensitivity to noxious stimuli in later life [5, 7]. Social, cultural, and ethnic differences in the experience of pain also are well documented [7-9]. A vivid example are the initiation rituals of many primitive tribes, which would be considered nothing short of torture if practiced by members of Western cultures.

Aristotle was the first to suggest that "pain is an emotion," as pervasive as anger, terror, or joy. For the early philosophers, the answer to the question "What is pain?" was "It is the opposite of pleasure." The emotional component of pain is inexorably bound to other aspects of the pain experience; for, anxiety and agitation are the natural consequence of a painful sensation that tells higher cognitive centers that "something is wrong." If the "something" can be clearly identified and appropriate corrective action can be taken, the (acute) pain experience is terminated.

However, for most patients with chronic pain, the "something" is vague, and fear of continued pain in an unknown future produces even greater anxiety. On a physiologic level, sympathetic hyperactivity develops, as manifested by increased heart rate, blood pressure, respiration, palmar sweating, and muscle tension [10]. In patients with musculoskeletal pain, this increased muscle tension often augments the sensation of pain, which further increases anxiety, which, in turn, produces even greater muscular tension and more pain. The relationship between pain and anxiety is well known to clinicians, for treatment of one frequently provides relief of the other as well [7-10].

With time, exhaustion of sympathetic hyperactivity is inevitable, and more vegetative signs and symptoms soon emerge, such as feelings of helplessness, hopelessness, and despair, sleep and appetite disturbances, irritability, decreased interests and libido, erosion of personal relationships with family and friends, as well as increased somatization of complaints [10]. Thus, acute pain and anxiety become chronic pain and depression. It is well-known that the most notable emotional change in patients with chronic pain is the development of reactive depression [10, 12]. This may be overt or masked to both patient and health practitioner alike. As with acute pain and anxiety, chronic pain is often relieved by treating the associated depression [13].

It is important to emphasize the psychophysiological basis of chronic pain; for, it is a complex subjective experience that involves physical, perceptual, cognitive, emotional, and spiritual factors. When a patient with arthritis of the spine reports, "My back hurts," his/her pain experience also may involve anxiety or depression (producing insomnia, loss of appetite, and decreased sexual desire), drug dependence or addiction, numerous secondary gains, separation from work, family, and friends, masochistic behavior, and a host of other problems. These may remain indelibly associated with the experience of back pain, even after the entire spine has been chemically anesthetized.

Thus, it is easy to see why no simple pill or shot can cure chronic pain. The most common error made by clinicians is to evaluate and treat only the physical aspect of the problem; for, they assume that the objective of therapy is to *treat pain* in people. To me, however, the objective of therapy is to *treat people* in pain. From this perspective, it is nonsensical to wonder if a patient has "real" versus "unreal" (imaginary) pain, "organic" versus "psychologic" pain, or "legitimate" versus "hysterical" pain. Pain is an intensely personal experience, and even if no physical explanation for it can be found, *all pain is real.*

The Purpose of Pain

Since the dawn of creation, pain has provided critically important information concerning man's relationship to his inner and outer environments. Pain strongly conveys the message that "something is wrong," and it encourages the body to take action to prevent further injury. From an evolutionary point of view, it is one of the most powerful ways to insure the survival of an organism in a dangerous world.

While most authorities acknowledge the positive aspects of acute pain, many believe that chronic pain is a "biological mistake," serving no useful purpose. In order to correct this "mistake," they recommend strong drugs or surgical procedures to obliterate the sensation of pain. The exact technique utilized is more likely to depend upon the type of specialist consulted than upon the unique needs of the patient. For example, an internist may prescribe medications; a psychologist, psychotherapy; an acupuncturist, needles; a chiropractor, manipulation; and so forth. As one of my teachers, Abraham Maslow used to say, "When you hold a hammer, you tend to look for nails."

In my opinion, the best long-term interests of the patient often are not served when the major goal of therapy is to artificially mask or suppress pain without attempting to understand its ultimate message. To do so is like responding to a ringing fire alarm by cutting its wires to stop the annoying clamor, rather than by leaving the burning building.

The "mistake" or "accident" notion of chronic pain is like saying that "the Martians did it." Sometimes, I suggest to a patient, "Perhaps you were just walking down the street when you accidentally stumbled into a Martian pain ray. I hope that this is not the case, for we don't yet have an antidote to the Martian ray, and we don't know how to contact them to ask that it be shut off."

I then suggest to them that there may be another explanation—that their own nervous system is generating the experience of pain *for a reason*. In essence, I believe that chronic pain is usually not a disease or a mistake; rather, it is a symptom generated through the wisdom of the body. In my opinion, symptoms are the way that the body tries to heal itself or prevent further injury. Once their message is heard and appropriate action is taken, symptoms usually will disappear, for they are no longer needed.

For example, a low-grade fever (under 103°) represents the body's attempt to raise its temperature in order to "burn out" an invading microbe. Practitioners of Oriental medicine consider fever to be a *healthy* response to danger, and they make no attempts to reduce it unless it rises to injurious levels (over 104°). But in the Western world, most people quickly reach for an aspirin.

Much of contemporary medicine is based on an "adjustment model" of therapy designed to suppress symptoms. If a patient has high blood pressure, drugs are prescribed to reduce it. If a patient is unable to sleep, sleeping pills are given for sedation at night. If a patient has excessive anxiety, tranquilizers are often utilized. But *why* does a given patient have hypertension, sleep disorders, or anxiety neurosis? What is the message that the symptoms are trying to convey?

I always have liked the concept of "organ language," the way the body communicates through symptoms. Examples are "pain in the neck," "a broken heart," and we all know what hemorrhoids mean.

Pain is a message that alerts us to danger. Through the primitive, survival-oriented wisdom of the nervous system, it also motivates us to correct the situation by changing and adapting to the shifting demands of the world in which we live. Through pain, we are warned about *all* of the dangers we face, and if we continue to ignore them, the intensity of pain will increase. Perhaps this is why many chronic pain patients receive only temporary relief after symptomatic treatment. Although the nervous system can be fooled for a short time by drugs or surgical treatment, if some subtle danger still remains, the pain will break through and, over time, continue to return until the message is heard and properly responded to.

What is the message that pain tries to convey? What is "wrong?" What sort of change is needed? The answers to these questions differ from person to person, but most commonly, the message has to do with the process of *change*.

THE TRANSFORMATIONAL PROCESS

Change is fundamental to all of life. If you step back and examine how your own life changes, you will see that it typically alternates between times of peace, contentment, and pleasure, and periods of pain and insecurity. Both are essential to life and health.

Life is filled with periods of dissolution in which old patterns are destroyed to let new ones develop. These transitional phases are painful, but without them, we would never grow, advance, and progress. As Abraham Maslow used to say, "There is no growth without pain. If you're not hurting, you're not growing."

When I interview people in pain, I attempt to gain a full understanding of their life cycles—that is, the patterns of change that characterize their lives. Amazingly, these patterns are quite typically spirals, for people seem destined to return to the same situational places through which they have struggled before. As Nietzsche stated, "If you have any character at all, you repeat the same crises throughout your life." A more contemporary version of this same notion is expressed by Barry Tydings: "You're always in the same game—only the players and the uniforms change."

People who suffer from chronic pain typically have difficulty dealing with the process of change. When confronted with a transformational crisis, they become immobilized, unwilling to let go of the old and make the hard but essential changes necessary for a meaningful new life.

Some think of the life cycle as a death/rebirth phenomenon. Whenever we reach a new plateau, something dies, but simultaneously, something new is born that replaces it. This death/rebirth process exists throughout the entire universe.

Take the human fetus, for example. In a sense, it is more like a plant than an animal. It lives in water and sends roots into the uterus from which it receives nourishment. But at the moment of birth, the water is released, the stalk is cut, and the roots are ripped up. At this precise instant, the "plant" has ceased to exist, and the infant is born. Something has died, but simultaneously, something else has begun to live. Is the death of the plant not synonymous with the birth of the fetus? Are they not just two aspects of the same process?

The same phenomenon is found throughout nature. The seed grows to become a tree, which, at the peak of its glory, gives forth its flowers. But can the tree cling forever to those blossoms? No. They soon wither and die. But is the death of the flowers not synonymous with the birth of the fruit—the real nourishment of the tree? And after the fruit reaches its full maturity, it withers and dies, too. But in the process, it distributes its seeds, which provide for the real immortality of the tree.

The life cycle occurs in our personal lives as well. For example, we confront the process of change time and time again in relationships. While we hope that our bonds to those closest to us will remain secure forever, all relationships must change sooner or later. The only permanent relationship we have is the relationship with ourselves. We value our interactions with others because they allow us to experience different parts of ourselves. As those relationships change, we, too, must change.

The experience of change is characterized by pain, anger, fear, and uncertainty. Psychologists often identify four phases in the transformational process. The first is denial: "This is not really happening. It's all a mistake." The second is anger: "Why me? I don't deserve this. It's not fair." The third is mourning: "What will I do now? How can I live without him/her/it?" The final stage is adjustment: "I wonder what lies ahead? Maybe things will be even better."

People who experience chronic pain typically get stuck in the first three stages of this process. In a literal sense, they allow their lives to grind to a halt, and all growth stops. *Pain does not make their lives unbearable. Rather, their lives make pain unbearable. Pain is not the cause of their lives stopping. It is the result.*

As a result of my personal experiences and my work with thousands of patients, I am convinced beyond a shadow of a doubt that *it is possible to feel pain and yet not suffer.* The critical difference is the manner of perceiving the reality of the pain experience.

THE NATURE OF REALITY

To understand modern perspectives of reality, we must turn to physics, the science of defining and quantifying reality. The Newtonian view of the universe was shattered by the theory of relativity which expanded the limits of our understanding of the real world. Albert Einstein postulated the equivalence of matter and energy in the classic law of relativity, and he explored the ways in which time influences our perception of events. I have always liked Einstein's definition which states, "When you sit on a hot stove for two seconds, it seems like two hours. But when you sit with a nice woman for two hours, it seems like two seconds. That's relativity."

The theory of quantum mechanics expands even further our concepts concerning the world in which we live. According to the principle of complementarity, the reality of an event is vague and ambiguous; for, it depends entirely upon the frame of reference through which it is viewed. In other words, what you experience depends entirely upon how you look at it. For example, imagine that two of your friends have just had a serious argument. After talking with the first friend, you feel outraged by the other friend's behavior. Yet, after talking with the second friend, you see his/her position as well. Who is *really* right? Both and neither. The reality of the situation is ambiguous, and the question of "Who is right?" depends upon your frame of reference. As Werner Heisenberg, one of modern physics' greatest theorists, has stated, "The universe is not completely knowable or predictable."

It is important to understand the practical implications of this concept, for it truly affects the ways in which we live. There is an old anecdote about two priests who approach their bishop with a question. "May I smoke while I pray?" asked the first priest, "Of course not", replied the bishop. "When you pray, all of your attention must be focused on the creator." The second priest then asked, "May I pray while I smoke?" and the bishop replied, "Of course. Prayer is appropriate during any activity."

When we understand that reality is vague and ambiguous, we are forced to view our lives in radically different ways. What may appear to be a tragedy from one frame of reference, may indeed be a blessing from another point of view. Remember, from the perspective of an egg, a chicken is just the way that one egg makes another egg.

Even more significantly, the theory of quantum mechanics stipulates that the act of observing influences what is seen. A classic illustration of this notion involves a small tank of water at an unknown temperature. How can you determine the *real* temperature of the water? You might use a thermometer. But the instant the thermometer touches the water, the temperature of the water is changed, even if the thermometer's temperature differs from that of the water by only a millionth of a degree.

In the same way, when you see yourself as a helpless, hopeless victim in an impossible situation, that is the way you experience your reality. If you change your way of looking at yourself and the world in which you live, you change the reality of your situation as well. This is why it is possible to hurt and yet not suffer. All of us must experience pain from time to time, but if we view the experience as an opportunity for growth and change rather than as a catastrophe, our reality can be a highly positive one.

There is an old saying in medicine, "The conviction of illness leads to illness, and the conviction of cure leads to cure." As John C. Lilly, a physician, once said, "In the realm of the mind, what you believe to be true *is* true, or becomes true, within certain experiential and experimental limits that remain to be transcended." To use the vernacular, what you see is what you get.

How, then, do we change our frame of reference? We do so by changing our beliefs, attitudes, and expectations about the world. This requires us to communicate with the deepest levels of the body, psyche, and soul, and to speak the language of the unconscious mind through images and symbolism. As we shall see, guided imagery is an effective technique for facilitating this type of communication and for promoting the healing experience [13-25].

THE IMPORTANCE OF
IMAGERY AND SYMBOLISM

Despite guided imagery's recent emergence as a therapeutic tool, the roots of this new technique may date back to the ancient Hebrew mystics, who recognized the relationship of images to events that went beyond normal experience. In more recent times, psychotherapists have utilized a variety of imagery techniques to tap the contents of the subconscious mind. For example, Hermann Rorschach, the Swiss psychiatrist, used standardized ink-blot designs to assess the psychological relevance of various images and emotions to his patients' mental states.

Freud developed a technique he called "free association" as a way of reading the unconscious. He believed that the unconscious was the storehouse of instinctual and forbidden desires and fears that were outside of conscious awareness, and that through the images produced in free association, much of this rich information could be evaluated.

Carl Jung contended that the unconscious held more than just our forbidden desires and fears, but also was the repository of our deepest, most positive hopes for fulfillment and self-actualization. He developed several innovative imagery techniques designed to explore these aspects of the unconscious.

More recently, O. Carl Simonton and Stephanie Matthews-Simonton have used guided imagery as an adjunct to conventional methods of treating cancer [26]. The Simontons compare patients' images of the power of their body to the power of their cancer. They report that often, the stronger image prevails in the real battle. For example, if the cancer is pictured as a dangerous animal and the white cells as puffs of snow or cotton, the prognosis is poor. As one aspect of their program, they frequently teach patients to imagine their white blood cells as warriors attacking and destroying the malignancies.

A family physician, Irving Oyle, D.O., has described a variety of guided-imagery techniques used to treat many different kinds of medical problems [14-16]. He believes that we are normally in contact with only 10 percent of our brain, and that guided imagery is a way to find out what the other 90 percent thinks about.

As a growing number of therapists acknowledge the potential benefits of guided imagery, new techniques constantly are being developed [13, 27]. While I cannot even begin to review them here, one basic approach involves having the patient draw a symbolic picture of his/her ailment. Such a picture can provide a more comprehensive perspective of the illness or symptom than any verbal description can.

One of my patients visualized her facial pain as her "mouth on fire." With this image in mind, I asked her to devise ways to put out the flames. The innovative ways available for extinguishing a fire are limited only by the patient's imagination, and she visualized herself absorbing those flames into cool, floating clouds of imaginary water. As she continued to practice this guided-imagery exercise, her pain gradually subsided. Remember, how you view the world determines how you experience it.

LANGUAGES OF THE NERVOUS SYSTEM

The human body is an enormously complex organism. Its nervous system contains at least seven to ten billion nerve cells, and an average cell has approximately 5,000 interconnections. Thus, according to neurophysiologist Charles Herrick, there are at least 10 to the 2,783,000 power possible connections for receiving, storing, correlating, and transmitting data [28]. How is this incredibly complex system regulated?

In a previous work, I have suggested that the answer may lie in the two fundamentally different ways the nervous system communicates with itself [13]. One higher-order communication system uses words and verbal thoughts. This is the "conscious mind," the little voice in your head that talks to you constantly. It has instant access to the somatic nervous system, the division that controls muscles and mediates voluntary movement.

For a quick demonstration of how this particular part of the nervous system works, try the following:

> First, raise your arm high into the air. Raise it as high as you can.
> Now, *how* did you do that? Did you have to tell your body how to go about raising your arm? Did you have to say, "Deltoids—contract! Latissium dorsi—relax?"
> No, your body knows exactly what to do. When your mind gives certain verbal commands—"I'm going to raise my arm"—you just do it. Verbal commands or thought have immediate access to functions controlled by your somatic nervous system.

Now, tell your body to raise your blood pressure. You're not having much success? My explanation for this is that the autonomic nervous system, the division that regulates blood pressure as well as heartbeat, blood chemistry, digestion, tissue regeneration, and immune/inflammatory responses among others, does not respond to the same language used to raise your arm. To increase blood pressure, a second type of communication system is involved—one that uses the language of symbolism and imagery.

If you would like to see how easily imagery can be used to raise your blood pressure, try the following exercise. (Note: If you already have high blood pressure, your nervous system apparently knows too well how to raise your blood pressure. Do not give it further encouragement.)

Sitting quietly and comfortably in a chair, imagine being in the deepest, darkest woods of Africa, alone on a cold, wet night, naked and shivering. You do not know what you are doing there, but you are lost and terribly frightened.

Then, suddenly, you realize that you are not alone! In the distance, you hear a crashing, pounding noise that is quickly becoming louder and louder, closer and closer. Your heart begins to beat faster, and as the sound becomes even louder, you panic and begin to run. You run slowly at first but then desperately faster as this "thing" in the woods comes even closer.

It is now clear that this beast is chasing *you*! As you race through the forest, faster and faster, with the brush tearing at your flesh, the beast is coming closer and closer, until you can feel its hot breath burning the back of your neck. As it reaches out to take you, you scream louder than you ever have in your life. . . .

What happened? If you were able to involve yourself in the scene described above, your mind almost certainly caused your blood pressure to rise. How did it do so? The results were produced in the same way you were able to raise your arm—by having an appropriate thought. But in this case, the language you used was not one of words but images.

Try another illustration of the difference between verbal commands and imagery: First, using verbal language, order yourself to "manufacture and secrete saliva." By thinking about this command, see how much you can generate. If you are like most people, you probably produced a little, but not much. It is not easy to do, because the parts of the nervous system that regulate salivation do not respond readily to verbal commands. Now try a different approach:

Imagine that you have a big, yellow, juicy lemon in your hand. Experience it in your mind's eye until you sense its fresh tartness. Now imagine taking a knife and slicing into the lemon. Carefully cut out a thick, juicy section. Now take a deep bite of the lemon slice and sense the sour lemon juice splashing in your mouth, saturating every taste bud of your tongue so fully that your lips and cheeks curl.

How much saliva did you create this time? If you were able to paint the picture vividly in your mind's eye, the image probably produced substantial salivation, for the autonomic nervous system easily understands and responds to the language of imagery. You do not have to tell it *how* to respond any more than you need to instruct your muscles how to raise your arm.

Here is the crux of this discussion: If thinking of a lemon makes you salivate, what happens when you think of yourself as a helpless victim of a hopeless problem? Does it not tell your nervous system to give up? In my opinion, negative expectations often become self-fulfilling prophecies; for, images have the power to create their own reality in the body. For example, if a patient experiences pain as a sizzling hot poker that is constantly being stabbed into his/her neck, or as a lion gnawing on his/her back, tearing deeper into the nerves with every bite, these images will contribute significantly to the experience of suffering and will interfere with the healing process.

THE BRAIN

The Brain's Two Hemispheres

Recent research studies suggest an anatomical explanation for the two languages used by the nervous system. This explanation may lie within the brain itself, which has two separate hemispheres. When viewed by the naked eye, these hemispheres appear identical, but functionally they are quite unique.

In most individuals, the left hemisphere is the seat of the conscious mind, for it is involved in the process of rational, logical, analytic, and evaluative thinking. Most importantly, the nerve centers that control speech are localized primarily in the left hemisphere, so its major communication system is a verbal one. It is the seat of the little voice in your head that constantly talks to you.

The right hemisphere, on the other hand, processes the information it receives in an abstract, symbolic manner, and appears to be involved in more creative, impulsive, intuitive, and instinctual thought processes. Its linguistic abilities are quite limited, so it communicates primarily through the language of imagery—most notably in dreams, daydreams, and intuitions. It is the seat of the unconscious mind, and although it does not communicate in words, do not assume that it is unintelligent or uninformed. Remember, "A picture is worth a thousand words."

Consciousness and the Brain

Although no one really knows what "consciousness" is, I believe that it is critically related to the process of "attention;" for, what we attend to is what we experience. Your attention is one of your most valued attributes; for, there is nothing you can give that is more intimate.

Children show us the truth of this notion. They will perform the most outrageous acts to attract our attention. And even if they are punished as a result, it is worth it, for nothing is more valuable than attention.

Over the years, most of us have learned to give our major attention to the conscious mind, the left hemisphere. We listen endlessly to the chatter of the little voice that maintains a logical, rational, analytic monologue concerning its perspective of the world. We quickly become lost in it, forgetting that any other part of us exists.

Nothing could be more counterproductive. You are *not* solely your conscious mind; it is no more (or less) important than any other aspect of your being. Your left hemisphere is just one part of your brain, and like other vital organs, it has a specialized function that aids survival—that is, it makes logical associations from Thought A to Thought B to Thought C, and so on.

Have you ever asked, "Now what made me think of that?" The conscious mind can race through a series of associations in a flash, and when you allow your attention to reside solely there, your total experience becomes that chain of thoughts.

However, you are much more than your conscious mind. You are also your intuition, emotions, and feelings, your drives and motivations, your goals and aspirations, your values and beliefs, your personality, and, of course, your physical body. To me, it makes no more sense to believe that you are primarily your conscious mind than to believe that you are primarily your liver or kidneys (or your anger, your appetite, and so forth).

How do you get in touch with the other parts of yourself? You do so simply by giving them your attention. Unfortunately, most of us do this only under strong coercion. When a part of us desperately needs to be heard, it briefly will capture our attention. For example, when we injure ourselves, the alarms go off and our attention is temporarily shifted to the body. But shortly thereafter, we wander back to the conscious mind, and the inner voice begins again.

Why do we allow the conscious mind to dominate our attention so thoroughly? We permit this because most of us have been rewarded for doing so. In the Western world, the accomplishments of the left hemisphere—our rational, logical, articulate side—usually are respected over all others. Our educational, social, and vocational systems offer great recognition and advancement to people who are logical, analytic, and articulate. True, athletes are rewarded for the accomplishments of their physical bodies (and as a result, their bodies receive much of their attention). In a similar manner, actors, writers, or artists may rely primarily on their intuitions and emotions.

But most of us receive little, if any, recognition for the achievements of the right hemisphere—our creative, intuitive, instinctive side. In fact, we usually are discouraged from "wasteful" activities such as daydreaming. Consequently, we suppress the most creative part of our nervous system and literally forget how to gain access to it. Thus, we identify almost exclusively with the conscious mind and allow it to keep our attention its prisoner.

If you think that you have control of your conscious mind, try these simple experiments. First, stop your conscious mind from thinking for 1 minute. Can you do it?

Next, tell your conscious mind to give you any *wrong* answer to the equation 2+2=( ). Do not let it return to the number "4."

These experiments illustrate the notion that the conscious mind is nothing more than a complex biocomputer, totally programmed by the rewards and punishments from past life experiences. Is it not important to let your attention explore the right hemipshere as well? Only in this way will you discover critical misconceptions about the nature of your personal reality that need to be corrected. For example, you may find that your right hemisphere is filled with negative beliefs and expectations that, in turn, are responsible for many or most of your negative experiences. These inappropriate expectations must be identified before they can be changed.

Through symbolism and imagery, you can readily access the autonomic nervous system and produce dramatic changes in your body. By learning to speak the language of the unconscious mind, you also may uncover new insights and information that will help you to optimize the quality of life that you experience.

GUIDED-IMAGERY TRAINING TECHNIQUES

Some people feel that they have little ability to create images in their minds, but everyone can cultivate this talent to an amazingly high degree. Many patients have told me that when they close their eyes, they see "nothing except blackness and some floating red, blue, or green dots." This is why I do not like the terms "visualization" or "visual fantasy." Although we are primarily visual creatures, imagery is a vicarious experience that does not necessarily involve seeing.

For example, think of the tune "Jingle Bells" for a moment. Can you remember how it goes? Now, where did you hear it? Was anyone playing it in the room? Or was it just an auditory image that you recalled? In the same way, we can experience olfactory images of burning leaves on an autumn day or of a favorite cologne.

To utilize guided imagery, it is not necessary to literally see, hear, taste, feel, or smell inside our heads. All that is required is to experience what the image might be like by becoming involved in a vicarious adventure.

Many people have not tapped their power of imagination since childhood. Getting in touch with images in the mind has become a difficult and awkward process, for their creative and intuitive abilities have long been ignored. Elsewhere, I have described several training exercises that can be used to strengthen imagery skills [13]. A prerequisite for maximum effectiveness of imagery techniques is the achievement of a state of deep relaxation. With diligent and conscientious practice, however, most people are easily able to utilize guided imagery.

Imagery and Pain Control

As a result of our work with thousands of people in pain over the past dozen years, my colleagues and I have developed a wide variety of imagery techniques designed to alleviate pain and suffering [13]. One approach is called "mind-controlled analgesia" (MCA); it uses the language of the unconscious mind to transform the pain experience in a positive way. Before beginning MCA, patients are asked to prepare two drawings that symbolize the experience of their discomfort at its worst and at its best. Then they are instructed to imagine how they would feel if they were experiencing the most intense pleasure possible and to draw a third picture that symbolizes this experience.

Next they are given a prerecorded cassette tape containing the MCA exercise and asked to practice it several times per day.[1] In essence, the exercise begins with a rapid-induction relaxation procedure, followed by a vivid experience of the first picture (pain at its worst). By means of systematic sensory enhancement, this experience is then transformed into the one symbolized by the second picture (pain at its best). Finally, patients are encouraged to unlock their maximum creative potential and to dissolve this experience into the image of pleasure, health, and healing. Over time, many people find that as the images change, so does their experience of the world in which they live.

Another pain control technique is called "glove anesthesia." It involves a two-step imagery exercise in which patients first are taught to develop feelings of numbness in the hand, as if it were in an imaginary anesthetic glove. Next, they learn to transfer these feelings of numbness to any part of the body that hurts, simply by placing the "anesthetized" hand on it.

Glove anesthesia is a symptomatic technique—that is, it reduces the physical symptoms of pain without concern for its cause. It is a useful alternative to analgesic medications, and it is used particularly when discomfort is so intense that the patient cannot concentrate enough to use other guided-imagery approaches. Glove anesthesia often helps to "take the edge off" the pain sensation, thus permitting patients to explore other aspects of the pain experience more fully.

In addition, glove anesthesia provides a dramatic illustration of the power of self-control. When patients realize that they can produce feelings of numbness in their hands at will, they recognize that they may be able to control their discomfort, too. This is profoundly therapeutic for pain sufferers who feel totally helpless and unable to affect their discomfort.

Symptom substitution is another symptomatic technique that permits the nervous system to move the discomfort to a new area of the body where it will be less disruptive. For example, patients can learn to experience their headaches in, say, the little finger instead of the head. This technique does not ask the

---

[1] Professionally recorded cassette tapes of these guided imagery exercises are available from Summerset Associates, Post Office Box 967, Pacific Palisades, California 90272.

nervous system to stop the experience of pain (or to cover up the message it is trying to communicate). Rather, it moves it to a less traumatized area so that patients can work more effectively to identify what is wrong.

These and other approaches encourage patients to utilize the intuitive side of the brain and all of their inner resources. In essence, guided imagery is the formation of personalized mental images that facilitate the healing process. Thus, its use is not restricted to pain problems. Because it can mobilize the autonomic nervous system and the immune/inflammatory response system, it is an important tool for any type of self-healing.

Remember, reality is vague and ambiguous. If you see your life as living torture, that is how you will experience it. But if you can see yourself in your mind's eye as being healthy, functional, and happy to be alive, that is the way your personal world will be.

THE INNER ADVISOR

One of the most powerful guided imagery techniques involves the creation of an "advisor," a "counselor," an "inner doctor," or a "spirit guide." During a session of guided imagery, the patient is taught to relax and then is instructed on how to locate an imaginary living creature in his/her unconscious mind, who thereafter will serve as his/her advisor. These advisors have taken the form of everything from dogs and frogs to religious figures—but of course, they are just a reflection of the person who is creating the image.

By definition, the advisor has access to the entire realm of the unconscious, the part of the brain which normally is outside the individual's awareness. Our unconscious is a valuable storehouse of insights, suggestions, and desires, and through regular communication with the advisors, critically important information about the inner world often emerges. Advisors frequently provide insights into past experiences that may have contributed to pain. They can offer advice on specific ways to relieve discomfort, and sometimes, they can even alleviate pain completely in an instant.

One of my patients, a fifty-two-year-old cardiologist named John, was suffering from excruciating low back pain following treatment for rectal cancer. Although surgery and radiation therapy apparently had eradicated the cancer, the pain that remained was "unbearable." Because the area had been so heavily irradiated, neither repeated nerve blocks nor further surgery could be used to help relieve his terrible discomfort, and he had long ago developed tolerance to his pain medications.

When John first came to see me, he already had narrowed down his personal alternatives to three: 1) successful treatment, 2) voluntary commitment to a mental institution, or 3) suicide. John was convinced that under no circumstances could he continue to live with pain and at the same time maintain his sanity.

In reviewing his medical records, I noticed that during a psychiatric workup, John had described his pain as "a dog chewing on my spine." This image was so vivid that I suggested we make contact with the dog, using guided imagery. With his training in traditional medicine, he thought the idea was silly, but he was willing to give it a try.

In John's case, our initial goal was to have the dog stop chewing on his spine. Over the next few sessions, the dog began to reveal critically important information. According to the dog (named Skippy), John never had wanted to be a physician—his own career choice was architecture—but he had been pressured into medical school by his mother. Consequently, he felt resentment not only toward his mother, but also toward his patients and colleagues. Skippy suggested that this hostility had in turn contributed to the development of his cancer and to the subsequent pain problem as well.

During one session, Skippy told John, "You're a damn good doctor. It may not be the career you wanted, but it's time you recognized how good you are at what you do. When you stop being so resentful and start accepting yourself, I'll stop chewing on your spine." These insights were accompanied by an immediate alleviation of the pain, and in only a few weeks' time, John became a new person, and his pain progressively subsided.

The Friend Inside

When I first was introduced to the advisor technique by Dr. Irving Oyle, I was as quick to challenge it as anyone. How could it do all the things he claimed? Also, it was so unorthodox that I doubted if the typical patient would accept it. After all, what would be your initial reaction to a doctor who encouraged you to start talking to little animals in your head?

However, I have been surprised, not only by the immense value of guided imagery, but also by the receptivity of most patients to the technique. In retrospect, this open-mindedness on their part is not as amazing as I had originally thought. Guided imagery is basically just a way of talking to ourselves, which is hardly a new concept.

I am sure that sometimes we react to a particular event by saying, "Damn! I knew that was going to happen!" Well, *how* did you know? Who told you? Of course, it was the intuitive part of your nervous system—in essence, an inner advisor. And you should have listened to it.

Interestingly, children are not as negligent of their unconscious mind as adults. They naturally communicate with that part of themselves and are constantly creating their own imaginary playmates. But unfortunately, parents often discourage such behavior ("It's not real, don't daydream, stop talking to imaginary things"). As a result, they unknowingly disconnect their offspring from this vital part of themselves. I think this situation is tragic. For when children communicate with their intuitive side, it is a very normal, healthy activity. How sad it is when children are outrightly told not to be impulsive, spontaneous, or creative.

Through guided imagery, however, people once again can make contact with inner "playmates" who are able to provide important insights about their lives. They can give advice on how to reduce stress and improve health. They can supply encouragement for decisions made, with an enthusiasm that friends or family members are unable or unwilling to offer. Because advisors are a reflection of their creators, they are always loyal and faithful.

Occasionally, however, communication problems do arise, but this is not really surprising. A dialogue with your advisor is just a reflection of what is going on inside of you. If your advisor acts timid or frightened, perhaps it is because you are feeling insecure. If your advisor will not talk to you, maybe it is because you are unwilling to open up about what really is going on inside.

Keep in mind that advisors always work on behalf of your best long-term survival-oriented interest. If an advisor will not cooperate with you, it may be a test of your sincerity. For example, Irving Oyle tells the case history of a psychiatrist who suffered from severe migraine headaches. Though highly skeptical of guided imagery, he found an advisor—a mermaid named Ethel—who insisted that in order for them to talk, he would have to swim out to her in the imaginary ocean where she lived. He refused at first, but at Dr. Oyle's urging, finally agreed. Once he had swum several hundred yards offshore, Ethel asked him to dive with her into the depths of the water so that their dialogue could begin. The psychiatrist began feeling even more silly. "How corny!" he exclaimed. "Sinking down into the sea of the subconscious. This whole thing is ridiculous!" Ethel responded curtly, "So sue me! Not only do I know about your headaches, but you deserve worse! You're even more ridiculous than I am." Later, after they had become friends, the psychiatrist asked Ethel why she had been so hostile initially. Ethel replied, "You were hostile, too, and it was the only way I could get your attention."

Ultimately, guided imagery boils down to making friends with your nervous system. When the technique is properly employed, it is safer than more invasive psychotherapeutic techniques, such as hypnosis. For example, if there is danger in breaking down a particular psychological safeguard or defense, the advisor usually will refuse to pursue the matter until the patient is able to deal with it more effectively. In my experience, advisors never tell patients something they are not psychologically equipped to handle. Even more important, advisors often can tell exactly what must first be accomplished in order to make this information safely available.

From my point of view, one of the great benefits of the technique is that it decreases dependency on the therapist. After all, it is clearly the advisor, not the therapist, who is providing the insights that facilitate healing.

Although there are no proven complications resulting from guided imagery therapy, I do not recommend it for people who are emotionally hysterical, mentally unstable, schizophrenic, or pre-psychotic. For these patients, guided imagery may some day prove to be as effective, or even more so, than conventional psychotherapy. But until more research has been conducted, it should be used with great discretion with such people.

THE ART OF MEDICINE

Guided imagery represents a different approach to health care, for it reflects more the art of medicine than the science of medicine. Rather than putting them into prolonged psychotherapy, guided imagery allows them to participate in a great adventure, an adventure in self-knowledge. That is why one of the most common prescriptions I write is: Four hugs per day———one before each meal and one at bedtime. Most of all, it is fun! While doctors are quick to review serum cholesterol and serum triglyceride levels, most people in pain need to increase their "serum fun levels."

To the extent that people in pain can laugh, have fun, and see the positive side of the world, they can be free from suffering.

REFERENCES

1. Arthritis Foundation, *Arthritis, The Basic Facts*, The Arthritis Foundation, Atlanta, 1976.
2. J. W. Pauley and D. J. Haskell, Treatment of Migraine without Drugs, *Journal of Psychosomatic Research, 19*, p. 367, 1975.
3. H. K. Beecher, *Measurement of Subjective Responses*, Oxford University Press, New York, 1959.
4. R. Melzack, *The Puzzle of Pain*, Basic Books, New York, 1973.
5. R. Melzack and T. H. Scott, The Effects of Early Experience on the Response to Pain, *Journal of Physiology and Comparative Psychology, 50*, p. 155, 1957.
6. H. W. Nissen, K. L. Chow, and J. Semmes, Effects of Restricted Opportunity for Tactual, Kinesthetic and Manipulative Experience on the Behavior of a Chimpanzee, *American Journal of Psychology, 64*, p. 485, 1951.
7. T. A. Gonda, The Relationship Between Complaints of Persistent Pain and Family Size, *Journal of Neurology, Neurosurgery and Psychiatry, 25*, p. 277, 1962.
8. R. A. Sternbach, *Pain: A Psychophysiological Analysis*, Academic Press, New York, 1968.
9. M. Zborowski, *People in Pain*, Jossey-Bass, San Francisco, 1969.
10. R. A. Sternbach, Psychology Factors in Pain, in *Advances in Pain Research and Therapy*, J. J. Bonica and D. Albe-Fessard (eds.), Raven Press, New York, pp. 293-299, 1976.
11. K. Jamison, M. T. Brechner, V. L. Brechner, and C. P. McCreary, Correlation of Personality Profile with Pain Syndrome, in *Advances in Pain Research and Therapy*, J. J. Bonica and D. Albe-Fessard (eds.), Raven Press, New York, pp. 317-321, 1976.

12. H. Merskey, Psychiatric Aspects of the Control of Pain, in *Advances in Pain Research and Therapy*, J. J. Bonica and D. Albe-Fessard (eds.), Raven Press, New York, pp. 711-716, 1976.
13. D. E. Bresler and R. Trubo, *Free Yourself From Pain*, Simon and Schuster, New York, 1979.
14. I. Oyle, *Magic, Mysticism and Modern Medicine*, Mesa Press, Bolinas, California, 1973.
15. I. Oyle, *The Healing Mind*, Celestial Arts, Millbrae, California, 1975.
16. I. Oyle, *Time, Space, and the Mind*, Celestial Arts, Millbrae, California, 1976.
17. J. E. Shorr, *Go See the Movie in Your Head*, Popular Library, New York, 1977.
18. R. H. McKim, *Experiences in Visual Thinking*, Brooks/Cole Publishing Co., Monterey, California, 1972.
19. M. Samuels and H. Bennett, *The Well Body Book*, Random House, New York, 1973.
20. M. Samuels and N. Samuels, *Seeing With the Mind's Eye*, Random House, New York, 1975.
21. J. L. Singer, *Imagery and Daydream Methods in Psychotherapy and Behavior Modification*, Academic Press, New York, 1974.
22. W. S. Kroger and W. D. Fezler, *Hypnosis and Behavior Modification: Imagery Conditioning*, J. B. Lippincott Co., Philadelphia, 1976.
23. R. Assagioli, *Psychosynthesis*, Viking Press, New York, 1971.
24. C. Jung, *Man and His Symbols*, Doubleday and Co., New York, 1964.
25. R. Sommer, *The Mind's Eye*, Delta Books, New York, 1978.
26. O. C. Simonton, S. Matthews-Simonton, and J. Creighton, *Getting Well Again*, J. P. Tarcher, Los Angeles, 1978.
27. D. T. Jaffe, *Healing From Within*, Alfred A. Knopf, Inc., New York, 1979.
28. C. J. Herrick, *The Evolution of Human Nature*, University of Texas Press, Austin, 1956.

CHAPTER 10

Imagine Health!
Imagery in Medical Self-Care

MARTIN L. ROSSMAN

Imagery has a long and varied history in the healing traditions of mankind. It is probably not too much to say that imagery is a central and omnipresent component of all healing when we consider the vital roles of placebo, suggestion and positive expectant faith. Imagery and suggestion are often carried covertly and unconsciously in the setting of medical communications and may well influence the treatment and outcome of illness. More conscious uses of imagery in medicine and in the self-care health movement involve techniques of relaxation, pain control, and autonomic self-regulation, as well as introspective, receptive imagery techniques aimed at fostering greater self-awareness in relation to some aspect of health. As a clinician working primarily either with people who have chronic or psychophysiologic illness or with basically healthy people who want to learn about health promotion and maintenance, I have been highly motivated to find educational methods and tools which can aid in attaining higher levels of competence in self-care. Over the past ten years, certain imagery skills have proven themselves so useful in practice, that my colleague, Naomi Remen, M.D., and I decided to put them in a format that could enable people to learn these skills by themselves. In this chapter I will briefly look at the relationship of self-care and professional care, review the range of uses of imagery in health care, discuss some models that may help explain the usefulness of imagery in this area, and finally present the rationale and format of our learning program, which we call *Imagine Health!* [1].

It is the premise of this chapter that the human imagination, perhaps the most subjective of all our therapeutic tools, is potentially one of the most useful in teaching people how to take better care of themselves. Historically, it is likely that the most ancient therapeutics arose out of vision and intuition as primitive patients and healers alike sought guidance and intervention from the spirit world. Whether the insights and instructions they received came from the gods or from somewhere in the right cerebral cortex is still a matter of neurotheological argument [2]. Nonetheless, history abounds with myths, legends, and "anecdotal case histories" that attest to guidance received when men cried out for help in the darkness of unknowing and suffering. It is in this empirical relationship to a higher level of organization, whether in our own nervous system or in the universe at large, that the great self-care potential of the human imagination may reside.

Imagery is receiving a tremendous resurgence of interest throughout the spectrum of the healing arts and is currently being researched in major medical centers and universities around the world in clinical situations ranging from the treatment of chronic pain to the management of patients with cancer. A large percentage of the methods involved consist of exercises and techniques that must be, or can be, learned by the patients themselves. An ever-increasing number of self-help books in all areas of psychology and medicine seems to reflect a growing desire of consumers to take more responsibility for their health and the increasing willingness of the professional community to teach them the skills that make it possible. Though professional expertise, guidance, and intervention will undoubtedly continue to be necessary and useful in future health care, the emergence of activated health consumers and educationally oriented health providers may mark a significant change in the nature of health care in this society.

SELF-CARE

The Need for Self-Care

The need and increasing desire for self-care skills stem from a variety of factors in contemporary American life. An overburdened, highly technological disease-oriented system of care often fails to satisfy the largely human needs of its consumers. Though health-related costs represent almost 10 percent of national expenditures and though health care (more accurately "disease care") costs are increasing at a rate *twice* that of any other significant public cost, the quality of care does not seem to be improving, and consumers and providers alike continue to express increasing levels of dissatisfaction with the system.

The "medicalization" of nonmedical issues [3-4] and a burgeoning reliance on technological solutions to largely emotional and social problems have resulted in a significant human as well as financial cost [5]. Iatrogenic illness is in itself a significant health problem in this country [3-6]. In addition, the cultural view of health and illness implicitly communicated through our predominantly biomedical approach is a factor which encourages somatization and medical presentation of such psychosocial complaints [7]. The emphasis that now exists on seeking specialized help for every problem tends to disempower the individuals and discourages them from taking an active role in determining their own fates. Unrealistic expectations on the part of both the public and professionals have resulted in mutual frustration, distrust, and hostility as evidenced by the malpractice crisis of the 1970's and rising levels of impaired and "burned-out" professionals [8].

One major reason for this disillusionment is the failure of American doctors to treat what Kleinman and others have called "the illness" suffered as well as the "disease" which has been diagnosed. Disease is defined as an observable pathologic change in organic function or form, and illness represents the experience and personal meaning of the problem [9]. Although pain may be caused by physical disease, a great deal of suffering stems from the personal meaning of the illness [10]. In failing to attend to the illness as well as to the disease, physicians often add to the suffering they are trying to alleviate. Kleinman, Cassel, Remen, and this author, among many [9-11] argue that medicine has the obligation not only to treat disease but also to relieve suffering; but emphasis on this function in medical education and practice will take time to effect even though it has been acknowledged as an important need. Methods of education that can help individuals identify, understand, and respect the nature of their own relationship to health and illness can both empower health consumers and relieve the besieged medical profession of its excessive burden.

The crux in many of the problems mentioned above lies in the accurate placement and acceptance of responsibility for health. Self-care is a twenty-four-hour-a-day process and no professional can assume it for anyone else. While expert, specialized, and caring guidance will always be needed in certain situations, the ability of people to help themselves in most health-related circumstances is a greatly underutilized health resource. In a civilization where the vast majority of all morbidity and mortality stems from "diseases of choice" and "diseases of civilization" [12], the burden and opportunity of responsibility must fall more squarely on the individual. As Knowles says,

> I believe that the idea of a 'right' to health should be replaced by that of a moral obligation to preserve one's own health. The individual then has the 'right' to expect help with information, accessible services of good quality, and minimum financial barriers [13].

I believe that professionals must contribute by helping to inform and instruct the public so that they can take better care of themselves, not only physically, but psychologically, emotionally, and socially. There now seems to be an unmistakable personal, social, economic and even ecological imperative for us to begin living more wisely if we are to survive and thrive, both individually and collectively.

The Advantages of Self-Care

The potential advantages of self-care are many. Decreased utilization of the health care system might be anticipated, especially for complaints that represent problems of living which are somatically expressed (the incidence of such somatization is thought to account for 50 to 75 percent of all visits to a primary medical practitioner [7, 14, 15]). We might expect a concomitant decrease in the frequency of toxic reactions to pharmaceuticals as the amount of prescribing is reduced. Likewise, a reduction in the amount of unnecessary surgery would be likely. Such decrease in iatrogenic illness alone would bring about a significant saving in health costs in both financial and human terms.

Professionals would be able to utilize their special expertise in a more realistic framework and not suffer as much from the inflated expectations of healing placed upon them by their patients and themselves. Less impairment and depression in physicians also might result in safer and more effective care. Professionals also would be less at risk as the irrational demand for pharmaceutical and surgical cure of suffering lessened.

Why then does there often seem to be such a reluctance to take more responsibility for one's health? Thomas Szasz has written succinctly to that issue:

> The crucial moral characteristic of the human condition is the dual experience of freedom of the will and personal responsibility. Since freedom and responsibility are two aspects of the same phenomenon, they invite comparison with the proverbial knife that cuts both ways. One of its edges implies options: we call it freedom. The other implies obligations: we call it responsibility. People like freedom because it gives them mastery over things and people. They dislike responsibility because it constrains them from satisfying their wants [16, p. xiii].

Individuals who accept the responsibility to take better care of themselves often have to face the possibility of giving up gains or functions served by the illness, unless they can develop healthy ways to meet those same needs. The increase in self-esteem, self-reliance, and independence that can come when individuals find that they can exert some control over their body and their life is therapeutic in itself. The lessened risk of drug toxicity and unnecessary surgery is a direct benefit to both individual and society. Beyond this, a shift in perspective that includes social and even global issues often occurs when individuals begin to notice and take care of themselves in a new way. As they become more sensitive and attuned to their own needs, it seems to become easier to perceive and respond to the needs of others as well.

Imagery, Psychophysiology, Self-Care, and Medicine

It is a rather well-established fact that imagery can be accompanied by a host of physiologic changes [17, 18]. The matrix in which much disease develops often is an unconscious process in which the taxing physiology of stress is produced in response to dysfunctional thought patterns. The ability to use imagery consciously to produce stress-relieving and potentially healing psychologic and change offers people an opportunity to play an active role in the outcome of their illness. Imagery has a valuable role to play in health care even if it were unaccompanied by physiologic change, a point that will be discussed later in this chapter. Yet, unsurprisingly, the imagery techniques that so far have received the most attention in the medical world are those that are associated with relaxation, pain relief, and autonomic self-regulation. These approaches, which all involve imagery to a significant extent, include, but are not limited to Benson's relaxation response [19], Jacobsen's progressive muscular relaxation [20], Transcendental Meditation [21], Autogenic Training [22], and hypnosis. The close relationship of imagery and hypnosis has been examined and elucidated by Barber, Sheehan, and others [18, 23]. Biofeedback training often involves visualization and guided imagery exercises in helping people learn to regulate autonomic processes [24-25]. Physiologic parameters that have been demonstrated to be affected by relaxation and imagery techniques include heart rate, blood pressure, respiratory rate, oxygen consumption, skin resistance, local blood flow, brain wave patterns, blood sugar, gastric acid secretion, salivation, gastrointestinal motility, pupillary size, sexual arousal, and muscle tension [17-25]. Placebo relief of pain has been associated with probable endorphin release from the pituitary [26]. Although therapeutic effectiveness and mechanism are not necessarily related to physiology, the vast range of physiologic functions which seems, within imagery's sphere of influence lends credence to the many reports of rapid, successful work with psychosomatic problems through imagery approaches.

Significantly, all of the above methods depend on one critical factor—the willingness of the clients to learn and use the techniques involved. Some methods are complex and require intensive special training to learn, others are easily explained through written materials or tapes. Though dose-response relationships for these techniques have not yet been determined, regular, frequent practice seems to be a factor stressed by all authors who have reported success with them. Prescribed frequency ranges from two sessions a day for hypertension control to twelve or more in working to relieve a chronic pain syndrome [19, 27].

The physician has an important role to play in the teaching of such self-care skills. For most people in our culture, the physician is still the ultimate authority on health care. While the methods need not be taught directly by a physician, the authority and reassurance that can be conveyed by the latter can lend a great deal of support to the effectiveness of the approach selected. The physician who realizes the value of involving patients in their treatment through relaxation and self-control methods can both motivate and support them to develop a higher level of competence in taking care of their own health.

Covert Roles of Imagery in Medicine and Self-Care

It seems important to point out that imagery plays an ongoing role in life and in health whether or not formal techniques are learned. Professionals and lay people alike need to be aware of the natural role of largely unconscious imagery in the way we perceive our world. Two important areas where imagery may often unconsciously influence health deserve particular mention—diagnosis and worry.

Diagnosis is the process of naming a disease or syndrome. Diagnosis is a system of classification dependent on the paradigm of the healing system in which it is made. The purpose of diagnosis, ideally, is to classify illnesses so that appropriate treatment can be administered. If such treatment is lacking, diagnosis still may serve a function in defining syndromes for research so that effective treatments can be found. Yet a third function of diagnosis is more magical than technical: Naming a syndrome often seems to convey to patients (and doctors) that some sense of control has been established over the process, and implies that they are no longer at the mercy of an unknown entity. Diagnosis, however, also carries with it a prognosis, and the range of prognosis is not always accurately explained to patients. Their private images of the meaning of a diagnosis may form the basis for very powerful, unconscious autosuggestion which may play a significant role in their response to the illness [28]. In most medical conditions there is a very wide variety of responses that patients have to their illnesses—some of this variety is attributable to our lack of knowledge about the diagnostic entity, and some to the individual physical and psychological resources of the patients. Yet frequently diagnosis is made and delivered more like a sentence than a description, and the image of a certain clinical course is overtly and covertly conveyed to patients by the health professionals. The latter must be aware of the real meaning (or lack of same) behind a diagnosis and must clearly explain to patients the range of prognoses and always leave room for hope and healing through mechanisms that are poorly understood but frequently witnessed.

The second special instance of unconscious imagery usage most important in health is worry. Worry may be seen as the repetitive anticipation of some form of disaster. Worrying is something we all do some of the time and some of us do all the time. Lewis Thomas has gone so far as to say that "man is the worrying animal" and that worry is a characteristic that distinguishes us from other life forms. Whether or not worry is unique to mankind, it certainly is a characteristic that plays a prominent role in health and illness. Worry is imagery and psychophysiology in action, and the rapid heart rate, sweaty palms, headaches, and upset stomachs that people bring on through worry can be the strongest evidence we can use to demonstrate that their thoughts do make a difference in how their bodies work. The first imagery skill I want chronically worried, tense patients with somatic complaints to learn is to *stop* using their habitual form of imagery. This may be done by instructing them to frequently stop and watch their thoughts [25], and by teaching them a basic relaxation exercise to practice two or more times a day. Barber gives his patients certain times in which to worry but instructs them to "worry in a new way," in a way that allows "new solutions, creative solutions to . . . problems to appear." [29]

Theories of Imagery

While it is not my purpose to exhaustively review theoretical speculations regarding the mechanism of imagery in psychology and medicine, it does seem worthwhile to look at several of the most useful models in explaining this phenomenon. Aristotle thought the imagination was a psychophysiologic aspect of the soul, a theory which is again finding consideration in some circles. Depth psychologist Ira Progoff has stated that imagery is the language of the psyche, and that the psyche is "the directive principle in the human being which guides its growth from the moment of conception forward." [30, p. 73] Lang refers to the image as a "conceptual network, controlling specific somatovisceral patterns, and constituting a prototype for overt behavioral expression." [31, p. 493]

This latter description is echoed in three similar models which, taken together, offer a good theoretical framework from which imagery may be explored. A model presented in Psychosynthesis Training [32] is schematically illustrated in Figure 1, where "P" represents a pattern of thoughts, feelings, or attitudes a person might hold consciously or unconsciously. This pattern, or belief system, would reflect itself in a person's daily life, "L", through patterns of behavior, including posture, activities, and ways of relating to people and events. The

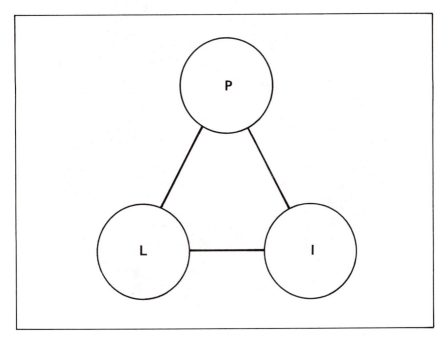

Figure 1. A psychosynthesis model of the relationship of thought patterns (P), imagery (I), and life (L).

thought pattern also would be reflected in the imagery, "I," that would attend it. When a person becomes aware, through illness or suffering, that something in "L" is amiss, he/she often seeks external help. By focusing on his/her imagery, "I," the individual may be able to access and work with thought patterns, hidden from consciousness, that may be underlying the symptoms. The symbolic dimension, expressed in imagery, may be more accessible and amenable to change than the pattern which underlies it, and a change in the imagery sphere then may be expected to be reflected both in the life situation and in the underlying belief system.

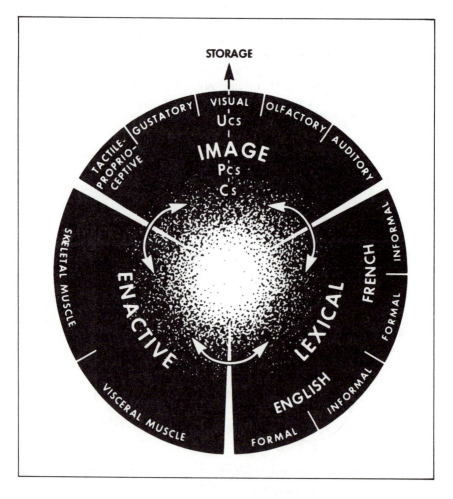

Figure 2. Systems of representation of thought (from M. J. Horowitz in Singer and Pope (eds.), *The Power of Human Imagination*, New York, Plenum, 1978.)

Another model of this process is presented by Mardi Horowitz (see Figure 2). Horowitz states that information entering the central nervous system is initially encoded in images and then may be translated into two other major forms of information storage and expression, which he terms the lexical and the enactive. The lexical mode is that type of thinking subserved by language and sequential, linear thinking. The enactive one is a kinesthetic mode represented by tension and movement patterns in the body, including facial expressions. Again, we see a tripartite model in which information can be encoded, retrieved, expressed, and exchanged among patterns of thought, images and physical reality. Horowitz also emphasizes that imagery is an effective mode in which to work with emotional issues, which, after all, are the main psychologic effectors of physiology. He states,

> The close relationship of images to wishes, fears and emotional processes may be regarded in three ways. Images (as thoughts in general) may be formed in response to emotions; images may express emotions; and images may evoke emotions [33, p. 73].

Eidetic therapy, described by Ahsen, Sheikh, and others, offers another triune model which not only emphasizes the connectedness of the image, the emotion, and the somatic state, but presents them as three aspects of a single psychosomatic entity, the eidetic. According to Ahsen, every important developmental event a person experiences is encoded in an eidetic, also called an ISM, which contains an image, a somatic response, and a meaning or emotional response. He considers that the image is the access piece that allows evocation of the entire eidetic, and that manipulation of the image can effect a change in the somatic and emotional response [34, 35].

A connecting thought seems to underlie these models, which simply stated is that as a person experiences life, perceptions and interpretations of his/her experiences are encoded in the nervous system in several ways: There is a verbal description or explanation, a pattern of symbols and images, and a somatic response. Since our descriptions and rationalizations about life are often tenaciously defended and since in illness the soma may act as the unconscious expressor of discomfort, imagery is the information system that may well offer us the easiest and most effective access to the understanding and resolution of the psychosomatic puzzle.

A fourth model, which is simpler, is one based on hemispheric differentiation. Though Galin appropriately warns about the development of a "neo-phrenology" by overemphasizing interhemispheric differences [36], what we know about the different ways the hemispheres process information allows us to construct a reasonable, functional model of imagery in the psychosomatic realm. While linear or "left-brain" thinking seems primarily oriented to activity and manipulation of the outside world, the symbolic thinking of the right hemisphere seems more closely related to emotions, body image, and internal equilibrium. While *naming*, a major function of lexical thinking, separates the world into component pieces, imagery seems to be able to represent a more complete gestalt of an event or situation. The right brain seems to be synthetic, holistic, and creative in its approach to the perceived world. Quieting "thinking," in its usual lexical sense, and evoking imagery offer a person the possibility of a fresh, creative viewpoint on a problem, such as an illness. We often encourage the patient to quiet his/her left brain and obtain a "second opinion" from the right one, through its language of imagery.

The Adaptive Potential of Illness

It is the premise of the approach described in this paper that symptoms, illness, and disease are not, by and large, capricious and random occurrences, but that they represent meaningful attempts on the part of the organism to reestablish a homeostatic balance which has been lost. When environmental, physical or emotional demands exceed a person's ability to cope, stress results, and when it is prolonged, structural and functional damage may ensue [37]. Though Selye's concept of stress points to a generalized, nonspecific physiologic pattern of reaction [38], others postulate a more specific and meaningful pattern in the response:

Any physiologic or pathologic change that disturbs the dynamic steady state of a living organism is likely to initiate activities of the organism as a whole or physiologic changes within the organism, which are aimed at maintaining the integrity of the organism and the integrity of its relation with the social groups of which it is a member. During this time we have also come to recognize that the adaptive reactions themselves are usually a part of—and often the most prominent part of—the pathology and pathophysiology of disease . . . the body can make highly specific, discrete and, in many cases, unique responses to demands arising either outside of it or within it by using its finite and nonspecific effector mechanisms in certain patterns and in certain orders. One might truly question if there is *ever* a truly nonspecific (that is, entirely random) response of a living organism to a demand: for it can be argued that the unique characteristic of living organisms is that they respond to change not randomly but with responses that are directed toward maintaining the dynamic steady state upon which their continued existence depends. [39, p. 194]

The Receptive Potential of Imagery

Though the previously mentioned psychophysiologic aspects of imagery represent a significant opportunity to those interested in self-care, a perhaps even more remarkable potential exists in the receptive and symbolic aspects of imagery. These functions of imagery have been utilized extensively in various forms of depth psychology, including Jungian analysis, where it is termed "active imagination," and in the work of Ira Progoff, who terms it "twilight imaging."

Gestalt psychologists and psychosyntheses guides make frequent use of imagery techniques to evoke, modulate, and transform psychically charged material. Imagery is used in psychology both to help identify and change dysfunctional thought patterns and to mobilize inner strengths and personal resources that may help the patient to become whole again [40].

As the models of imagery that I have described indicate, imagery not only seems to affect physiology, but it also may represent it and its needs for adaptation. This afferent aspect of imagery provides us with an opportunity to understand the needs of an organism that are being somatically expressed. People with tendencies to somatize seem to have an underdeveloped internal emotional language [41], and their somatization often expresses or fills needs which are primarily emotional and social. Since we are essentially ignorant of the boundaries of the somatization process, and since our interest is in any case the treatment of the whole person, this dimension of a person's problem always deserves exploration. It may be that the symbolic language of imagery, bypassing the usual verbal information processing system, can give both patients and therapists pertinent information regarding those needs and how they might be filled without resorting to illness.

Imagery may be regarded as an access system which can allow us a 360° view of our inner landscape. By looking into what Assagioli termed the lower and middle aspects of the unconscious, we can identify needs, drives, and beliefs that may be either harming or helping us. By looking to the higher unconscious, we can draw on inspiration, illumination, creativity, and the transpersonal qualities available to us. By looking to the past, we can recall consequences of dysfunctional patterns and also evoke personal strengths and resources. In looking forward in imagery, we have the opportunity to anticipate and rehearse possible events, and to energize and affirm our chosen path.

IMAGINE HEALTH!

Imagine Health! is the name of a graduated learning program in self-care relaxation and imagery skills developed by Dr. Naomi Remen and I over the past six years. Since we utilized certain basic techniques and approaches repeatedly, we decided to create a learning system that could enable patients to learn and practice fundamental imagery skills at home between visits. The advantages to using such a teaching aid include reduced cost to patients; the provision of structure to patients' homework, which along with the reinforcement of the therapist encourages participation; the availability to patients of specific guidance and instruction when the guidance is needed; and a reduction in repetition and consequent boredom for the professional teaching these skills. In addition, it seems that attachment to the therapist is reduced and self-reliance encouraged by giving patients self-care tools as early as they are able to use them. Our system has been designed both to help people learn these skills on their own, and to be used as a teaching aid by therapists and health professionals. It consists of three audiocassettes containing six guided relaxation and imagery exercises, and a thirty-two-page instructional booklet. The specific elements of the program will be described below, with a few brief case histories that illustrate the potential value of such an approach.

Element 1: Relaxation Skills

A simple relaxation technique consisting of progressive relaxation of major muscle groups from the feet to the head is the first skill we teach. Most people take to this technique very readily and only a few need personal instruction beyond that contained in the first cassette and instruction booklet. This simple relaxation technique surprisingly often produces relief of a wide variety of stress-related syndromes, including tension and migraine headaches; chronic pain syndromes of all types; functional gastrointestinal disturbances; atopic symptoms including hay fever, eczema, and asthma; mild hypertension; menstrual dysfunction; and symptoms directly attributable to anxiety. Given the pervasive influence of stress and tension in medical and psychiatric patients and in the "worried well" in modern society, it seems that relaxation skills should be something we all learn in elementary school. It would be difficult, if not impossible, to name the full range of clinical syndromes in which the patient's ability to relax can be beneficial—because it is almost always beneficial, though by no means curative.

Case 1: A thirty-three-year-old mother of two small children had been hospitalized for several weeks in the ICU. Her diagnosis was primary pulmonary hypertension, a progressive, fatal lung disease for which there is no known cause or cure. She had lost about 25 percent of her body weight, she had in place two intravenous lines, a nasogastric tube through which she was fed, a urinary catheter, and a nasal oxygen delivery tube. She was weak, intermittently disoriented, complaining of a continuous pain in different areas of her body, and had been vomiting every 1 1/2 to 2 hours for two days. Everyone felt powerless to help her in her suffering. Pain medications and tranquilizers could only be offered in very small doses because of their effects on respiration, and she had vomited even the small doses of medications for days. Her internist and her husband requested that I see her, knowing of my interest in alternative medical approaches. After talking with this woman for a while, it became very obvious to me that there was no curative magic I could offer her. I did, however, ask her the simple question "Would you like to learn to become more comfortable?"[1] She did, and I led her through the basic relaxation exercise I have described. She relaxed surprisingly easily and drifted off to sleep. I left a cassette with the staff and instructed the staff to invite her to relax when she became uncomfortable.

---

[1] This invitation to relaxation is attributed to Dr. Joseph Barber.

Mercifully, the woman died four days later. In the intervening period, she did not vomit again, nor did she complain of pain. The nurses said she spent a fair amount of time resting peacefully and had been able to talk with her husband and children calmly before she died.

I believe the above case illustrates dramatically the potential of relaxation in a range of clinical situations where it might be overlooked or devalued because it is neither specific nor curative for the problem. In a society where over 160,000,000 prescriptions were written in 1976 for tranquilizers [42], it would seem that a simple, nontoxic method of relaxation would have a place in every professional and lay person's repertoire of health skills. This patently excessive reliance on pharmaceutical solutions to life problems is not without significant human and financial cost. Tranquilizers are the single largest class of drugs we prescribe and take, and adverse drug reactions nationwide kill more people than cancer of the breast (130,000 deaths per year in the U.S. alone), and rank as the seventh leading cause of hospital admission [6]. A portion of these fatalities are due to unavoidable risk, but a great many unfortunately are due to professional and public ignorance of effective, safe, nondrug alternatives for a large number of common clinical conditions.

Case 2: A fifty-five-year-old woman with a thirty-year history of mixed tension and sinus headaches consulted me because of my acupuncture practice. She suffered from bilateral fronto-occipital headaches five to seven times a week, with intensities ranging from nagging to near-disabling. Her headaches were more intense during the summer when smog levels in her area were higher. She had been tested for allergies and found to have numerous seasonal and perennial sensitivities. Several years of hyposensitization had not helped with her headaches. She took antihistamines religiously three times a day though she did not know if they helped. She disliked tranquilizers, since they made her too sleepy and she preferred to stay active. She took aspirin, Tylenol or Darvon almost daily yet still had headaches. After our initial visit, I suggested she begin relaxaing, using the Basic Relaxation cassette, twice a day. We scheduled her for some acupuncture treatments as well. When she returned, she stated happily that in the two weeks since she began the relaxation her headaches were 90 percent better. After several acupuncture treatments she was completely relieved. After seven years, she continues to relax twice a day and only has very occasional "stuffiness" in her forehead in the summertime. She takes no medications, feels very pleased with her own ability to help herself and has taught all of her family to relax. Her husband has attributed breaking what was developing into a serious drinking problem to discovering that he could relax without a drink.

There are many simple ways to teach and achieve relaxation. The method we have chosen seems especially easy, nonsecular, and nonthreatening to most people. We encourage people to practice regularly for several weeks until they are confident in their ability to relax, and then to modify and adapt the ability to their specific life patterns. We also encourage them to keep a journal in which they can subjectively assess their ability to relax, the way they feel, and any experiences they have, in either imagery or life that sheds light on their situation. For some people, a more structured evaluation method, such as the one presented in Bresler's *Free Yourself From Pain*, is recommended [42].

Along with potential relief from specific symptoms and a greater ability to cope with stress, people also often develop an enhanced awareness of their bodies and physical needs through relaxation alone. As they notice the difference between feeling relaxed and feeling stressed (many people have told me that they never knew they were so tense until they learned to relax), it becomes easier to identify stressful situations and interactions. Once identified, there is an opportunity to make changes in the situations or to relax during them rather than to tense unconsciously.

The first side of our first cassette teaches a twenty-two-minute technique of muscular relaxation. The second side, to be used after the first side is felt to be mastered, repeats this same process in ten minutes, then teaches two simple deepening techniques—counting backwards from ten to one, allowing deeper relaxation with each descending number, and imagining a beautiful, quiet, peaceful place of relaxation. This imaginary setting is effective both in inducing relaxation [43] and in introducing imagery in a nonthreatening way. This peaceful imaginary place also provides a starting place for the more involved imagery processes taught later in the program.

Element 2: The Inner Advisor

A technique we have found extremely valuable is the dialogue with what we term an "inner advisor," a figure of wisdom and caring evoked in imagery. Jung used a variant of this approach which he described in Mysterium Coniunctionis,

> What I call coming to terms with the unconscious, the alchemists call 'Meditation'. . . [Ruland says of this] : 'Meditation, the name of an internal talk of one person with another who is invisible, as in the invocation of the Deity, or communion with one's self, or with one's good angel [p. 497, 44].

Catholics learn in catechism that they have a guardian angel available to them in times of need. Spirits and spirit guides are a part of the belief system of a surprising number of people in this culture. Bresler uses this technique in his work with chronic pain patients and believes it is a good starting place for work with imagery because it helps to "prevent traumatic insight." [45] As the cases below illustrate, the advisor can be a helpful source of not only psychological and spiritual but also physical guidance.

It is important to evoke the patient's reaction to and interpretation of the advisor to make best use of it. If the aura of the spiritual is bothersome to someone a neurological model is stressed, and the advisor is presented as a way of evoking right-brain activity that may provide new pertinent information. In *Imagine Health!* a nondogmatic model of this phenomenon that accommodates most belief systems is described. If, however, the patient has specific spiritual beliefs about the advisor, these beliefs must be respected, since we really do not know exactly what this phenomenon represents. Interestingly, the only complaint we ever have received from anyone using this technique came from a woman who apparently was a devout spiritualist; she objected strongly to our use of the term "imaginary" when referring to the advisor, stating that such guides were real entities and that we were missing the boat. Dr. Irving Oyle, who introduced me to the technique, once explained it to me by saying,

> The brain contains approximately 13 billion nerve cells. Maybe two billion are tied up in the speech areas, the parts of ourselves that think rationally, verbally, and call ourselves by our names—the Advisor is the way the other 11 billion cells communicate with those 2 billion.

Whatever the mechanism of the inner advisor, it has proven to be a useful introduction to imagery. Once people can relax with some confidence and imagine themselves in a quiet place, they are encouraged to invite into their awareness an image which represents the qualities of great wisdom and caring. This figure may be someone familiar or unfamiliar to the person, an old man or woman, a religious figure, a child, an animal, plant, ball of light, or just a sense of a wise presence. The image need not be visual, though it usually is. When the advisor appears, the individuals should invite it to be comfortable and should talk with it and ask it questions about their problem or illness. They should allow themselves to be receptive to the answers they receive in response, whether through thoughts, auditory imagery, or in mime or symbolism. Further dialogue is encouraged until it seems that some clear contact or resolution of at least some aspect of the problem is reached. Individuals are asked to record in their journal these experiences with the advisor, noting insights, feelings, and questions that seem relevant to the problem.

Case 3: A twenty-nine-year-old woman, who worked as a secretary, complained of severe tension headaches which had been occurring several times a week for ten years. Relaxation training helped somewhat, but her headaches continued at a reduced frequency and intensity for several weeks. One day she came in with a severe, generalized headache she had developed the night before. I asked her to relax and ask her inner mind for an inner advisor, a figure that could help her understand the headache and what she could do about it. Immediately the image of a mynah bird came to her mind. She said it was like one she had had when she was 9 years old and had died because she did not know how to nurture it. The imaginary mynah was friendly however, and when she asked it about her headache it began to peck her all over her head. The message she received was that she let people pick on her too much. Specifically, the day before she had heard that a fellow employee, a man whom she had helped obtain a job in her office, had been slandering her behind her back to her boss and other office staff. She became infuriated, but instead of expressing her anger, began to feel sick and went home with a headache. She then asked the mynah what to do—it told her to assert herself, to tell the man to his face to stop slandering her, and to apologize. She visualized herself doing that (it was a very frightening idea for her) and was surprised to see the man sheepishly apologize and shrink in size. She laughed as she saw this, and to her surprise, she found that her headache was gone. The next day she confronted this man in real life and found to her amazement that he acted very much as she had seen him act in her imagery. In a later talk with the mynah, it told her that she should not have been surprised at that man's reaction because she had known all along that he was this type of person, and she had recommended him for a job because of what she thought others thought of him. She recognized that often her personal assessment of people was accurate, yet she had ignored it and had related to people according to the opinions of others. Consequently, she had been consistently disappointed in relationships and work situations. The continuing process of inner dialogue, leading to growing self-respect and assertiveness resulted in far fewer and less severe headaches and in an ability to respond effectively when a headache did occur.

Case 4: A thirty-year-old psychiatrist complained of aching in his shoulders, neck, and head, which radiated throughout his whole body when it was most severe. The problem increased when he was seeing patients. A physical examination and screening laboratory tests revealed general tension, soreness, and multiple trigger points in the shoulders, neck, and back without other abnormal findings. His advisor, a male figure reminiscent of a combination of his brother and his "shadow," told him, "You are a healer, but before you can heal others you have to learn to heal yourself." At this, tears flowed down the patient's cheeks, and he experienced a sensation of relaxation in the areas the tears had crossed. In the conversation with his advisor, he had a spontaneous image of himself with armor on his shoulders. He was told that the armor was made of "thinking and planning" and was there to protect him from his feelings. He was instructed that the armor was old and was not necessary anymore. His advisor told him that to stop having pain he would have to stop thinking in his usual manner and learn to pay direct attention to his feelings, which would then reveal themselves to him. He experienced significant relief of pain during the session and for the next week while he met with his advisor.

Case 5: A thirty-year-old woman lawyer with multiple severe allergies complained of constant fatigue, abdominal bloating and cramping, skin rashes, and sinus congestion. Allergy testing had revealed her to be sensitive to almost every inhalant and food product tested. Several years of environmental manipulation, rotary elimination diets, hyposensitization, and psychotherapy had helped little, if at all. A course of acupuncture treatments was only somewhat helpful. Her advisor was a thin, willowy young woman who called herself Laura. When asked if she knew anything about this patient's allergies, Laura answered, "You have light compression." Neither the patient nor I understood this enigmatic answer and we asked Laura for more information. She refused, however, to say more, but offered in her outstretched hand a prism, which was refracting a beam of white light into the seven colors of the spectrum. She gave this to the patient and then disappeared. The patient was instructed to meet with Laura again and ask her for more guidance and also to be aware of possible meanings in this image that might occur to her over the next few days. Three days later she called excitedly saying she was browsing through some old books and found one which cited evidence of the adverse effect of less than full spectrum lighting on the immune system [46]. The author emphasized the possible role this might play in allergies, among other illnesses. The patient consulted with her advisor who confirmed the meaning of the imagery. She advised the patient to spend one hour a day in the sun when possible and to replace all her light bulbs at home and in the office with full-spectrum bulbs. After three weeks the patient reported that she was "95 percent" better, and follow-up 1 1/2 years later revealed that she had stayed well.

Information received from the inner advisor needs to be evaluated before it is put into action. We do not advocate that people abandon their responsibility to their inner advisors any more than we encourage them to abandon it to anyone else. In fact, we tell people that they need not do whatever the advisor recommends but to consider it carefully. If the advice seems reasonable and the risk is acceptable, we encourage people to act on it and see how it works.

The relationship with the advisor is an ongoing one, and in time, a person may develop several advisors, each with a different area of expertise. I encourage people who have reached this point to think of the entire unconscious mind as an advisor, which can appear in different forms to deliver different messages. Thus people attain a conscious attitude which, as Jung said, "allows the unconscious to cooperate instead of being driven into opposition." [47]

Element 3: Listening To Your Symptom

As people become comfortable and successful with the inner advisor technique, they are invited to progress to the next step in the program which involves them in an inner dialogue with an image representing the symptom or problem itself. Their attention is focused directly on the sensations, feelings, and ideas that attend the problem, and an image is allowed to emerge. They are encouraged to accept whatever develops in a nonjudgmental fashion. This, of course, is the technique Jung called "active imagination." No attempt is made to differentiate between somatic and psychological complaints as long as no necessary medical treatment is overlooked. The symptoms, however they present,

Andrea,

are regarded as feedback from the organism signalling the need for adaptation. Persons with a chronic or recurrent illness, are told that they have an ongoing relationship with their problem, whether they like it or not, but that the potential exists to improve that relationship. Communication is an important factor in any relationship, and the inner dialogue process is presented as an aid to developing better communication with an unconscious aspect of themselves that may be signalling for attention through symptoms. This inner dialogue is an opportunity to come to terms with the illness and to learn what it would take to become healthier. Jung, speaking of the legend of St. George and the dragon as an allegory for encountering potentially threatening aspects of the unconscious, said, "In myths the hero is the one who conquers the dragon, not the one who is devoured by it. And yet both have to deal with the same dragon." [47, p. 178]

Jung also speaks of active imagination as a natural process, "used by nature herself," which tends to occur spontaneously when "the opposites [have been constellated] so powerfully that a union or synthesis of the personality becomes an imperative necessity." [48, p. 494] By focusing directly on their symptoms in a way that fosters insight, people are a step closer to identifying and clarifying unconscious conflicts, to developing understanding and empathy for their own needs, and to creating a healthy synthesis of the natural qualities struggling in opposition.

Specifically, once an image has emerged for the symptom or problem, people are encouraged to thoroughly examine it, noting its form, size, colors, textures, and energetic qualities, as well as any feelings they have toward it. A closer inspection is then suggested, including touching the image and focusing more closely on the qualities it seems to convey. Any feelings the image itself may be expressing are explored. Then people are instructed to "give the image a voice" and to ask it *what it wants*, allowing it to answer. *"What does it need?"* is the next question, followed by: *"What does it have to offer* if its needs were met?" At this point, listeners are asked to stop the tape and to make notes in their journal of what has happened so far. However, some people prefer to complete the entire process and then record their experiences, thoughts, and questions.

The image is again evoked, and a deeper exploration is encouraged: people are asked to "become the image" in imagination, noticing what that is like, what the world looks like from this perspective, how it feels toward life and specifically toward the person doing the imagery. This is frequently a powerful part of the experience and often evokes empathy between the conscious identity and the unconscious aspect represented by the image. As the image, individuals tell themselves what they need and then become themselves again. They are then asked to look at the image again and to notice if they observe or feel anything they did not before. Are they willing to give the image what it says it needs? If not, what stands in the way? What are the problems or objections to doing this?[2]

[2] This same process, "Listening to your Symptom," may be repeated, focusing on "what gets in the way" as the symptom in order to help understand and resolve resistance.

To complete this part of the process, the person is asked to imagine what it would look like if they decided to act in accord with what they had learned in the imagery. Who and what might they have to contend with and how might they handle those situations? A more detailed method for making practical use of any insights is taught in the fourth element of the program, which will be discussed later in detail. At this point, notes are made again, which encourages individuals to go over what they have learned, helps them to retain it, evokes further insight, and commits the experience to a tangible form for later review.

Finally, the inner advisor is invited to appear and the experience is discussed. Questions the individual might have about what happened or about future plans and directions can be asked here. This process closes with an encouragement to "ground" any insight they decide to act on by putting it to use in their daily life.

Case 6:   A twenty-seven-year-old registered nurse had separated from her husband nine months before consultation and had not had a menstrual period since. Previously she had always had regular, moderate periods without problems. A complete gynecologic workup was normal. She focused on her problem and had an image that looked something like she imagined the pituitary gland would look like—"sort of peanut shaped." It told her, to "Love your reproductive organs more" and gave her a "feathery light broom" with which she was to sweep out her uterus daily. As she did this, she felt a pleasant warm tingle in her pelvic area. Through the next week, though, she complained of feeling "disjointed" and "pulled apart" when she did this. She concentrated on the disjointed feeling and had two images: one representing the part of her that wanted to have babies, which appeared as Cinderella, and one portraying the part that did not, which took the shape of a witch. The Cinderella image promised her "love, fulfillment, happiness, and pride" if she would become pregnant. The witch turned out not to be evil in any way but rather a magical character who "expressed herself through my healing abilities." The witch was afraid of not receiving enough attention if the woman became pregnant. A temporary agreement was made that she would not become pregnant without consulting the witch, and she agreed to meet daily with both characters so they could come to a harmonious understanding. Her periods started six days later and resumed their regularity. Six months later she called to say that she was feeling well and had decided to take postgraduate training to become a midwife.

The case below illustrates a point I find comforting. The "guiding principle" within the psyche, with which we seem to be working, will often redirect a person who unintentionally has been led off the mark by a well-meaning but misdirected guide.

Case 7:   A thirty-year-old woman complained of a kidney infection: "I ache all over, my back aches, my head and nose are stuffy and I have had no energy for over a week." A medical examination showed her to have a viral upper respiratory infection. A history revealed that she had been working exceptionally long hours for many months, doing secretarial work at low pay for an institute to which she was deeply committed, even though she was a trained psychotherapist. She had been smoking heavily, skipping meals, not exercising, and had taken no time for herself or her recent marriage.

I asked her to relax and develop an image for her body—she pictured it as a horse. She asked it how it was doing and it replied, "Oh, I'm doing OK. You could smoke less and walk more, but you better pay attention to your feelings—they're really upset."

She immediately had an image for her feelings—it looked like her and was very angry. It said it was angry because it had not been included in her decision to do what she had been doing. She apologized, and as the dialogue continued, she decided, with the agreement of her body and feeling images, to go on doing what she had been doing for a while, but to take several breaks during the day, breathe deeply, relax, and pay special attention to her feelings during those times.

Over that weekend she fully recovered and went on to complete the project she had started without further distress and with a great deal more enjoyment and satisfaction.

Of course, these cases are not meant to be examples of "miracle healing" of an intractable disease. They may illustrate, however, the releasing of natural healing mechanisms which occur after the needs that were expressed in their illnesses have been met. Both of these women not only recovered, which they undoubtedly would have done without intervention, but they learned something about taking care of themselves, and about how much they know about themselves. Both of them, like the majority of people who have worked with this process, expressed that they actually felt more whole and more self-sufficient after these experiences than they had ever felt before.

Illness, Suffering and Meaning

In the first case report in this chapter, simple relaxation and imagery seemed to relieve a great deal of the patient's suffering, without affecting her disease process at all. It is important to emphasize that imagery can play a great role in medicine and healing even if it has no physiologic effects whatsoever, because of its many uses in addressing the dimensions of a human being where the majority of suffering occurs—the mind, the emotions, and the spirit. Suffering is an intensely personal experience which may include but is not limited to physical pain. Cassell defines suffering as "the state of severe distress associated with events that threaten the intactness of the person." Among the many dimensions of "personhood," he includes the individual's personality, social roles, family roles, abilities to act and create, abilities to understand events and relationship to his/her body [10].

Imagery, in its various forms, often can help when the integrity of many of the above mentioned aspects of self are threatened. Many times it can help by permitting a new perspective on the events attending an illness. The transcendent dimension is often tapped in work with imagery and people often are able to find meaning for their suffering which is, in itself, therapeutic.

Cassell also states that suffering is increased in a number of situations,

> . . . when (people) feel out of control, when the pain is overwhelming, when the source of the pain is unknown, when the meaning of the pain is dire or when the pain is chronic.

Relaxation and imagery techniques can address several of these variables by helping people to gain a locus of control, a sense of meaning, and a perception of a relationship to their pain, which in itself may reduce their suffering.

The potential of visualization and imagery in regulating physiologic functions and reversing pathologic changes is just beginning to be seriously researched. The prospects of finding that physical healing can be engendered through imagery are good, yet hard evidence is still lacking. The perhaps distinctly human problem of suffering, however, is an area in which the integrative and symbolic roles of imagery have a definite and powerful role to play.

Element 4: Turning Insight Into Action

Gaining insight into the dynamics of an illness and suffering is often the first step in the healing process. Too often, however, the insight remains purely intellectual in nature and no real change in attitude or behavior results. In order to realize the benefits of what has been learned, the lessions need to be put to use in daily life. For some this is an instinctive process, others need to be taught how to do this. The process of consciously "grounding the insight" encourages people to choose and to act in a manner that supports and affirms their movement toward greater self-sufficiency and wholeness. The method of grounding we teach in *Imagine Health!* is based largely on the work of Roberto Assagioli on will and choice [50, 51].

This last tape begins with an example of grounding, that is, a woman finds her headaches are due to tension, experienced mostly in her work setting. She sees that she needs to reduce tension at work and considers ways she could do that. She sees several options—she could reduce her intake of coffee, ask for a reduction in responsibility, ask for more vacation time, learn and practice a relaxation technique, and/or quit her job. She decides to begin with eliminating coffee. She affirms this choice and decides to have an apple instead at her morning break. She mentally rehearses this plan, but as she imagines sitting in the coffee room eating her apple, she becomes aware of a strong temptation to drink coffee. She alters her plan by choosing to eat her apple outside by herself. She then carries out her plan and notices that it helps. If she still wants to reduce tension, she may then choose to take another step, perhaps learning to relax, and might repeat the grounding process to make that part of her daily routine.

The first step in the process of grounding is to *clarify the insight*. People are instructed to write down the clearest sentence that expresses the insight upon which they wish to act. Careful attention is paid to each word, making sure it expresses exactly what is meant. It is often helpful to choose the most important word in the sentence.

The next step is to *think about the options*, to brainstorm and list all the possible ways of meeting the needs discovered through the insight process. Options are then reviewed, combined if possible, and examined for practicality, ease of accomplishment, and promise of success.

Once the options seem clear, individuals are asked to *choose* the most realistic and promising course of action. The size of the step decided upon is important. It should be large enough so that tangible benefit can be expected, yet not so large as to be overwhelming.

After the choice has been made, persons are encouraged to *affirm the choice* and put their energy and resolve behind it. We ask them to affirm their choice out loud several times and also commit it to paper.

The fifth step is to *make a concrete plan* for carrying out the chosen action, including specific steps that will have to be taken. The plan is written down, clearly and in appropriate detail.

Next, *the plan is rehearsed in imagination* from beginning to end. This is a chance to become aware of unanticipated obstacles. If such obstacles are identified, the plan is adjusted and modified accordingly. Once it has been adjusted and is successful in imagination, it is rehearsed several times until it feels comfortable and familiar.

The final step is to *act* and carry out the plan in real life. It is crucial to maintain a high level of awareness of thoughts, feelings, and actions as the plan is carried out. It is also very important to be observant of the reactions of others to it. Grounding is a matter of continual refinement until the desired results are achieved.

Initially, we ask individuals to ground an insight for a very short period—an hour or so a day. Once successful over these periods of time, longer-range plans for establishing new ways of acting can be made and carried out.

Two other techniques useful in grounding over a long period of time are then explained—the "morning preview" and the "evening review." In the morning preview people visualize and mentally rehearse the chosen plan, imagining events and interactions with people anticipated for that day. This preview energizes and reinforces the plan, and allows it to be custom tailored to that particular day's activities. In the evening review, the day is visualized backwards, an hour at a time, beginning with the most recent hour until the hour of awakening is reached. Nonjudgmental attention is paid to what went well and what did not, and ways of doing better are considered for tomorrow.

The following case illustrates the importance, though not the specific steps, of grounding in healing.

Case 8: An attractive woman in her mid-thirties, married fourteen years with two children, had severe, disfiguring psoriasis covering her abdomen, back and legs. Many types of both conventional medical and alternative treatments failed to give more than some palliative relief. A counselor herself, she was familiar with imagery techniques. Her inner advisor consistently told her she "had to follow her inner wisdom and be true to herself," and to assert herself as an individual. The major source of stress in her life was her marriage: Her perception of her husband's unwillingness or inability to change was extremely frustrating to her and she struggled incessantly to change herself to improve the relationship.

Visit after visit the issue of the unresolved relationship emerged. Though compromises of various types were struck with her advisor and with images representing her skin, she never improved more than marginally.

She discontinued regular visits and did not return until a year later. She was calm, self-assured, and radiant. She stated that three months earlier she had made an internal commitment to follow her guidance, wherever it led her. She was separating from her husband and establishing her own practice of counseling. She said, "I feel whole—I'm not trying to be someone I'm not anymore." Her psoriasis was gone with the exception of two or three small spots in the process of resolving.

In the next case, some of the specific steps of the grounding process made it easier for a man to free himself from addiction to cigarette smoking.

Case 9: A thirty-year-old man had been smoking one and a half to two packs of unfiltered cigarettes a day for fifteen years and wanted to quit. His advisor told him not to try to quit, but to notice, in great deatil, the process of smoking and the consequences of each individual cigarette he smoked, and to choose, each time, whether to smoke or not. He was to evaluate whether each cigarette was going to make him feel better or worse and then to decide whether to smoke it. If he did decide to smoke, he was to do so without guilt and then to notice again how it made him feel.

"Notice" and "choose" seemed to be the key words to him, and he agreed to try the method. After the first few days, he altered the plan, because he noticed that after a few cigarettes he became progressively less able to notice what effects they had on him. He decided to pay special attention to the first cigarette of each day. After nine months, during which he sometimes smoked a lot and sometimes less he noticed that cigarettes made him emotionally numb, created an uncomfortable feeling in his chest and made him tired. He began to smoke less and less and gave it up completely within another month.

Seven years later he reported smoking "one to twelve cigarettes a *year*, without any struggle." He still thought about, and chose whether to smoke each cigarette individually. Occasionally he enjoyed it, but usually he did not and put out the cigarette without finishing it.

Grounding is perhaps the most important step in this self-care process. People who choose to take responsibility for themselves need courage, determination, and support, especially at the beginning. Family members, friends, even health professionals may unconsciously or consciously contribute to or sabotage efforts to move toward better health. We encourage people to be frank and to enlist as much support as they can among people sympathetic to this approach, and not to disclose their efforts to people likely to discourage them. The keeping of a journal is especially important in grounding, as it provides a record of insights, plans, successes, and failures, as well as of the state of health.

Cautions and Precautions

Imagery approaches and especially self-care approaches through imagery are not for everyone. In general people will self-select in this regard according to their interest, understanding and intuition about the approach. Therapists will use their clinical judgment in deciding whether or not to introduce patients to imagery techniques. Patients already overinvolved in fantasy may not be good candidates. Obviously, psychotic and prepsychotic patients need to be handled very carefully if these approaches are tried with them at all. People with organic brain syndromes or those with difficulty in concentrating may not do well, unless their concentration can be improved through other exercises [50].

One of the major cautions in working with the method described centers around the issue of responsibility. Many clinicians are concerned, and rightfully so, about the feeling of guilt for creating an illness that patients might develop [52]. This is certainly a sensitive area and one that requires thoughtfulness, discretion and a thorough understanding of the notion of responsibility on the part of the professional presenting this approach. We define "responsibility" as "the ability to respond," and we encourage patients to become actively involved in responding to their illness, stressing that their personal resources can positively affect its course. We point to the lessons that their body, or unconscious mind, may be pointing out to them and their opportunity to learn to understand their physical, emotional, psychological, and spiritual needs more clearly. The models mentioned before, of right- and left-brain function or of the conscious and unconscious mind, may offer paradigms in which patients are allowed to take responsibility without having to accept blame. If the illness or symptom is seen as feedback to the conscious mind, it is not regarded as evil but merely as advisory. People with marked masochistic and self-blaming tendencies should be directed to use imagery to look for strengths, resources, and solutions within themselves that can help them improve their health.

Patients who choose to work with self-care programs probably have some aptitude for them. We advise people to respect significant fear and perhaps learn to understand their fear before progressing in an inner dialogue technique. In the past two years, over 1000 people have purchased and used *Imagine Health!*. We have not had one report of an adverse effect from either professionals or lay persons. Other professionals who have published guided imagery experiences for self-care have reported no known adverse effects with over 10,000 users [53].

Questions and Directions

Many questions and directions for research occur as the issues discussed in this paper are considered. What type of people seek out self-care tools like the one I have presented? How successful are they in using these methods? What can we learn from them that would allow us to teach others to use these approaches?

How effective is this method? We, among others, have a great deal of clinical indication that it can be helpful, yet it needs more formal study. Does it help to engender self-respect, self-efficacy and a greater sense of well-being? Does it have any measurable effect on the course of organically demonstrable disease?

What are the physiologic accompaniments of inner dialogue techniques? Are there differential hemispheric or intrahemispheric patterns during an imagery process?

These are just a few of the many questions in need of investigation. A questionnaire survey of people who have worked with *Imagine Health!* over the past two years is presently being taken. We will collect demographic and subjective data relating to the above questions about users and efficacy.

Conclusion

From a pragmatic interest in methods that can help medical patients with common complaints, the path has led to awareness techniques that can relieve suffering and seem closely connected with the process of healing. Methods from depth psychology seem to be effective in dealing with somatically presented illnesses in people who accept the challenge of taking responsibility for their health. Pain and suffering, the great motivators, often lead people to assume this responsibility, and when they have done so, deep healing and growth may begin.

We are constantly being informed that we live in the midst of a paradigm shift, a shift of worldview promising to bring a new order out of the chaos perceived through the limitations of our perspective. Indeed, throughout the sciences and humanities a resurgent holistic view of man and life is emerging, a view that points out connections rather than distinctions, whether between subatomic particles and energetic fields or between man and his family, society, and environment. The dehumanizing effects of scientific reductionism are beginning to be tempered by a more comprehensive psychosocial or even biopsycho-social-spiritual view of humanity. In medicine and psychology, the rift between body and mind is being allowed to heal. It is in this fundamental process of communion of body, mind, and spirit that imagery plays its primary role.

Individual consciousness is an infant relative to the billions of years of evolutionary experience contained in what we may call the unconscious aspects of mind. The unconscious contains, among other things, the patterns and thoughts that motivate us and the potential we can realize as we fully unfold. It also contains the organizational intelligence that shapes and maintains the physical body.

Imagery is one of its natural languages and a major key to understanding and directing its operations. In this time of epidemic alienation, apathy, and fragmentation in individuals and society, we must seek and travel the path that leads back to our essential integrity. We need to become more conscious of the world within us and around us and to realize how powerful imagination and choice can be. We also need to learn to use them well, with respect for ourselves and others. In a personal sense, imagery can be our contact with our deeper selves and can help us use our energy and creativity to better our world. In a social sense, personal transformation and healing is a step forward in social transformation. Everyone who takes responsibility for his/her well-being lightens the load and encourages others to do likewise.

It is clear that more self-sufficiency and responsibility for health is needed in Western culture, and the opportunity to take this responsibility is available. Though imagery and insight techniques do not replace either appropriate professional care or physical self-care, they offer a potent medium for self-regulation, self-exploration, and self-knowledge, processes that can engender and nurture healing of the whole person.

REFERENCES

1. M. L. Rossman and N. Remen, *Imagine Health!*, Insight Publishing, Belmont, California, 1981.
2. J. Jaynes, *The Origin of Consciousness in the Breakdown of the Bicameral Mind*, Houghton-Mifflin, New York, 1978.
3. I. Illich, *Medical Nemesis*, Pantheon, New York, 1976.
4. T. Szasz, *The Myth of Mental Illness*, Harper and Row, New York, 1961.
5. F. Ingelfinger, Medicine: Meritorious or Meretricious?, *Science, 200*, p. 945, May 26, 1978.
6. M. Silverman and P. Lee, *Pills, Profits and Politics*, University of California Press, Berkeley, California, 1974.
7. G. Rosen, A. Kleinman, and W. Katon, Somatization in Family Practice: A Biopsychosocial Approach, *Journal of Family Practice, 14*:3, pp. 493-502, 1982.
8. J. Green, Responsibility for Health, *Journal of Holistic Health*, pp. 76-79, 1977.
9. A. Kleinman, L. Eisenberg, and B. Good, Culture, Illness, and Care: Clinical Lessons from Anthropologic and Cross-Cultural Research, *Annals of Internal Medicine, 88*:2, pp. 251-258, February 1978.
10. E. J. Cassel, The Nature of Suffering and the Goals of Medicine, *New England Journal of Medicine, 306*, pp. 639-645, 1982.
11. N. Remen, *The Human Patient*, Doubleday, New York, 1980.
12. J. Goodfield, Humanity in Science: A Perspective and a Plea, *Science, 198*, pp. 580-585, 1977.
13. J. H. Knowles, The Responsibility of the Individual, *Science*, masthead page, December 16, 1977.

14. B. H. Roberts and N. M. Norton, Prevalence of Psychiatric Illness in a Medical Outpatient Clinic, *New England Journal of Medicine, 245*, pp. 82f, 1952.
15. J. D. Stoeckle, I. K. Zola, and G. E. Davidson, The Quantity and Significance of Psychological Distress in Medical Patients, *Journal of Chronic Disease, 17*, p. 959, 1964.
16. T. Szasz, *The Theology of Medicine*, Harper Colophon, New York, 1977.
17. A. A. Sheikh, P. Richardson, and L. M. Moleski, Psychosomatics and Mental Imagery, in *The Potential of Fantasy and Imagination*, A. A. Sheikh and J. T. Shaffer (eds.), Brandon House, New York, 1979.
18. T. X. Barber, Physiologic Effects of "Hypnotic Suggestions": A Critical Review of Recent Research, *Psychological Bulletin, 63*, pp. 201-222, 1965.
19. H. Benson, *The Relaxation Response*, William Morrow, New York, 1975.
20. E. Jacobsen, *You Must Relax*, University of Chicago Press, Chicago, 1934.
21. R. K. Wallace, The Physiology of Meditation, *Scientific American*, pp. 64-92, 1972.
22. J. Schultz and W. Luthe, *Autogenic Training: A Psychophysiologic Approach in Psychotherapy*, Grune and Stratton, New York, 1959.
23. P. W. Sheehan, Imagery Processes and Hypnosis: An Experiential Analysis of Phenomena, in *The Potential of Fantasy and Imagination*, A. A. Sheikh, and J. T. Shaffer (eds.), Brandon House, New York, 1979.
24. K. Pelletier, *Mind as Healer, Mind as Slayer*, Delta, New York, 1977.
25. J. L. Singer and K. S. Pope, The Use of Fantasy and Imagery Techniques in Psychotherapy, in *The Power of Human Imagination*, J. L. Singer and K. S. Pope (eds.), pp. 3-34, Plenum Press, New York, 1978.
26. J. D. Levine, N. C. Gordon, and H. L. Fields, The Mechanism of Placebo Analgesia, *Lancet*, pp. 654-657, September 23, 1978.
27. N. Shealy, *The Pain Game*, Celestial Arts, Millbrae, California, 1976.
28. T. Miller, Psychophysiologic Aspects of Cancer, *Cancer, 39*, pp. 413-418, 1977.
29. T. X. Barber, *Imagery, Hypnosis and Psychosomatic Health*, tape of lecture delivered at The Power of Imagination Conference, April 1, 1982, Insight Publishing, Belmont, California, 1982.
30. I. Progoff, *The Symbolic and the Real*, McGraw-Hill, 1973.
31. P. J. Lang, A Bioinformational Theory of Emotional Imagery, *Psychophysiology, 16*:6, pp. 495-511, November 1979.
32. Psychosynthesis Training Seminar, Psychosynthesis Institute, San Francisco, 1979.
33. M. J. Horowitz, *Image Formation and Cognition*, Meredith Corporation, New York, 1970.
34. A. Ahsen, *Basic Concepts in Eidetic Psychotherapy*, Brandon House, New York, 1968.
35. A. A. Sheikh, Eidetic Psychotherapy, in *The Power of Human Imagination*, J. L. Singer and K. S. Pope (eds.), Plenum, New York, 1978.
36. D. Galin, Implications for Psychiatry of Left and Right Cerebral Specialization, *Archives of General Psychiatry, 31*, pp. 572-583, 1974.
37. T. Cox, *Stress*, Macmillan, London, 1978.
38. H. Selye, *The Stress of Life*, McGraw-Hill, New York, 1956.

39. L. E. Hinckle, Jr., Commentary . . . , *Cardiovascular Medicine*, pp. 192-201, February, 1979.
40. N. Remen and C. Peters, Invalidism or Rehabilitation: The Importance of Meaning, *New Physician*, 1975.
41. J. Nemiah, H. Freyberger, and P. Sifneos, Alexithymia: A View of the Psychosomatic Process, in *Modern Trends in Psychosomatic Medicine*, Vol. 3, Oscar Hill (ed.), Butterworths, London, 1976.
42. D. Bresler, *Free Yourself From Pain*, Simon and Shuster, New York, 1979.
43. J. L. Singer, *Imagery and Daydream Methods in Psychotherapy and Behavior Modification*, Academic Press, New York, 1974.
44. C. G. Jung, *Mysterium Coniunctionis*, Princeton University Press, 1970.
45. D. Bresler, *Mind-Controlled Analgesia: Imagery in the Treatment of Chronic Pain*, tape of lecture delivered at The Power of Imagination Conference, April 2, 1982, Insight Publishing, Belmont, California, 1982.
46. J. Ott, *Light and Health*,
47. C. G. Jung, *Practice of Psychotherapy*, Princeton University Press, 1975.
48. C. G. Jung, *Mysterium Coniunctionis*, Princeton University Press, 1970.
49. R. Assagioli, *Psychosynthesis*, Viking, New York, 1971.
50. R. Assagioli, *The Act of Will*, Viking, New York, 1973.
51. J. C. Holland, Why Patients Seek Unproven Cancer Remedies: A Psychological Perspective, *CA—A Cancer Journal for Clinicians*, *32*:1, Jan/Feb 1982.
52. E. Miller, personal communication, 1982.

CHAPTER 11

Imagery, Body, and Space in Focusing

EUGENE T. GENDLIN
WITH DORALEE GRINDLER
AND MARY McGUIRE

After a short theoretical statement we will present some recently developed procedures and describe their use with a cancer patient and two suicidal patients [1-5].

Although theory and practice are deeply related, the need and mood for them may differ. Some readers might want to turn directly to the clinical section.

THEORY

Readers of a book like this can agree that visual imagery is a bodily process, that it is symbolic, and that symbols are real and physical events. We know that visual imagery can play a role in bodily healing and physical change [2, 3, 6, 7]. Although we know it, we cannot understand this with the current concepts of imagery, symbol, object, space, and body.

The objects and space of medicine and physiology cannot be thought clearly together with how we experience the body, imagery, and symbols. To bring them together we must understand how science's "objects" and "space" are generated *together* and *from the living body*.

Current physics still renders anything as located at space-time points defined in relation to an abstract observer. We might think that a single particle courses independently through space, but "it" is "one particle" only by being continuous from "this one here" to "the one that is now over there." "It" is differentiated from others just like it only if an observer adds this continuity which is the observer's grid of space-time points. Relativity theory only provides equations for several such observers [8].

The human sciences study the observer and therefore cannot assume a constant and abstracted observer-continuity. We must see how this observer-continuity is generated. Then we can relate science's space and objects to other kinds of space and objects that also can be generated.

Without such an understanding, the focusing process [9] described later in this chapter would be very puzzling indeed. The body-sense of a problem as a whole is an odd kind of "object" which can be "moved" and "put down" in an odd kind of space that was not there, moments before. As with the particle in physics, object and space are made together. They share the same continuity.

The space-time continuity of the observer in physics is abstracted from the continuity of living bodies. Body life has *its own* continuity, not only a continuity imposed on it from outside.

Body-Process "Implies" in Two Ways

First, the body's own continuity is expressed in the word "implying"— any present bodily event *is* also an *implying* of the body's *next* events. In the inhaling the exhaling is implied. The feeding *is* also the implying of defecating, ground-scratching, burying, and getting hungry again. Hunger *is* an implying of food-finding and feeding.

Second, body-events are always also environment-events. The implying of further body-process also implies the environmental aspects involved in those body-events, for example the food, and the ground.

If the animal is hungry and there is no food, feeding cannot happen even though it is the body's implied next event. The bodily implied feeding is very complex, but cannot happen without food. Food seems a simple occurrence, but when it happens, the whole complex feeding process occurs. The food *carries the body forward* into its already implied next events.

The food becomes "an object" by enabling and lasting through the feeding process. Carrying forward takes time or, we can say, makes time. An object has its continuity from the body-process which it carries forward.

We can define an "object" as what carries the implied body-process forward.

Do not assume one reality of independent objects in one space. Each species lives *in* its own *mesh of objects* which cannot be perceived by other species in the same way. For example, the complexity of the body's implying *makes* a food-object with the environment's cooperation. That object is not just there that way independently in the environment.

We cannot begin with perception as if objects were there waiting simply to be photographed. What a living body perceives is first made with that body's own complex implying.

The Body Originates Complex Forms

It used to be thought that imagery was a left-over from previous external perception. This old theory ignored the obviously wild imagery everyone has in dreams and other states. A rearranged copy of externals seemed to be the only explanation for imagery. How could the body *originate* pictures before perception? *But the forms of the perceived objects also do not originate externally!* They are formed in interaction. The body's complexity is implicit in them.

The body's implying is always more than what occurs. The usual events are only one way the implying can be carried forward. What has occurred has a fixed form and also implies further. The now implied is not a fixed form. We think the implied is what we often have seen coming next. Indeed, if the environment cooperates in the same way, the same object may be made again. Almost anything else will fail to carry forward. But new ways of carrying forward are always possible as long as a next step has not yet occurred. The body's implicit organization is much more complex and capable of many more possible further events, than those that have ever occurred.

Symbolic Purely Visual Objects

In one species of fish the males have a red circle on their bellies. When a male sees another, they fight. The male also will fight a floating toothpick that has a little red paper circle suspended from it. We scientists say that the fish responds to the red circle. But of course the fish responds to another fish. Their bodies do not imply such purely visual things as red circles.

Only humans respond to pure looks, something purely visual. For example, a little painting on the wall shows a vast mountain scene. My chest expands as I see this vast space. Behind me the owner of the painting is waiting for my comment, and I also hear car noises from the street. I respond to the picture *as a picture* and never lose track of being in the room, not in the mountains. The mountain scene is "purely visual," just its looks, *because* I also see the wooden painted thing on the wall in the room.

The picture is purely visual only in that its look is not part of the space in the room. The picture's own *different* space, which it brings, of course is not purely visual. I generate the vast space with my body. My chest feels expansive, and I "hear" the quiet in the scene. My body also implies how what is painted would feel if I touched it. The picture brings its own body-experience and is not purely visual.

The so-called "purely visual" depends on our living in more than one situation *at once*, so that something visual here belongs actually to its own different situation. *The human capacity to live in more than one situation at the same time brings the separation of the five senses.* Something can be just visual, or just a sound, or a texture, if it brings its own bodily wholeness of a different situation into this one.

We do not experience ordinary objects by putting the five separate senses together. On the contrary, their separation is only a result of two situations at once. *The symbolic capacity* is a bodily living in physically absent situations. Purely visual sensations, or auditory ones, are products from living symbolically in absent situations. Humans do not live in the space of the physical behavior objects but in a symbolic space. We live not in one situation at a time, but in all our situations. Let us see what new space is made thereby.

Symbolic Space: Internal/External

The many absent situations are each their own space. My body implies possible actions in the absent situation. I imagine the action *there*, as I sit here.

That is how there is an *inner space*. Even in the present situation, I can privately live one action, and then outwardly do another. All situations, including the present one, are a symbolic inner space.

Symbolic space is first of all inner space. But we will now see how an external empty space is derived along with symbolic inner space: The early proto-humans made hunting tools only when they were already out on the hunt. Then they left them on the hunting site, because once the hunting process was over the tools were no longer perceived objects. Only later after the symbolic power had developed, could they appreciate the hunting tools after the hunt and did they take them home. Then they also spent time at home making hunting tools. This involves living neither on the hunt nor at home, but imaging one while in the other. When archeologists find hunting tools on home sites, they know they are dealing with a later human, one which lived after the last great brain expansion.

The last great physical brain development came after the beginnings of culture and happened in a cultural context. Just sound, the purely visual, and symbolizing are a late *physical* development.

So we understand that the simple "object" that just fills a slot in empty space is a symbolic product. For example, only as the tools remain perceived on the hunt *and* at home, do they come to be "things" that just remain, and thereby make a mere placement-space. Their remaining generates a space of remaining-slots. If we move such a thing, its space-slot seems to remain.

The *external empty space* that consists of empty slots is a result of "things" that exist in more than one situation. The "thing" falls out from the several situations we can live in and lasts across them. The thing is then neither in this nor in that situation, but in a new *empty* and *external* space.

The internal/external distinction is one development. The external space depends on the internal situational imaging.

Inner Objects

As I said, even a *present* situation is an inner space. It is much more than the outer objects one can see. The executed action is only one among many we can consider.

Even without so-called reflecting, our bodies "feel" the implying and the doing of our actions. But *a feeling* is a newly made object that carries the body forward differently. When we spend time attending to *a feeling*, we live some aspect of the situation differently than in acts.

The Usual Inner Objects Are Only Parts

An image places us at some spot within a situation. *A thought* is only one of many meanings we could make in the situation. *An action* is only one of many ways to change the situation. *A memory* is only one bit of our past that is involved in how we imply this situation now.

Similarly, *a feeling* comes in the body as we live *in* the situational space where a certain event might happen. We feel the heart pounding in the body, as we live *in the situation*. Or, we recall how someone treated us, and anger comes.

The fear is never the whole situation. We need to overcome it to find a course of action other than fleeing. Similarly, we are taught to count to ten when angry . . . because the angry feeling carries forward only part of the situation. Later we are sorry about what we did or said in anger.

Would it not be good, if in addition to these objects which carry forward certain aspects within a situation, we also could sense the whole situation? Our bodies, after all, imply the whole situation! Why can we not feel that, have it, live it as an object, an it, a datum? The *focusing* process described in the next sections makes this possible, but ordinarily we cannot.

Without *some* object, the implying is not carried forward or sensed at all. But with ordinary visual imagery or sound-thought we either imagine this *or* that, either this action and its consequences or that one. We make a feeling from this part of the situation or from that. We live in some one formed way and never sense the *whole* bodily implying at once and *as implicit*.

But there can be a very odd "object" whose occurring is a carrying forward of the *whole* bodily implying of a situation, so that we can feel *all that*. Such a sense *of* the whole situation does not come *in* the space of the situation. It generates a new space, *in* which it is a new kind of "object."

Two Kinds of "Wild" Imagery

We live in situations with the usual imagery. But there are also two "wild" kinds of imagery which picture what could never happen.

When environmental interaction is greatly restricted (by sleep, drugs, deep relaxation, "altered states,") the bodily process is narrowed. The usual totaling which makes the familiar objects cannot occur. Instead, very primitive ancient sequences that are always implicit, actually occur. Any outer event then comes into these.

These experiences can be very valuable. The individual's and the species' pasts are implicitly part of the make-up of the usual objects. One finds out some of that vast richness when some usually implicit sequences visibly occur. But what one finds out is "not integrated," that is to say it is not totaled in the usual more inclusive process. So this kind of imagery is less whole than the usual kind.

But there is another kind of "wild" image that does come from the body's wholistic implying of a whole situation. If you now think of several of your own ongoing situations, (your work, one of your friends, your major relationship, what you must do tomorrow . . .) you may find that one of them feels expansive and energy freeing. With another of them a heaviness might come in your stomach and chest.

From this heaviness you might get an image, for example, of a large leaden ball which seems to *be* the heaviness in your stomach, although the ball also is larger than your stomach. It is in your stomach and also in its own new space where it is larger.

This leaden ball directly pictures your body-sense *of that whole situation.* In this type of process (which we will describe in practical terms) one is not as deeply relaxed as in altered states. It has great depths, however, on a different continuum of depth. One is open to the "wild" richness of altered states, but what forms is always already "integrated," already a new *whole.*

There is no leaden ball in the actual situation. It is not *part* of the situation, nor is it an old implicit sequence. The fresh bodily totaling of the whole situation now creates a new wholistic image from that "wild" implicit richness. Therefore it is "already integrated" *if* the image comes *from* first sensing the bodily implying of a whole situation.

If the image comes before wholistic bodily sensing, one needs to move from the image to the coming of such a body sense, (as we will explain in the next sections).

In the altered states, even during mere relaxation, there is often a stream of images, a whole mass of material which must then be interpreted. For example, in Jung's procedure a great deal comes which the therapist must interpret or which the person interprets as it comes. But there is always a great deal of material and change. On the other hand, the bodily-feeling side is often ignored or even missing; for, in deeply relaxed states the body "melts away," at times.

In contrast, in focusing the relaxation is kept sufficiently light so that the body sense is always there. Other ways also are used to insure the presence of the body sense. There is an emphasis on one specific situation or aspect of living. The result is that the leaden ball, for example, *stays.* Rather than a flood of material and many images that follow each other rapidly, there is one image along with one body sense. And this body sense is that person's sense of that one, *whole situation.*

All of the person's implicit sense of the situation is sensed in a bodily way, more not less than usually. A specific new kind of object arises, the *felt sense* (which might be pictured also, but is a body sense.) The leaden ball is *the whole situation*, and is in the stomach, as well as in a new space of its own. The body makes this odd kind of object which is a single one and thus permits the person to deal with the whole situation as a single thing.

Instead of having to interpret later and having to deal with a mass of different material, there is one felt sense of the whole situation and one way it is in image space. And one can feel in a bodily way that this is how the situation now is. It is a picture of how one is, just now, in that unique situation.

But as an "object" (see our earlier discussion) the very having and seeing and feeling this image is in itself a bit of further living. It is not a thing separately but a bit of further living.

In this odd space of focusing, the body can live *on*, in a way it cannot in the situation with others, (just yet). The body's whole implying and bringing of this situation can move past the point at which it is now stuck.

Jung already said that imagery (as in dreams) is "compensatory." He meant it brings a bit of living and being which is missing and needed by the conscious person's usual living. The whole organism or the whole psyche can live the situation somewhat differently than the usually functioning "everything" affected by "everything" does.

But, as I said, this poses the problem of how to go on from there. Jung frequently analyzed dreams of someone to illustrate his theory of symbols. Then he would often say something like: "But this patient is not developed enough, as a conscious person, to use these symbols at all. So they will just continue to come in dreams and make little difference."

With the present theory, we can understand this compensatory function more clearly. The body always implies the further continuation of its living processes, including the symbolic human interactions we call situations.

In forming a *felt sense* in its own space, the body makes the object it needs to live that whole situation further, as it is implied.

Humans, especially modern urban humans, live many situations in unique ways. The old stories and patterns are not sufficient to handle modern situations. We become aware, therefore, of our own unique texture underneath or implicit in what at first seem to be the usual stories. We say, "Anyone would be disappointed . . . he promised." But just after that, we can sense our own unique complexity in this unique situation. "And just when I was trying to be this new way, and just after that other thing happened, and now, the way I am, I don't know what to do, because usually when I try, what happens to me is . . . and so I can't, and that makes me feel helpless, and . . . and . . . ." All this is "the situation," each unique and much more than the simple social story pattern, promise-disappointment.

A felt sense (which may also have an image with it, as we will explain now, but is always in an image space of its own) is *all that*, all the implicit complexity which we can never have thought out separately, and yet it is also one single sense, one single object with which we live that whole situation a little bit further. Now, the big question is the practical one: How can we go on from that?

CLINICAL PROCEDURE AND EXAMPLES

In the rather unusual and very specific process called *focusing*, the body forms an odd object called a *felt sense*. It is felt directly in the body as a certain physical quality, such as heaviness, jumpiness, tightness. Soon it turns out that this body-sense is a new kind of "this" and brings with it a new kind of space, *in* which the felt sense can be moved. We will clarify this.

A felt sense (the body sense of a whole situation) is always at first fuzzy, unclear, murky, unrecognizable; it is a unique quality which comes in the body and reflects how the situation is lived in the body. This unrecognizable character clearly distinguishes it from the usual emotions, gut feelings, such as anger, sadness, or joy, which we can recognize.

Focusing instructions are rather specific and complex. We will summarize them later on. Most people need two or three days of instruction followed by practice with subsequent further instruction. The *Focusing* book also offers a great many suggestions about what to do when certain difficulties are encountered [9].

The clinical procedures developed recently and to be presented here constitute a way around this teaching difficulty, especially with people in difficult situations. But something new also developed, of interest to anyone.

Focusing is divided into six specific "movements." In a difficult situation, it was natural to attempt only the very first one, which we always considered merely preliminary, called "clearing a space;" it is now far more than preliminary.

This preliminary movement already had become important in its own right a few years ago, when we found, over and over again, that it very often leads to a very large space which is often experienced with a spiritual quality.

Next we learned, just last year, that focusing can be taught successfully in a weekend, if all of Friday—that is to say, about one-third of the time available—is spent just in learning this first movement exactly. To teach and learn nothing but that, first, has made our intensive teaching weekends successful with nearly every person; whereas, before many people went home without having really found focusing.

What, then, is this first movement, or rather, what is its expanded version as we teach it now? If I can make that clear here, then perhaps, you may also carry these developments further. The first movement, clearing a space, used to consist simply of a few moments during which a person sensed what just then was being carried in the body and "put" these concerns "down."

For example, I wish to focus on a major relational problem I just now have with another person. I know I want to focus on that. Or, perhaps, I do not yet know exactly what there will be to focus on. Either way, I *first* sense what I am carrying just now, perhaps four or five concerns. Perhaps I have just come from a tense meeting, and even though next week it will not matter, right now it is still with me. "Well, that's one thing . . ." I say with a breath of recognition, and I put that aside. I feel a slight easing in my body. "Another thing . . . uhm . . . my work got stuck last time, I have to get back to it as I left it, stuck . . ." another breath. Each time I recognize, acknowledge, "Yes, that's there . . . that's another one." Perhaps a few more, small ones like some call I have to make, perhaps one more big one, too, mixed. When I have finished finding and putting down each thing my body is carrying just then, I move on into actual focusing. I pick *one* concern, and focus on the unclear felt sense of that.

So, in one paragraph, I can describe that first movement. It sometimes leads to a genuinely, physically sensed good feeling, good energy, and sometimes one feels only slightly better. No matter, it is only a preliminary to focusing. Or so it seemed.

In this form, clearing a space (also called "putting things down") was and is an important *stress reduction* method, as well as a way to be ready for each new thing in the day. One uses just this first movement in the times between one setting and another, that is to say on the bus, or while waiting for the elevator, or while waiting for food in a restaurant. One senses what one's body is just then carrying, puts it down one by one, and feels a physical relief. One works on no problem at all. Just putting them all down enables one to clear oneself of accumulated tension and unease. One is then ready for the next activity. Most people spend every day chronically at maximum tension, so that one more troubled situation does not make any more difference. They never feel the physical easing and reduction of stress which this first movement alone can bring, if done several times during the day. So the first movement in its simple form became a method of stress reduction, and it still is.

Then another wrinkle was added: At the end of the series of problems or concerns, we learned to ask, "What is the background feeling?" We came to this, because often one has indeed put down each concern and still one feels not very much better. Most people have a chronic, ever-present feeling tone that is so constant that they do not notice it anymore, like the wallpaper that one doesn't notice because it is always there. "What is your always-there feeling?" We found it important to ask that. Some examples are: "always cautious," "always a little sad," "always trying hard" . . . When you find it, "put it down" also. Just ask, in your body: What would come, in my body, if this weren't there?

The first movement of focusing very often leads to a really major positive energy coming in the body. (*"Herzaufgehend,"* a woman in Munich called it— heart-opening-up—the German language has such words.) Most people describe it with a motion of the hand and arms, beginning with both hands at the chest and then opening out, arms apart. "A big space" is another metaphor for it. Life energy moves, you can also say.

Of course this feeling may last only a little while. Of course one has not made any progress on any problem, one only has allowed the body to exist *as it would, if* life were going perfectly. (For humans, it hardly ever can.)

Our difficulties cramp the body. We "carry" our situations in the body, as constriction, as weights we feel or *can* feel, as a fixed set, sometimes an unfeeling one, of steady tension. We *are* difficulties then. When one puts each thing down in this way one discovers quite directly, "Oh . . . I am not these things. I am here, they are there. . . ." One is alive, temporarily without them, as it seems; However, to have this experience, they must be put down *right there*. They must not slip back into an underground existence.

Now we have become much more able to teach this first movement *exactly*. First we found, that, for this movement and focusing generally, people must be able to sense their bodies from inside. This is natural and obvious to some, unknown to others. Here now was a discovery: those who naturally sense from within their bodies find it very odd that some people do not know how to do that, and those who never did this find it odd and mysterious when first asked to do it. "Can you sense your stomach and chest from inside? Is it warm and fuzzy, tight, heavy, jumpy?" Some people wonder what that phrasing means! If some cannot feel it, we ask them to move to their right big toe. Everyone can, and everyone's attention is then *in* the toe. We move up to the knee and try to sense it without moving it. Some find it difficult. We progress to the groin and then up to the stomach.

What is the use of teaching focusing to people who cannot, as yet, sense within their bodies? Now we find this out early on.

Next we found that the first movement of focusing must include checking the body each time something is put down. Does the body feel physically different now? If not, the problem has not really gone down, even though in an imagery space one visually has put it down. Not the visual image but the physical relief indicates that one has put something down successfully.

Now when we teach putting things down, we include checking whether physical relief indeed ensued. Each act of putting down needs this physical release. If there is none, one of many other ways of putting down needs to be tried, until there is. We now have developed many different ways which fit different people at different times.

Examples of Ways to Put Things Down

After having put the problem down, one should ask, "What would come, in my body, if this trouble were somehow solved in just the right way?" (This is asked *without* knowing what that way would be.) This requires attending within the body, letting one's first thoughts go by ("Of course, I'd feel great . . .") and *waiting* for what will come, more slowly, within the body, physically.

One may have to let each problem (or some of them) show a little of how it is, now, before it will permit itself to be put down. ("Oh . . . I see . . . I got discouraged when that happened, yesterday . . . as if that meant the whole thing can't be fixed. . . .") The whole problem now may let itself be put down.

The superego, the critic, the negative inward attacking that goes on in most people may have to be put aside a little. "Yes . . . ," one says in response to inward attacking, "that may all be so, but move over, wait, I want to hear from underneath just now."

The causal order can go either way. One may find in putting problems down that the usual self-attacking also has moved over. Or, it may help the putting down to move the superego over, if possible.

There is a need and a way to be friendly with each problem, however much one may dislike the problem. It needs to be acknowledged like an old friend. ("Oh . . . yes, sure . . . that *is* heavy . . ." one might say in an understanding way, to comfort the body.)

Sometimes the metaphor "putting things down" is ineffective, and others are needed. Stepping back from the problem is another version. Some people like "find where you are, in relation to the whole thing." It turns out that any number of such metaphors can be devised by each person, as you will see in the reports.

Imagery may help: "Imagine a slanting board with steel rollers in it, such as truckers use to unload heavy boxes. One end leans on the back of the truck, the other on the ground. Let this problem slide down that ramp . . . (Now, is it physically better?)"

Moving back and putting down can be combined, as in: "Sit forward on the edge of the chair. O.K., now very slowly, slowly, let the heavy feeling remain where it is, in space, and move slowly back in the chair."

After any imagery one must, of course, check in the body if the physical easing has come. Imagery alone does not decide if the problem indeed has been put down.

Asking "What would come, in my body, if this trouble were somehow fixed?" requires, of course, attending within the body, *and waiting there* for what takes a minute to come, physically.

There is also a specific learning needed even to imagine that one could have a better relation to a problem that feels very bad or very hurt. That is a relation of sensing it, but not being all the way in it. It takes most people a day to discover this relation.

The Third Position:
Neither in the Problem Nor Away From It

In learning to put problems down, one learns a specific relation to problems: sensing them but not being in them. It takes most people a day to discover that such a relation is possible.

The relation is neither running away (so that one no longer feels the problem) nor being in it (at more intensity than one can bear just then.) The relation is not just some distance but the right distance, where one can still sense all that. At that distance the whole thing is, as it were, in front of one, not all over, and not suffusing one's body.

That distance enables one to relate to the problem as a whole. ("All that,"

"This whole thing," "Whatever all goes with it, more than I know.") From that third position one still senses the problem, but from *a spot a little outside it.*

Putting Down is a Kind of Working Too

A person may then consider whether to move further into it, or to wait, to try to sense it from this distance. Perhaps that is as much as one can do now, perhaps right at this place small steps come.

Most people do not know that relating to a problem as a whole, in this way, *is* working on the problem. Even though one thinks only about whether to enter into it or not, or when, one touches this whole a little, pulls back, touches again. This is in fact a way of working in which the whole of it changes.

From this place one may feel, "Wow, what a lot of sadness!" or "What a huge anger . . ." or "This will take more than one day. . . ." In the very act of sensing the whole this way one finds onself stepped back. Or some other way of making the space might come first.

This third position is a different place from which to work on a problem. Whether it is an all-good feeling or merely bearable, it always feels better than either being overwhelmed or out of touch.

Life Energy

Finding the space is indeed a very good feeling; life energy flows again, one physically rediscovers onself as not just this problem.

These two events can happen in either order. One may discover this all-good life energy coming in after one has put things down. Or the putting down may become possible from first having found a different, all-good place.

And now I move closer to where the latest developments begin.

When have you last felt really wonderful? It would be a long time ago. Many people have to search their memories, way back.

But the first movement of focusing (and really, every movement of it) depends on having a good feeling as a background against which the problem is sensed. Here is more exactly what this means:

One asks, in effect, "What would it take to feel good? What would be a step toward feeling better?" Or "What is *now* between me and feeling all fine?"

We have found that many people do not ask in this way and then the first movement does not work as I described. Instead, they either run through their list of known problems (quite long for most people). Or they sense their body just by itself, the belt tight here, a gurgling inside there . . . just physical feelings not about anything. Or they sense the heaviness of a problem, but heavy pure and simple, not heavy-in-relation-to-a-better-way-I-wish-I-did-feel.

The instruction now is phrased: "Suppose *your life* is going just perfectly . . . you feel glorious . . . now wait for your body to talk back and give you, how you now *do* feel. Then see, one by one, what that is about, *in your life.*"

The first movement should not involve all one's problems but only whatever the body is now carrying. How does one find that? It is by having at least some trace of an all-good feeling, against the memory of which one can sense what is in the way of feeling good.

If one has such an all-good feeling, even a trace of it, to begin with, putting things down is much more likely to be effective.

On the other hand, by putting things down one may arrive at such an all-good feeling.

What matters most is that for the rest of focusing, it helps greatly if there is such a good feeling, or open space, or new energy *from which* then to work on whatever problem.

As long as a person is and lives as the problem, the body is cramped by the problem, duplicates how the problem is, and the problem cannot be worked on. Instead, one is trapped within it, and one swims around rather helplessly in it.

From feeling and living as the body is without the problem, one can best work on the problem.

This is obviously true sometimes of many problems: "If I could first be as I would be if it were solved, in that way of being I could solve it...." For example, confidence is like that. "If I were already confident, I could get the success experiences which would then make me confident, so that I could then do things well."

This twist about confidence, which everyone knows, is an example of a more general physical principle: We identify with our life situations and problems, and that blocks the instinctual life-energy which is needed to change these situations and problems. If we could first be as if these problems were already solved, we could solve them.

This all-good feeling (or all-good place, or space, or energy), which we first reached by putting each thing down, and then the deeper background feeling, is the basis for further focusing.

The felt sense (the second movement of focusing) forms and comes as one's body sense of *the whole of* the problem. To sense a whole one is no longer identified with or inside the problem, but one senses *it* as *there*, a breathing space is between oneself and the problem.

Forming the wholeness of a felt sense is therefore greatly facilitated, if one is outside the problem in the preliminary movement.

Also, at every step of focusing one really asks: "What's in the way of feeling good?" or "What would be a step toward feeling better?" All the while there is an all-good feeling, *from which* one asks about this *whole* problem.

A felt sense is usually much less intense than the familiar emotions, although new and changed very intense emotions may come from a felt sense. It is less intense (often so tenuous that one easily loses hold of it) just because one is outside the problem, touching it *from* another place.

For all these reasons, once one has physically experienced this making a space, the rest of focusing becomes easy to find.

Once the all-good feeling is here, the rest of focusing needs to be done *from* it, without totally losing it. Of course, as one senses the problem, it feels bad, but tolerably bad because one maintains the good place and a slight distance between that and the problem.

This positive energy is not optimism or preference for the positive. It comes, in fact, as one is both separate from *and in touch with* one's negatives. That is what the third position is.

But is it always right to engender this all positive life energy? What if someone is dying, or very aged, or if reality and limitations are to be accepted? From our experience, it is always right to let life energy flow!

The most debilitating thing about many problems and situations is not the loss or limitation but the overall stymying and backing up of life energy.

You may not be able to imagine how you would live a given situation *with* this life-energy, but there is nothing unrealistic about it. If you had 5 minutes left to live you would want it, as well as if you had 50 years.

Some clients spend every hour over a long period of therapy, making this transition from backed-up energy to sensing it flow forward again. They come to each hour very negative and backed-in, then they find again the positive place from which the difficulties can be processed much more effectively. One can see a total physical change in the person. Yet this making a space is not alone a miracle cure, as if it needs to happen only once. It may have to be worked for in each hour,enabling it to grow, and enabling a long series of different problems to be worked on, one by one.

Why is this energy stopped in us? Why do we not usually live from this place, or in this space, or with our heavy problems put down? We do not know. To put each down, one by one, may be a capacity most people have not learned.

Sometimes a person also disapproves of that positive energy before it can come in fully enough to be sensed directly. Perhaps sexuality is with it, and the person disapproves of the particular form of that sexuality. Perhaps joy and a sense of being alive seems—at first—childish, or selfish, or unrealistic in relation to the superego type of reality. Perhaps it is mixed with being power hungry or irresponsible or feeling superior or other ways of feeling that the person considers bad. Never mind! Let the whole energy through, you need not give up your value system, you can decide later about actions and choices. For now, sense life coming through! Then the problem can be worked on.

A Guide to the Reports

Many therapists know about and have written about the value of asking troubled people to recall a time in their lives when they felt really good. This is something everyone can do, and it has at least a temporary effect. I had always thought of it as overly simple and superficial.

Now McGuire has found that one can take that situation when the person felt really good, *both* as a way to provide something like the first movement, and more importantly, *by using it as a metaphor*, the further steps of focusing can be instituted *from* the good feeling, just as is needed in focusing.

McGuire's first client thought of a time when she went sailing. Notice that the client was first asked to make this physically vivid in herself now. But after that, McGuire used the sailing situation as a way to work on the problem from the good feeling: *She put the problem on the shore, so that it could be worked with at some distance, and so that the patient remained in her good feeling while working on it* [10].

This produced the usual release and steps of the therapeutic process in a situation in which it would have been quite impossible to introduce focusing in the usual way, with all the jargon and required learning.

Here then is a procedure everyone can do immediately without having to learn anything first. This procedure in very different words includes all our ways of clearing a space—the inward bodily attention (by vivifying the physical feeling of the good situation), the good life energy coming, the making one whole out of the problem by putting it over there, and the steps of working with it as a whole, *from* the position of the good feeling, so that it does not overwhelm and yet can be felt clearly.

In the report on the cancer patient we see again the direct way of allowing the powerful positive life energy to come. Illness constricts most people, so that the life energy is even less able to flow through than ordinarily. The therapist flatly insists that the horror is not all. There also can be a good place. It takes work but that good place is found. From it, much can be therapeutically processed, which could not be touched at all before, and would have overwhelmed the person if it had been felt.

The cancer patient also discovered that she had been totally cut off from that part of her body which was ill. This discovery raises profound but empirically answerable questions: Is illness more likely in parts of the body one does not or cannot sense from inside?

Cancer patients quite commonly "cut off" the part of the body that has the cancer, giving it as little as possible bodily sensed attention from the inside. Most patients are also angry at that part. Will it aid in healing to sense that part of the body from inside? Does it make a difference if there is a kind of compassion with that body part which is having to suffer the cancer?

Does discovering the ability to do these things, and then the step-by-step focusing and processing the many gradually coming emotional meanings aid in healing? It is too soon to say, but these are eminently answerable empirical questions. We are publishing this work with cancer patients at such an early stage because this enables others to go further, perhaps much sooner than we will be able to do. In the following, the therapists who created these innovations will describe them in their own way.

Finally, consider what this humble preliminary putting down movement is now seen to contain! It leads to a spiritual place which one does not need to announce as such. It enables life energy (probably healing energy) to flow through the body and a given part of the body. It permits people to process therapeutically certain material which is otherwise utterly too overwhelming to touch.

Illnesses have long been thought to have as one causal dimension how one lives life. This public understanding can lead to a foolish prejudice against the physically ill. Someone said to me recently, "We used to make ill people utterly helpless, now we blame them." It is foolish to burden an ill person with the supposed shame of having somehow caused the illness by being neurotic or living less optimally. Who is not neurotic or lives optimally? Different ways of being neurotic might have led to less visible, but not necessarily less unfortunate results. If certain ways of being human lead to physical illnesses, others lead to other human suffering, either one's own or someone else's.

No one can say which way of being human and inevitably fallible is better or worse than another. If we try to decide that we could say: People who have to learn to care more for themselves are, if anything, better than those who still have to learn to care about others.

But we do not know what causes illnesses. We do know that the psychic way of being can contribute a great deal to getting well, in very many cases beyond what medicine has so far conceptualized. Today most medical people know that and are attempting to integrate that factor into healing.

We are publishing early reports, long before being sure, because doing so enables others to test and try new ways and develop better ones. Please notice, these are very early reports with no implication that one ought to work just this way, and without claims.

CLEARING A SPACE
WITH TWO SUICIDAL CLIENTS

by Mary McGuire

The first step of focusing called "Clearing a Space" is vital to the rest of the process. Why? In putting concerns, problems down, or outside of oneself, or stepping back, or leaving the problem there and moving away, some space of one's own, separate from the problem, is created. There is an *I-It* relationship. A solid *I* stands in relation to *It*, the problem. One is much more than one's problem, yet before clearing space one may not feel this "more." One can be so overwhelmed by a problem that one loses touch with the sense of *self*.

For example, a forty-two-year-old woman came to the emergency room in crisis. She was extremely suicidal/homicidal. She had a plan to shoot her husband and then herself. The only emotion she could feel was *sheer* anger and hate. She and her hate were inseparable. I knew she would be unable to place this outside of herself. After a few hours of listening to her acute rage, I could sense that underneath was a very scared, hurt person.

The question was how to help her touch that part that was crying out to be heard. I asked her if there ever had been a time in her life when she had felt completely happy and at peace. After a long silence (2 minutes) she said, "Yes. A few years ago my twenty-eight-year-old son and I went sailing." I had her imagine the scene with all its beauty—the color of the sky, the clouds, the color of the water, the sounds, the smells, the wind, the temperature of the water, the touch of the water. Only after that did I ask her if she, her son, and I could go sailing now, and we would leave her husband on shore. I took her through guided imagery using her description of that happy time. After we had put some distance between ourselves and the shore, I asked her to glance at her husband now and then. She did and sensed anger at first, but it was less intense. Next she sensed a feeling of being trapped, boxed in. She stayed with that and from it came a flood of tears and deep hurt. I could see the easing in her whole body, her facial expression was changed. She no longer felt like killing herself or her husband, but she also knew that she could easily feel that way again. She decided that it would not be safe for her to go home today. She agreed to stay with her aunt. We drew up a written suicidal contract in which she agreed to call me if she felt suicidal during the night. She signed the contract, and I witnessed it. At 4:00 a.m. she called; she was upset. After talking for a half hour on the phone, she felt better and went to sleep.

In moving some distance away from the problem, then glancing toward it, a felt sense of the whole could come. It was "trapped," staying with "trapped" allowed it to open and pour out the tears and hurts of many years. True, this is only one step, but it is a long way from how she was when she came. There will be many more. Putting her anger and hatred for her husband outside of herself was crucial. As long as that was inside her, she would kill him and kill herself. Touching and tapping, moving back was important so that she was no longer overwhelmed nor sunk in her feelings.

I went in the boat with her because it seemed that she could have little sense of self apart from the problem. In going with her I was a "borrowed ego" and together we could separate *I* from *It*.

I worked with a second client, a thirty-six-year-old male, who came into treatment very depressed. He had made one serious suicide attempt a few years ago. During the first five sessions, he talked about the misfortunes in his life in great detail. He was very intelligent, sat rigidly in the chair, and never once allowed himself to experience a feeling. He *talked about* feeling hopeless, having nothing to live for, but always immediately gave an intellectual reason for each feeling. Even when he talked about being sad, his affect was flat. I taught him progressive relaxation; he was able to do it but expressed a *fear* of losing control. This was the closest he had come to allowing himself to experience a feeling.

For the subsequent session, he arrived very depressed and talked of suicide. I asked him if he could remember a time in his life when he had felt relaxed and happy. He quickly said "No." I said, "That was fast, could you just go back slowly through the years and see if there was even one time?" He paused for 2 minutes and then he said, "Yes, when I was twelve years old, my uncle took me to Disneyland." And then he said, slowly with sadness, "My father never took me anywhere." I felt that if I would touch that sadness there would be too much pain and he would back off. So I asked him to describe Disneyland. What he remembered best was a little rowboat he and his uncle paddled on a small body of water. He described the rocks, flowers, smells in the air, trees with the sun shining through them, slight breeze blowing, little colored fish popping up and down. I now felt contact with him, and his stern look was gone. He was enjoying telling this. I had never seen him like this before.

I asked him if he, his uncle, and I could go in that little boat now. He looked more relaxed, smiled and said, "Sure." I did a guided fantasy, using his imagery, but as I went on, I added, "And your father, who never took you anywhere, is standing on the shore. Can you see him?" He said, "No, I don't want to look at him." I said, "Fine, you don't need to right now, we will go way out on the water, and you can then see if it feels OK for you to just glance at him on the shore." I went on with the imagery, and after a few minutes he said, "When I think of him on the shore I get tense, I feel a hard rock in my chest." I said, "Can you just glance at him, then turn away so it won't feel so tense." He was able to do that, and his whole body eased. I asked him to stay with the easy feeling for as long as he wanted.

After a few minutes the tears started dropping down his cheeks, and he said, "I feel so hurt about my father. I loved him, but I could never reach him." For 2 minutes he sat in silence, crying. "I love him, right now I *feel* I hate him. I am so angry at him for what he did to me." He went on to tell me some of the wounds and hurts of the past. He cried and cried as he talked, at the end he looked and felt more at ease then he had up to this time.

CLEARING A SPACE
WITH SOMEONE WHO HAS CANCER

by Doralee Grindler

I am presenting current work in this ongoing case because it may be of value to others working with cancer patients. At this time we have no medical outcome on this or any other patient.

S. has had cancer for one and one-half years. When the cancer was first discovered, she underwent a bowel resection and the removal of her ovaries, uterus, and cervix. During the preoperative time, S. became acquainted with Simonton's imagery process and made attempts to use it as part of her healing process. However, her attempts were not always successful. She said that it was difficult for her to have the discipline to do it regularly and frequently and, in addition, she had trouble working with the kind of imagery they were suggesting (aggressive/violent). After her surgery, she was told that she was cured, and she did begin practicing another imagery process in which she would relax and then find images of health. A year later the cancer returned. She underwent a colostomy and began an eight-week treatment program of chemotherapy, radiation, and hyperthermia directed at the pelvis.

When she came to see me, which was in the middle of her treatment program, she was depressed and suffered from extreme anxiety attacks. The attacks were associated with anticipation of the next painful treatment. She had two main concerns: "I want to find something that will help me live through these treatments, and I want to find something like the Simonton imagery that would be more compatible to me." I have seen S. for twenty sessions of focusing, and during this time she has changed considerably. In applying focusing to S.'s struggle with a physical illness, I discovered a new significance and power to the first step of focusing—clearing a space.

Clearing a Space

I already knew from my own experience that the process of putting down each concern one is carrying and looking for that place where one is "all OK" profoundly links one to an essential life force, which brings new energy to deal with problems and concerns. But S. showed me how crucial this movement may be for a physically ill person. This step in fact became the pivot around which I worked with S.

S. is a very intelligent woman in her forties who has had many experiences exploring herself psychologically. She was already skilled at self-reflection, could easily be in touch with feelings, and had access to the imagery level within herself. In fact, several years ago she had been in a focusing group that I had led and had found the experience worthwhile. In those days we always began with relaxation instructions. (Since then we have learned that some people become too relaxed to do focusing, while for others, relaxation is an important first step toward focusing.)

In our first meeting S. spoke mostly of the physically distressing details of her illness and treatments. There was concern and anxiety in her voice, and I sensed a very deep vulnerability in her courageous struggle to cope successfully with the treatments and to find a way to face a life-threatening illness.

Both as a way to begin the focusing and as a way to respond to the vulnerability (you can feel safe here), I suggested that we begin with a time of guided relaxation. I asked her to lie down on the floor (on a sleeping bag covered with a soft comforter), and she remained in this position for the whole session.

I then led her in a process of total relaxation which lasted about 8 minutes, and in its course, I specifically mentioned the pelvic areas as a part of the body to relax.

After the relaxation, I asked her to let me know by raising her hand when she wanted to begin focusing. But she first needed to talk. Tears came to her eyes as she told me how hard it was for her to relax her pelvic area. The relaxation itself led to a discovery.

> S: I can't believe it!
>   I just cut that part off! (crying)[1]

There was real shock in her voice as it suddenly hit her that since she had learned of her cancer, it frightened her so much that she just had cut off that part of her body. . . . Then slowly there emerged a mournful tone, as she experienced how hard it was to be caring toward that part of herself.

It was as if, all along, she had been blaming her body for the illness. Now something had shifted. That part of her body was no longer the enemy. Instead there was a desire to care about that part. In this process of recognition, there was a seed for developing a new relationship with her body.

After a while I asked again if she wanted to proceed with the focusing and she said, "Yes." I asked her to:

> D: Put your attention in the center of your body and very gently ask yourself, "How am I right now?" and then wait and see what comes. We just want to see what's there, what your body is carrying right now. We aren't going to work on anything.

After a period of silence S. said:

> S: I can't do it. When I put my attention there nothing comes. It's dead inside!

S. was in touch with her pelvic area,[2] but I could feel how overwhelming this was to her. I saw fear on her face. She was terrified because what came was the feeling that it was dead in there.

> D: It's very scary to feel the deadness there!

I knew that at this point in the focusing she needed to obtain a little space between this "dead place" and herself. In addition, she needed to find an OK place

[1] Unless otherwise indicated, the speech is paraphrased.

[2] The pelvic area is certainly part of what we mean by the "center of your body" and since she was concerned with that area, she went there.

to stand in. I also knew that I could not go into a long explanation at this intense moment. How do I help her put that down? I made this suggestion:

> D: Why don't you look around and move to another place in your body, a place where you sense more energy and movement.

She agreed, and then after a long period of silence what she said was surprising to me. In her own way she was searching for that OK place.

> S: I'm in my heart area now but there is a lot of tension here.
> D: So, in your heart area there's a lot of tension.... Can you mark that? Say to yourself, "Yes, there is tension here." Then go see if there is a better place.
> S: MmMm
> (Long silence)
> I had some trouble at first, I went up to my neck and got stuck in a whole lot of tension. I thought, "How can I find any good energy. I'm sick! So much of me is wrapped up in thinking of myself as sick! Like I'm bad in some way because of that!
> D: It feels like that's all of you, being sick. And so there is no good energy.
> S: Yes, but the amazing thing is that somehow I managed to move past that, and I got to a place in my head where I feel some creative energy. It feels *really good!* (with surprise and relief in her voice).[3]

What was surprising to me as well was that S., all on her own, found what stood in the way of finding any good energy. It was this all-encompassing sense of "I'm sick." Then she put that down, and in this movement the good energy emerged. This is exactly what we teach about focusing. Once you find what is in the way of feeling good and make a place for it, the good energy has space to come in. This is what we call the "OK place." Sometimes we call it "the big space" or "the open space." Each is a short-hand description of an inner bodily experience of expansion and well-being. This is a direct experience of one's essential self distinct from problems, circumstances, and limitations.

Yet, once S. found that OK place, I did not stop there, but suggested that she apply the next steps of focusing.[4]

---

[3] The OK place is not usually found in a different body location. One focuses in a particular location in the center of the body, and finding the good place does not usually mean moving to a different location. We call it a "place" but the space in which this movement usually happens is metaphorical. With S., I changed the instructions and asked her to move to another part of her body because it was the original body location itself which was so terrifying. This was an easy way of making a place for the part that felt dead without having to do a lot of explaining of what I meant. Later S.'s OK place began to emerge out of where she was originally focusing.

[4] This is a recent innovation in the use of focusing. Usually one does Step 1 as a preparation to work on a particular issue. To apply the rest of the focusing steps to the OK place, we are learning, actually results in activating and intensifying the good energy.

D: Is there a word that captures that good energy?
S: (Silence)
   Connection . . . (deep breath)[5]
D: Your breathing really changed and became deeper at that point.
S: I'm glad you said that because "breath" seems to be another part of it.
   (Silence)
   I'm taking this good place and sending my breathing into my pelvic area.

In this process, S. found two "handle" words for the OK place ("connection" and "breath"): They further activated the good energy, which I could literally see in the change in her breathing pattern. She then, on her own, saw this breath as a healing force and directed it to her diseased area. Our first session ended at this point, and S. left feeling much less anxious with a new base for relating to her body.

In this first session, I observed three important factors. The first is the importance of putting one's attention in the body. S. did this, both during the period of relaxation and in Step 1 of focusing. This process of going inside the body and letting the body tell what it is carrying, began to nurture a positive relationship to the body (and specifically, with S., to the diseased part of the body). I also was struck by the fact that S. had cut herself off from the diseased part, and I wondered whether this might be a common reaction among people with cancer.

Secondly, I noted the power of the self-image of being sick. It was a very strong self-definition that took up all the space. I would compare it to what we now call "that background feeling," or "that thing that's always there," or "the wallpaper on the wall." The background feeling is usually such an implicit part of us that we do not even know it's there, except subliminally. It is in the process of looking for the OK place and not being able to find it because something is in the way, that we discover this background sense. It is often when one takes that problem out and puts it down, that the big space opens up. S. was able to put that sense of sickness down, and then she found the good energy. I thought that, in working with other people who are physically ill, I might try specifically instructing them to put their sense of being sick down.

Finally, it was clear to me that S.'s discovery of the OK place was very significant for her. It was both physically relieving and led to the release of a positive energy. Also, I noted the importance of going through the next steps of focusing while staying with the good place. Instead of "picking a problem," which is the Step 2 of focusing, I asked her to stay with her body sense of the good energy. Then, with her attention on that, I asked her to find a handle word

---

[5] I knew that S. had found what we call a "handle word" because the word "connection" accurately described the feeling quality of the good energy, and because I observed her head nodding involuntarily and her breathing was noticeably deeper.

(Step 3)–a word which captures the quality of the body sense. From this, she was able to say that word to herself (Step 4) and experience the word resonating with her body. It was in this process that the good energy intensified and became more available to her. Step 5 is "asking an open question" like, for example, "What would help here?" We did not do this step directly, but she intuitively grasped that this energy could help, and she directed the energy to her pelvic area. Step 6, "receiving what comes," also was implicit in her process, because she was receiving and welcoming the good energy. I felt that a self-generating process with potential for healing began that day.

Gradually, by observing how powerful this process continued to be, I began to postulate that essentially my role was to guide her to this OK place, to strengthen this place, and then she would use this energy to relate more positively to the part of her body that was carrying the illness.

She began to bring to our sessions intense and often anxiety-provoking images of darkness, death, demons–all of which seemed to symbolize the life-threatening nature of her illness. Since she realized that she had cut herself off from the sick part of her body, she desperately wanted to look at the darkness to find out what it meant, yet at the same time the images were frightening and overwhelming. I continued to apply my hypothesis. I *did* not have her go into the darkness, but instead I consistently had her make a place for it and then go and find the OK place.

> D: Make a place for the darkness. Yes, that's there, but put it out there. Get some space from it because it's not all of you . . . Now go find that place where you are OK.

Of course, in focusing, we always make a place or put something down or put it out there with the understanding that we will come back to it. We are not trying to avoid it or get rid of it. We only want to *first* create a bigger space within which to work on the problem. For S. the first result of putting the darkness down was an immediate diminishing of the anxiety and fear. Furthermore there was a gradual strengthening of the "I" which was not the illness. Through consistently guiding S. to make a place for each problem and then to find the OK place, this "I" did become much stronger and she continued to use this energy to relate to the darkness.

The following is taken verbatim from one session during which S. discovered a way to begin to relate to the darkness. After 8 minutes of relaxation, I asked her to put her attention in her body to see what is there.

> S: It feels very hard to get in. I feel scattered. Just odd little meaningless things. . . . The images feel so disconnected, disparate, fleeting. I deduce from that, that I'm not getting in touch with anything.

D: The images that are coming up aren't connecting you to a deeper place in you.

S: Right.

D: Then you have a sense of wanting to touch deeper. . . . Can you just be with that sense?

S: You mean the wanting?

D: Yes. My guess is, that it is in the wanting, the sense that you want to go deeper, that something could come from that.

S: I feel calmer. I sort of sense going down into light, layers of reflected light, as if I were going into a cave and lights bouncing off.

D: A visual sense of going deeper you have now.

S: HmHm. I have more satisfaction with that. It's quieter. And there is darkness too.

As I mentioned earlier, S. is very adept at imagery. This ability is very positive in that it could potentially stimulate a deep process, but not necessarily. The felt sense of the image is what I really want her to work with, and my responses always are pointing to the sense itself, not just to the image.

S: (Silence)

D: You are being with your sense of wanting to touch deeper. And in that place is some light and some darkness.

S: HmHm

D: Is there a word to describe the quality of how that feels in your body?

S: I'm trying to be with the darkness. Just feeling I want to be with it. I'm a little afraid of that anxiety we talked about last time. And part of me wants to be with it. Just let me feel it.

D: A real want to be with the darkness even though there's anxiety.

S: I can see it. It has visual qualities. It's nothing impenetrable. Shapes and edges. A lighter darkness. It makes me think of velvet, which is more like a touching thing. I have a sense of wanting to get closer.

S: (Silence)
Poignant (sigh, tears). Like there is this slightly uncertain person who wants to stay open to this. It's kind of touching—that duality.

D: There is the *you* that's risking being open to this place.

S: HmHm
(Silence)
I had a little shift there. It's as if there are two parts—there's me and there's this darkness and I said to myself something like: 'In the earlier images there seemed to be a lot about the darkness but now there's me here too.' I said that in a stronger voice, not quite so childlike.

D: It's almost like being able to recognize the strength of the *you* that's starting to relate to the darkness; so it becomes more true to say there's *you* and then there's the *darkness* over here.

S: MmMm. Yes, that felt good.

D: It seemed like something new came there that was both releasing and strengthening. Can you really welcome that and let
that live for a moment?

S: (Silence)
The sense of myself growing in relation to the darkness, the
strengthening of the part that's me, that's observing the experiencing. . . . The darkness just assumes a different kind of proportion.

D: You can feel your self growing stronger and that puts a different light on the darkness.

S: That feels like a really good shift.

D: Just stay with that as long as it feels right.

S: (Silence)
I was thinking about the way you ask sometimes to find that
place where you feel all right, and I thought that's a very good
place—that I got to where I can keep clear between myself and
my experience and my surroundings or other feelings or any of
that. It's a much calmer and more satisfying way to live.

D: It's like that inner place where you are all OK, where you're
distinct from anything else. It's like you've tapped that place
again now and you're recognzing it when you get here—and it
feels good.

As S. describes what happened inside her, it strikes me how very specifically
distinct the process is, of finding that inner place that is separate from one's
problems. It's awesome, it brings peace, calm, and strength. S. now has more
energy to bring to her struggle with the darkness.

At the time of our sixth session, S. happened to be in the middle of a setback.
She had severe diarrhea and was physically so weak that she was confined to
bed. (This is a common side-effect of radiation.) She was anxious about not getting any nutrition, until she was given a synthetic complete food which she
could drink. This improved her diarrhea and physical strength. Still for the sixth
session, she was too weak to leave home and therefore I made a house call.

I began, as usual, with a guided relaxation. Afterwards, she talked about how
difficult the last week had been for her, but once this was out she looked visibly
more relaxed. There was a long pause, after which she said:

S: I think I'm ready to hear from the darkness. (her pelvic area).

I was surprised that she was saying this now, given her physical distress; yet,
I trusted what she said. I knew that she had been building up to this moment
during all our previous sessions. Previously, we had been working mostly in a
middle ground, always staying in both places at the same time: "There's the
darkness over there," and "There's the OK place over here." Even her handle
word "poignant" was not from the darkness itself, but rather it captured what it

was like trying to be in relation to the darkness. A change had occurred. There now seemed to be a readiness from inside her to hear from the darkness directly.

As we began with the focusing, she first sensed a lot of impatience with the pace of her recovery. Her body was carrying that impatience, and once it had been stated, there was a little more space. She then was able to put her attention back down inside, and clear words came from her pelvic area which said:

> S: We're doing the best we can . . . we just need more time to rest.

Here was a change. Before this moment, the darkness had remained threatening, the imagery had been vague, and there had been no words. Now words actually came from her sense of this darkness and the message was positive. I experienced the healing potential of the body, especially now, when the body clearly spoke as an ally instead of as the enemy.

This continued:

> S: I feel so peaceful. (deep breath)
> (Silence)
> I'm getting an image. . . . It reminds me of when my husband and I were in a canyon one summer. We were just walking along. . . I'll never forget this experience . . . and we came upon a valley. It was so incredibly peaceful and beautiful.
> This feels so good. I can't believe all this came from my pelvic area.
> (Silence)
> Now I'm getting another image. It has a different quality. It's like soft velvet . . . it feels very sensual, like I want to touch it and wrap myself in it.
> (Silence)

I waited in silence out of respect for the powerful experience she was having, allowing her to stay with the positive feelings.

After a while I was still concerned that her experience was very visual, and I wanted her to clearly touch her body sense. So I asked her to go back to both images and see if she could find a handle word or words that would capture the body sense of both together.

She became quiet again and closed her eyes. By her expression, she seemed to be concentrating on finding her sense of the images in her body. The task was not easy, because she had to sense both images together, and it does take time for the sense to form. Then she struggled with a couple of words which did not really fit. She went back to the sense again, and then it came:

> S: There's life here! . . . (silence) . . . (tears) . . .

S. has stated to me that she experiences this process of clearing a space as healing. When S. was given this report to check for accuracy, her main comment was that it did not strongly enough communicate her sense of this positive energy as a healing energy. (Of course, since there is as yet no medical evidence; even in this one case, I cannot claim that this experience is in fact healing.)

While S. experienced this as healing, I did not want her to neglect any other process that also could be helpful; so recently I strongly suggested to her that she again try the Simonton method [1] which she had rejected early on. I reported research findings to her that indicate strongly the power of mental imagery in affecting cellular healing processes in the body [2].

S. decided that she would first clear a space and find the good energy, and then, while in this place, she would do the Simonton method. I work with her until she has an active image of the kind that the Simonton method involves. This continues to be hard work on both our parts. We now spend about one quarter of most hours on this.

The combination of focusing and the Simonton method involves both reaching the OK place first and also working, in a focusing way, to move from merely visual pictures passively experienced to a genuine bodily felt active experience.

Still, clearing a space continues to be the most important part of S.'s work with me. We continue to meet and her process continues to evolve, but I want to end here, for the purpose of this paper is to illustrate merely the first step of focusing.

She began her process with the shocking experience of feeling that the part of her body that has cancer is dead. This recognition filled her with anxiety. Together we struggled to make a place for each of these difficult experiences, while searching for a place inside her that was free from and not fully identified with her life-threatening illness. From this OK place she received new life and energy which she brought to the "dead" place. Gradually, she began to experience life in the part of her body that she had felt was dead.

This change from deadness to life energy also brought with it relief of her anxiety, pain, and depression.

She had been very anxious about the painful treatments (radiation, chemotherapy, and hyperthermia) and the ordeal of having them five times a week. She felt almost no anxiety after our second session and continued without it through the remaining weeks of treatment. The pain during the treatments lessened to little or none.

S. came to me very depressed. By the 11th session her depression lifted. Her mental attitude was positive and hopeful, and she felt more in control of her life.

What happened in this focusing process? It is clear to me that the focusing process taps into some power or force of life. . . . Is it healing power? Did some kind of healing occur that brought life back to the pelvic area for S.? Maybe, we cannot answer this question yet. But I *do* know that this process brings a profound gift of strength, peace, and further meaning . . . even to someone whose life is threatened.

REFERENCES

1. *A Process Model.* Available from E. T. Gendlin, University of Chicago, Chicago, Illinois 60637.
2. E. T. Gendlin, Imagery Is More Powerful with Focusing, in *Imagery—Its Many Dimensions and Applications*, Shorr, Sobel, Robin, and Connella (eds.), Plenum Press, New York and London, 1980.
3. E. T. Gendlin, The Body's Releasing Steps in Experiential Process, in *Healing*, J. L. Fosshage and P. Olsen (eds.), Human Sciences Press, New York, 1978.
4. E. T. Gendlin, Experiential Phenomenology, in *Phenomenology and the Social Sciences*, Natanson (ed.), Northwestern University Press, Evanston, 1973.
5. E. T. Gendlin, The Client's Client, in *Client-Centered Therapy and the Person-Centered Approach*, (Theory Section), J. M. Shlien and R. Levant (eds.), Praeger, New York, in press.
6. O. C. Simonton, S. Mathew-Simonton and J. Creighton, *Getting Well Again*, J. P. Tarcher, Inc., Los Angeles, 1978.
7. W. Smith, J. Schneider, C. Minning, and B. A. Witcher, Imagery and Neutrophil Function Studies: A Preliminary Report, Department of Psychology, Michigan State University, 1980.
8. E. T. Gendlin and J. Lemke, A Critique of Relativity and Localization, *Mathematical Modeling*, 4:1, pp. 61-72, 1983.
9. E. T. Gendlin, *Focusing*, Bantam Books, New York, 1981.
10. The Focusing Folio, *Journal of the Focusing Institute*, Chicago, Illinois. (These and other reports of practice first appeared there.)

SUBJECT INDEX

ACKNOWLEDGMENTS

Permission to reproduce material from the following sources is gratefully acknowledged:

1. P. Hughe, Mind, *Omni*, p. 20, August, 1982 (Copyright 1982 by Omni Publications International Ltd.).

2. J. R. Cautela, Covert Reinforcement, *Behavior Therapy*, *1*, pp. 35-50, 1970 (Copyright 1970 by Academic Press).

3. K. D. Schultz, Imagery and the Control of Depression, in *The Power of Human Imagination*, J. L. Singer and K. S. Pope (eds.), Plenum, New York, 1978 (Copyright 1978 by Plenum Press).

4. H. S. Akisal and W. J. McKinney, Overview of Recent Research in Depression: Integration of Ten Conceptual Models into a Comprehensive Clinical Frame, *Archives of General Psychiatry*, *32*, pp. 285-305, 1975.

5. M. J. Horowitz, Controls of Visual Imagery and Therapist Intervention, in *The Power of Human Imagination*, J. L. Singer and K. S. Pope (eds.), Plenum, New York, 1978 (Copyright 1978 by Plenum Press).